Schriftenreihe
„Studien zur Politischen Soziologie"

herausgegeben von

Prof. Dr. Andrew Arato,
The New School for Social Research, New York
Prof. Dr. Hauke Brunkhorst, Universität Flensburg
Dr. Regina Kreide,
Goethe-Universität Frankfurt am Main

Band 6

Wissenschaftlicher Beirat
Amy Allen (Dartmouth College, USA)
Gurminder Bhambra K. (University of Warwick, GB)
Craig Calhoun (Social Science Research Council an der New York University, USA)
Sergio Costa (Freie Universität Berlin)
Robert Fine (University of Warwick, GB)
Gerd Grözinger (Universität Flensburg)
Christian Joerges (Universität Bremen)
Ina Kerner (Humboldt Universität Berlin)
Christoph Möllers (Freie Universität Berlin)
Marcelo Neves (Universität São Paulo, Brasilien)
Patrizia Nanz (Universität Bremen)
Uta Ruppert (Goethe-Universität Frankfurt am Main)
Rainer Schmalz-Bruns (Leibniz Universität Hannover)

Chris Thornhill | Samantha Ashenden (eds.)

Legality and Legitimacy: Normative and Sociological Approaches

Die Deutsche Nationalbibliothek verzeichnet diese Publikation in
der Deutschen Nationalbibliografie; detaillierte bibliografische
Daten sind im Internet über http://dnb.d-nb.de abrufbar.

Die Deutsche Nationalbibliothek lists this publication in the Deutsche
Nationalbibliografie; detailed bibliographic data is available
in the Internet at http://dnb.d-nb.de .

ISBN 978-3-8329-5354-6

1. Auflage 2010
© Nomos Verlagsgesellschaft, Baden-Baden 2010. Printed in Germany. Alle Rechte, auch die des Nachdrucks von Auszügen, der fotomechanischen Wiedergabe und der Übersetzung, vorbehalten. Gedruckt auf alterungsbeständigem Papier.

This work is subject to copyright. All rights are reserved, whether the whole or part of the material is concerned, specifically those of translation, reprinting, re-use of illustrations, broadcasting, reproduction by photocopying machine or similar means, and storage in data banks. Under § 54 of the German Copyright Law where copies are made for other than private use a fee is payable to »Verwertungsgesellschaft Wort«, Munich.

Contents

Introduction 7

Section I: Legality and legitimacy: The form of the problem

Chapter 1
Blandine Kriegel
The legal and sociological construction of norms 21

Chapter 2
Chris Thornhill
Legality, legitimacy and the constitution: A historical-functionalist approach 29

Chapter 3
Samantha Ashenden
Legality, legitimacy and the circumstances of sociology 57

Chapter 4
Pierre Guibentif
Sociology among the third-order observers in legitimation processes 79

Chapter 5
David Sciulli
Societal constitutionalism: Procedural legality and legitimation in global
and civil society 103

Chapter 6
Darrow Schecter
The critique of instrumental reason: Between normative and sociological
approaches to legitimate law 125

**Section II: Legitimacy as a problem in international law: Critical and
               cosmopolitan approaches**

Chapter 7
Inger-Johanne Sand
Legitimacy in global and international law: A sociological critique 147

Chapter 8
Hauke Brunkhorst
Cosmopolitanism and democratic freedom 171

Chapter 9
Robert Fine
Political argument and the legitimacy of international law:
A case of distorted modernization 197

Chapter 10
Costas Douzinas
Saving cosmopolitanism? Legality without legitimacy 215

Chapter 11
Gavin W. Anderson
Post-colonial legality and legitimacy: The challenge of indigenous people 235

Chapter 12
Kirsten Campbell
From legitimacy to legality: The problem of the global legal form 255

Section III: Legitimacy as an institutional problem

Chapter 13
William Outhwaite
Legality and legitimacy in the European Union 279

Chapter 14
Andreas Hess
From Philadelphia to Vitoria via Bonn? Why there is no Constitutional
Patriotism in the Basque Country 291

Chapter 15
David Saunders
The necessary secularism of legitimate authority 307

Chapter 16
Nicholas Turnbull
Legitimation in terms of questioning: Integrating political rhetoric
and the sociology of law 323

Notes on contributors 341

Introduction: Legality and legitimacy – Between political theory and theoretical sociology

The themes of the book

The question about the relation between legality and legitimacy – that is, about the necessary legal and judicial preconditions for the general exercise of power – is, to quote Niklas Luhmann, both the 'basic question' of modern legal and political philosophy and one of the most deeply constitutive conceptual problems in the history of theoretical sociology.[1] The point of general convergence in post-Enlightenment political-philosophical debate is the claim that general laws are required to constitute or enshrine power as *legitimate power*, and that laws secure and transmit legitimacy insofar as they reflect rationally acceded norms or universally tenable values. Political philosophy, at least in its post-Enlightenment guise, is consistently fixed on the attempt to deduce and explain the legal-normative preconditions of legitimate power. Analogously, though, the initial impetus behind the formation of sociology as an academic discipline was also shaped by debate over ideals of legality and principles of political legitimacy. In fact, it is arguable that sociology first emerged as a corpus of theoretical analysis that opposed the normativism, the prescriptive rationalism, and the formal ius-naturalism of post-Enlightenment political philosophy,[2] and that sought to examine political legitimacy, and the fabric of laws and rights sustaining and expressing legitimacy, in the many embedded and factual sites of its societal production and experience.[3] Throughout the methodological consolidation of sociology, in consequence, the concern with political legitimacy and its legal prerequisites has remained at the centre of sociological inquiry, and the different formative stages in the evolution of legal and political sociology have been articulated through different accounts of law and legitimacy.[4] The question of the relation between legality and legitimacy, in other words, marks the central or constitutive point in the two dominant avenues of theoretical inquiry in the social sciences; in addition, though, it

---

1 *Luhmann*, Soziologie des politischen Systems, p. 159
2 For this view, see *Luhmann*, Soziologische Aufklärung. However, for divergent comments on the emergence of social theory from the moral philosophy of the Enlightenment, see *Manent*, La Cité de l'Homme, p. 73; *Heilbron*, The Rise of Social Theory, p. 86; *Fletcher*, The Making of Sociology, I, p. 645. In his history of the Enlightenment, Peter Gay simply referred to the theorists of the Scottish Enlightenment as 'Scottish sociologists'. See *Gay*, The Enlightenment, p. 34. It has even been argued in this respect that sociology was born in a 'state of hostility to law'. See *Timasheff*, An Introduction to the Sociology of Law, p. 45.
3 See Deflem, *Sociology of Law*, p. 6.
4 See for example *Weber*, Wirtschaft und Gesellschaft, pp. 122-76; *Pareto*, Treatise on General Sociology, pp. 1299-1300; *Parsons*, Politics and Social Structure, p. 362

also marks the point of critical distance and variance between them. This book thus takes as its theme one of the central controversies in the history of the theoretical social sciences, and it aims to offer new perspectives, both objective and methodological, to illuminate this controversy.

In addressing the question of legality and legitimacy, this book as a whole and the individual chapters that it contains are shaped in particular by two distinct perceptions.

First, the book is motivated by the sense that throughout the history of reflection on law and legitimacy both political philosophy and legal and political sociology, although focused on internally related problems, have constructed their inquiries in unnecessarily and unhelpfully discrete analytical frameworks. To be sure, there are certain clear positional overlaps between the two theoretical lineages. Both political philosophers and legal and political sociologists, for example, normally subscribe to the idea that legitimacy depends on laws that obtain generalized acceptance, and that purely coercive laws are unlikely to be perceived as legitimate. Both also usually accept that legitimate power is tied to the common recognition and enablement of social freedoms, and even that legitimate power might necessarily be power underpinned by articulated principles of right and framed within the public order of a constitution. Indeed, modern philosophical and sociological analyses of legitimacy might both, whatever their subsequent variations, be seen to have originated in the endeavour, in and after the Enlightenment, to interpret legitimacy as a condition of constitutional rule.[5] Beyond these elementary points of convergence, however, there is much seemingly irreconcilable methodological indifference and disagreement between normative and sociological accounts of law and legitimacy. Both lines of analysis tend to avail themselves of a rather limited and self-contained set of instruments, both tend to proceed from pre-determined preconditions in analyzing legitimacy and its legal substructure, and the accounts of legitimacy produced in one discipline are always unlikely either to contribute to the research or even to withstand the critical scrutiny of theorists working in the other.[6]

---

5 Constitutional rule is usually perceived mainly as the object of normative analysis. For the clearest expression of this, see *Finn*, Constitutions in Crisis, p. 36. Early social theorists interested in law and legal validity also usually rejected formal constitutionalism. As points of departure for this analysis, see De Maistre's seminal response to the constitutionalism of French Revolution: that is, his claim that all legal rights of persons are founded either in the concessions of monarchical personality or in the 'anterior rights' of historical tradition (*De Maistre*, Considérations sur la France, p. 81) and Burke's claim that rights are 'metaphysically true' but 'morally and politically false' (*Burke*, Reflections on the Revolution in France, p. 59). See also Savigny's view that the 'production of law' is a process of natural-historical self-interpretation, in which the 'natural whole' or the integral spirit of the people externalizes its defining characteristics and its specific rationality in the form of law (*v. Savigny*, System des heutigen Römischen Rechts, I, pp. 21-2. However, early sociology also contained a very clear, albeit still contextual and relativistic, vision of constitutional governance. See for example *Durkheim*, De la Division du Travail Sociale, p. 199; *Duguit*, Le Droit constitutionnel et la Sociologie.

6 John Rawls is perhaps the most salient example of a normative theorist of legitimate rule who attempted to incorporate a sociological dimension in his work. But his theory of the reasona-

In particular, pure normative/philosophical analysis of legality and legitimacy necessarily accentuates the deductive foundations of law, it is intent on obtaining categorical certainty in determining the norms that are definitive of legitimacy, and it usually arrives at its account of law's necessity from prior and socially abstracted first principles. Normative reflections on legitimacy are consequently disposed towards critical corrective assessment and adjudication of prevailing legal-political conditions; however, they habitually derive their critical-normative substance from hypostatic postulates or at least from singular normative principles, and because of this they struggle to provide plausible objective evidence to support their normative claims. In contrast to this, sociological reflection on the same questions necessarily ascribes to the law a factually positive, and more contextually variable role in forming legitimacy. It tends to observe law's legitimatory function as a capacity for expressing pre-existing societal orientations or for condensing positive societal motivations, and it is in principle prepared to accept a high degree of multi-valence in the law: many laws can form the legitimacy of power, power can be exercised as legitimate in many ways, and the normative status of norms is determined through their motivational, not their deductive, content. Sociological perspectives on legitimacy might thus also offer critical analysis of existing legal-political conditions; however, as they accept pluralism as a constitutive feature of society's laws they lack the internal concepts to provide justification for determinate or binding normative critique, and they too struggle to provide compelling evidence to accompany their claims and observations. Because of these primary distinctions, then, each line of analysis tends to occlude itself against the insights produced in the other, and the accounts of legitimacy emerging in each discipline – either normative/deductive or factual/motivational – rarely reflect on or incorporate elements of analysis from outside their own conceptual structure. In consequence of this, moreover, it is arguable that neither line of inquiry on its own provides a fully convincing (that is, at once normative and factual) structure for analyzing conditions under which power and law may or may not be legitimate. Indeed, both lines of inquiry suffer from distinct evidential deficiencies, which can only be overcome if a method is used that constructively incorporates elements of both. The chapters in this volume are devoted, therefore, to opening a more consistent dialogue between rival traditions of reflection on law and legitimacy, they aim to counteract the methodological closure between these lineages, and, in some cases, they propose normative/factual arguments that traverse the evidential distinctions separating these lines of analysis.

In this respect, in fact, many of the chapters in this volume also have the distinction that, even as they employ sociological methods to question more conventional normative assumptions, they remain attenive to the inner juridical dimensions of legitimacy. Sociological reflection on legitimacy has tended to be relatively indifferent to law: the prevailing sociological accounts of legitimacy are located in the realm of pure political sociology or the sociology of states, they have tended to observe legitimacy through a broad analysis of social structure, political formation and

ble society as a normative foundation for government can hardly be viewed as a success. See *Rawls*, Political Liberalism, p. 223

human motivation, and they have not normally accorded a specific force to the law as a precondition for legitimacy.[7] Indeed, additionally, the sociology of law itself has not yet provided anything more than very tentative paradigms for examining legitimacy as a distinct *socio-legal* condition, and legal sociology still awaits an analysis of law's distinctive capacity for allowing power to construct and present itself as legitimate. In the most prominent cases in which sociological theorists endeavour to explain the legitimatory force of legal norms they either (as exemplified by Habermas) cease to think in distinctively sociological categories,[8] or (as exemplified by Luhmann) they accept extreme normative latitude in their definition of a political system able to assume legitimacy.[9] The chapters in this volume, however, all correct the common sociological devaluation of law, and all seek, in diverse ways, to illuminate the specifically formative relation between law, power, and the construction of power's legitimacy. Indeed, connecting many of the chapters in this volume is an attempt both to question the more simplistic perspectives of normative theory yet also to place law at the centre of sociological analysis of power and to give due sociological prominence to law's role in the constitution of legitimate power.

Second, the book is also shaped by the sense that the necessity of reconfiguring philosophical and sociological analysis in addressing law, power and legitimacy has been rendered particularly pressing through the fact that the societal conditions in which, conventionally, legitimacy could either be philosophically defined or sociologically observed have in recent years become increasingly unsettled and precarious. That is to say, the last decades have witnessed a fundamental transformation both in the societal location and experience of legitimacy and in the institutions producing or obligated to legal norms designed to secure legitimacy. As a result of this, debate about legitimacy must also re-reflect and refine its basic preconditions. Debate about legitimacy can longer presuppose the existence of static state structures or unitary societies as its objects of analysis; it can no longer attach its construction of norms to simple and easily identifiable, territorially dominant, uniform institutions; it can no longer anticipate evidence of the validity of its prescriptions or observations in easily discernable social socio-institutional settings; it can no longer presuppose a stable *demos* to underwrite its power, and it must explain itself through reference to multiple modes of agency, subjectivity and normativity. Above all, the fact that law now originates in many diverse environments and that political power is routinely applied across national limits and outside enforceable legal constraints means that the central normative presupposition that law is a simple and controllable medium for constituting, rationalizing and regulating power as legitimate has be-

---

7   Most seminal is again *Weber*, Wirtschaft und Gesellschaft. For Weber, the legal dimension of legitimacy possesses insubstantial motivational force.
8   Contrast the account of legitimacy contained in *Habermas*, Faktizität und Geltung, with that contained in *Habermas*, Strukturwandel der Öffentlichkeit.
9   At some points, Luhmann indicates that the second-coding of power by law might be a factual precondition of legitimacy. See *Luhmann*, Die Gesellschaft der Gesellschaft, p. 357. However, Luhmann finally resolves the question of legitimacy by observing legitimacy as the outcome of effective self-description in the political system. See *Luhmann*, Staat und Politik, 102; *Luhmann*, Politik der Gesellschaft, pp. 319-371.

come problematic: indeed, it is simply no longer tenable.[10] In consequence of this, analysis of legitimacy and legitimatory norms must now position itself in relation to the processes of socio-political and economic change that have recently assumed formative importance in modern societies, and it must necessarily deploy a sociological methodology to assess the transformations affecting the origin and application of laws. In particular, analysis of legitimacy must seek to adjust its perspectives to examine the contours of legitimacy within a horizon marked by societal pluralization, economic globalization, the dislocation of law and legislation from national frameworks, the division of judicial and legislative power between national and trans-national institutions, and the multi-causality of objective juridical norms. For theory to be *plausibly normative*, in sum, it must also, arguably, be *internally sociological*, - do you take this to be the argument of all the papers? And, equally arguably, it is only theory that can maintain a high level of sociological sensitivity that can propose sustainable normative outlooks.

These perceptions converge in a more general intuition, which is also at the centre of this book. This is the intuition that traditional theoretical vocabularies, either normative or sociological, can no longer plausibly be applied to the contexts and problems of legitimacy in contemporary, increasingly international and heterarchical societies, and that a thorough and substantial revision of the methods used to approach legitimacy is now indispensable as a precondition for adequate theoretical debate. The last decade has witnessed a proliferation of new methodologies for determining legitimacy and new conceptual models for imagining a legitimatory recoupling of law and politics.[11] Despite this, however, most social-scientific disciplines and sub-disciplines have failed to propose transferable paradigms for accounting for the changing realities of legitimacy and for the changing role of law in creating or reflecting legitimacy. In fact, even in most recent inquiry the analysis of the relation between law and legitimacy has tended still to fall on one or other side of an inherited or relatively simple facts/norms dichotomy: that is, it has tended either to view the laws of modern society as normatively suspended or contingent, or, even as it seeks to account for law sociologically, it has been inclined to uphold substantial or foundational assumptions in order to account for law's normative legitimatory content.[12] Albeit in occasionally surreptitious form, therefore, the traditional dichotomy between sociological and normative accounts of legality and legitimacy persists in pervasive fashion in current debate – even at a time where new, reactively complex and multi-disciplinary paradigms are pressingly required to comprehend the changing relations between law, statehood and legitimate power. The papers contained in this volume, in consequence, all position themselves in express relation to the antinomical structure of this methodological dichotomy. All are shaped by the recognition that it is necessary to mediate between these two sets of paradigms, that it is essential critically to fuse sociological and philosophical analysis of legitimacy,

---

10   See *Fischer-Lescano/Teubner*, Regime-Kollisionen.
11   At the most theoretically refined end of these recent discussions, see *Teubner*, Globale Zivilverfassungen, p. 138; *Brunkhorst*, Rights and the Sovereignty of the People, p. 55.
12   Egregiously open to this accusation is *Alexander*, The Civil Sphere, p. 153.

and that this objective has, in existing theories, not yet been adequately fulfilled and requires further theoretical labour.

Though varying greatly in focus and ranging from highly contemporary analysis to broad-ranging historical or philosophical reconstruction, in sum, all the chapters in this volume combine sociological examination of the changing conditions of legitimacy with the insistence that legitimate power needs to be accounted for as possessing determinate normative features and preconditions. Some of the contributions in this book are devoted to constructing and reconstructing the relation between sociological and normative analysis of law and legitimacy. Some seek to show how the conflict between these approaches rests on false or artificial preconceptions, and they suggest ways in which the form of the problem of legitimacy might need to be rephrased. Some offer new socio-theoretical models for evaluating or envisioning legitimacy. All chapters, however, are structured either around an interdisciplinary analysis of the normative preconditions for the legitimation of political power or around a cross-disciplinary attempt to re-devise the theoretical constructions employed to evaluate legitimacy.

The structure of the book

For the sake of thematic and methodological coherence, the papers in this volume are organized under the following sectional headings:

Section I.   The form of the problem of legitimacy: Critiques and alternative paradigms.

Section II.   Legitimacy as a problem in international law: Critical and cosmopolitan approaches.

Section III. Legitimacy as an institutional problem.

Section I: The form of the problem of legitimacy: Critiques and alternative paradigms

The chapters in the first section all focus on the customary formulations of the question of legitimacy. Most suggest ways in which the question of legitimacy might be reconsidered, and all present critical analyses of the inherited paradigms through which legitimacy is analyzed and propose alternative theoretical constructions for approaching problems of legitimacy.

From a position based in the history of the philosophical tradition, Blandine Kriegel outlines an opening approach that draws wide parameters for addressing questions of legality and legitimacy. She argues that, across the distinctions between different theorists, classical philosophy was *in toto* oriented towards a conception of the legitimate state as a state exercising power in uniform laws. In contrast to this, she views the rise of sociological theories of law both as accentuating the pluralism of modern law, yet also as eroding the quest for a unity of legality and legitimacy within the state of law. She argues provocatively that the increasing prevalence of sociological analysis of norms 'has simultaneously made norms relative and undermined the law', and so requires correction through a new 'legal construction of norms'.

Chris Thornhill examines the question of legality and legitimacy from a standpoint derived from a historical-functionalist sociology of power. He argues that analysis of legality and legitimacy has necessarily concentrated on accounting for the role of constitutions in modern societies, and that constitutions are usually seen as documents that condense societal norms into a heightened legitimatory expression. However, he suggests that to date neither purely normative nor avowedly sociological methodologies have been able convincingly to interpret the ways in which constitutions generate normative reserves of legitimacy for political systems. To resolve this, he proposes a historical paradigm to examine how constitutions have allowed societies at once factually to respond to and normatively to organize their wider processes of evolution and functional costruction. He concludes that constitutions act as vital repositories of *factual norms*, through which modern societies support and legitimize their political functions.

Samantha Ashenden phrases the argument in her chapter as a set of critical reflections on the standard methodological self-comprehension of sociology. She questions the widespread assumption that sociology is an analytical-descriptive scientific discipline, which is strictly counterposed to normatively organized jurisprudence and political philosophy. She traces the emergence of the idea of 'social-scientific laws', and she notes that these laws, though they share nothing with classical jurisprudence, provide the immanent norms of 'the social'. In particular, she claims that the legitimacy of modern forms of governance is often premised on norms and legal constructs constituted through ostensibly value-free social scientific knowledge. She concludes that legality and legitimacy need to be construed as effects of multiple practices of governance, in which the social sciences play an active and normalising role.

Pierre Guibentif argues that a fourfold sociological perspective is required in order adequately to examine the legitimacy of the contemporary political system. First, he argues, this perspective must incorporate the participant's perspective: it must acknowledge that legitimacy depends on the inner conviction of social actors 'that there are good reasons to accept a given social order or, in particular, a certain rule.' Second, this perspective must contain an observational dimension: it must recognize that legitimacy depends on the fact that people are motivated to accept an order as legitimate through 'observation of the behaviour of other people.' Third, this perspective must also include awareness of the fact that legitimacy depends on the fact that collective social actors, i.e. states, 'develop means to enhance the global level of ceptance of certain rules.' Fourth, then, this perspective must also reflect the fact that legitimacy necessarily involves the third-order 'justification of social rules'. In particular, Guibentif concludes that social-scientific analysis needs to be placed within the fourth dimension of this perspective, and has the role of third-order observer, able to stimulate substantive normative inquiry into the legitimacy or otherwise of given and explicit social rules.

David Sciulli also challenges and modifies the common frame of reference for examining legitimacy. Building on his earlier research on societal constitutionalism, he claims that standard explanations of state power are inadequate for understanding the conditions of legitimacy in contemporary societies. Examining the weaknesses of state-centred positivist and voluntaristic/foundational constitutional constructions of state power and its legitimacy, he argues for a societal-organizational approach to the formation of democratic authority and the procedural-legitimatory limitation of state coercion. He concludes that the establishment and maintenance of lawfulness in society arises from the 'immediate positional and corporate interest' that is brought to bear on public institutions by 'societal constituents'.

Darrow Schecter's chapter concludes this section with a far-reaching analysis of the theoretical constructions that underlie the question of political legitimacy. He argues that if legitimacy in law is to be conceptualized in terms that are normatively and sociologically tenable it is necessary to abandon simple positive observation of the 'legitimacy-neutral legal order' of current capitalist societies and to adopt a foundational analysis of the social and epistemological preconditions of legitimate law. In this respect, Schecter's approach presents a counterpart to Hauke Brunkhorst's method of extracting categories of law and legitimacy from the epistemological aspects of Critical Theory. He argues that the outstanding positions in modern social philosophy have pointed – either intuitively or expressly – to the fact that legitimacy does not merely reside in a positive relation between law and power, but must also possess a 'marked rational and epistemological dimension'.

Section II: Legitimacy as a problem in international law: Critical and cosmopolitan approaches

The chapters in this section all address questions of legitimacy in the context of international law and in theoretical frameworks relating to international law. Common to all these chapters is the attempt to assert new models of legitimacy to capture the evolving reality of post-national societies. However, all chapters also reflect on the instruments offered by cosmopolitan patterns for theorizing transnational governance, and all engage critically with and seek to revise and reconstruct the normative ideas of international law that support the prevalent outlooks of cosmopolitanism.

Inger-Johanne Sand's chapter concentrates on the legitimatory resources that law presupposes, and she argues that through recent societal transformations the contexts of law's validation and application have been substantially altered. One consequence of this is that the ability of law to draw legitimacy from its correlation with democratically legitimized states has been undermined, so that an intensified contingency has been instituted at the centre of the law. As a result of this, although in contemporary society law does not renounce its need for legitimization, the foundations of law and its supporting semantics tend to become highly precarious and variable. For these reasons, she observes that a 'new way of thinking about legitimacy' is needed, which abandons its attachment to transparently applicable norms. This approach 'may have to deal more profoundly with multiple and more complex and conflictual meanings and situations'.

Hauke Brunkhorst expands his theory of critical cosmopolitanism to argue for the necessity of a new conception of democratic legitimacy. He argues that in recent decades the legitimatory accomplishments of national states have been eroded by changes in the relation between state and other social systems, especially the system of the international economy. Chief amongst these changes is the 'complete transformation of the state-embedded markets of regional late capitalism into the market-embedded states of global turbo-capitalism'. To combat the loss of legitimacy that was historically preserved in traditional (national) state structures, Brunkhorst argues that classical dualist constructs of democracy as representative or pure constitutional democracy need to be abandoned: that is, the dualistic 'power-limiting constitutionalism' of classical democracy needs to be replaced by 'power-founding constitutionalism.' This, he argues, will form the foundation for a political reality in which legitimacy in the static classical sense gives way to 'a legally organized procedure of egalitarian and inclusive legitimization'.

In his chapter on concepts of legitimacy in international law, Robert Fine questions the validity of the assumption that international law can be invariably invoked as a higher legitimatory norm for determining legal and political rulings. On one hand, he concedes that the 'appeal to international humanitarian and human rights law as an authoritative ground of political argument [...] offers an essential response to escalating dangers that were inherent in the structure of the nation state.' Yet he adds the cautionary note that the idealization of international law and international jurisdictional procedures for guaranteeing human rights obscures the relations of power inscribed in law, and in positing absolute standards of legal normativity it effectively erodes the law-determining force of political argument itself. He concludes that the (allegedly) supra-positive forms of human-rights legislation always need to be supplemented and in fact 'stand in need of a politics able to give them the recognition that is their due'.

Costas Douzinas responds to the claims made by Fine, and he sets out a far-reaching critique of cosmopolitan theories of government. In particular, he argues that the dream of universal law that supports cosmopolitanism is a fictitious ideal, and he explains how the concepts of humanity, rights and generic equality that sustain it falsify the conditions of human liberty. The cosmopolitan construction of all humans as bearers of rights, most especially, has, he asserts, led to a depletion of freedom, through which human beings encounter only an ideological mirage of themselves, tuned to the ideological exigencies of international capitalism. Douzinas then proposes a corrective to more established cosmopolitan theory by proposing an ethic of singular solidarity, based in 'respect' for 'the singularity of the other'.

Gavin Anderson's chapter reflects Douzinas's scepticism about the capacity of international legal rules for generating and expressing legitimacy, and he uses analysis of the legal status of indigenous peoples, and the relation between colonial and indigenous law, to identify the oppressive functions of law's universalism. In this respect, Anderson also echoes Schecter's claim that legal constructs need to be viewed as articulating knowledge strategies and as founded in a distinct epistemological dimension'. He concludes by arguing that a 'normative development of the ethic of constitutional pluralism' is required, and that legitimate application of law presupposes a legal apparatus capable of sustaining a plurality of rights and of accommodating diverse modes of legal cognition and recognition as the substrate for rights.

Kirsten Campbell focuses on the question of legitimacy, and its sociological determinacy, in the context of international criminal law. She uses an analytical method derived from Pashukanis to examine law as a 'historical form of regulation' that has emerged from, and incessantly refracts, the social relations of international capitalism. In particular, she claims that the principles of validity and legitimacy underlying contemporary international criminal law need to be analyzed as the legal form of 'emergent force-relations', which expresses 'global relations as juridical relations'. She concludes by arguing that normative claims for legitimacy in criminal law can only be accurately comprehended if they are seen as elements of the global legal form.

Section III: Legitimacy as an institutional problem

The chapters in this section aim to elucidate contemporary problems of political legitimacy by examining specific – and specifically problematic – institutional settings and expanding this analysis to form the basis for wider-range theoretical inquiries. In particular, the chapters in this section probe at the fragility of the legitimatory foundations of contemporary institutions, and they examine and propose different methodologies both interpretively to account for and normatively to promote an enhancement of state legtimacy.

William Outhwaite addresses the legitimatory problematics of the EU. He argues first that the democratic or legitimatory deficit in the EU has to be examined both as resulting from the 'the relatively unpolitical (though of course politically relevant) spheres of EU policy-making' and from the internal policies of 'the member states themselves'. He responds to the legitimatory weaknesses of EU institutions by advocating a restatement of the Habermasian project of constitutional patriotism, and he concludes by asserting that the EU can consolidate itself as a fully legitimate polity only if the 'already shaky identification of modern Europeans with democratic parliamentary politics' is overcome both at European and at member-state level.

Andreas Hess replies to Outhwaite's approach by using an examination of the question of transitional legitimacy in the Basque country to set out a far-reaching critique of the doctrine of constitutional patriotism. He explains how the one-size-fits-all model of social integration through identification with the normative substance of constitutions cannot be adapted to all traditions of state- and nation-building in Europe. He concludes with the claim that if the construction of legitimacy through constitutional integration is a desirable goal, then the US-American model of constitutional patriotism might be considered more easily transportable than the primarily (West) German vision of moral-constitutional identity.

In similar vein, David Saunders explores a particular question of institutional analysis in order to conduct a wide, historically reconstructive survey of the legitimatory preconditions of modern states. His argument focuses primarily on the principle of post-secularity in contemporary political and ethical discourse, and he questions the seeming neutrality with which 'the assimilation and the reflexive transformation of both religious and secular mentalities' is accepted in current analysis of law and power. His conclusion is a strong statement of the conviction that the foundations of state legitimacy are essentially incompatible with any public commitment to the traces – however 'post-secular' – of religious disposition and belief patterns.

Nicholas Turnbull also adopts a simultaneously theoretical and institutional approach to legitimacy: he describes this as a 'philosophical and political orientation towards public problems'. As a general explanatory framework for understanding the legitimatory structure of contemporary states, he proposes a theory of problematology, which considers the state as the fulcrum of a set of rhetorical or problematic social relations within society. He claims that the problematological method makes it possible to appreciate states as institutions that possess both normative and contingent or rhetorical instruments for obtaining legitimacy. He concludes by claiming that states secure their legitimacy through a dual process: both by establishing firm legal parameters and by evolving rhetorical procedures for addressing questions of 'shared contingency'.

Acknowledgements

Earlier versions of the chapters in this volume by Hauke Brunkhorst, Kirsten Campbell, Robert Fine, Pierre Guibentif, Andreas Hess, Blandine Kriegel, William Outhwaite, Inger-Johanne Sand, David Saunders, Darrow Schecter and Nicholas Turnbull were originally presented at a symposium that was held in late April 2008 at the *International Institute for the Sociology of Law* in Oñati, Spain. The editors thank the staff at the Institute for their help in organizing the symposium.

Bibliography

Alexander, Jeffrey C., The Civil Sphere, Oxford, 2006.
Brunkhorst, Hauke, Rights and the Sovereignty of the People in the Crisis of the Nation State, Ratio Juris 13(1) (2000), pp. 49-62.
Burke, Edmund, Reflections on the Revolution in France, London, 1910.
Deflem, Mathieu, Sociology of Law. Visions of a Scholarly Tradition, Cambridge, 2008.
De Maistre, Joseph, Considérations sur la France, Lyon, 1847.
Duguit, Léon, Le Droit constitutionnel et la Sociologie, Revue internationale de l'Enseignement 18 (1889), pp. 484-505.
Durkheim, Émile, De la Division du Travail Sociale, 7th edition, Paris, 1960.
Finn, John E., Constitutions in Crisis. Political Violence and the Rule of Law, Oxford, 1991.
Fischer-Lescano, Andreas/Teubner, Gunther, Regime-Kollisionen. Zur Fragmentierung des globalen Rechts, Frankfurt am Main, 2006.
Fletcher, Ronald, The Making of Sociology. A Study of Sociological Theory, vol. I: Beginnings and Foundations, London, 1971.
Gay, Peter, The Enlightenment: An Interpretation. The Rise of Modern Paganism, London, 1966.
Habermas, Jürgen, Strukturwandel der Öffentlichkeit. Untersuchungen zu einer Kategorie der bürgerlichen Gesellschaft, Frankfurt am Main, 1990.
Habermas, Jürgen, Faktizität und Geltung. Beiträge zur Diskurstheorie des Rechts und des demokratischen Rechtsstaats, Frankfurt am Main, 1992.
Heilbron, Johan, The Rise of Social Theory, vol. I: Contradictions of Modernity, translated by S. Gogol, Minneapolis, 1995.
Luhmann, Niklas, Soziologische Aufklärung, Soziale Welt 18(2/3) (1967), pp. 97-123.
Luhmann, Niklas, Soziologie des politischen Systems, in Luhmann, Soziologische Aufklärung, vol. I. Aufsätze zur Theorie sozialer Systeme, Cologne, 1970, pp. 154-177.
Luhmann, Niklas, Staat und Politik. Zur Semantik der Selbstbeschreibung politischer Systeme, Politische Vierteljahresschrift, Sonderheft 15, Politische Theoriengeschichte. Probleme einer Teildisziplin der Politischen Wissensschaft (1984), pp. 99-125.
Luhmann, Niklas, Die Politik der Gesellschaft, Frankfurt am Main, 2000.
Manent, Pierre, La Cité de l'Homme, Paris, 1997.
Pareto, Vilfredo, The Mind and Society: A Treatise on General Sociology, translated by A. Bongiorno and A. Livingston New York, 1935.
Parsons, Talcott, Politics and Social Structure New York, 1969.
Rawls, John, Political Liberalism, New York, 1993.
v. Savigny, Friedrich Carl, System des heutigen Römischen Rechts, in 9 vols., Berlin, 1840.
Teubner, Gunther, Globale Zivilverfassungen: Alternativen zur staatszentrierten Verfassungstheorie, in Neves, Marcelo and Voigt, Rüdiger (eds), Die Staaten der Weltgesellschaft. Niklas Luhmanns Staatsverständnis, Baden-Baden, 2007, pp. 117-147.
Timasheff, N.S., An Introduction to the Sociology of Law. Westport, CONN., 1974.
Weber, Max, Wirtschaft und Gesellschaft. Grundriß der verstehenden Soziologie, Tübingen, 1921

Section I:
The form of the problem

The legal and sociological construction of norms

Blandine Kriegel

That there is a divergence between legal and sociological approaches to the twin concepts of legality and legitimacy can hardly be doubted. Legality is compliance with the law, legitimacy is consent to a norm acknowledged to be just. If legality does not invariably entail legitimacy (a law may be considered unjust), legitimacy similarly does not invariably presuppose the existence of a law (a law does not necessarily take legislative form). Legitimate authority is authority whose source is just (Rousseau), and legal authority is authority whose exercise is dependent on the law. At this point, we should briefly set out two approaches: the legal construction of norms, and the sociological investigation of norms.

The legal construction of norms

Rousseau argued that "Every legitimate government is republican". Classical legal philosophy narrowed the gap between legality and legitimacy to the point of its disappearance. We can summarise this concisely here.

In the view of classical political philosophy from Bodin to Rousseau, the production of norms – i.e. laws – is first and foremost the prerogative of the sovereign. The sovereign may be the monarch alone, as it is for Hobbes or Bodin, the monarch in association with parliament for Locke, or the people alone, as is the case for Rousseau, but it is the function of the sovereign and the sovereign alone to promulgate and decide upon the laws. The legal construction of sovereignty results from the efforts of Bodin (in *Methodus ad facilem historiarum cognitionem* or *A Method for the Easy Understanding of History* [1566], *Six livres de la République* or *Six Books of the Commonwealth* [1576]) to shape and reformulate the ancient and medieval doctrine of imperium and merum imperium, that is to say the essence of the political, shifting it from potestas to auctoritas, from force to law. Sovereign power is a power whose key attribute is no longer war but the law, and the sovereign state is first and foremost a state ruled by laws, a legal state, a commonwealth defined in opposition to empire. This definition of sovereignty as defined in laws and the endeavour to maintain peace are essential components of the legitimacy of the republic according to Bodin. His successors went further, emphasising the legitimacy of the republican state ruled by laws, strengthening its construction by adding the notion of the contract, an originating pact presiding over its institution. The contract itself derives, according to various commentators, from a dual legitimacy. For the theorists of will such as Grotius and Rousseau, the key notion is that of free consent to the legal order and the birth of the civil society that is the foundation of the legitimacy of the institution of legal norms. But for believers in natural law, Hobbes, Spinoza or Locke for example, the central concept is, as Hobbes expresses it so admirably in chapter XIV of *Leviathan*: 'A law of nature [...] is a precept [...] found out by reason, by which a man is forbidden to do that which is destructive of his life',[1] which provides the foundation for the true legitimacy of the civil construction, the shift from the state of nature to the civil state.

The legitimacy of the norms produced by the sovereign is to be found in the procedure whereby civil laws in effect generate natural laws that would remain virtual in a state of nature, a time of conflict in which 'the life of man [is] solitary, poor, nasty, brutish, and short'.[2] In other words, legal norms, laws promoted by the mechanism of alienation of the will to power and the natural rights of each in favour of the government of the state alone, are simply a system to ensure that each individual is able to enjoy his or her rights: security for Hobbes, liberty for Spinoza, property for Locke, and equality for Rousseau. The law is thus transformed into rights; it guarantees the rights of man that must be declared if the life of the citizen is to become a truly human life.

Under the mechanism of the social pact thus conceived, free consent, the contractual dimension at the root of legality, is combined with a rational dimension whereby, far from being invented from scratch, the civil laws are a rediscovery, a reformulation of natural laws already present in human nature and which the philosophers of ius naturalis, poring over the Decalogue and the Gospels, express in so many words. The human contribution to legal norms resides in declaration (discovery), implementation and interpretation, but fundamentally there is no difference between such norms and natural laws. In this way, an equation also defined by Hobbes and Locke is established between civil law, natural law, common goods and the general interest; civil law thus conceived embodies both legality and legitimacy simultaneously.

Hobbes provides a perfect explanation of this in *The Leviathan*, where he states:

> [T]he laws of nature, which consist in equity, justice, gratitude, and other moral virtues on these depending, in the condition of mere nature [...] are not properly laws, but qualities that dispose men to peace and to obedience. When a Commonwealth is once settled, then are they actually laws, and not before; as being then the commands of the Commonwealth; and therefore also civil laws. [...] The law of nature therefore is a part of the civil law in all Commonwealths of the world. Reciprocally also, the civil law is a part of the dictates of nature. For justice, that is to say, *performance of covenant*, and giving to every man his own, is *a dictate of the law of nature*. But every subject in a Commonwealth hath covenanted to obey the civil law [...]; and therefore obedience to the civil law is part also of the law of nature'.[3]

---

1   *Hobbes*, Leviathan, p. 66.
2   *Hobbes*, Leviathan, p. 65.
3   *Hobbes*, Leviathan, p. 141. Emphasis is added by author.

The sociological investigation of norms

In the more contemporary sociological model such as one finds in the writings of Émile Durkheim or Max Weber, norms are seen as a fact of human society. Compared with the undeniable dogmatism of the notion of legal construction, when the latter had made more and more room for the will, for decision or for absolute power, when society came to be seen as dominated by the conflict of class interests (only the viewpoint of the proletariat and the party representing it being deemed just and legitimate), sociology's labours permitted diversity and plurality to be recognised. Whether norms are deemed to be founded on a contract or on enforcement, as in Durkheim, or as deriving from tradition, custom or convention, as Max Weber argues, they are invariably seen as being plural.

This is the explanation for the fact that several types of legitimacy can be invoked. Weber points to three: legal rational legitimacy, which recognises the authority of law; traditionalist legitimacy, based on custom and the authority of the past; and, lastly, charismatic legitimacy, based on the personal charm of exceptional individuals. In this context, it is undoubtedly legality reduced to itself alone that is questioned, but the supremacy of the law and the transcendence of norms are also suspect. Max Weber describes a battle of the gods, an eternal conflict leading into a tragic arena. The upsurge in the sociological approach to norms was preceded by the destruction or marginalisation of legal construction. For some, the supremacy assigned to social emancipation entails the annihilation of law ('The spirit of the laws is property' – Marx). Legal norms are always a superstructure, when they are not seen purely and simply as a form of alienation. Previously, the attempt to reconcile the plurality of society desired by Rousseau in *Émile* presupposed the existence of distinct social spheres: the sphere of the family, that of work and material interests, and that of citizenship and the State. The same idea leads in the work of Hegel to an admirable effort to promote pluralism and balance between different ethical norms: family morality founded on faith, ethical life in civil society founded on self-interest, the rationality of the State founded on reason. All of which is to be understood as meaning that the complexity of society leads to layered norms. However, and unfortunately, plurality is not the final word in Hegel's *Elements of the Philosophy of Right*. The return to unity is brought about through the pre-eminence of the 'Spirit of the People', which is invariably religious in essence. Each society is dominated at a given point in its existence by an organic 'Spirit of the People', a superior norm that battles with other 'spirits of the people'. What will decide upon their respective degrees of legitimacy? In the end, war and victory alone: 'The world's history is the world's tribunal'. Marx and Nietzsche did not have far to go before observing that 'revolutions are the locomotives of history' (Marx) and: 'A state is called the coldest of all cold monsters' (Nietzsche). Here we return to the aporia denounced by Rousseau in the contradiction inherent in the right of the strongest:

> The strongest is never strong enough to be always the master, unless he transforms strength into right, and obedience into duty. Hence the right of the strongest [...]

> Suppose for a moment that this so-called 'right' exists. I maintain that the sole result is a mass of inexplicable nonsense [...] As soon as it is possible to disobey with impunity, disobedience is legitimate; and, the strongest being always in the right, the only thing that matters is to act so as to become the strongest. [...] Clearly, the word 'right' adds nothing to force [...] Obey the powers that be. If this means yield to force, it is a good precept, but superfluous, I can answer for its never being violated [...] Let us then admit that might does not create right, and that we are obliged to obey only legitimate powers.[4]

Where then does the refusal to see norms as transcendent lead? To a gap between legality and legitimacy. This is a gap that is particularly evident in the contemporary, albeit recessive, currents of thought in the philosophy of law.

On the one hand, there is the legal positivism of Hans Kelsen, who looks only to a form of legalism that eliminates the issue of legitimacy (all norms are just). On the other, we have the decisionism of Carl Schmitt, who relies totally on the legitimatisation of the sovereign will and argues that: 'Sovereign is he who decides on the exception'.[5] In this development, not only is the opposition lost between republic and empire (the state ruled by laws and the despotic state), but justice is also left aside.

This reminder, albeit brief, of what separates legal construction from the sociological construction of norms requires a further comment that touches on a preliminary difficulty: the legal construction of norms belongs essentially to the classical age. The sociological approach is linked to the contemporary period, achieving wide dominance in the nineteenth and twentieth centuries, although a dialogue seems to have been restored between the two eras in the latter part of the twentieth century in the philosophies of Leo Strauss and John Rawls.

What we are seeking here is an answer to the question whether the unchallenged dominance of the sociological standpoint as the point of view of diversity and plurality might not originate in a problem intrinsic to the classical legal construction itself.

The criticisms levelled at the notion of the legal construction of norms in the French republican theory of the infallible general will, of the one and indivisible republic (the French school) as well as in the Bismarckian Prussian theory of the power of the state as the sole source of norms, target one of the models of the classical doctrine but not that doctrine in its entirety.

In the distinction that opposes republic to empire, between the state ruled by laws and the despotic state, it is undeniable that the whole of classical political philosophy stands on one side, on that of the republican state ruled by laws. From Bodin to Kant, we see described one and the same construction, that of a state whose function is expressed through law (legal norms) and not force, a state that guarantees essential rights for its citizens and which is founded on consent (the contract). Nevertheless, looking beyond this unanimity, one fundamental difference separates the doctrinarians of sovereignty from the proponents of the separation of powers. We

---

4   *Rousseau*, Du Contrat Social, p. 44.
5   *Schmitt*, Politische Theologie, p. 13.

should not believe that the dividing line between the two runs down the English Channel or out in the Atlantic. At the time when the model, a republican model, was being conceived, the division between the two zigzagged beyond the seas, splitting the whole of Europe. Any concise summary may approach it from several different angles: from the philosophical angle for example, with on the one hand the philosophers of the subject and the will (the Cartesians, Grotius, Pufendorf, Kant), and, on the other, the philosophers of natural law and understanding (Hobbes, Spinoza, Locke). Then there is the political angle, with those favouring the just State on one side (Locke), and the zealots of the administrative State on the other (Bodin); and finally, from the legal angle, with the philosophers of citizenship reduced to itself alone and founded on decision (Kant), and the philosophers of the rights of man (Hobbes, Spinoza, Locke).

It is manifestly the case that many other nuances of opinion separate these theorists, but from the standpoint that is of interest to us here, that is to say the construction of legality in a search for legitimacy, it is striking that supporters of sovereignty such as Bodin ground it in the decisions of the sovereign and put forward an administrative model of the state whereas the theorists of the separation of powers such as Sidney and Locke allow for empirical, exploratory diversity in the construction of norms. We might add that only the philosophers of natural law defend the rights of man, and that the latter cease to exist for the philosophers of the subject.

Until the end of the seventeenth century and the arrival of the crisis in European consciousness, and during the eighteenth century in the reflections of Montesquieu, the debate continued between the proponents of infallible sovereignty and those of the empirical, pluralistic construction of norms, but it is undeniable that in France, even under the Jacobin Republic, and in the Germany of Romanticism, where the imperial state was reborn, the standpoint of the plural legal construction of norms breaks down. If the general will cannot err (as Rousseau claims), how then do we account for the legal accession to power of Hitler and Pétain?

It is this unanswered question and the necessity of restoring the link between legitimacy and legality that have forced the republican states of the twentieth century to return to the issue of the legal construction of norms and find a pluralist, transcendent approach. The first step was to include transcendent and legitimate norms in the preamble to European constitutions: human rights, precisely those rights that pure political will had claimed to abolish. Alas, in the meantime, the empirical view of diversity had had time to extend the battle of all against all and decree that universalism is an ethnocentric projection of the Western world. Seeing diversity as absolute leads to the idea, already present in Romantic philosophy, of the shock of cultures and the battle to the death between 'spirits of the peoples'. Nevertheless, what underpins it is a total absence of any recognition of diversity, a claimed colonial entitlement to impose from outside a model arbitrarily decreed as better, the triumph of the will and the negation of the finite.

The great merit of the sociological approach is to have reminded us, often in a democratic spirit, of the priority to be assigned to social diversity, the necessity of construction after the fact, and in doing so, to have obliged the will to lower its sights, as well as having forced the will to absolute power to reveal its artificial and monstrous nature. But while going down this road it has simultaneously made norms relative and undermined the law. What needs to be done today is to revitalise them and ensure the rebirth of a legal construction of norms that leaves room for plurality and diversity.

This, however, naturally entails a requirement to redefine the angles of approach described above. Primarily, it necessitates a redefinition of the philosophical approach. The Cartesian philosophy of pure domination of nature ('to make ourselves the masters and possessors of nature'), which has taken human beings out of nature and exiled them from it, thus preparing the way for the misfortunes visited upon us by the will to absolute power in the twentieth century, has been radically undermined by the natural disasters that we have brought upon ourselves. But what has been noticed less is that psychology and politics have suffered similarly from this sense of absolute power: psychology, in the triumph of the infinite will over finite understanding, which denies our finite nature or sees it as relative and humbles our reason, developing all the diseases of desire, the will to power and narcissism; politics, in the continuation of the administrative state, which, while it is highly compatible with monarchy, aristocracy and corporatism, is out of step with democracy, which must assign a place to all citizens in all their plurality and diversity. The keystone of this reconstruction may perhaps be found in a new philosophy of nature that would reconcile norms with human diversity and prove capable at last of adapting the legal construction of norms to their sociological investigation.

Bibliography

Hobbes, Thomas, Leviathan, London, 1914.
Rousseau, Jean-Jacques, Du Contrat Social, Paris, 1966.
Schmitt, Carl, Politische Theologie, Berlin, 1922.

Legality, legitimacy and the constitution:
A historical-functionalist approach

Chris Thornhill

Introduction

This chapter attempts to comprehend the role of constitutions in modern society. In particular, it examines why in modern societies the interactions between law and politics are usually arranged in the form of a constitution, it assesses why modern political institutions tend to organize themselves around relatively stable constitutional norms, and it seeks to reconstruct the reasons why constitutions and constitutional rights act as dominant elements in the legitimatory grammar of modern politics. On this basis, this chapter also seeks to contribute to the understanding of political legitimacy quite generally, and it aims to account both for the form of legitimacy in modern society and for the correlation between legitimacy, rights and constitutions.

In addressing these questions, this chapter proceeds from the argument that standard modes of normative constitutional analysis are rather simplistic and do little to elucidate questions of legitimacy. This applies in particular to the claims deriving from the Enlightenment that constitutions are normative forms that stipulate principles of rational accountability by which the legitimacy of state power is measured and preserved.[1] To a lesser extent, this also applies to the more practical political-scientific claim that constitutions are patterns of institutional design, which secure legitimacy for political power by aligning the political system to prior models of stable and efficient government.[2] These theories throw little light on the broad societal foundations of constitutions, and they are not sensitive to the underlying or internal societal motives that lead political systems to adopt, and obtain legitimacy through, constitutions and constitutional rights. In different ways, both these theoretical approaches are structured around a formal antinomy between legality and legitimacy (or between norms and facts), and they simplify analysis of legitimacy by transforming factually evolved patterns of legitimacy into abstracted normative standards, which are then defined as external indicators of sustainable and valid authority. In the final analysis, these views postulate antinomically generalized laws as preconditions for legitimacy, and they can only give a rather reductive and eviden-

---

1 See my critique in *Thornhill*, Towards a Historical Sociology of Constitutional Legitimacy.
2 See the classic work of political science: *Sartori*, Comparative Constitutional Engineering, p. 196.

tially impoverished account of the function of constitutional norms in generating legitimacy for the state.

In consequence, this chapter responds to the deficiencies of conventional normative inquiries by endeavouring to propose a sociological approach to constitutions and their legitimatory status. Indeed, it argues that the nexus between constitutions, rights and political legitimacy can only persuasively be illuminated if constitutions and constitutional norms are examined in a very strict sociological perspective: that is, as factually emergent elements within *the constitution of society* as a whole. In the first instance, therefore, this endeavour picks up the threads of early constitutional sociology that are present, albeit rather inchoately, in the works of Durkheim, Weber and Léon Duguit. Constitutional sociology in fact began as an important subfield of sociology, but it was never consolidated as such, and this chapter might be viewed as an attempt to re-vivify some methodological aspects of classical constitutional sociology. At the same time, however, this endeavour also relates closely to other work in the contemporary social sciences that also aims to analyze constitutions from a sociological vantage point. In current theoretical research, it is possible to identify two broad theoretical lineages that approach constitutions from a sociological view, and together these have already generated a body of outstanding theoretical research. One of these lineages has a primarily systems-theoretical orientation: it is represented by (among other notable theorists) Gunther Teubner and Andreas Fischer-Lescano. The works of David Sciulli might also be cautiously placed in the margins of this lineage, as Sciulli also employs elements of functionalist institutionalism to assess the constitutional conditions of society.[3] The other of these lineages has a more obviously normative emphasis: it is stimulated originally by Habermas, and it is now represented most significantly by Hauke Brunkhorst.[4] In referring to this recent research on constitutional sociology, however, the analysis in this chapter attempts to set the terrain for an alternative sociological approach to constitutions and their legitimatory functions, and it proposes and utilizes a method that is substantially distinct from that used in both these lines of inquiry.

The sociological analysis of constitutions provided by recent theories in the systems-theoretical tradition, for example, has the striking benefit that it draws attention to new sources of quasi-public legislation in modern society, and it examines the laws articulating the constitutionality of public power as socially produced and highly variable and contingent forms, which often originate outside the conventional

---

3   For example, see *Teubner*, Societal Constitutionalism; *Teubner*, Die anonyme Matrix. For a US-American theory close to this milieu, see *Sciulli*, Theory of Societal Constitutionalism, pp. 78-80. See also David Sciulli's chapter in this voume.
4   Brunkhorst's work modifies Habermas's more strictly normative approach, and it accentuates ways in which constitutions bring legitimacy to society's politics by refracting and stabilizing underlying societal dynamics. See *Brunkhorst*, Solidarität, pp. 113-39. See also Brunkhorst's chapter in this volume.

spheres of state authority.[5] The primary yield of this work resides in the fact that it subjects more common state-centred perspectives on the sources of public law to a powerful revision, and it proposes a multi-focal and multi-causal account of the legal/normative structure of modern society. Although it uses a normative perspective in reflecting new modes of legal agency that limit or construct political power,[6] however, this research does not take as its object the deeper structural sources and the wider social functions of constitutions: in particular, it is not primarily concerned with the specific normative qualities of constitutions as documents of public law, and it does not identify written constitutions, or *constitutions of state*, as privileged sources of legal normativity in modern society. Moreover, this research does not explicate the central historical role of constitutions in the political stabilization of modern societies and in the production of legitimacy for modern political systems. In this theoretical lineage, neither the position of constitutions in the broader constitution of society nor the determinate normative status and functions of constitutions form the central object of inquiry. Although it promotes inquiry of the highest value into societal constitutionalism, therefore, this line of this theory does not offer a comprehensive sociological examination of constitutions and their societal functions. In conjunction with this, it is also arguable that, outside the systems-theoretical milieu more conventional normative approaches to constitutional sociology, such as those emerging in the wake of Habermas, also, for all their outstanding importance, fall slightly short of providing a general sociological method for interpreting constitutions. In fact, it is arguable that these theories ultimately move outside the terrain of strict sociological inquiry when examining the legitimatory reliance of modern societies on constitutional norms. Arguably, these works investigate the formation and function of constitutional norms in society by proceeding from the prior presupposition that agents within society possess a fundamental inclination towards the construction of normative or even quasi-consensual public institutions.[7] The constitutional formalization of public power provides political legitimacy for a society, then, because it articulates and gives realized and generalized form to this prior consensual inclination of social agents. In consequence, it can be argued that theories in the Habermasian lineage only, in the last analysis, account for the importance and the legitimatory status of constitutions because they pre-

---

5   Fischer-Lescano's analysis of how the 'political global constitution' of international society arises both from 'private governance regimes' and 'public governance regimes': *Fischer-Lescano*, Die Emergenz der Globalverfassung', p. 755. Together, Teubner and Fischer-Lescano also argue that the fragmented legal apparatus of modern world-society creates a number of auto-constitutionalized quasi-polities, existing in parallel to or interdependence with classical state forms. See *Fischer-Lescano/Teubner*, Fragmentierung des Weltrechts.
6   *Fischer-Lescano*, Emergenz der Globalverfassung, p. 721
7   Habermas's legal humanism revolves around the claim that a 'post-metaphysical understanding of the world' sees power as legitimate where it is formed in the 'language of law', through the 'discursive opinion- and will-formation of equal citizens' (*Habermas*, Faktizität und Geltung, p. 429).

construct an *anthropological* (that is, not *sociological*) body of practices and moral requirements as the common substrate of social life. Then, simply, they designate this substrate as bringing forth a normative order in society and as necessarily culminating in a normative-constitutional structure, to which states refer as the basis of their legitimacy.[8] For all their focus, on constitutions as factual institutions, therefore, these views do not yet comprehensively analyze constitutions as aspects of the more general constitution of society: in fact, in tacitly indicating that the terms of legitimacy are normatively external to states they suppress the social dimension of constitutions and constitutional norms and the post-Habermasian theory of the constitution resorts, lastly, to persistently antinomical constructions of constitutional legitimacy.

As a result of this, it is arguable that we still await a fully evolved *sociological* method for analyzing constitutions. That is to say, we await a method that examines the constitutions of modern societies in a manner that recognizes the distinction of constitutions as legal orders organizing state power and that does justice to their functions in generating quite specific normative resources of legitimacy for states, yet that also reflects the normative/legitimatory role of constitutions as embedded in deep-lying social structures or deep-lying social functions and so as not simply deducible through externally rationalized procedures or privileged cognitive acts. The sociological approaches to constitutions that have been proposed to date necessarily fall on one side of a strict (though often only half-articulated) facts/norms dichotomy. They necessarily observe constitutions either as *normatively contingent* (although, in the case of Teubner, most categorically *not* normatively indifferent) or as deduced and imposed through essentially *asocial normative prescription*. What might be viewed as missing from both lines of approach is the ability to construe the normative forms enshrined in constitutions as expressions of *society's norms*: that is as normative forms which are essential to society, upon which society experiences a particular legitimatory reliance, and which are relatively generalizable and invariable across society, yet also as forms that a society produces for itself in response to its internal functions and exigencies. Because of this, then, both current lines of sociological constitutional analysis, for all the ground-breaking quality of their research, do not accord specific objective meaning to the condition of legitimacy in the political system, and they either construe legitimacy in highly unspecified and variable terms or they deduce its conditions by means of external procedures. To assess constitutions and their normative/legitimatory functions as conclusively innersocietal realities, in consequence, a method is required that pursues a macrosociological approach to political constitutions and their legitimatory operations, and

---

8   See the argument in *Habermas*, Erkenntnis und Interesse. Brunkhorst's work is much more sociologically nuanced and less anthropologically hypostatic than that of Habermas. Yet his account of society's norms also relies on the assumption that 'communicative power' and 'democratic solidarity' are relatively constant fundaments of social practice: *Brunkhorst*, Solidarität, pp. 216-217.

that observes these operations as reflexive aspects of the constitution of society as a whole. This method, then, might establish parameters for constitutional sociology or the sociology of constitutions as a distinct sub-discipline of sociological inquiry. It might offer a theoretical perspective that positions itself outside the fact/norms dichotomy of much constitutional inquiry, and it might be able cogently to account for the legal-normative sources of legitimacy in a manner that does not either depreciate or externally prescribe the normative features of a society. This method, moreover, might even be authorized to use sociological analyses of constitutions to offer generalized models for examining the probable preconditions of legitimacy and the probable functions of effectively legitimatory constitutions in contemporary societies.

To provide a sociological method for addressing the question of political legitimacy and its relation to constitutions and constitutional norms, however, it is also essential to observe the processes underlying the historical formation of modern societies, and to evaluate the constitutions as objective constitutions arising in the course of modern societal formation. A sociology of constitutions, therefore, must also include a strong historical-sociological dimension. Here again, however, we encounter in many dominant sociologixcal methods a number of theoretical aporia that obstruct plausible sociological analysis of constitutions. One reason why the sociology of constitutions has not developed as a distinct element of sociology as a whole is because historical sociology is widely overshadowed by the sociology of states, and this body of literature habitually closes itself against normatively inflected inquiry. Analyses in this theoretical lineage usually argue, first, that modern states are formed through a process in which, in a given society, prepotent social agents deploy strategies of coercion and extraction in order to arrogate more or less exclusive power to themselves: this power is then concentrated in the institutions of the state.[9] On this conventional account, the condition of political modernity specifically depends upon the fact that a state produces directives for all members of a society, so that, across its sectoral variations, a modern society is inevitably forced into convergence around the coercive power of the state. Second, sociological analyses of the state also generally argue that, as the state is primarily an organ of political coercion and concentration, the precise institutional forms in which states elect to legitimize themselves are the results either of instrumental strategy or of highly contingent historical and cultural variations, and they cannot be assessed through any normative,

---

[9] For my critique of this literature, see again *Thornhill*, Towards a Historical Sociology of Constitutional Legitimacy. For a history of state formation that abandons the normal fiscal/military focus, see *Corrigan/Sayer*, The Great Arch. This account, based mainly in the sociology of culture, has nothing in common with the analysis offered here. A further exception to the standard patterns of historical-sociological inquiry is Otto Hintze's analysis of the evolution of modern constitutional rights from earlier constitutional forms. See *Hintze*, Staat und Verfassung, p. 147. I am deeply impressed by Hintze's work, but my analysis here borrows nothing from it.

deductive or generalizable analysis.[10] In general, therefore, the sociology of states only rarely addresses the precise role that legal-normative institutes play in the organization of statehood, and it is widely indifferent to the normative structures, such as rights and political constitutions, that condense around state power and around which state power arranges and legitimizes itself. Indeed, whilst the broader evolutionary trajectory of modern social reality has tended manifestly toward a consolidation of the nexus between states and legal norms (especially in the form of constitutional rights), the sociology of states has been largely obdurate in refusing to fix its gaze on this fact, and it has, with some exceptions, persisted in its construction of the state as a coercive order and as detached from stable or fundamental normative legal form.[11]

In consequence, the attempt to counter-pose to other current sociological views a fully sociological method for examining constitutions and their normative/ legitimatory functions must also respond critically to the more traditional sociology of states. In particular, in attempting to elucidate how constitutions and constitutional norms evolve, and perform legitimatory functions, in the wider contours of societal formation sociological inquiry must begin to re-examine the historical formation of states, and it must seek to interpret the ways in which states depend on, and in fact even directly generate, constitutions and constitutional norms. The sociology of constitutions, thus, also presupposes a revision of classical views of the state, and it requires a thorough reconstruction of many standard positions in historical-political sociology. The analysis below, in consequence, seeks to comprehend and demonstrate how constitutions and their normative functions are interwoven with the structure of a modern society. To this end, it observes the relation between the historical formation of states and the normative processes of constitutionalization, and it examines ways in which states habitually obtain constitutional norms for their functional support and their reflexive legitimacy. In so doing, as well as illuminating the specific social functions of constitutions, this analysis seeks to offer a fully sociological account of the sources of the legitimacy of the modern political apparatus.

---

10 See, for example *Weber*, Wirtschaft und Gesellschaft, pp. 122-76. Of course, some sociological analysis of states has a pronounced normative bias. See *Parsons*, Sociological Theory and Modern Society, pp. 7-8. However, Parsons also suggests that the normative content of states can only be examined, not as resting on explicitly justifiable principles, but through reference to variable values embedded in social structure and residual cultural patterns of integration.
11 See *Tilly*, Reflections on the History of European State-Making, p. 37.

States, rights and political differentiation

Medieval constitutions

On this theoretical basis, it can be observed, first, that constitutions initially began to evolve in nascent European societies as responses to an incremental, although not always linear, process of *functional differentiation*.[12] This was a process that, as it initially commenced, exercised a deep and formative impact on the structure of European societies as a whole. Most significantly, this process was reflected, first, in the differentiation of political power from ecclesiastical power; second, in the (incipient) differentiation of the economy as a distinct, expanding and broadly specialized set of monetary transactions;[13] and, third, in the separation of an (emergent) public apparatus, containing vertically applicable power, from the private and local masses of agreements, privileges and overlapping jurisdictions that structured early feudal society. It is in this relation to this process of differentiation, then, that we can discern the first indications of a growing constitutional order in the political apparatus of European societies, and that we can observe the first legitimatory functions of constitutions. Indeed, the earliest European constitutions began to emerge as institutions that allowed societies, in a number of ways, to reflect on and to adjust to the evolutionary transformations that they experienced because of this complex differentiatory process, and they enabled societies to construct a political order that was sensitive and responsive to the increasingly differentiated pluralization of society's functions. In this respect, of course, it needs to be stated that there is some ambiguity attached to the use of the term 'constitution' in this context: this term, arguably, was not widely employed in its modern sense until the seventeenth century.[14] However, if a constitution is generally taken to include both a set of relatively stable and acceded legal circumscriptions placed on the use of political power, and a body of legally or customarily formalized arrangements for securing political consensus in major directive decisions, constitutions were factually widespread in the more centralized European societies by the fourteenth, and perhaps even by the thirteenth, century. The existence of such constitutions can be identified in most proto-modern European polities, from the Holy Roman Empire, to the monarchy of Castile-Léon, to the cities of medieval Lombardy, to later Norman and Angevin England, and to mid-

---

12   This argument refers to Niklas Luhmann's theory that there is a demonstrable 'connection between social differentiation and the development of constitutions'. See *Luhmann*, Politische Verfassungen im Kontext des Gesellschaftssystems, p. 6. Some points in the following historical sections discuss, in extremely condensed form, aspects of material that I am also treating in the earlier chapters of my forthcoming book: *Thornhill*, A Sociology of Constitutions. The context, the precise content, and the focus of the present analysis are different from those contained in the forthcoming book.
13   See *Lousse*, La Societé d'Ancien Régime, p. 123.
14   *McIlwain*, Constitutionalism Ancient and Modern, p. 97.

to late-Capetian France. In each of these settings, constitutions played a vital role in enabling growing centres of political agency to detach themselves both from the church and from the privatistic and functionally interlocking foundations of feudal order, and they made it possible for societies gradually to evolve a political apparatus adequately adapted to, and capable of asserting legitimacy within, an increasingly differentiated and functionally specialized societal setting.

The earliest constitutions helped early European societies to adjust to their underlying differentiation, first, because they provided legal-technical arrangements, usually in written form, that enacted a function of *political abstraction* for society. That is to say, early constitutions acted as documents that protected the liberties of some social groups, that identified some social practices and personal attributes as beyond the reach of state power, that regularized procedures used by political actors for utilizing and applying power through society, and that gradually stabilized basic principles or agreements concerning the origins, functions and ends of state power. In these respects, on one hand, these early constitutions served to mark out terms of *inclusion* for the political system, and they allowed early states to construct themselves as possessing acceded collective personalities, in which (politically relevant) parts of society were implicitly present.[15] For this reason, constitutions also acted, crucially, to delineate the political system of society as a relatively independent and thematically specialized realm of social exchange, whose functions could be disembedded from highly privatistic concerns, prerogatives and milieux. In some cases, in fact, these constitutions also instituted devices for resolving conflicts at the boundaries between the political system and other parts of society (especially at the boundaries between polity and religion and polity and economy: i.e. in conflicts over ecclesiastical jurisdiction and fiscal revenue, the resolution of which, more than any other factor, allowed states to evolve as possessing central jurisdictional power in a given society).[16] In doing this, early constitutions began to reformulate private rights and immunities as rights recognizable and reflected through states, and thus also to transform centrifugal rights into inclusive principles of public order. In each of these respects, therefore, it can be observed that the fact that in medieval society bearers

---

15 On the religious origins of the state's transpersonal personality, see *Black*, Monarchy and Community, p. 14. This point was made most famously by Gierke. See *Gierke*, Das deutsche Genossenschaftsrecht, III, p. 275.

16 The Holy Roman Empire gave conclusive constitutional form to the Imperial office in the Golden Bull of 1356. Subsequently, the princely states within the Empire also assumed (less formalized) constitutional structure, as through the later fourteenth and the fifteenth century these states often developed patterns of delegation of territorial estates [*Landstände*]. Indeed, as early as 1231 it was forbidden by Imperial decree for German princes to raise taxes without consent of the Landstände. In Spain, the kings of Castile-Léon began to convene meetings of estates after 1188, and delegates at these meetings had extensive quasi-legislative powers. In France, the differences between Philip IV and Pope Boniface VIII before and after 1300 led to the first convocations of the Estates-General. In England, the Magna Carta of 1215 set out an early constitutional design for the state, and by 1300 parliamentary assemblies, with extensive fiscal powers, were regularly convened.

of political power began to surround themselves with legal/constitutional arrangements specifically enabled these actors to concentrate their power in the inclusive form of early statehood or proto-statehood, and to consolidate society's political functions as an increasingly self-contained body of interactions, distinct from other realms of social practice. Indeed, this fact permitted early states internally to formulate the principles underscoring their power, and it played a crucial role both in the first differentiation of states from the overlayered functional structures of feudal political order and in the broader de-feudalization of society more generally. These constitutions allowed the political system to incorporate a mass of decisions that could be abstractly specified and transmitted quite quickly and without incessant renegotiation across society, and they ensured that the political system could operate as a political or proto-public apparatus that no longer, in the fashion of power under feudal regimes, relied on highly privatized acts of agreement and recognition in order to mobilize collective resources.[17] The first consolidation of a differentiated and centralized polity, using power as an abstracted and differentiated commodity, was, in short, only possible because the early form of the polity mobilized constitutional forms in order to sustain its social abstraction.[18]

In relation to this, second, early constitutions also allowed European societies to react to their underlying differentiation because they enacted a process of *political generalization* for society. In separating the political apparatus from other exchanges and, in particular, in giving normative-legal form to the boundaries and limits of states and the procedures for transmitting political power, constitutions made it feasible for the state to use its power in reliably inclusive and relatively reproducible manner.[19] The fact that constitutions conferred a general legal form on political power made it possible for states to emerge as institutions that were able to extend their power across societal divisions, positively to underwrite the circulation of their power in very different societal settings, and, in so doing, constantly to reconstitute their own operative preconditions. Crucial to this aspect of constitutional formation was the fact that in specifying legal forms for the use of power and mobilizing manifest consent for important decisions constitutions allowed states to pass laws at an increasingly high level of positivity: that is, in the form of *statutes*. The very earliest

---

17 On the emergence of a concept of public law, see *Post*, The Theory of Public Law and the State, p. 52.
18 See *Major*, Representative Institutions in Renaissance France; *Spangenberg*, Vom Lehnstaat zum Ständestaat, p. 130; *Koenigsberger*, Parliaments and Estates.
19 In this, we can identify the cause of the structural nexus between increasing legal regularity and reinforced constitutional arrangement in later medieval societies. Societies that possessed relatively centralized polities in later medieval Europe – i.e. France, England, Spain, Sweden, the Holy Roman Empire, some Italian cities – also implemented increasingly generalized law codes and obtained increasingly regular legal systems, and they incorporated widening mechanisms of constitutional integration to support their legislative and jurisdictional acts. Notable amongst these codes were the Siete Partidas in Spain (mid thirteenth century), the Swedish Land Law (1350s), the refined construction of the English common law commissioned by Henry II, and the Sachsenspiegel in some parts of Germany (1220-35).

legal structure of European societies was determined by the fact that laws were of essentially customary or consuetudinal character, and proto-state actors had only limited freedom to alter customs or to legislate in autonomous or positive fashion.[20] As states increasingly began to function as positively differentiated political actors, however, it also became essential for states to legislate at a growing level of positive autonomy, and to apply law, more variably, to more disparate social themes: that is, primarily to apply law through statutes. The ability of a state to construct and to refer to itself as possessing a constitutional or consensual structure was fundamental for its ability to pass laws in positive form and to legitimize new statutory acts.[21] Indeed, it can clearly be observed that the emergent European states with the most elaborate constitutional apparatus and the most uniform legal order were also the states that were best equipped positively to pass and authorize statutory laws, and so rapidly to transmit power through society. The consolidation of the state as an institutional body able to generalize power across society in the form of positive law thus also presupposed that the state could act in compliance with a constitutional form, that it could account for itself as containing a legal personality distinct from any particular bearer of its power, and that it could regulate its power through constitutional norms.

In addition to this, third, constitutions helped early European societies to adapt to their widening differentiation because they provided instruments that performed a service of incremental *political selection* or even of *social de-politicization* for society as a whole. In demarcating the peripheries of the political order and in formulating normative principles to trace out or even to govern the points of intersection between the political system and other social spheres, constitutions created normatively stabilized legal devices in which societies were able to stipulate in relatively regular manner what was and what was not subject to immediate inclusion in the po-

20 *Reynolds*, Law and Communities.
21 It is of course not possible here to cover all the literature on statutes and their contribution to the emergence of a modern society. However, two salient cases can be noted. First, the Italian cities of high medieval Europe might be seen as trailblazers in the promotion of statutory legislation. As, after the wars of the Lombard League, a legal vacuum emerged between the Holy Roman Empire, the papacy, and local territorial powers, the cities of northern Italy obtained a legal concession of statutory power [*ius statuendi*], and they began progressively to transform their customary laws into constitutional statutes. For a tiny sample of the literature on this, see *Pini*, Dal comune città-stato al commune ente amministrativa, pp. 471-2; *Zorzi*, La giustizia imperiale nell'Italia comunale, p. 89. At a later stage, in England the use of statutes as instruments for introducing new laws increased exponentially through the thirteenth century and this culminated in the extensive swathes of statutory legislation introduced during the reign of Edward I. See *Plucknett*, Legislation of Edward I, p. 10; *Plucknett*, Statutes and their Interpretation, p. 30. The Second Statute of Westminster introduced by Edward I in 1285 is seen as marking a seminal moment in the 'transformation of the law of England from a basis of custom to a basis of statute'. See *Wilkinson*, Constitutional History of Medieval England, I, p. 44. In both these cases of accelerated legal positivization, notably, the promulgation of positive statutes was made possible by the fact that states, either in the form of the consoli in Italy or the parliament in England, evolved an extensive constitutional apparatus for supporting and legitimizing their laws.

litical system. Most obviously, this enabled political systems to reinforce their abstracted independence of privately or locally embedded agreements. However, this also enabled political systems to withdraw many social exchanges from unabated internalization in their exchanges, and to ensure that many conflicts and contests in society were not placed immediately under political jurisdiction. In consequence, this function of constitutions also allowed emergent political systems to make decisions in thematically selective manner, to focus their power on a specific set of social phenomena, and to limit the degree to which they encountered (or stimulated) societally amorphous or unpredictably resonant obstructions in their use of power. Indeed, where the societal boundaries between the growing political system and other systems were precarious or prone to conflict (especially, for instance, in religious or fiscal questions), constitutions widely acted to provide mechanisms for the pacified resolution of antagonism, and they offered utensils for the formal *exclusion* of some exchanges from the inner structure of politics. Not lastly, therefore, the earliest constitutions evolved as normative documents that ensured that not all of society needed to be ceaselessly immersed in political power, and that those exchanges to which power was relevant could be accurately described and proportionately included in differentiated acts of political jurisdiction. In this respect again, the limiting of state power performed by the legal arrangements formalized as early constitutions might be seen as marking a crucial juncture in the evolutionary transition of early European society from the relatively undifferentiated, highly privatized condition of feudalism towards the differentiated and functionally specialized reality of modern society and modern political order. It was only as a result of the limiting function of constitutions, or through the controlled and proceduralized political in- and exclusion of different social exchanges, that societies that were rapidly expanding across differences of time and place were able to form and explain their power as a commodity that could be used in a reliable and effective manner in a differentiated society.

In each of these respects, in sum, constitutions brought great functional advantages to the gradually modernizing modern societies of medieval Europe. In particular, they helped the political systems of these societies to develop a body of normative arrangements in which they were able to employ power at an appropriate level of differentiated abstraction and inclusive generality. Constitutions and constitutional norms thus contributed directly to forming the reserves of *practical-functional legitimacy* for early political systems: that is, they allowed political systems to obtain legitimacy for themselves by establishing an apparatus in which they could stabilize their exchanges, effectively and inclusively utilize their power, and adjust both to the pluralistic environments in which they were located and to the functional demands directed to them. In addition to this, however, constitutions also brought benefits to European societies because they instilled – or at least began to instil – within the political system a body of norms from which it could project constant and reproducible accounts of itself and its power, and so, gradually, they allowed the political system both to internalize and articulate, *from within itself*, positive principles to support and simplify its activities and to accompany its particular acts of legislation across society.[22] In stabilizing a normative account of the political system in objectively differentiated and internalized legal principles, in other words, early constitutions also allowed nascent political systems to call upon an inner reservoir of *conceptual or reflexive legitimacy*: that is, they permitted political institutions to incorporate a stable and organically constructed account of their functions, to which they could refer to explain their power, and which enabled them to perform their operations for society at an increasingly high level of abstraction, generality, and iterability. Most especially, the fact that they obtained from constitutions a set of inner principles for formulating their legitimacy meant that evolving political systems were able, with some reliability, to project preconditions, to pre-structure the social terrain, and to provide constant and pre-emptive explanations, for the future use of their power. In addition to promoting political abstraction, political generalization and social de-politicization as prerequisites of the first formation of a political system in a differentiated society, therefore, early European constitutions had the function that they offered to states a stable, consistent, and socially withdrawn normative formula through which they could freely consume and reproduce their legitimacy while conducting their concrete societal functions.[23] The *normative* principles that underpinned earliest European constitutions, thus, were also *functional* elements of society, and these norms allowed the political apparatus of society at once to internalize plausible descriptions of itself and to simplify the general transmission of its power. The antinomy between facts and norms that perennially perplexes the established tradition of political and constitutional theory thus appears in this perspective to be a misconstructed antinomy.[24] In fact, in analyzing constitutions from a historical-sociological perspective we can observe that constitutions originally emerged as institutions in which evolving modern societies first learned to bring their functional requirements and their normative requirements into convergence, and this made it possible for societies, and political systems within these societies, to develop in their essential modern (i.e. differentiated and positivized) form. From the period of their earliest formation, therefore, constitutions were evidently defined by their normative structure, and they articulated an abstracted corpus of norms around which a society could shape its political functions. Yet this structure was not imported into society as an external check on the power of society's political system. On the contrary, consti-

---

22 This argument is influenced by Niklas Luhmann's claim that, through the positivization of law, law and politics were forced to devise patterns or semantics for their 'self-foundation' [*Selbstbegründung*]: Luhmann, Die Gesellschaft der Gesellschaft, p. 976.
23 This theory of legal positivization as formative of modern society has its origins in Luhmann's legal sociology. Yet note that my account of positivization – that is, the translocation of law onto autonomous and self-generated foundations – sees the beginnings of this process at a much earlier historical stage than Luhmann, who makes a distinction between positive law and natural and sees the former assuming dominance in the eighteenth century. See *Luhmann*, Das Recht der Gesellschaft, pp. 38-9.
24 The longest rumination on this perplexity is *Habermas*, Faktizität und Geltung.

tutions evolved as the adaptive functional form in which political power was able to abstract, generalize and positivize itself for those functions in society requiring power. Constitutional norms, in other words, first emerged as the adequate form of *society's norms*.

To summarize these points, therefore, we might conclude – to argue at a high level of generality – that the formation of constitutions (that is, the relatively formal and stable interpenetration of politics and law) played a crucial role in allowing nascent European societies to form themselves as characteristically modern (differentiated) societies. Indeed, we might also say that a society assumes modern (differentiated) form through certain primary acts of *inclusion* and *exclusion*, and that both these acts were tied to constitutions.[25] In particular, we can say, first, that a society emerges in its proto-modern structure as it develops patterns of extensive and simplified *inclusion*: that is, as it learns to reproduce certain modes of exchange (both juridical and political, but increasingly also monetary) across widening local and temporal spaces, and as it acquires the facility to incorporate social agents in these exchanges without being forced constantly to adjust the form of these exchanges to all the structural particularities of those agents included in them. Then we can say, second, that a society develops the features of a proto-modern society because, by virtue of its inclusivity, it constructs its members in a relatively positive and generalized fashion, its members recognize themselves as generally and quite uniformly identifiable with this society and as included within its patterns of exchange, and because media of social exchange can be used in relatively uniform and internally reproducible fashion, so that these media do not have to be re-formulated in every act of their application. A society becomes a modern society as a shared aggregate of functional horizons, in which persons are transformed from bearers of highly local or particularized expectations into subjects of extensible media of exchange, which presuppose the uniform *inclusion* of their addressees as a basis for their own self-reproduction or iterability. The generality and inclusive iterability that give foundation to a proto-modern society, thus, first resulted – at least in part – from the ability of the emergent political system in society to include its addresses under generalized, uniform and positive laws: in fact, the formation of a political system as a relatively independent centre of legal order initially both accompanied and reinforced the wider generalization and increasing inclusivity of society as a whole.[26]

---

25 For recent analysis of inclusion as the formative dimension of society, see *Stichweh*, Inklusion und Exklusion, p. 71. Unlike Stichweh (and Luhmann before him), my analysis here emphasizes the function of exclusion as the correlative of inclusion.
26 The emergence of sovereign states as a process correlated with a widening of societal inclusivity can be seen in most stages of state building. In Capetian France, for example, the increasing exercise of quasi-sovereign power by the state was flanked by the delocalization of societal structures, by the increasing dissemination of law, articulated as positive law by the légistes, as a general medium, and by the increasingly public organization of the state's foundations. See *Aubert*, Le Parlement de Paris, pp. 7-11; *Bardoux*, Les Légistes, p. 34. In the German territories, the construction of inclusive societies was also specifically linked to the

More particularly, though, these processes of inclusion also resulted from the formation of the state as a group of institutions endowed with a constitutional order, and the state's ability to construct itself as a uniform legal personality was central to society's capacity for utilizing power as an inclusive and reproducible medium of exchange and for stabilizing itself over aver large geographical and temporal spaces. In addition to this, however, this general process of inclusion also presupposes that a political system in society can clearly differentiate those dimensions of the exchanges conducted by its addressees that are susceptible to assimilation under law and under power from those that are not, that it can eliminate from its functions those social exchanges that are not (normally) articulated as politically relevant, and that it can avoid the recurrent or internal *controversialization* of the procedures in which it uses power and law. In this respect, for instance, it might be argued that nascent modern societies gradually learned to limit the degree to which they defined economic exchanges as primary objects of political inclusion, that these societies also very gradually (with many lapses) found ways of disengaging religious contents from legal and political procedures, and that these societies managed to separate power from informal spheres of private practice and arrangement. Each of these processes was a precondition for the capacity of a society to use power as a generalizable and differentiated facility. The element of legal-political *inclusivity* at the core of an emerging modern society, in consequence, also requires certain acts of primary *exclusion* on the part of a political system, and it presupposes that the political system can recognize that in order to *include* certain exchanges it must also *exclude* others. In both these respects, the status of early constitutions is vitally formative of modern society. In identifying and formalizing the boundaries of the political

emergence of states and to the formation of constitutional mechanisms within these states. The constitutional arrangements of the Landstände in some German territories specifically acted to detach the exercise of power from private persons, to consolidate power in one social setting, and to delineate in relative permanence the territorial locations subject to power. For classic commentary on constitutions as the hinge between the formation of states and the emergence of inclusive societies, see *v. Below*, Territorium und Stadt, p. 55. At a later stage, England under the Tudors might be seen to mark an early culminating of this process. Although the formal concept of sovereignty was not yet established at this time, in the early 1530s Thomas Cromwell was able to describe the polity of England in terms that accorded to it a status close to de facto sovereignty, asserting that it was able to provide justice in all matters and without any superior. See *Dickens*, The English Reformation, p. 117; *Lehmberg*, The Reformation Parliament 1529-1536, p. 164. Though on the limits of sovereignty see also *Loades*, Tudor Government, pp. 1-4. This process fell well short of constituting the Tudor state as an exclusive centre of social control. However, through the course of the Tudor period the power of royal courts was substantially reinforced, and monarchical control both of the fiscal system and of the means of jurisdiction was tightened. See *Richardson*, Tudor Chamber Administration, pp. 79-80. Of particular importance was the fact that the edifice of state emerging under the Tudors was beginning to assume features of a fully public apparatus: that is, it was effectively distinct from the model of semi-private government characteristic of the Middle Ages, and it organized its administrative (and especially its fiscal) mechanisms as devices for general rule across a national kingdom. See *Elton*, The Tudor Revolution in Government, pp. 4, 150.

system, in reflecting the immunity of social agents in their non-political activities, in specifying activities relevant for political inclusion, and in abstracting political power as a distinct and distilled societal resource, early constitutions enacted the exclusion required to complement the state's inclusion, and in so doing they acted (as far as possible) to immunize society against experiences of undifferentiated political saturation. In both respects, constitutions served to extend and augment the resources of usable power over which the incipiently differentiated political system disposed.

A constitution, in sum, might be seen, in its essential and original social functions, as an objective normative construction in which societies first began to balance the necessary inclusionary and the necessary exclusionary functions of a modern political system. It was only through the ability of political systems to use constitutions to found adequate normative self-constructions for their functions that modern society as a whole, as a selectively in- and exclusive aggregate of exchanges, was able to evolve and sustain its typically differentiated form.

Early modern constitutions

The constitutions of European states that emerged during the early modern period also performed their primary function through the fact that they allowed developing political systems further to adapt to the accelerating differentiation of the societies in which they were located. At the caesura between medieval and modern Europe, most particularly, it can be observed that states were now approaching a condition of relatively high autonomy in relation to other social exchanges. Accordingly, the constitutions that evolved at this time acted in different ways to provide refined support for the adequately abstracted and positive organization of the functions of these states, and they again helped states, both in- and exclusively, to sensibilize themselves to the complexly differentiated social realities to which they applied their power.

First, for example, most constitutions of the early modern era were conceived as documents that specified the limits of monarchical, or imperial prerogative, and that ensured that particular persons (i.e. regents) could not detach the form of the state from the public-legal order established by practical legal consensus or convention. These constitutions, and the ideas surrounding them, had their normative emphasis in the principle that there existed *basic laws* of state, which even those personally utilizing the state's power could not contravene.[27] In this regard, constitutions of this

---

27 For the classic case of this, England, see *Eusden*, Puritans, Lawyers, and Politics, pp. 44-49. The idea that there are basic laws, whose recognition involves rights that can be invoked against the state, is at the core of the original meaning of the concept: constitution. This idea was also widespread across most early modern European states. The Dutch jurist, Ulrich Huber, explained constitutions as laws that irrevocably founded the structure of the state. See

period were intended to make sure that political power was conclusively condensed in the public/organic form of a *body politic*, and that it could not re-converge with the private objectives or proprietary claims of individually powerful political actors. In consequence, early modern constitutions contributed directly to the differentiated and specifically political construction of the state, and they instituted procedures and legal forms that substantially reinforced the abstraction of the state's societal boundaries. Moreover, in framing political power in acceded public norms these constitutions also reinforced the legal personality of the state, which had been more tentatively elaborated in medieval constitutional texts: in so doing, they articulated a firmly inclusionary and transplantable support for society's power, and they simplified the generalized transmission of power across society.

Second, however, the truly salient point in this epoch of constitutional foundation was that these constitutions were organized – though, as yet, only to a limited degree – around the incipient principle that constitutions were required to enshrine and guarantee *rights*. That is to say, the most progressive and elaborated constitutions of this period had the distinctive dimension (albeit with extreme regional variations) that they gave formalized and uniform recognition to claims over property ownership and personal autonomy and judicial integrity, and they sought to preserve attributes of personal autonomy by rendering general and permanent hitherto sporadic or informal agreements over customary freedoms between established political actors around the state and consolidated or emergent interests in the economy.[28] The most advanced early modern constitutions, in consequence, extended beyond merely practical provisions for basic laws. In addition to this, they also offered normative sanctions for proprietary freedoms throughout all society (i.e. they cemented rights against non-mandated taxation and expropriation); they enshrined general procedural entitlements (i.e. they granted rights of protection from judicial irregularity) for legal subjects (or for a select number of legal subjects); in some instances, they acted to uphold delegatory rights for members of an exclusively circumscribed (i.e. independently property-holding) political class.[29]

It can be observed from a socio-functional viewpoint that the advent of rights as dominant norms in the legitimatory grammar of politics brought a large number of

---

Huber, De Jure Civitatis, I, p. 125. In Germany, Althusius had already moved this idea closer to a doctrine of popular sovereignty. See *Althusius*, Politica, p. 169. This idea is also evident in slightly earlier principles of French constitutionalism. See *de Haillan*, De l'Estat et Succes des Affaires de France, III, p. 43.

28 The English constitution can be seen as the classic case of this. See *Ogilvie*, The King's Government and the Common Law, pp. 4, 6.

29 England is again the main example. For England's constitution in nuce, see *Aylmer*, The Struggle for the Constitution, pp. 222-229. These principles were stated in the Petition of Right, which defined 'common consent by Act of Parliament' as the basis for new taxes, and it was refined in Article 4 of the Bill of Rights. See Kenyon (ed), The Stuart Constitution, p. 84. Sweden was also an example of a state guaranteeing formal constitutional rights and the general rule of law. See Roberts (ed), Sweden as a Great Power, pp. 20, 26; *Roberts*, Gustavus Adolphus and the Rise of Sweden, p. 85.

adaptive benefits to evolving European societies, and they strongly reinforced the functions of constitutional norms that are described above. First, these constitutional rights acted to translate particular freedoms into freedoms invoked and obtained through the state. In this respect, rights both consolidated the publicly differentiated form of the state and consolidated its inclusive organic personality. Second, in instituting generalized procedures in which power had to be utilized and in defining addressees of law as bearers of like status, rights greatly simplified the generalization of power through society. Most important amongst the social functions fulfilled by rights, however, was the fact that constitutional rights also served dramatically to strengthen the tendencies towards inclusionary political selection and exclusionary societal de-politicization, which modern societies, and the modern political systems situated in these societies, structurally presuppose. The constitutions and constitutional rights of early modern Europe accomplished this, most evidently, because they clarified and perpetuated the conditions of articulation between the state and other social domains, and in recognizing certain activities as protected from political encroachment by rights they limited the tendency of social themes indiscriminately to migrate towards the political system and they reduced the extent to which themes originating in different parts of society (notably in religion or in the economy) had to be ceaselessly regulated by or internalized, as *political*, within the state.[30] Additionally, moreover, the constitutions and constitutional rights that were gradually formulated during this period also created clusters of sanctioned legal formulae and procedures at the periphery of the state, which also helped to regulate exchanges between the state and other social domains and generally served society's depoliticization. The fact that states now began to incorporate clear provisions over rights meant that the political system acquired a corpus of norms and precedents, in reference to which debates about pressing social themes could be conducted and which could be invoked to deflate moments of intense political controversy. Indeed, these constitutions engendered conventions by means of which many controversial issues could be directed to sub-sectors of the state administration (usually to legislatures or courts of law, with constitutionally prescribed realms of competency) and so resolved in placatory procedural fashion.[31] Under pre-modern constitutions, therefore, state execu-

---

30   Here again, it should be noted that my account of rights is indebted to Luhmann's work on the sociology of rights. It should also be clear, though, that I ascribe a stable normative function to rights that Luhmann is not willing to countenance. For Luhmann's analysis of rights, see *Luhmann*, Grundrechte als Institution, p. 135.

31   Before the concession of formal constitutional rights, courts contributed widely to the destabilization of the state, and states struggled to bring their own judicial apparatus under control. In England, for example, the courts of common law were central to the constitutional conflicts prior to the Civil War. For contemporary insistence on the integrity of judicial procedure as a check on the state, see *Coke*, Selected Writings, III, p. 1271. For the implications of this, see *Judson*, The Crisis of the Constitution, pp. 191, 211; *Hart*, The Rule of Law, esp. p. 39; Kenyon (ed), The Stuart Constitution, p. 92. In France, the conflict between the monarchy and the sovereign courts was also one main constitutional cause of the revolution of 1789. France's belated evolution of a constitution was one reason why the monarchy was structural-

tives had usually been objects of constant and sporadic personal *petition* by particular social agents, and actors in the executive had been recurrently forced, in often personalized and irregularly intensified manner, to pursue statutory functions in response to individual complaints or demands.[32] Under early modern rights-based constitutions, in contrast, it gradually became possible for states regularly to transport political decisions into subordinate courts, into separate legislatures, or, as far as these can be distinguished from legislatures and courts, into the (politically neutralized) civil service.[33] This greatly expanded the administrative flexibility of the state, and it greatly diminished the political volatility attached to the boundaries between the political system and the rest of society. In consequence, the tendency in many early modern constitutions exponentially to reinforce (and constitutionally to protect: i.e. *through rights*) parliamentary authority, increasingly to separate parliaments from royal courts, and to transform royal appointees into professionalized civil servants, might be viewed, in a functional light, as a process that limited the overt

    ly weak. For samples of the literature on this, see *Hamscher*, The Parlement of Paris after the Fronde, p. 119; *Hurt*, Louis XIV and the Parlements, pp. 149-172; *Stone*, The French Parlements, p. 76. In Germany, notably, even many of the most powerful states did not possess full jurisdictional supremacy in their territories until well after 1648. On the tortuous conflict over the formation of a jurisdictional-constitutional balance between territories and Empire in the German context see: Ulrich Eisenhardt (ed), Die kaiserlichen Privilegia de non appellando; *Weitzel*, Der Kampf um die Appellation, p. 87; *Diestelkamp*, Zur Krise des Reichsrechts. Chronologically inaccurate in its analysis of the emergence of early statehood in Germany is *Berman*, Law and Revolution, vol. II, p. 62. In each of these cases, the consolidation of statehood depended on the internalization of the courts of law into the state by means of a regular constitutional system.

32   On this general aspect of very early parliamentary activity in different settings, see *Wilkinson*, Constitutional History of Medieval England, II, p. 6; *Procter*, Curia and Cortes, p. 206; *de Dios*, El Consejo real de Castilla, p. 67; *Moraw*, Versuch über die Entstehung des Reichstags; *Neuhaus*, Reichsständische Repräsentativformen, p. 26

33   Here again, I argue against widespread orthodoxy in historical sociology. The emergence of a centralized state bureaucracy is usually seen as a sign of increasing societal convergence around the state (Here again, my argument is respectfully opposed to Weber. See *Weber*, Wirtschaft und Gesellschaft, p. 825). In my view, the emergence of a powerful state bureaucracy in European societies reflected a process of functional sub-division within the state, which enabled the state to store administrative reserves towards which it could deflect volatile social exchanges. On this process in England, see *Stone*, Crisis of the Aristocracy, p. 10. On the professionalization of the English civil service, see *Aylmer*, The Crown's Servants, p. 101. In France, the emergence of state bureaucracy was hampered by the fact that many public offices were venal, and the French monarchy, owing to its personalized constitution, struggled to form an independent civil service. For commentary, see *Mousnier*, Les Institutions de la France sous la Monarchie Absolue, p. 466; *Zeller*, Les Institutions de la France au XVI siècle, p. 142. Sweden might be seen as an early example of way in which states used constitutions to integrate oppositional forces in the state administration. See *Lindegren*, The Swedish military state, p. 309; *Buchholz*, Staat und Ständegesellschaft in Schweden, p. 127. The classic, though somewhat later, example of this process is Prussia, in which the belated course of constitutional formation famously consummated a move to government by a 'parliament of civil servants' [*Beamtenparlament*] that was placed next to the monarch. See *Vogel*, Allgemeine Gewerbefreiheit, p. 132.

politicization of social themes, that exclusively reduced the intensity of political conflict around the executive apparatus of states, and that augmented the positive statutory power of the state. Quite evidently, in fact, this constitutional process – entailing, but not exhausted in, an early separation of powers – helped secure a positive sphere of operative freedom around the administrative organs of the state. As a result of this, the particular actors situated in this administrative body were not encumbered by an excessively large or excessively politicized mass of commitments,[34] and states obtaining a parliamentary constitution were able integrate complex yet politically withdrawn procedures for responding to social exchanges. The proclamation of legitimate state power as residing in a rights-based parliamentary constitutional state thus dramatically expanded the positive power of the state, and it exponentially increased the facility with which power could be employed and disseminated through society.

To conclude this section, it can be seen that the more refined constitutions of early modern European states helped to stabilize society's differentiated political form because they began (albeit still gradually and rudimentarily) to implant within the state a normative construction of those persons subject to its power as *holders of rights*. This norm performed the practical function that it helped to minimize fractious controversy about the terms of exchange between the political system and other social systems, and it facilitated processes of sub-division in the political system: both of these processes augmented the differentiated stability and the positive/technical efficacy of the political system. In addition, these constitutions brought the still greater, but less apparent, benefit for early modern states that they dramatically enlarged the reflexive resources of positive legitimacy that states could obtain and employ. As they learned to refer to their addressees as entitled claimants over rights and as they then evolved constitutions that normatively formalized and perpetuated this recognition, early modern states slowly acquired an internally consistent and reproducible *vocabulary of inclusion and exclusion*, which had inestimable functional and legitimatory advantages for their further development. That is to say, as they began to define and include those subject to their power as endowed with rights, political systems began, first, to integrate a reflexive/normative apparatus through which they could administer the application of political power to their addressees in categories that were at once replicable, flexible, uncontroversially generalizable and internally differentiated. Second, through this process they began to account for themselves as possessing a perennial and generalized legal personality, and this meant that they could project themselves as positively entitled to pass laws across all social differences of region, status or time. Third, they also began to ela-

---

34 On the overlapping of delegatory and judicial functions in pre-modern states in different national contexts, see *de Dios*, El Consejo real de Castilla, p. 18; *Schubert*, König und Reich, pp. 323-4; *McIlwain*, The High Court of Parliament and its Supremacy; *Brown*, The Governance of Late Medieval England, p. 159; *Pollard*, The Evolution of Parliament, p. 149. Pollard sees the strong fusion of judicial and parliamentary functions in England as a root of English democracy. This fusion was quite general, however.

borate permanent and routinized procedures in which they could utilize their power across very diverse exchanges with a minimum of societal disruption and convergence. In these respects again, therefore, the normative/legitimatory dimension of a state's constitution should not be viewed as an external attribute of the state or as a formal standard of legitimacy, against which state power should be measured. On the contrary, the normative/legitimatory aspect of the constitutions of developing European societies acted as a primary functional precondition of the state's emergence as a differentiated fulcrum of inclusive political power.

Revolutionary constitutions

During the seminal period of revolutionary constitution writing between the 1770s and the 1790s, it can again be seen that states acquired constitutions as instruments that helped them to formalize, generalize and positively to organize their power as a differentiated social facility. In fact, it was through these constitutions that states were able to bring towards a conclusion their slow emergence as differentiated centres of abstracted, generalizable, functionally specified and positive political agency.

The functions enacted by the revolutionary constitutions can be seen, first, in the fact that they took decisive steps to eliminate reference to monetary status and private social standing as foundations for legal inclusion, and they ensured that states recognized those subject to their power as holding rights of equality before law, which were usually guaranteed by a separate and independent judiciary.[35] As in earlier constitutions, the recognition of these rights meant that states acquired a legislative and judicial apparatus that allowed them, positively and generally, to introduce laws in a form that was not shaped by unnecessary sensitivity to the personal or economic situation of law's addressees and that effectively effaced the last traces of private or structural singularity from the state's legal apparatus. This greatly increased both the abstraction and the flexibility of the state, and it substantially expanded the state's ability to apply and sustain power as a generalizable resource across society. Second, the functions performed by these constitutions can also be seen in the fact that these constitutions accentuated earlier rights of proprietary integrity and personal autonomy, and they gave uniform validity to rights of free contract, free belief, free assembly and free expression of opinion. Indeed, these constitutions greatly reinforced and extended the status of constitutional rights, and they began to explain and conserve these rights by defining them as irreducible foundations for law and as

---

35 The correlation between the constitutionalization of rights and the reinforcement of public authority is observed in some of the historical literature on the American constitution. See *Wood*, The Radicalism of the American Revolution, p. 324. On the reinforcement of the French state administration in the years after 1789, see *Bosher*, French Finances, pp. 232, 295; *Garaud*, La Révolution et L'Égalité Civile, pp. 131-33; *White*, The French Revolution and the Politics of Government Finance, pp. 227-255.

invariably attributable to *all persons* through society: that is, as *subjective rights* or *human rights*. In sanctioning extended rights of autonomy as pertaining to every member of society, then, these constitutions, acted to remove vast swathes of social activity from the state's own structure, and to construct, through the law, a firm universal boundary between itself and the rest of society. In one universalizing moment, in fact, the constitutionalized concept of human rights spectacularly reduced the volume of social exchanges that states were required to regulate, and this ensured that most activities of social agents, imagined as bearers of rights, were necessarily perceived by the political system as belonging to other areas of social life and so as excluded from direct political inclusion or manifest politicization. Provisions over civil rights, thus, curtailed the extent to which states could be called to account for or destabilized by exchanges arising in those parts of society comprising activities covered by rights (i.e. in religion, employment, the press and publishing, science). Moreover, these provisions allowed the political system narrowly to pre-define those exchanges that it was expected to recognize as relevant for its legislative acts, and to apply its power solely to those exchanges that it observed as political. The status of rights as institutions of societal – and, in particular, political – differentiation, in short, was suddenly and powerfully intensified at this time. This dramatically heightened the adequacy of the political system to the differentiated societal landscape in which it found itself, and it dramatically increased the volume of positively usable power that the political system contained.

In addition to this, however, these revolutionary constitutions also had the function that they provided new normative and reflexive reserves for the political system. Indeed, they instituted at the centre of the political system heightened facilities for generating positive political legitimacy, and in so doing they greatly enhanced the capacity of the political system for positively applying its laws, for stimulating legal-political compliance through society, and for responding adaptively and positively to pluralized societal demands. The revolutionary constitutions performed this function of legitimatory positivization in two particularly important ways.

First, in enunciating the normative principle that the state obtains its legitimacy through its *inclusion* of the popular will of society (often configured as *the nation*, *the sovereign nation*, or the *nation of citizens*), the constitutions of the late eighteenth century enabled the state to describe itself as incorporating a concrete yet fully abstracted public source, and they permitted the state finally to internalize a reference for itself through which it could easily and positively reproduce its power across society. Indeed, the idea of civil inclusion expressed by these constitutions had the specific importance that it offered to states an image of their legitimacy, which they could conserve in simple fashion, and which ensured that their explanation of their power could not easily be disrupted or destabilized by external challenges or principles. That is to say, these constitutions derived the legitimacy of states from the claim that those to whom laws of the state were objectively applied were also the subjective origins or the authors of these laws, and that law's legitimacy was thus generated by a real and material identity between law's subject and law's object, both of whom the law, as the law of an inclusive and constitutionally legitimized state, always factually contained within itself. In storing this principle for the state, then, these constitutions performed the immeasurably important service for modern society that they ensured that states could, in each act of legal application, explain their laws as automatically, internally and reproducibly legitimized,[36] and they permitted states, in their everyday processes of legislation, to use and describe laws as universally adjusted to, subjectively authorized by, and in fact always internally *including*, their objective addressees. The civil inclusivity of law promoted by the revolutionary constitutions was thus, in the first instance, an idea through which the state discovered a rounded formula, in which, at one level, it could plausibly include and indefinitely presuppose its inner legitimation, and through which, at a different level, it could harden its legitimacy against external interference and in fact freely pre-construct its addressees and manufacture the differentiated social horizons on which it expended its power. In the principle of proto-democratic political formation implied in the idea of law's inclusion, in fact, the modern state obtained a conceptual norm through which – finally – it could produce, authorize, and consume its power as a narrowly abstracted, positively justified, and (to a large extent) internalized and depoliticized commodity: this, once again, greatly intensified the positive abstraction of the state, and it vastly expanded the resources of internally differentiated and positively usable power that the modern state possessed.

Second, it can also be observed in this respect that, although they purported to draw legitimacy from the practical *inclusion* of national citizens, the constitutions of the late eighteenth century actually located the source of the state's normative/inclusionary authority, neither in the existing nation nor in the wills of its particular constituents, but in a formal written document (and the subjectively ascribed rights that this document contained), which remained largely static against the people and its highly varied acts of volition. In consequence of this, these constitutions ensured that the legitimatory norm of inclusion underlying the state remained at all times highly dialectical, depoliticized, or even chimerical. In fact, they allowed the state to refer to its inclusive legitimatory source and constantly to utilize and further to positivize its power through reference to this source whilst also endlessly *excluding* the purported origin of legitimacy from the concrete apparatus of the state and ensuring that the constituent origin of the state's power could not meaningfully act as a formative, or even integrated, element of the political system. In defining members of the people or nation as constitutionally acknowledged protected *rights-holders*, therefore, these constitutions served restrictively to pre-construct the activities and the judicial procedures in which members of the nation could appear as relevant for the political system. In this again, they acted, as far as possible, to offset the concentrated politicization of any given site of power within the state or in socie-

---

36 Rousseau first formulated this idea in Du Contrat Social. It also informs all post-Rousseauian democratic thought.

ty more generally, and they conferred abiding stability upon the state's form by dislocating the state both from the factual persons named as originary bearers of power and from the particular or emergent demands of members of its constituent body.[37] Once more, therefore, these constitutions offered to the state a legitimatory norm from which it could further positivize its power whilst averting any specific increase in its politicality, whilst holding itself in a condition of high abstraction in relation to other social spheres, and whilst substantially closing itself against external interference.

The revolutionary constitutions in the USA and France, in short, enacted the structurally indispensable feat for emergent modern societies that they allowed the power of the political system to reflect and legitimize itself, in entirely differentiated manner, as *political* (that is, as conclusively distinct from private, colonial or dynastic power and so as fully adapted to and generally applicable in a differentiated society). In so doing, they created a norm of self-reflection in which the political system was able recursively to generalize and to positivize both its broad foundations and its particular statutory acts. However, at the same time, in locating the sources of power's inclusivity and legitimacy in formal catalogues of rights these constitutions also ensured – to a large degree at least – that the everyday mechanics of state activity did not need to be interrupted by any socially expansive claims, by perceived civil obligations, or by precariously unfiltered social conflicts. In consequence, these constitutions allowed the state to express and reproduce the legitimatory origin of its power at a low level of internal and external political intensity, so that its legitimacy could not be challenged or questioned in any but the most exceptional crises or moments of conflict. The normative fusion of the *inclusionary* republican concept of *citizenship* with the *exclusionary* liberal concept of *rights*, above all, was the positivizing normative mainspring of the legitimatory functions performed by these constitutions. In these constitutions, the differentiatory dynamic underlying earlier constitutions came towards its culmination, and both the abstracted political design and the legitimatory reserves required to sustain a modern pluralistically differentiated society were put in place.

---

37 On this phenomenon in France, see *Deslandres*, Histoire Constitutionelle de la France, III, pp. 78-9; *Thompson*, Popular Sovereignty and the French Constituent Assembly, p. 25. On the difficulties attached to this reduction of the state's political emphasis, also, see *Gooch*, Parliamentary Government in France, p. 251. On the USA, see *Wood*, The Creation of The American Republic, p. 266; *Wills*, Explaining America, p. 213. On the early function of the US-American constitution as promoting the 'establishment and acceptance' of limits on social politicization, see *Sharp*, American Politics in the Early Republic, p. 13. On the similar role performed in France by the constitution of 1791, see *Duclos*, La Notion de Constitution, p. 11.

Conclusion

On these grounds, it is possible to propose foundations for a tentatively generalized sociology of constitutions, and for a macro-sociological approach both to the rights and to the juridical norms that constitutions commonly contain and the legitimatory functions that they habitually fulfil. The constitutional-sociological thesis proposed here suggests – first – that constitutions are produced by relatively uniform processes of socio-functional causality, which, with evident variations, are formative and deep-lying in all modern societies. As a result of these processes, constitutions are indispensable for the functional organization of modern societies and the politics of these societies. Modern societies have a functional *need for constitutions* and for the interlinked web of functions and norms that these provide. Constitutions perform functions of abstraction, generalization, depoliticization and positivization for the political power of a modern society. The functional and reflexive reserves of legitimacy produced by constitutions are among the main reasons why modern society is able to exist, politically, in a functionally differentiated and pluralistic. Second, the analysis proposed here also suggests that in approaching constitutions it is essential both to observe and fully to appreciate their specific normative component, yet also to recognize that norms enshrined in constitutions are not external to society or to society's political functions. The normative apparatus of a constitution might in fact be seen as the reflexive form into which a society adaptively distils its functional exigencies. The norms of a constitution are always *society's norms*, and they allow a society both functionally and reflexively to adjust to its underlying differentiatory processes. Indeed, the extent to which a constitution permits a society to respond to its differentiation might be viewed, both functionally and normatively, as the primary index of its legitimacy (or otherwise).

In this respect, it might also be tentatively suggested that the sociology of constitutions outlined here contains a partial corrective to more widespread inquiries into the constitutional origins of political legitimacy. At one level, this approach opposes standard normative theory in arguing that normative analysis must be grounded in a functional and structurally adequate reconstruction of the constitution of society as a whole, and it is only if it accounts for norms as reflecting the wider constitution of society that analysis can account for the preconditions of a constitution likely to help secure legitimacy for society's political system. At a different level, however, this approach might be viewed as a sociological theory that identifies and seeks concretely to explicate the correlation between political legitimacy and constitutional norms, and it argues that sociological analysis cannot remain blind to the legitimatory status of norms (as social facts), and it needs to interpret norms – and even quite specific norms – as key elements of society and as preconditions of political legitimacy. On this account, in fact, sociology is also entitled to propose a generalized theory of political norms, and, in examining norms as adaptive articulations of societal process, it might offer grounds to evaluate different constitutional norms in light of their reflexive contribution to the legitimacy of the political system.

On the basis of the above reconstruction, then, the approach outlined here indicates that a constitution capable of obtaining and preserving legitimacy will probably be one that effectively responds to and facilitates the processes of political abstraction, generalization, selective de-politicization and positivization, which usually act in modern societies as preconditions for the adequate construction of political power. Naturally, it is necessary to observe here that after the period of classical constitution writing, constitutions have recurrently been required to respond to new social demands. In particular, the constitutions of the early decades of the twentieth century deviated from earlier constitutions in that they addressed questions of social rights and material citizenship; the constitutions drafted in the three waves of democratic transition in the late 1940s, the 1970s and the 1990s were substantially devoted to problems attached to the de-coupling of state, economy, military and judiciary; very contemporary processes of constitution writing, then, have focused on problems of overlapping statehood, on the splitting of power between multi-levelled executives, and on the emergence of sites of soft law as new patterns of constitutionality. Despite this, however, the earlier processes of constitutional reflection laid out in very general terms both the basic functionnal/evolutionary and the basic normative/legitimatory template for the politics of a modern society, and the functional exigencies to which these constitutions reacted still remain structurally formative, even in later-modern societies. Indeed, if we observe that in contemporary societies states enjoying legitimacy are primarily those that guarantee a limited set of rights, that avoid the amorphous, arbitrary or functionally indeterminate exercise of power, that transmit power in adequately generalizable legal form, and that contain plausible and easily internalized descriptions of their authority, we might also observe that this is because these states have a constitution with a design that allows a political system to sustain itself, both functionally and normatively, in the conditions of a pluralistically differentiated society. To this extent, the historical/functionalist approach proposed here might be invoked as a premise for analysis of contemporary constitutions, and it might (within broad parameters) explain, using both normative and sociological evidence, why some constitutional norms are likely to promote legitimacy and others are not. Above all, however, the approach outlined here might insist that conventional analysis of constitutions habitually struggles to explain the constitutional sources of legitimacy because it views constitutional norms as distinct from the societal functions that require legitimacy. The legitimatory function of norms can be best comprehended and evaluated as an articulated expression of societal functions: a fully sociological method, however, is required for this.

Bibliography

Althusius, Johannes, Politica, third edition, Herborn, 1614.
Aubert, Félix, Le Parlement de Paris. De Philippe le Bel a Charles VII (1314–1422). Sa Compétence, ses attributions, Geneva, 1977.
Aylmer, G.E., The Struggle for the Constitution. England in the Seventeenth Century, London, 1963.
Aylmer, G.E., The Crown's Servants. Government and Civil Service under Charles II, 1660-1685, Oxford, 2002.
Bardoux, Agénor, Les Légistes. Leur Influence sur la Société Française, Paris, 1877.
v. Below, Georg, Territorium und Stadt, Munich, 1923.
Berman, Harold J., Law and Revolution, vol. II: The Impact of the Protestant Reformations on the Western Legal Tradition Cambridge, MASS, 2003.
Black, Anthony, Monarchy and Community. Political Ideas in the Later Conciliar Controversy 1430–1450, Cambridge, 1970.
Bosher, J.F., French Finances 1770–1795. From Business to Bureaucracy, Cambridge, 1970.
Brown, A.L., The Governance of Late Medieval England, London, 1989.
Brunkhorst, Hauke, Solidarität. Von der Bürgerfreundschaft zur globalen Rechtsgenossenschaft, Frankfurt am Main, 2002.
Buchholz, Werner, Staat und Ständegesellschaft in Schweden zur Zeit des Überganges vom Absolutismus zum Ständeparlamentarismus, 1718-1720, Stockholm, 1979.
Coke, Edward, Selected Writings, edited by Steve Sheppard, in 3 vols., Indianapolis, 2003.
Corrigan, Philip/Sayer, Derek, The Great Arch: English State Formation as Cultural Revolution, Oxford, 1985.
Deslandres, Maurice, Histoire Constitutionelle de la France de 1789 à 1870, in 3 vols. Paris, 1932.
Dickens, A.G., The English Reformation, London, 1964.
Diestelkamp, Bernhard, Zur Krise des Reichsrechts im 16. Jahrhundert, in Angermeier, Heinz (ed), Säkulare Aspekte der Reformationszeit, Munich, 1983, pp. 49-63.
de Dios, Salustiano, El Consejo real de Castilla (1385–1522), Madrid, 1982.
Duclos, Pierre, La Notion de Constitution dans l'Oeuvre de l'Assemblée Constituante de 1789, Paris, 1932.
Eisenhardt, Ulrich (ed), Die kaiserlichen Privilegia de non appellando, Cologne, 1980.
Elton, G.R., The Tudor Revolution in Government. Administrative Changes in the Reign of Henry VIII, Cambridge, 1966.
Eusden, John Dykstra, Puritans, Lawyers, and Politics in Early Seventeenth-Century England, New Haven, 1958.
Fischer-Lescano, Andreas, Die Emergenz der Globalverfassung, in Zeitschrift für ausländisches öffentliches Recht und Völkerrecht 63 (2003), pp. 717- 760.
Fischer-Lescano, Andreas/Teubner, Gunther, Fragmentierung des Weltrechts: Vernetzung globaler Regimes statt etatistischer Reichtseinheit, in Albert, Matthias and Stichweh, Rudolf (eds), Weltstaat und Weltstaatlichkeit: Beobachtungen globaler politischer Strukturbildung, Wiesbaden, 2007, pp. 37-61.
Garaud, Marcel, La Révolution et L'Égalité Civile: Histoire Générale du Droit privé francais (de 1789 á 1804), Paris, 1953.
v. Gierke, Otto, Das deutsche Genossenschaftsrecht, vol. III: Die Staats- und Korporationslehre des Althertums und des Mittelalters, Berlin, 1881.

Gooch, R.K., Parliamentary Government in France: Revolutionary Origins, 1789-1791, Ithaca, NY, 1960.
Habermas, Jürgen, Erkenntnis und Interesse, Frankfurt am Main: 1968.
Habermas, Jürgen, Faktizität und Geltung. Beiträge zur Diskurstheorie des Rechts und des demokratischen Rechtsstaats, Frankfurt am Main, 1992.
de Haillan, Bernard de Girard, De l'Estat et Succes des Affaires de France, in 4 vols., Paris, 1572.
Hamscher, Albert N., The Parlement of Paris after the Fronde 1653-1673, Pittsburgh, 1976.
Hart, James S. Jr, The Rule of Law, 1603-1660: Crowns, Courts and Judges, London, 2003.
Hintze, Otto, Staat und Verfassung. Gesammelte Aufsätze zur allgemeinen Verfassungsgeschichte, edited by Gerhard Oestreich, 2nd edition, Göttingen, 1962.
Huber, Ulrich, De Jure Civitatis, in 3 vols. Franeker, 1684.
Hurt, J.J., Louis XIV and the Parlements. The Assertion of Royal Authority, Manchester, 2002.
Judson, Margaret A., The Crisis of the Constitution. An Essay in Constitutional and Political Thought in England, 1603-1645, New Brunswick/London, 1949.
Kenyon, J.P. (ed), The Stuart Constitution 1603–1688, Cambridge, 1966.
Koenigsberger, H.G., Parliaments and Estates, in Davis, R.W. (ed), The Origins of Modern Freedom in the West, Stanford, CA, 1995, pp. 135-177.
Lehmberg, Stanford E., The Reformation Parliament 1529-1536, Cambridge, 1970.
Lindegren, Jan, The Swedish military state, 1560-1720, Scandinavian Journal of History 10(4) (1985), pp. 305-336.
Loades, David, Tudor Government. Structures of Authority in the Sixteenth Century, Oxford, 1997.
Lousse, Émile, La Societé d'Ancien Régime. Organisation et représentation corporatives, Paris, 1943.
Luhmann, Niklas, Grundrechte als Institution. Ein Beitrag zur politischen Soziologie, Berlin, 1965.
Luhmann, Niklas, Politische Verfassungen im Kontext des Gesellschaftssystems, I, Der Staat 12(2) (1973), pp. 1-22.
Luhmann, Niklas, Das Recht der Gesellschaft, Frankfurt am Main, 1993.
Luhmann, Niklas, Die Gesellschaft der Gesellschaft, Frankfurt am Main, 1997.
Major, J. Russell, Representative Institutions in Renaissance France 1421–1559, Madison WIS, 1960.
McIlwain, Charles Howard, The High Court of Parliament and its Supremacy. An Historical Essay on the Boundaries between Legislation and Adjudication in England, New Haven, 1910.
McIlwain, Charles Howard, Constitutionalism Ancient and Modern, Ithaca, 1947.
Moraw, Peter, Versuch über die Entstehung des Reichstags, in Weber, Hermann (ed), Politische Ordnungen und soziale Kräfte im alten Reich, Wiesbaden, 1980, pp. 1-36.
Mousnier, Roland, Les Institutions de la France sous la Monarchie Absolue 1598-1789, in 2 vols. Paris, 1974.
Neuhaus, Helmut, Reichsständische Repräsentativformen im 16. Jahrhundert. Reichstag – Reichskreistag – Reichsdeputationstag, Berlin, 1982.
Ogilvie, Charles, The King's Government and the Common Law 1471–1641, Oxford, 1958.
Parsons, Talcott, Sociological Theory and Modern Society, New York, 1967.
Pini, Antonio Ivan, Dal comune città-stato al commune ente amministrativa, in Galasso, Giuseppe (ed), Storia di Italia, vol. 4: Comuni e Signorie: Istituzioni, società e lotte per l'egemonia, Turin, 1981, pp. 451-590.
Plucknett, T.F.T., Statutes and their Interpretation in the first Half of the Fourteenth Century, Cambridge, 1922.
Plucknett, T.F.T., Legislation of Edward I, Oxford, 1949.
Pollard, A.F., The Evolution of Parliament, London, 1920.
Post, Gaines, The Theory of Public Law and the State in the Thirteenth Century, Seminar 6 (1948), pp. 42-59.
Procter, Evelyn S., Curia and Cortes in León and Castile 1072–1295, Cambridge, 1980.

Reynolds, Susan, Law and Communities in Western Christendom, c. 900-1140, The American Journal of Legal History 25(3) (1981), pp. 205-224.
Richardson, W.C., Tudor Chamber Administration 1485-1547, Baton Rouge, 1952.
Roberts, Michael (ed), Sweden as a Great Power 1611-1697. Government: Society: Foreign Policy, New York, 1968.
Roberts, Michael, Gustavus Adolphus and the Rise of Sweden, London, 1973.
Sartori, Giovanni, Comparative Constitutional Engineering. An Inquiry into Structures, Incentives and Outcomes, second edition, Basingstoke, 1997.
Schubert, Ernst, König und Reich. Studien zur spätmittelalterlichen deutschen Verfassungsgeschichte, Göttingen, 1979.
Sciulli, David, Theory of Societal Constitutionalism. Foundations of a non-Marxist Critical Theory, Cambridge, 1992.
Sharp, James Roger, American Politics in the Early Republic. The New Nation in Crisis, New Haven, 1993.
Spangenberg, Hans, Vom Lehnstaat zum Ständestaat. Ein Beitrag zur Entstehung der landständischen Verfassung, Munich, 1912.
Stichweh, Rudolf, Inklusion und Exklusion. Studien zur Gesellschaftstheorie, Bielefeld, 2005.
Stone, Bradley, The French Parlements and the Crisis of the Old Regime, Chapel Hill/London, 1986.
Teubner, Gunther, Societal Constitutionalism: Alternatives to State-Centred Constitutional Theory?', in Joerges, Christian, Sand, Inger-Johanne and Teubner, Gunther (eds), Transnational Governance and Constitutionalism, Oxford/Portland OR, 2005, pp. 3-28.
Teubner, Gunther, Die anonyme Matrix: Zu Menschenrechtsverletzung durch 'private' transnationale Akteure, Der Staat 45 (2006), pp. 161-187.
Thompson, Eric, Popular Sovereignty and the French Constituent Assembly 1789-91, Manchester, 1952.
Thornhill, Chris, Towards a Historical Sociology of Constitutional Legitimacy, Theory and Society 37(2) (2008), pp. 161-197.
Thornhill, Chris, A Sociology of Constitutions. Constitutions and State Legitimacy in Historical-Sociological Perspective, Cambridge, forthcoming.
Tilly, Charles, Reflections on the History of European State-Making, in Tilly, Charles (ed), The Formation of National States in Western Europe, Princeton, NJ, 1975, pp. 3-83.
Vogel, Barbara, Allgemeine Gewerbefreiheit. Die Reformpolitik des preußischen Staatskanzlers Hardenberg (1810–1820), Göttingen, 1983.
Weber, Max, Wirtschaft und Gesellschaft. Grundriß der verstehenden Soziologie, Tübingen, 1921.
Weitzel, Jürgen, Der Kampf um die Appellation ans Reichskammergericht. Zur politischen Geschichte der Rechtsmittel in Deutschland, Cologne, 1976.
White, Eugene Nelson, The French Revolution and the Politics of Government Finance, 1770–1815, Journal of Economic History 55(2) (1995), pp. 227-255.
Wilkinson, Bertie, Constitutional History of Medieval England, 1216–1399, in 3 vols.: vol. I: Politics and the Constitution 1216–1307, London, 1948-58.
Wilkinson, Bertie, Constitutional History of Medieval England, 1216–1399, in 3 vols.: vol. II: Politics and the Constitution 1307–1399, London, 1948-58.
Wills, Garry, Explaining America: The Federalist, London, 1982.
Wood, Gordon S., The Creation of The American Republic 1776–1787, New York/London, 1969.
Wood, Gordon S., The Radicalism of the American Revolution, New York, 1992.
Zeller, Gaston, Les Institutions de la France au XVI siècle, Paris, 1948.
Zorzi, Andrea, La giustizia imperiale nell'Italia comunale, in Toubert, Pierre and Bagliani, Agostino Paravicini (eds), Federico II e le città italiane, Palermo, 1994, pp. 85-103

Legality, legitimacy, and the circumstances of sociology

Samantha Ashenden

> Laws, taken in their broadest meaning, are the necessary relations deriving from the nature of things; and in this sense, all beings have their laws: the divinity has its laws, the material world has its laws, the intelligences superior to man have their laws, the beasts have their laws, man has his laws.[1]

As Montesquieu observes in the above quotation the concept of laws has multiple possible meanings.[2] This paper makes an argument for the constitutive role of sociological and other social-scientific knowledge in modern governance. In particular it argues that the claimed legitimacy of modern forms of governance, whilst legally coded, is reliant to a great extent on normative laws constructed through social-scientific knowledge. These normative laws are neither laws of nature nor commands of a sovereign, but laws of development, of equilibrium and of change. Such laws are discerned on the foundation of the assumption that society exists as a totality of relations, and that these relations are amenable to analysis in terms of differentiation, regularity, normal distribution around the mean, evolution, homeostasis, and so on. In contrast to those accounts that privilege legality and democratic process in discussion of the ways in which legitimacy is achieved in contemporary practices of government, and to those accounts that stress the analytical as opposed to normative role of the social sciences, therefore, this paper views legality and legitimacy as effects of multiple practices of governance, in which the social sciences play an active and 'normalising' role.[3] Underlying the argument proposed in this chapter, in consequence, is a challenge to views of law and legitimacy that posit a simple dichotomy between legal/normative and factual/sociological analyses of power and the reasons for its acceptance as legitimate: it argues that social-scientific knowledge plays a vital role in the multifarious processes and procedures of legitimation that underpin the power of modern states, and that the laws discerned by sociology assume a quasi-normative role in the legal order of modern polities.

My claim, in short, is, in its first formation, that sociology inherits the classical question: *How should we live?* However, it inherits this question in a context in

---

1 *Montesquieu*, Book 1, ch 1, p. 3. Thanks are due to James Brown, Deborah Mabbett, Tom Osborne, and Chris Thornhill for comments on earlier drafts of this argument.
2 My title borrows from Waldron's discussion of the 'circumstances of politics' in *Waldron, Law and Disagreement*, and *Waldron, The Dignity of Legislation*.
3 The claim here is not that law and democratic processes are unimportant, but that focusing on them alone does not allow us to see the substantial normative role of social science and scientific knowledge in legitimising contemporary governance.

which previous ways of responding are no longer tenable: that is, in which classical and modern natural law cease to provide convincing responses, and legal positivism leaves standing the question of the foundation of right. Sociology, with its conception of society as a totality of relations, offers an account of normal functioning that provides and is sustained by *immanent norms*. Whilst developing as positive forms of knowledge of the social, the social sciences have on the whole claimed an analytical rather than a normative orientation to their objects. Nonetheless, the claim that I wish to elaborate here is that sociology and the other social sciences are intrinsically normative discourses: they are discourses of the norm that commonly disavow their own normativity.

In order to pursue this argument, we need to examine how the concepts *legality*, *legitimacy*, *normative* and *sociological* are held in particular constellations in the present. What work do these sets of relations do? There is a longstanding relation between law and legitimacy,[4] but what concerns us here is the specific form in which this relation is articulated in the present. In terms of definition, both legality and legitimacy might be said to resolve into 'conformity to law', but legitimacy is often understood also to imply conformity to principles or norms, and it can consequently exist in tension with posited law.[5] The problem of the relationship between modern legality and legitimacy might be stated thus: in modernity legality gives form to legitimacy, and this raises the question: *What founds legality?*[6] At its most general level, the issue might be taken as one of the arbitrariness of authority after the demise of theology and metaphysics;[7] as Arendt wryly observed, our era is characterised by the unprecedented contingency of authority.[8] If we turn to the relation between the normative and the sociological, then we see that these are widely regarded as entirely distinct and even antagonistic to one another. As a result, for example, from Timasheff to Luhmann the sociology of law has been observed as an empirical-analytical rather than a normative exercise: there is an insoluble tension between normatively organised law and jurisprudence on the one hand, and analytical-descriptive sociological explanation of law on the other.[9]

---

4   *Berman*, Law and Revolution.
5   See, for example, *Habermas*, Between Facts and Norms. But also see *Luhmann*, A Sociological Theory of Law; *Thornhill*, On Norms as Social Facts.
6   See, amongst many, Loughlin and Walker (eds), The Paradox of Constitutionalism; *McVeigh*, Jurisprudence of Jurisdiction. As Luhmann put it, the juridical bestowal of form does not equate to giving an account of the source of law; see *Luhmann*, Are There Still Indispensable Norms in Our Society? p.33. See also *Schmitt*, Legality and Legitimacy; *Kelsen*, Pure Theory of Law; *Habermas*, Between facts and Norms; *Luhmann*, A Sociological Theory of Law; *Dyzenhaus*, Legality and Legitimacy.
7   *Nietzsche*, The Gay Science, pp. 119-20, s. 125.
8   *Arendt*, Responsibility and Judgement, p. xxvi.
9   *Timasheff*, Introduction to the Sociology of Law, p. 367, argues that 'Sociology is a nomographic, not normative science. It is not the task of sociology to tell us whether one or another social institution is rational, just, useful and the like.' Luhmann echoes this in his statement

In the context of the contingency of authority and the apparent contradiction between the normative and the sociological, sociology and social-scientific knowledge more generally have come to play a crucial role in providing justifications for, and orientations of, governance. In modern liberal democracies, claims to legitimate governance can only be produced and sustained through specific combinations of simultaneously legally and scientifically ordered forms of knowledge and practice: legitimacy is achieved through claims to legality plus scientificity, such that claims to *legitimate jurisdiction* and to *scientific veridiction* are intimately linked. Here, for example, we might think of the manner in which contemporary public-policy initiatives stake claims to legitimacy through reference to their 'evidence base' or 'sound science'. In turn, this implies that social-scientific knowledge, notwithstanding protestations by some of its practitioners to the contrary, can itself be both normative and normalising. In consequence, whilst in modern societies legitimacy is rendered in terms of legality, social-scientific and other normalising knowledge is often a precondition for the exercise of legitimate power. One might say, following Weber, that in modernity legitimacy necessarily has legal form. However, following Foucault, one might add that this legal form is often supplemented and made effective through forms of knowledge and practice extraneous to law: for example, through economics, natural science, demography, psychology, and sociology and so on.[10] My suspicion, guided by Foucault, is that in modern liberal polities the knowledge of regularities produced by the social sciences constructs an 'infra-law' which grounds the legitimacy of legality.[11] That is to say, the knowledge of regularities and normal functioning (of 'society', the 'economy' and so on) proposed by the social sciences both constitutes objects of governance and provides immanent norms of judgement of those objects. Social-scientific work thus contains a kind of normative or legal knowledge that owes nothing to the normativity found in classical jurisprudence.[12] This normativity, however, contributes to the legitimation of government to at least the same degree as the deductive norms of philosophical jurisprudence.

A number of sociologically oriented writers have focused on changes in the relations between legality and legitimacy that have attended the rise of the modern state. In particular, Arendt, Habermas and Bobbio all, in slightly different but largely consonant terms, pinpoint the eighteenth-century European constitutional state as articulating a transformed and delimited conception of political legitimacy in the separation of state and society. After this time, the state assumed a definite, constitutional-

---

    that whilst the legal system works with a division between norms and facts, 'sociology treats norms as facts.' *Luhmann*, Are There Still Indispensable Norms?, p. 20.

10 See, for example, *Nelken/Pribán*, Law's New Boundaries, *Freeman/Reece*, Science in Court.

11 See *Foucault*, The History of Sexuality Volume 1. Also see *Foucault*, Discipline and Punish, where Foucault makes the case that disciplinary norms are a precondition for the successful operation of modern forms of law.

12 Referring to Kelsen, Foucault directly contrasts the 'normativity intrinsic to legal imperative' with 'techniques of normalization [that] develop from and below a system of law, in its margins and maybe even against it.' *Foucault*, Security, Territory, Population, p. 56.

ly constrained form, counterpoised to the society of which it was a part. These theorists proceed to argue that through the nineteenth century this separation of state and society was undermined by the encroachment of the social administrative state, such that state-society relations were re-fused in a manner which resulted in a tension between the protected and participating citizen.[13] In a related way, Habermas and Luhmann take up the problem of legitimacy in terms both of law's 'positivisation' and its expansion through legislation during the nineteenth and twentieth centuries. Luhmann argues that with the decline of natural-law arguments and the development of legislation in the nineteenth century the concept of legitimacy was recast on a purely factual basis: from this time on, legitimation has been secured *through procedure*.[14] Habermas for his part distinguishes two forms of juridification: that is, codification of already formally constituted relations on the one hand, and the expansion of legislation and administrative regulations into previously informally regulated spheres on the other.[15] He suggests that new administrative instruments developed from the nineteenth century on suffer a lack of legitimacy insofar as they represent the instrumentalisation of law as a medium of communication cut off from the communicative infrastructure of the lifeworld. Therefore, whilst for Luhmann modernity consists in the functional differentiation and autopoiesis of different systems of communication, and the question of legitimacy retreats either into inner-systemic self-descriptions or into proceduralised law and its structural coupling to other systems of communication such as politics, for Habermas the issue of legitimacy in modernity is framed in terms of the democratic genesis of legal norms. One refuses a normative stance; the other develops an avowedly normative theory. However, both Habermas and Luhmann share vital assumptions in centring the issue of legitimacy on legality.

Foucault approaches this matter rather differently. In marked contrast to those who construe legitimacy fundamentally as a question of legality and democratic process, he presses us to examine legitimacy as an effect of multiple practices of governance. Remarking on the tendency within political theory to frame power in terms of sovereignty, and thus to construct legitimacy in terms of juridical order, Foucault complains that such conceptions reflect a refusal to 'cut off the King's head':[16] that is, they refuse to recognise the productivity of power and the multiple ways in which it is articulated through claims to knowledge. This refusal in turn prevents us from bringing into view the ways in which we are governed through norms seemingly immanent to our own individual and collective wellbeing. His analysis of biopolitics, and of the relationship between 'law and order' in modern

---

13 *Arendt*, On Revolution; *Habermas*, Structural Transformation; *Bobbio*, Future of Democracy.
14 *Luhmann*, Sociological Theory of Law, pp. 199-206; *Luhmann*, Legitimation durch Verfahren.
15 *Habermas*, Theory of Communicative Action, Volume 2. See also Teubner (ed), Dilemmas of Law in the Welfare State; Teubner (ed), Juridification of Social Spheres.
16 *Foucault*, Truth and Power, p. 121.

political formations, is an attempt to do just this.[17] For Foucault, modern political rationalities combine attention to juridical principles of right and to biopolitical norms of population; they combine the binary division permitted/forbidden with distribution around the mean. Norms of population are diametrically opposed to juridical norms, yet in modern forms of governance they come to fulfil a normative and normalising role with respect to legitimacy.

For Foucault in the context of the biopolitical regulation of population, law becomes part of a forward-looking apparatus of government.[18] According to Foucault, the problem of population is vital to the reorganisations of knowledge that since the eighteenth century have produced the human sciences and modern systems of rule. He argues:

> The theme of man and the 'human sciences' that analyze him as a living being, working individual, and speaking subject, should be understood on the basis of the emergence of population as the correlate of power and the object of knowledge [...] man, as he is thought and defined by the so-called human sciences of the nineteenth century [...] is nothing other than a figure of population. Or let us say again: If, on the one hand, it is true that man could not exist, and that only the juridical notion of the subject of right could exist when the problem of power was formulated within the theory of sovereignty, on the other hand, when population becomes the vis-à-vis of government, the art of government, rather than of sovereignty, then I think we can say that man is to population what the subject of right was to the sovereign.[19]

The development of the human sciences is, through disciplines such as social administration, instrumental to the development of the modern nation state and its claims to legitimacy. Social-scientific knowledge brings forth new objects for governance, and it enables liberal governance to function in the name of the governed, by sustaining and enhancing population. Foucault, in consqeuence, talks of a *doubling* of forms of rule, whereby we are simultaneously juridically and biopolitically constituted: the modern state simultaneously addresses us as citizens with rights and as subjects capable of supervision and reform according to appropriate norms of behaviour.[20] He characterises our present in terms of a political rationality that com-

---

17 For more detailed treatments of Foucault's conception of the relation between law and biopolitics see *Hunt/Wickham*, Foucault and Law, and *Golder/Fitzpatrick*, Foucault's Law.
18 Biopolitics is the term Foucault uses to characterise power over life; it refers to the multitude of ways in which the life and vitality of a population is enhanced. Foucault develops the idea of biopolitics most fully in Discipline and Punish and The History of Sexuality Volume 1. In the latter text he uses the term 'biopower' 'to designate what brought life and its mechanisms into the realm of explicit calculations and made knowledge-power an agent of transformation of human life.' *Foucault*, History of Sexuality, p. 143.
19 *Foucault*, Security, Territory, Population, p. 79.
20 For example, with respect to crime our judgements of guilt are based on legal responsibility for acts committed, but we also ask of the criminal the question 'who are you?' and this is

bines law and norms, where this combination constitutes a 'hybridized monster'.[21] Like asking for 'lemon and milk' in our tea, we ask for the simultaneous enactment of two models of political community: the city-citizen game of juridical equals and the shepherd-flock game of a secularised Christian pastoral, where the latter is found, for example, in the normalising branches of a therapeutic state organised through social-scientific and other positive knowledge. Foucault argues that these divergent models are combined in modern forms of government: we are simultaneously citizens possessing civil and political rights and subjects of pastoral supervision, regulation and reform (both individually and as a population). We are subject both to the laws of a juridical polity and to the norms of a welfare society. By examining the topography of this dual conception of political community that animates our present we can disclose how it is that sociology, even where it disavows normative/legitimatory functions, is implicated in the claims to legitimacy of contemporary rationalities and practices of governance.

Foucault's observation that two divergent models of political community, the city-citizen and shepherd-flock games, animate our vision underpins his diagnosis of the problems of the modern state that we have seen treated as a matter of legal legitimacy above. For Foucault, the problem of the modern state is that it combines 'the tricky adjustment between political power wielded over legal subjects and pastoral power wielded over live individuals'.[22] This formulation gives us a distinctive way of analysing the problem of legitimacy. To comprehend the manner in which we are governed we need to look, not only at the legal coding of power, but also at the operation of the social sciences in constituting 'man' as a site of and for governance.

My argument proceeds from this insight. In the analysis below, I suggest that the circumstances of sociology's emergence produced a doubling of sociology's relation to law such that sociology looks both to philosophical anthropology and to statistical regularities in understanding its object: that is, *society*. This doubled relation, to the idea of laws of man as such, and to statistically derived laws of tendency, underpins the complex interconnection between the sciences of the social and the claims to legitimacy of modern forms of governance. In order to develop this case I begin by examining the emergence of sociological thinking in Europe in the eighteenth and nineteenth centuries. This is followed by an attempt to tease apart the natural-law and natural-scientific inputs in sociology: here I also examine the types of law that exist modernity, and I consider their relationships to different sorts of norms. The final section looks at the political role of sociology and other social scientific knowledge, and it concludes by suggesting that it is a mistake to comprehend contemporary debates about legality and legitimacy as divided between analytical/descriptive social-scientific arguments and normative political theory and jurisprudence. Soci-

    bound up with attempts to know, and possibly reform, the criminal. See *Foucault*, About the concept of the "dangerous individual" in 19th century legal psychiatry.
21   *Foucault*, Lemon and Milk, p. 438.
22   *Foucault*, Politics and Reason, p. 67.

ology is set to remain a truth-producing practice that straddles claims to empirical truth and normative justifiability.

The circumstances of sociology

> If, as Comte remarked, metaphysics was the ghost of dead theology, sociology was in a similar way the ghost of jurisprudence past.[23]

At the beginning of *The Theory of Communicative Action* Jürgen Habermas reflects on the origins of sociology as 'a discipline responsible for the problems that politics and economics pushed to one side on their way to becoming specialized sciences.' He comments that:

> Its theme was the changes in social integration brought about within the structure of old European societies by the rise of the modern system of national states and by the differentiation of a market-regulated economy. Sociology became the science of crisis par excellence; it concerned itself above all with the anomic aspects of the dissolution of traditional social systems and the development of modern ones.[24]

As such, Habermas observes, sociology retains a relation to society considered as a whole.[25] It is the circumstances of sociology's emergence, its comprehension of society as a totality of relations, and its attempt to constitute itself as the science of that totality of relations that is the object of investigation in this and the next section.

Sociology and social theory were established in the historical context of Europe in the eighteenth and nineteenth centuries in response to a particular set of problems: that is, to problems of social order and its sustenance. In many ways, the rise of social theory marks the emergence of a species of political and moral theory under modern conditions. Increasingly through the nineteenth century it was sociology that developed in response to the classical moral-philosophical question: *How should we live?*[26] Early sociology, and the social sciences more generally, emerged in the context of a newly differentiated state/society constellation, and they formed an attempt to understand, theorise, and justify these changed social relations. Social science, in turn, had an effect on the constitution of this new entity called 'society'. Itself a product of the transformative dynamics of modern society, sociology developed as an analysis of the social and political problems of modernity that broke with the ear-

---

23 *Kelley*, The Human Measure, p. 275.
24 *Habermas*, Theory of Communicative Action, Volume 1, p. 4.
25 *Habermas*, Theory of Communicative Action, Volume 1, p. 5. Notwithstanding Luhmann's de-centred account of social systems, in his sociology totality is still at work in the concept of 'society'; see *Luhmann*, Social Systems, p. 408.
26 *Hawthorn*, Enlightenment and Despair.

lier normative tradition of political theory, but which in turn helped create the ground for new norms of the social. For these reasons, sociology bears a complex relation to the normative and normalising, and in this respect it also contributes to the legitimatory dimensions of modern society and the modern state.

In this respect, in particular, we can make a number of distinctions between social thought after the eighteenth century and that of preceding centuries.[27] First, from the ancient world to the seventeenth century the dominant concern of social analysis was to map the relation between human nature and government; society as such was not conceptualised as something distinct from political institutions. In the eighteenth century, as exemplified by figures such as Adam Smith and Rousseau, but more generally by the Enlightenments, the idea of man as radically conditioned by his social existence became prominent, and because of this human social existence was increasingly viewed as preceding politics, and theory was marked by a growing concern with analysing the forms of that existence. Secondly, at the end of the eighteenth century cyclical views of history, common since classical antiquity, were displaced by conceptions of history as a process of development. This break was necessary to the idea of the modern as a novel social form and to ideas of progress and evolutionary development that gave shape to much classical and contemporary social theory.[28] Thirdly, the idea that classical antiquity had conclusively identified human nature and the range of social forms was broken by Enlightenment. Enlightenment can in this sense be epitomised by Kant's motto *'sapere aude'* [*dare to know*].[29] Or, as Hegel put it in the introduction to the *Philosophy of Right*, it was reflected in the sense that modernity must create its moral framework out of itself, without reference to tradition. This produced an unending quest for determinate accounts of human subjectivity; it generated new questions concerning education and political organisation; it also created enduring problems of political justification and authority.

Social theory and sociology, therefore, are products of the emergence of the idea of 'society' as such: that is, of a concept derived from a number of sources, which took shape during the eighteenth century. Prior to this time the word 'society' primarily referred to companionship and fellowship. From the eighteenth century, however, economic, political and scientific developments began to produce notions of society as a system of interconnections between strangers.[30] Sociology, as an intellectual discipline, can be regarded as an attempt to understand these developments. However, it can itself also be observed as one of the products of these developments in the idea of society as such. The backdrop to these developments was the eighteenth-century experience of new commercial activities and the French Revolu-

---

27 For an overview see *Callinicos*, Social Theory.
28 See *Gellner*, Time and Validity; *Hall/Jarvie*, Transition to Modernity; *Nisbet*, History of the idea of Progress.
29 *Kant*, What is Enlightenment?
30 *Williams*, Keywords, p. 244.

tion. Both of these phenomena added to the perception that there existed a distinct realm between the public world of law and politics, and the private realm of the household: the social realm of civil society. This idea of a realm separate from and preceding government underlined the centrality of the belief that the state had certain limits, and the legitimacy or otherwise of public power depended on the recognition of these limits. However, this idea also added to the conviction that the methods of the natural sciences could and should be applied to the social realm: that is that there could be a social 'science' that might discern dynamics opaque to sovereignty.

From natural law to natural science?

This development of sociology, starting in the eighteenth century, implies that the objects of sociology have a distinct history. Sociology's 'society' is an artefact produced since the eighteenth century: in particular, it is a product of the division of state and society. It is worth noting that from its inception sociology inverted the usual assumption of previously existing political and legal theory that a primary moment of legal or political foundation was always constitutive of society. Instead of arguing that society is legally and politically instituted, the proto-sociological ideas of writers such as Montesquieu, Smith and Marx conceived (commercial) society as existing prior to and as determining political and legal forms. Sociology therefore overturned the tendency of classical political and legal theory to assert that society is politically constituted in the first instance, and it looked to the societally grounded preconditions of particular legal and political systems.

What shape, however, did this new science assume? Discussing the rise of social theory, on one hand, Heilbron argues that Montesquieu and Rousseau, as progenitors of sociology, followed, not natural science, but natural law. They each attempted to develop an account of a law independent of local customs, which could be discerned by reason based on suppositions about human nature.[31] Heilbron notes, further, that in France in particular sociology came into existence as a moral science. He argues that it succeeded and developed from the literature of the *moralistes* and the decline of natural-law theories.[32] He goes as far as to suggest that social theory emerged from attempts to integrate political and legal theory with moral theory, and he points to Montesquieu as central to this in the French context.[33] In this regard, one might follow Manent in reading Montesquieu's work precisely as registering a shift occurring in the conceptions of law available at the time;[34] Montesquieu, as the epigraph

---

31 *Heilbron*, The Rise of Social Theory, p. 96.
32 See also *Collini*, Liberalism and Sociology; *Hawthorn*, Enlightenment and Despair.
33 *Heilbron*, The Rise of Social Theory, p. 80.
34 *Manent*, The City of Man, p. 85.

to this chapter indicates, stands at a point when discourses of law as rules of action and as regularities of population are both in play for the first time.

On the other hand, however, sociology has also been understood as modelled on the natural sciences, and many who might be called social theorists and sociologists have understood their work as the elaboration of a scientific account or explanation of the laws of society understood as a system. The idea of sociology as a successor to the natural sciences of mathematics, physics, astronomy, and chemistry of course gained its first thorough expression in Comte's 'social physics',[35] and this was further articulated in the works of Durkheim. However, we should take care to note that for Durkheim it is not strictly true that the methods of the natural sciences formed the model for sociological inquiry. In fact, for Durkheim sociology, as the science of the social, has its own rules of method corresponding to its distinctive object of investigation.[36] It is worth exploring this since examining Durkheim's conception of sociology reveals a complex relation between early sociology and the idea of laws of nature. As Durkheim explains, it was a precondition for the emergence of the science of sociology that 'the concept of natural laws had [...] to be enlarged to include human phenomena.' On one hand, this involved asserting the 'unity of nature' (Newton had shown that matter obeyed a single law). But this in itself was insufficient to found the new science, since on its own it simply implied that social phenomena could be reduced to their 'material substratum':

> For sociology to arise, it was therefore not enough to proclaim the unity of reality and knowledge: that unity had also to be affirmed by a philosophy which acknowledges the natural heterogeneity of things. It was not sufficient to establish that social facts are subject to laws. It had also to be made clear that they have their own laws, specific in nature, and comparable to physical or biological laws, without being directly reducible to the latter [...] Thus, by the one fact that sociology was placed on an equal footing with the natural sciences, its own individuality was assured.[37]

On this basis, we can see that for Durkheim the methods of sociology implied an extension of the methods of the natural sciences in order to encompass the specific object of sociological investigation: the totality of social facts, in their full complexity. In this respect, it is worth comparing Habermas's assessment of the circumstances of sociology noted earlier with Durkheim's robust discussion of its necessary predicament. Durkheim asserts: 'Sociology is nothing if it is not the science of societies considered concurrently in their organisation, functioning and development.' He recognises that this prospectus requires that sociology draw on a number of specialised disciplines (such as political economy and history). Yet he also insists that sociology

---

35 *Comte*, Cours de philosophie positive.
36 *Durkheim*, The Rules of the Sociological Method.
37 *Durkheim*, Sociology and the Social Sciences (1903), pp. 177-8.

is not a new label for a category of things that has long existed: on the contrary, 'the term "sociology" sums up and implies a whole new set of ideas, namely that social facts are solidly linked to each other and above all must be treated as natural phenomena, subject to necessary laws'. In this process the more specialised social sciences are to become branches of sociology.[38] Durkheim goes on to state that a hostility between sociology and the social sciences of history and political economy was being overcome by the turn toward sociology of these disciplines in the development of comparative history and in the analysis of national economy. Nonetheless, he argues that each studies a portion of the whole that is society without cognising the totality and that working to make the sociological idea 'a more conscious one' is 'the urgent problem for sociology'.[39] In the face of fragmentation, the sociological idea 'must penetrate more deeply these various technological disciplines.'[40] In effect, Durkheim suggests that sociology must encompass and give form to the social sciences, with the anticipation that by doing so it will provide a privileged route to social progress.

We can reflect on this by observing that, whereas in the natural-law tradition the relation of factual to normative questions is constructed universalistically, and it is moved away from a focus on mores and customs and toward an idea of human nature *per se*, in the strand of sociology often mistakenly labelled 'positivist' the question of sociology's relation to normative questions is attenuated or rather occluded by a drive to scientific explanation, to analytic-descriptive statements capable of law-like replication, and to the framing notion of totality. This orientation existed in proto-sociological form in Smith and Marx. But whereas in early analyses, such as that set out by Smith, an assumption of natural sympathy bound together the normative and the analytic, in later arguments these appeared to part company. For example, for Durkheim and for Weber the sociological task was construed as one of objective scientific analysis (even if this aspiration was not realised), and Luhmann viewed the normative resources of the modern world as decisively decentred, and he argued that the task of theory is, not to moralise, but to analyse.[41] Nonetheless, from these ostensibly analytic arguments normative criteria can be retrieved; for Durkheim we need only think of the 'abnormal forms' of the division of labour diagnosed from an assumption of sociological 'homeostasis', and for Luhmann the concern

---

38 *Durkheim*, Sociology and the Social Sciences (1903), pp. 194-5.
39 *Durkheim*, Sociology and the Social Sciences (1903), p. 206
40 *Durkheim*, Sociology and the Social Sciences (1903), p. 206
41 Writing of law and sociology Luhmann observes that 'It does not lie in the sociologist's competence either to make a decision or even simply to recommend a certain decision ("after weighing all factors" as jurists say). As a sociologist, one is interested in the *problem*; or, as one could say, owing to particular theoretical guidelines, in the *form of the problem*.' *Luhmann*, Are there still indispensable norms? p. 19.

with the possibility of de-differentiation, understood as regression from the evolutionary advance represented by modernity.[42]

The normativity of sociology and the other social sciences should now be clear. Social scientific norms of population are diametrically opposed to juridical norms,[43] and yet in modern forms of governance they come to fulfil a normative and normalising role with respect to legitimacy. The way in which this is so can be briefly clarified by comparing classical and modern natural- law arguments with the social laws discerned by the social sciences. Whereas in classical natural law, arguably deriving from Aristotle, political community was conceived as a natural end, and the common good was viewed as part of an ordered cosmos of meaning,[44] the so-called 'scientific revolution' changed the epistemological assumptions underpinning these ideas. The modern natural-law arguments of writers such as Grotius, Hobbes and Locke relate, not to the idea of the cosmos as a well-ordered whole, but to Euclidean geometry and to the newly mechanising conception of nature, in which space was conceived as homogenous and its extension infinite. In this conception, the 'facts' of nature themselves bear no relation to schemes of value. Significantly, as Ewald notes,[45] the problem of political community surfaces here (or is it perhaps thematised here for the first time?) as a problem concerning the question of how it is possible to construct a common frame of reference out of a state of nature (for which one can read state of war). In the tradition of modern natural law, the political power of the sovereign is artefactual, stemming from reason and contract, and the form of the political community that it makes possible is one that is conceived as universal, reciprocal, and founded on equality. Consequently, modern natural-law arguments conceive community as a coming together of subjects of right, where these subjects are unified by virtue of the fact that they share the capacity for reason. However, the universality inscribed by the idea of the willing subject of natural-law arguments typical of the later eighteenth century was undermined by nationalism, historicism and the systematic mapping of differences between and within societies conducted in part by the emerging social sciences in the next century. This mapping of differences undermined the capacity of modern natural law arguments to compel agreement, and revealed the contingency of authority noted by Arendt and cited at the beginning of this chapter.

It is in this context that social science's conception of laws of development, derived from the analysis of populations, has taken hold. This is because statistical and other norms of the social develop with reference only to that which is observed. Such norms thus produce a rule of judgement immanent to the object itself, rather than relying upon external sources of authority such as arguments from deductive

---

42 *Luhmann*, Differentiation of Society; *Durkheim*, The Division of Labour in Society, esp. Book III: The Abnormal Forms.
43 As Foucault points out in discussing Kelsen; see *Foucault*, Security, Territory, Population, p. 56.
44 *Douzinas*, The End of Human Rights.
45 *Ewald*, Justice, Equality, Judgement: On "Social Justice".

legal principles. As Ewald notes, 'Once human nature loses its metaphyscial status, individuals can be judged only with reference to the social and, more precisely, with reference to the average man.'[46] Moreover, norms demand their own extension, they are dynamic:

> In any case the property of an object or fact, called normal in reference to an external or immanent norm, is the ability to be considered, in its turn, as the reference for objects or facts which have yet to be in a position to be called such. The normal is then at once the extension and the exhibition of the norm. It increases the rule at the same time that it points it out. It asks for everything outside, beside and against it that still escapes it. A norm draws its meaning, function and value from the fact of the existence, outside itself, of what does not meet the requirement it serves. The normal is not a static or peaceful, but a dynamic and polemical concept.[47]

A community demonstrated statistically is not a property created by subjects of right coming together as in natural-law arguments. On the contrary, it is a community that is produced by the analysis of the dynamics of the population concerned. The resultant knowledge does not produce a division between the legal and the illegal, but organises a distribution around the mean. The knowledge produced is a normalising knowledge that works through the polarity normal-abnormal and is articulated through the social and natural sciences, not through juridically conceived law. However, this absence of a relation to juridically conceived law does not imply a lack of relation to value. In fact, as Hacking has noted, the concepts 'norm' and 'normal' function to reconnect fact and value: 'normal' implies both average and right.[48]

Different types of law?

Eighteenth-century writers were keenly aware of the different meanings of the term law. Compare, for example, the quotation from Montesquieu at the outset of this chapter with this statement from Blackstone:

> Law, in its most general and comprehensive sense signifies a rule of action; and it is applied indiscriminately to all kinds of action, whether animate or inanimate, rational or irrational. Thus we say, the laws of motion, of gravitation, of optics, or mechanics, as well as the laws of nature and of nations. And it is that rule of action, which is prescribed by some superior, and which the inferior is bound to obey.[49]

---

46 *Ewald*, Norms, Discipline, and the Law.
47 *Canguilheim*, The Normal and the Pathological, pp. 238-39.
48 *Hacking*, The Taming of Chance, ch. 19.
49 *Blackstone*, The Sovereignty of the Law, p. 27.

We regularly encounter *a doubling* in the meaning of the term law. On one hand, in the idea of positive and natural laws one finds the idea of law used to describe the rules formulated by some authority; on the other hand, in the idea of scientific laws or laws of nature we encounter the idea of regularities potentially capable of nomothetic explanation. Sociology occupies a complex and ambiguous territory between these two perspectives. It attempts to be the positive science of the social, and as such it aims to discern the laws of motion of society; so to some extent then it models itself on natural science. But at the same time it promises to be a successor to classical natural law: from its inception sociology has promised to enable us to govern in the name of that which is governed, in terms of the nature of society as such, without recourse to metaphysical or religious values.[50] And in this there is an important sense in which it also constitutes its objects.[51] This is the reason for the doubling of man, as both subject and object of knowledge, that Foucault recognised as key to the human sciences.[52]

We have noted Heilbron's argument that natural law and natural science are opposites. The latter is premised upon empirically testable regularities and is analytic-descriptive whereas the former consists of normative rules, is based on a priori reasoning concerning the nature of man or society, and is evaluative.[53] In one sense this is right. But if the account of sociology's emergence just put forward is accepted it suggests that the empirically testable regularities that it has generated have been the ground for the development of norms, and these in turn are the basis of what might tentatively be called a latter-day natural law.

If we take categories of legal rule and statistical methods each to imply epistemologies (i.e. ways of knowing and thus governing – or attempting to govern– the social world)[54] then Montesquieu's equivocation between using the concept law to refer to pure political command and to refer to sociological necessity merely discloses that something happened to the concept of law and its relation to norms in the course of the eighteenth century. One might argue that from the eighteenth century onward there occurred a doubling of 'law' in terms of both authoritative rules and regularities of nature, and a doubling of norms as mores or even as prescriptions for action and as regularities (and within regularities between 'best' and most common). 'Law' refers both to authoritative rules and to regularities, and 'norm' refers both to usual and to right. Sociology is simultaneously the fleshing out of questions derived from philosophical anthropology concerning the nature of 'man', and the plotting of empirical regularities of populations. Both are necessary to the claim to legitimacy of modern forms of governance: to govern legitimately is to govern in name of that governed, and this requires positive knowledge.

50   See *Rose*, The Politics of Life Itself, and *Dean*, Governmentality, p. 119.
51   On the impossibility of a theoretical formulation of sociology as a science of the given see *Hirst*, Bernard, Durkheim and Epistemology. See also *Hacking*, Historical Ontology.
52   *Foucault*, The Order of Things.
53   *Heilbron*, The Rise of Social Theory, p. 98
54   *Shapin/Schaffer*, The Leviathan and the Air-Pump.

Sociology moves back and forth between structural analyses of mores, and accounts of the subject and of agency that are indebted to the sense, prevalent since the eighteenth century, that mores are formed by the will.[55] One could say that sociology at once inherits and transforms a problem posed by Kant in his assertion of the willing subject as the ground of morality: that is, it inherits the idea that norms are founded in acts of self-legislation, but it renounces the Kantian containment of this idea in the principle of reason's universality.[56] Sociology seeks universals, but it is also founded on a necessary quantum of relativism and on attention to individuation and social and cultural difference.[57] In sociology, in consequence, the fact/value distinction splits normativity and reason; the turn to the subjective both introduces the arbitrariness of *Willkür* and it creates the conditions for the normalising forms of knowledge with which to govern; and, overall, *normative reason* is replaced by positive law and *normalising reason*.

Sociology, in short, expresses a desire for and concern regarding social order, and it endeavours to produce accounts of society as a totality of relations, where these relations cannot be reduced to sovereignty. As a discipline it has often been understood as a science of processes taking place behind the backs of actors and as a value-free science or at least as analytical rather than evaluative work.[58] But it is important to note how this embodies a dualism from the start. The normative and factual are bound together. For example, Durkheim's attempt to found a science of sociology produced a richly idealist philosophy.[59] Likewise, Weber's attempt to hold apart fact and value in a world that is value-free [*wertfrei*] produced enduring controversy. In other words, it is inaccurate to state that sociology is empirical-analytical and that political and legal theory is normative. The matter is substantially more complex. Conditions of argumentation are structured by the assumption of, and yet the impossibility of achieving, clear divisions of fact and value for both.[60] Ideas of normality, pathology, homeostasis, autopoiesis, and so on in social theory are not innocent metaphors. These ideas assume the functions of a displaced normativism.

Sociology has been, since its inception, part of a process both of societal construction and nation-state building. In proposing the idea of expertise in the functioning of society, it has promised to resolve the problem of morality: the question

---

55   See *Dawe*, The Two Sociologies.
56   Though see *Habermas* The Unity of Reason in the Diversity of Its Voices.
57   *Geertz*, Anti Anti-Relativism.
58   See, for example, Weber's careful distinction between a 'value relation' and a 'valuation' in *Weber*, Science as a Vocation.
59   In a late essay reflecting on the recently published Elementary Forms, Durkheim asserts that 'the traditional antithesis of body and soul is not a vain mythological concept that is without foundation in reality. It is true that we are double, that we are the realization of an antinomy.' And: 'It is not without reason, therefore, that man feels himself to be double: he actually is double': *Durkheim*, The Dualism of Human Nature and its Social Conditions, pp. 330, 337.
60   See *Williams*, Ethics and the Limits of Philosophy, pp. 141-2, on thick terms and the fact/value distinction. On the historical epistemology of the fact/value distinction see *Poovey*, A History of the Modern Fact.

of how we should live. Durkheim is explicit about this; for him the sociologist is the expert and the statesman the doctor: 'The duty of the statesman is no longer to propel societies violently towards an ideal which appears attractive to him. His role is rather that of the doctor: he forestalls the outbreak of sickness by maintaining good hygiene, or when it does break out, seeks to cure it.'[61] Sociology takes its place here as perhaps the pre-eminent knowledge of the social. Sociology, in its attempt to understand and explain the dynamics of the 'social', that totality which is not amenable to analysis in terms of sovereignty, has helped provide positive knowledge with which social relations can be managed without direct reference to politics. This suggests a doubling of forms of rule (or a series of tensions and mutual dependencies in the relation of sociology and liberalism, and between descriptive and evaluative conceptions of legitimacy): modern polities are governed simultaneously through the normative/legal idea that as citizens of a polity we are equal with one another, and through statistical mappings of populations, their abnormalities and dangers. We are simultaneously citizens possessing civil and political rights and subjects of pastoral supervision, regulation and reform; we are subject both to the laws of a juridical polity and the norms of a welfare society. Norm and fact are bound together here, but in a way quite distinct form classical philosophy's normativism. If we look through the lens of contemporary normative political philosophy we are likely to miss this point, just as we do if we look through the lens of an attempted purely positivist social science; if 'biopolitics is a condition of liberalism',[62] then sociology has been a condition of biopolitics.[63]

Conclusions

> Solutions to the problem of knowledge are solutions to the problem of social order.[64]

One could recount a history of legal forms as a history of the ways in which customs have been turned into legal rules, and these have been invested with metaphysical and religious significance. This history might also include the development of natural-law arguments as part of a process of secularisation, and it might conclude by examining the search for empirical regularities using the methods of the natural sciences as inspiration for a legal code. One would then have to say that this history is split between a procedural philosophy of law as right (exemplified by Kant and

---

61 *Durkheim*, Rules for the Distinction of the Normal from the Pathological, p. 104. In this formulation presumably sociology is equivalent to the corpus of medical knowledge.
62 *Dean*, Governmentality, p. 113.
63 Both Campbell and Douzinas's papers in this collection resonate with this idea, and suggest that the biopolitical is currently being refigured through developments in the idea of international order.
64 *Shapin/Schaffer*, The Leviathan and the Air-Pump, p. 332.

Habermas) on one hand, and attempts to produce a 'jurisprudence' owing nothing to the tradition of jurisprudence and all to a social physics (for instance, Bentham, Posner) on the other. One might then say that law originates in fact, but that legal interpretation builds a normative system on this customary basis. Facts and norms are thus interwoven from the start.

The natural-law arguments of the seventeenth and eighteenth centuries are usually understood as bound together with the progress toward a secularisation of political authority that took place in early modern Europe.[65] These arguments can be conceived as responses to a series of crises of legal authority, and as providing a secularising discourse that nonetheless looked to sustain universality through the idea of reason. By contrast, the natural sciences emerged in the seventeenth century by breaking away from older methods of finding knowledge through the prioritising of experiment.[66] Shapin goes so far as to suggest that for parts of the seventeenth century, especially in England in the context of the breakdown of other forms of civility and authority, it was science, in the context of the Royal Society, that provided the space for continued public discourse.[67]

Both models for knowledge production, natural law and natural science, feed into sociology. On one hand, from the eighteenth century onward the sciences of man developed through philosophical anthropology: that is, through speculation on the question of the nature of man. On the other hand, increasingly from the nineteenth century these sciences developed through observation-based knowledge of behaviour. Modern anthropology, psychology and sociology all rest on a relativising move that renounces, or at least brackets, the question '*What is man?*' in order descriptively to map human variety. We see a doubling of the empirical and transcendental. And from the eighteenth century on, with the development of programmes for the governance of populations, both sets of ideas are operative. Contemporary governance appeals to us simultaneously as subjects of right and as members of populations.

In consequence, we can conclude by observing a twin genesis of norms: in the idea of normative reason that runs from Rousseau, through the French Revolution, through Kant, and down to Habermas in the present, and in the idea of the norms of a population derived from detailed statistical description of its patterns. Both feed the development of systems of rule, and both provide potential justifications for political policies. But the supposedly analytic-descriptive knowledge of the social sciences is normative and normalising in a distinct way from the normativity of political philosophy. Natural-legal and social-scientific norms claim to be derived from the thing observed, they are immanent to it, and they provide knowledge of normal functioning, homeostasis, pathology and so on. On these grounds, we can even pose the question: Is the normalising, statistically derived, knowledge of man that one

---

65 *Tuck*, Natural Rights Theories.
66 *Shapin/Schaffer*, The Leviathan and the Air-Pump.
67 *Shapin*, A Social History of Truth.

finds in contemporary empirical sociology a modern 'natural law'? It is certainly the root and branch of the justification for and legitimacy of much evidence based public policy.

In addition, then, we can also conclude that the idea that sociology is analytical/descriptive, and that political theory and jurisprudence are normative, is a mistake that is generated by a positivist approach to the matter. One might say that objects and evaluations are indissolubly linked.[68] In this sense, pace Habermas, one cannot be 'between facts and norms', any more than, following Luhmann, legality and legitimacy can be considered sealed off as internal to the legal system; rather, repeated attempts at such demarcations are demonstrative of the peculiar instabilities wrought by modern attempts to distinguish a brute order of 'facts' from their evaluative significance. Solutions to the problem of knowledge are indeed solutions to the problem of social order. Sociology is a truth-producing practice which straddles the propositionally true and the normatively justifiable. And in the present the legal system regularly draws on forms of knowledge extraneous to itself: legality and legitimacy are achieved (if that is factually the case) through a combination of law that acts as command or rule, of reason, or of the sovereign, and the laws of normal functioning of that which is governed. Jurisdiction and veridiction are tied together in the production of legitimacy; sociology is a necessary part of liberal legal order.

---

68 See, in very different modes but supporting the same point concerning the un-sustainability of the fact/value distinction, *Canguilheim*, The Normal and the Pathological, and *Williams* Ethics and the Limits of Philosophy.

Bibliography

Arendt, Hannah, On Revolution, London, 1963.
Arendt, Hannah, Responsibility and Judgement, New York, 2003.
Berman, Harold, Law and Revolution: The Formation of the Western Legal Tradition, Harvard, 1983.
Blackstone, William, The Sovereignty of the Law. Selections from Blackstone's Commentaries on the Laws of England, London, 1973.
Bobbio, Norberto, The Future of Democracy: A Defence of the Rules of the Game, Cambridge, 1987.
Callinicos, Alex, Social Theory: A Historical Introduction, Oxford, 1999.
Canguilheim, Georges, The Normal and the Pathological, New York, 1991.
Collini, Stephan, Liberalism and Sociology, Cambridge, 1979.
Comte, Auguste, Cours de philosophie positive, Paris, 1830.
Dawe, Alan, The Two Sociologies, The British Journal of Sociology 21(2) (1970), pp. 207-218.
Dean, Mitchell, Governmentality, London, 1999.
Douzinas, Costas, The End of Human Rights, Oxford, 2000.
Durkheim, Emile, The Dualism of Human Nature and its Social Conditions, in Wolff, Kurt H (ed), Émile Durkheim: Essays on Sociology and Philosophy, New York, 1960, pp. 325-340.
Durkheim, Emile, Sociology and the Social Sciences, in Lukes, Stephen (ed) The Rules of the Sociological Method, Basingstoke, 1982, pp. 175-208.
Durkheim, Emile, Rules for the Distinction of the Normal from the Pathological, in Lukes, Stephen (ed), The Rules of the Sociological Method, Basingstoke, 1982, pp. 85-107.
Durkheim, Emile, The Division of Labour in Society, London, 1984
Dyzenhaus, David, Legality and Legitimacy: Carl Schmitt, Hans Kelsen and Herman Heller in Weimar, Oxford, 1997.
Ewald, Francois, Justice, Equality, Judgement: On "Social Justice", in Teubner, Gunther (ed) Juridification of Social Spheres: A comparative analysis of the areas of labor, corporate, antitrust and social welfare law, Berlin, 1987, pp. 91-110.
Ewald, Francois, Norms, Discipline, and the Law, in Post, Robert (ed), Law and the Order of Culture, Oxford, 1991, pp. 138-161.
Foucault, Michel, The Order of Things: An archaeology of the human sciences, London, 1970.
Foucault, Michel, Discipline and Punish: the Birth of the Prison, Harmondsworth, 1977.
Foucault, Michel, About the concept of the "dangerous individual" in 19th century legal psychiatry, International Journal of Law and Psychiatry, 1 (1978) pp. 1-18.
Foucault, Michel, The History of Sexuality Volume 1: An introduction, Harmondsworth, 1979.
Foucault, Michel, Truth and Power, in Gordon, Colin (ed), Michel Foucault: Power/Knowledge: Selected Writings 1972-1977, Hemel Hempsted, 1980, pp. 109-133.
Foucault, Michel, Politics and Reason, in Kritzman, Laurence (ed) Michel Foucault: Politics, Philosophy, Culture: Interviews and Other Writings 1977-1984, London, 1988, pp. 57-85.
Foucault, Michel, Lemon and Milk, in Faubion, James (ed), Michel Foucault – Power: The essential works of Foucault volume three, London, 2001, pp. 435-438.
Foucault, Michel, Security, Territory, Population: lectures at the College de France 1977-1978, Basingstoke, 2007.
Freeman, Michael, and Reece, Helen, Science in Court, Dartmouth, 1998.
Geertz, Clifford, Anti Anti-Relativism, American Anthropologist 89(4) (1984) pp. 263-278.

Gellner, Ernest, Time and Validity, in Thought and Change, London, 1964, pp. 1-32.
Golder, Ben, and Fitzpatrick, Peter, Foucault's Law, Abingdon, 2009.
Habermas, Jürgen, The Theory of Communicative Action Volume 1: Reason and the Rationalization of Society, Boston, 1981.
Habermas, Jürgen, The Theory of Communicative Action Volume 2: Lifeworld and System, Cambridge, 1987.
Habermas, Jürgen, The Structural Transformation of the Public Sphere: An Inquiry into a Category of Bourgeois Society, Cambridge, 1989.
Habermas, Jürgen, The Unity of Reason in the Diversity of Its Voices, in Postmetaphysical Thinking, Cambridge, 1992, pp. 115-148.
Habermas, Jürgen, Between Facts and Norms, Cambridge, 1996.
Hacking, Ian, The Taming of Chance, Cambridge, 1990.
Hacking, Ian, Historical Ontology, Harvard, 2002.
Hall, John A and Jarvie, IC (eds), Transition to Modernity: essays on power, wealth and belief, Cambridge, 1992.
Hawthorn, Geoffrey, Enlightenment and Despair: A history of sociology, Cambridge, 1976.
Heilbron, Johan, The Rise of Social Theory, Cambridge, 1995.
Hirst, Paul, Bernard, Durkheim and Epistemology, London, 1975.
Hunt, Alan, and Wickham, Gary, Foucault and Law: Towards a Sociology of Law as Governance, London, 1994.
Kant, Immanuel, An Answer to the Question 'What is Enlightenment?' in Reiss, Hans (ed), Immanual Kant: Political Writings, Cambridge, 1970, pp. 54-60.
Kelley, Donald, The Human Measure. Social Thought in the Western Legal Tradition, Cambridge, Massachusetts, 1990.
Kelsen, Hans, Pure Theory of Law, Berkeley, 1967.
Loughlin, Martin and Walker, Neil (eds), The Paradox of Constitutionalism: Constituent Power and Constitutional Form, Oxford, 2007.
Luhmann, Niklas, Legitimation durch Verfahren, Berlin, 1969.
Luhmann, Niklas, Differentiation of Society, New York, 1982.
Luhmann, Niklas, A Sociological Theory of Law, London, 1985.
Luhmann, Niklas, Social Systems, California, 1995.
Luhmann, Niklas, Are There Still Indispensable Norms in Our Society?, Soziale Systeme: Zeitschrift für Soziologische Theorie, 14 (2008), pp. 18-37.
Manent, Pierre, The City of Man, Princeton, 1998.
McVeigh, Shaun (ed), Jurisprudence of Jurisdiction, Abingdon, 2007.
Montesquieu, Charles-Louis de, The Spirit of the Laws, Cambridge, 1989.
Nelken, David, and Pribán, Jirí, Law's New Boundaries, Aldershot, 2001.
Nietzsche, Friedrich, The Gay Science, Cambridge, 2001.
Nisbet, Robert A, History of the idea of Progress, London, 1980.
Poovey, Mary, A History of the Modern Fact: Problems of Knowledge in the Sciences of Wealth and Society, London, 1998.
Rose, Nikolas, The Politics of Life Itself, Princeton, 2007.
Schmitt, Carl, Legality and Legitimacy, London, 2004.
Shapin, Steven, and Schaffer, Simon, The Leviathan and the Air-Pump: Hobbes, Boyle and the Experimental Life, Princeton, 1985.
Shapin, Steven, A Social History of Truth: Civility and Science in Seventeenth Century England, Chicago, 1994.
Teubner, Gunther (ed), Dilemmas of Law in the Welfare State, Berlin, 1986.
Teubner, Gunther (ed), Juridification of Social Spheres: A comparative analysis of the areas of labor, corporate, antitrust and social welfare law, Berlin, 1987.

Thornhill, Chris, On Norms as Social Facts: A view from historical political science, Soziale Systeme: Zeitschrift für Soziologische Theorie, 14 (2008), pp. 47-67.
Timasheff, Nicholas Sergeyevitch, An Introduction to the Sociology of Law, New Jersey, [1939] 2002.
Tuck, Richard, Natural Rights Theories: Their origin and development, Cambridge, 1979.
Waldron, Jeremy, Law and Disagreement, Oxford, 1999.
Waldron, Jeremy, The Dignity of Legislation, Cambridge, 1999.
Weber, Max, Science as a Vocation, in Gerth, Hans H, and Wright Mills, Charles (eds), From Max Weber. Essays in Sociology, London, [1948] 1991, pp. 129-156.
Williams, Bernard, Ethics and the Limits of Philosophy, Cambridge Massachusetts, 1985.
Williams, Raymond, Keywords, London, 1976.

Sociology among the third-order observers in legitimation processes

Pierre Guibentif

'Legitimacy' is one of these words that belong both to common language and to scholarly discourse. Therefore, if we wish effectively to control the impact of common-sense assumptions on our reasoning, and thus to be able to produce a vision of the phenomena under discussion different from the one of the people engaged in the social contexts we are called to analyse, we need to exercise particular care in defining a precise concept that can be linked to this word. Within the framework of a discussion of Max Weber's classic concept, I have already compared the concepts used by two of his most famous successors, Jürgen Habermas and Niklas Luhmann.[1] My participation in this edited work provides a good opportunity to test and possibly to develop the rather complex concept that emerged from this exercise.

In a first section, I shall introduce the results of the comparison between Habermas and Luhmann and confront them with the concepts used in other contributions contained in the present volume. As we shall see, this confrontation confirms the proposed concept. A more convincing test, however, is to use it in the analysis of a concrete issue and to appreciate how useful it is for this analysis. Such an issue, suggested by several papers contained in this volume, is the legitimacy of international law. This analysis, to be presented in the second section, will give more substance to one specific component of the concept of legitimacy outlined in the first section: the role of theories of society developed by philosophers and social scientists, a role that will be addressed in the third, concluding section of this essay.

A concept of legitimacy based on Habermas and Luhmann

Jürgen Habermas and Niklas Luhmann both wrote influential books on the subject of legitimacy,[2] and the issue was tackled at several occasions in the course of the life-long dialogue between them. And, as many readers have had the occasion to witness, and as I had the opportunity to test in former empirical researches,[3] there is a striking complementarity between their two theoretical proposals. A systematic comparison between their works leads to the following analysis.[4] Legitimacy might

---

1   *Guibentif*, La légitimité des mouvements sociaux.
2   *Luhmann*, Legitimation durch Verfahren; *Habermas*, Legitimationsprobleme im Spätkapitalismus.
3   See especially *Guibentif*, La pratique du droit international et communautaire de la sécurité sociale.
4   Comparison presented in *Guibentif*, La légitimité des mouvements sociaux.

be the result of processes in which four different perspectives are likely to be adopted; and, as a total social phenomenon, it deserves to be conceived as a composition of what is experienced or observed under these four different perspectives.

The four perspectives in legitimation processes

A first perspective has been named by Habermas the *participant's perspective*. One may be convinced, after a rational discussion of a concretely experienced situation, that there are good reasons to accept a given social order or, in particular, a certain rule (we shall come back later in this paper to the distinction between these two scales of the legitimization problems). That is, according to Habermas' reconstruction of our modern 'discourses' (here in the German sense of *Diskurs*, i.e. discussion),[5] what happens when someone accepts the validity claim on legitimacy defended by somebody else.

The second perspective is analyzed by Luhmann in *Legitimation durch Verfahren* [*Legitimation by Procedure*].[6] This work does not analyse the subjective motives that lead people rationally to recognize certain rules. Instead, it addresses the fact that rules are accepted because of the perception people have of other people's behaviour. If we witness that other people generally obey certain legal rules, we might admit that these other people have substantial motives to do so, and that it will be more risky to adopt a deviant behaviour. Procedures are mechanisms that make it more probable for people to see that other people do accept the rules currently in force, and for people opposed to certain rules to admit that it will be difficult to find allies likely to join them in their opposition. Thus, Luhmann analyses the way people orient their actions according to what they think other people actually do, or to what they presume, on the basis of what they see, that other people think. Positive law contributes to this mechanism. Where people do what has to be done according to positive law, the others are likely to admit that, firstly, they know the legal rule, and, secondly, they act in accordance with it because they have good reasons to accept it, even if one also admits that other, less substantial reasons – fear of punishment, for instance – might also play a role. The legitimacy of an order, according to Luhmann, is the result of the fact that people act as if they accepted it, and that they are motivated to this acceptance by the fact that they observe, just as sociologists also observe this, that other people also act in accordance with this order. In this case, legitimacy is promoted, not by participation in a discussion, but by observation of the behaviour of other people.

---

5   *Habermas*, Moralbewusstsein und kommunikatives Handeln; *Habermas*, Erläuterungen zur Diskursethik.
6   *Luhmann*, Legitimation durch Verfahren.

To separate and integrate in one sole model these two perspectives is a simple way of dealing with a well-known ambivalence of the legitimacy concept.[7] In order for it not to become simplistic, one should emphasize that these two perspectives have to be separated logically and they raise quite different questions, from a philosophical point of view, but that, at the same time, they designate realities that are merged in concrete situations. The empirical observation of legitimization processes has to take these mixtures into account. Participants in a discussion are at any time likely to observe each other, just if they were not actually involved in the debate. People observing other people interpret their behaviour on the assumption that this behaviour, at least to some extent, is motivated by justifications that could have been expressed in discussions, even if only in monological *in petto* discussions.

A third perspective is taken into account notably when Habermas discusses the 'legitimization problems' of late capitalism.[8] Collective social actors, in the first place the state, develop means to enhance the global level of acceptance of certain rules. This can be done by trying to persuade people rationally to adhere; but also by trying to give more visibility to the cases of apparent compliance. Here we have entities observing people who, themselves, are observing other people. In this sense, who adopts a legitimization strategy has to put himself in the position of a second-order observer. Here we use a concept that belongs to systems theory. Luhmann himself uses it to deal with an issue related to the legitimization problems analysed by Habermas: the role of public opinion, as a device allowing second order observation in the political system.[9]

Reading the works of Habermas and Luhmann we are led to identify a fourth perspective, adopted by researchers who specialize in the observation of complex social reality: this reality includes actors designing legitimization strategies, people guiding their actions according to what they see other people doing, and people discussing substantively the justification of social rules (that is, researchers who make cognitive and normative statements on this reality). In such cases, we see people who observe actors implementing legitimization strategies, and who thereby observe – see above – a group of persons observing each other. This means that we are here on the level of third-order observers. This perspective is adopted by Habermas in *Between Facts and Norms*, where he tries to reconstruct the role of legal procedures in modern complex societies, examining the extent to which, and the conditions under which, these procedures are likely to work as mechanisms that enable these societies to act upon themselves.[10] Luhmann also adopts a perspective of this kind, though without emphasizing its normative and political implications.[11] This political relevance becomes more noticeable in his later writings, in which he admits, among

---

7 On this ambivalence, see *Turnbull*, Legitimization in terms of questioning; *Peters*, Public discourse, identity, and the problem of democratic legitimacy.
8 *Habermas*, Legitimationsprobleme im Spätkapitalismus.
9 *Luhmann*, Die Politik der Gesellschaft, p. 287ff.
10 *Habermas*, Faktizität und Geltung.
11 *Thornhill*, Niklas Luhmann's Political Theory, p. 98.

other assumptions, that theory might bring about some structural coupling between social systems, notably between law and science, thus favouring, to some, even if minimal, extent, a co-evolution of these systems.[12] His late statements on persons as part of the neglected environment of social systems,[13] or on the evolution of the relationship between organization and functional social systems also suggest normative appreciations of contemporary social reality, even if they remain implicit.[14]

What is at stake here is the question of whether we can develop this four-perspectives concept of legitimacy, and in particular whether we can more accurately identify what structures experience and observations in all the four perspectives, how these perspectives came to be differentiated one from the other, and how they relate to each other.

Other relevant distinctions

When we talk about legitimacy, we necessarily imply some distinctions, which cut across the four perspectives. First of all, legitimacy, as it is recalled in the title of the present volume, has to be distinguished from legality. This distinction has been subject to thorough discussion in Luhmann's *Rechtssoziologie* in relation to the notion of *positivization* of the law.[15] This historical process leads to a notion of legal validity based on the sole ground of legality itself: legislation is valid as long as it has been first enacted, and later published according to procedures ruled by positive law. Through this process, the actual validity of legal provisions ceases to be linked to any substantial justification. From this moment on, it makes sense to discuss, separately, the question of the justification of this validity. Without a clearly differentiated notion of validity, the question of whether a legal provision is justified becomes identical with the question of its recognition as a rule to be obeyed. This is still the way Kant tackles the concept of law in his *Metaphysics of Morals*, published a few decades before the completion of the historical process of legal positivization: in his view, law is not what is currently being applied by the courts; it is what reason is able to justify.[16] According to this definition, reason performs two things that we nowadays perceive as discrete: it justifies legal rules and grounds them as valid.

As a matter of fact, this reconstruction of our notions of legality and legitimacy misses some crucial points, to which we shall come back in the next sub-section, notably the question of the factual power relations that, together with other factors, contribute to the historical experience of a legal order being empirically valid.[17] But

12 *Luhmann*, Das Recht der Gesellschaft, pp. 543f.
13 *Luhmann*, Globalization of World Society.
14 *Luhmann*, Die Politik der Gesellschaft, p. 81.
15 *Luhmann*, Rechtssoziologie.
16 *Kant*, Metaphysik der Sitten, p. 65.
17 Let us remember that this experience is the starting point of Max Weber's sociology of law, as connected to a sociology of legitimacy in modern society: *Coutu*, Le droit du travail

these points do not touch the essential fact here: that we are nowadays able to, and obliged to, distinguish the question of legal validity from the question of the legitimacy of law.

Both notions, legality and legitimacy, imply a third one: the reality that has, under certain circumstances, to be qualified as legal, and as legitimate. Here the structure of modern law obliges us to deal with two distinctions: first, the distinction between the whole legal order, on the one hand, and single legal provisions, on the other; second, the distinction between the law and the facts. Crossing these two distinctions leads to four types of social reality that are likely to be subject to the question of legitimacy.

The discussion of two of them seems, at first glance, to be not too difficult. We can easily imagine an appreciation of the legitimacy of a specific piece of legislation, or of a concrete act of behaviour or a particular measure taken. In the first case, the more detailed formulation of the question would be: is this legislation, even if validly enacted, also legitimate: that is, acceptable from a substantive point of view? In the second case, it would be: even if an act of behaviour is required or allowed by valid legislation, is it legitimate? Or, alternatively, even if an act of behaviour is prohibited by valid legislation, might we consider it legitimate? The discussion of the two other types of realities raises several problems. In logical terms, it makes sense to question the legitimacy of a legal order as a whole. The question, however, loses its relevance if we admit that the only function of it is to give validity to single legal provisions. This would simply bring us back to the question of the legitimacy of the single provisions. The question makes sense again if we admit that legal systems also perform other – substantial – functions, such as: warranting normative homogeneity in a pluralist context; making foundational societal violence invisible, or else recognizing and protecting human rights. On the other hand, to pose the question of the legitimacy of a social order that, as a whole, corresponds to the legal order is to pose *the* classical question of legitimacy. However, only under quite specific conditions will it be possible to identify a social order with a unity that justifies global discussion of its legitimacy. Things look quite different if we give up a sharp distinction between legal and social order. Indeed, it makes sense to question the legitimacy of the legal order if we take it, not as an abstract entity, nor as a mere discourse (here in the French sense of the word, as an identifiable set of propositions), but as an acting device: that is, as including the authorities charged with its enforcement (courts and administration). But by so doing, we are merging social elements in our definition of the legal system. The other way round, we may question the legitimacy of a social order with an acceptable unity if we define it according to the borders traced by the legal system. But by so doing, we are merging legal elements in our definition of the social order. In other words, it seems that the question of legitimacy arises at that moment that we recognize a separate notion of legality, which reproduction would be the only vocation of the legal system; but we only

comme ordre légitime, p. 339.

have an object likely to be submitted to this question if we abandon the separation of facts and legal norms, or else the notion of law existing merely for its own sake. This is a paradox that would not have surprised Niklas Luhmann.

Historical evolution

So legitimacy, on the one hand, is a problem that can only be discussed nowadays if we make distinctions that seem to be the result of a historical process – that is, of the 'positivization of the law'. On the other hand, legitimization issues seem to be a composition of four perspectives. A method for reconnecting these two analyses is to revisit the four-perspective concept, by adopting an evolutionary approach. The aim of this is to reconstruct how, in concrete terms, the perspectives under which legitimacy problems might be viewed, and the distinctions needed for the use of this concept, were generated. This is what I would like to do in the following points.

(a) The French dictionary *Le Grand Robert* dates the political use of the word back to 1797,[18] quoting Chateaubriand: there, for the first time, it seems, the word was applied to a political regime. Up to that moment, it only did apply to private social bonds: marriage as creating a legitimate union between man and woman, or establishing a legitimate relationship between parents and children. In the nineteenth century, the word became part of the usual political vocabulary, providing the root for the name of a political grouping: the *légitimistes*, who supported one specific branch of the Bourbon dynasty. This semantic step may be related to the following institutional evolution. At the end of the eighteenth century, the European type of political state had acquired its main features. One is the definition of a specific realm of 'governmentality',[19] differentiated from the realm of traditional authority relationship to be found at the macro level in the church or, at the micro level, in the family. 'Governmentality' means the exercise of a specific kind of command, based mainly on material means of enforcement, and aiming at a detailed coordination of individual actions by the way it addresses individual consciences. The other is the fact that this new form of power practice develops in parallel in different territories, in the context of a competition between different 'states'. States, from the outset, were experienced as a plurality of competing entities.[20] In this context, the American and French Revolutions gave rise to a divide between two types of state: between republics claiming to be grounded on the will of nations, expressed in the legal form of a constitution, on the one hand, and monarchies, on the other hand, invoking traditional

---

18 Rey (ed), Le grand Robert de la langue française. A more comprehensive analysis would require us to take also former uses of the Latin word into account, a survey that I was not in condition to carry out in writing the present paper.
19 *Foucault*, La gouvernementalité.
20 *Foucault*, Sécurité, territoire et population, p. 302.

foundations of social order.[21] This divide could be experienced both in comparing different states, and, within the borders of the same country, where regimes changed through episodes of revolution or restoration, as was the case in France.[22]

These developments created the conditions for a political discussion about the preferable foundations of political order, and, more specifically, the conditions for a differentiation of the specific question of legitimacy. Indeed, the fact that state governments ruled with similar instruments (written commands and specialized staff in charge with their enforcement) in all territories gave concrete foundations to a separate notion of the *validity* of state rules. In all the countries likely to be compared in these discussions, rules were enforced with a considerable level of effectiveness, that is: were *valid*. But, at the same time, these rules, with their similar validity, were justified with two radically different arguments: the political will of a nation, on the one hand, the traditional authority of the monarch, on the other hand. The different foundations of an identical mechanism of power made it possible and necessary to discuss the question of legitimacy, beyond the question of the validity of the rules. So the word 'legitimacy' was probably shaped by the competition between political orders that took place in the first decade of the nineteenth century.[23]

(b) The setting up of a democratic political regime led to the refinement of an institution that has older roots: representation.[24] Elected people gather in the political assembly, representing those who elected them, and what happens there is witnessed by a broader public. The distinction between those inside and those outside the Parliament – remember the relevance of the distinction of those inside and those outside the procedure in Luhmann's *Legitimation durch Verfahren* – could well be considered as the source of the distinction between participants and observers in experiences of legitimacy. Actually, the distinction is likely to come into effect in several different ways. Its most obvious application is the distinction between politicians participating in the discussion, and other people observing the debate. But the existence of a political arena makes also possible distinctions outside of it. In the 'world out there', people knowing that there is a parliament are likely to establish, in their informal encounters, the following difference. There are moments in which we just do what we have to do, and, besides, pay attention to the acceptance by others of the

---

21 This evolutionary step was certainly favoured by the earlier process of secularization discussed by *Saunders*, The Necessary Secularism of Legitimate Authority.
22 Rightly emphasizing the frequent constitutional changes that occurred in France over the 19th and 20th centuries: *Hess*, From Philadelphia to Vitoria via Bonn?.
23 This reconstruction of the political discourse in the early century is based on a continental experience. For elements on the corresponding evolution in the United Kingdom and in the United States of America, see *Hess*, From Philadelphia to Vitoria via Bonn?'. The profound differences between continental and Anglo-American experiences of the State are also discussed by *Sciulli*, Societal Constitutionalism.
24 The link between the mechanism of political representation and the issue of legitimacy is rightly emphasized in *Brunkhorst*, Cosmopolitanism and democratic freedom.

rules we should obey; and there are moments in which, just as if we would be in the Parliament, we debate about the world, and about the rules we should obey.

It should be noticed here that these mechanisms only work when related to a certain notion of citizenry. Firstly, those inside the parliament have to share the notion that what happens out there matters. This was probably not the case, or not to the same extent, in former monarchical regimes, and acquired obvious relevance only from the moment on people out there were those who elected the insiders. Secondly, it must be possible to assume that people out there do show what they think. This is not the case to the same extent in non democratic regimes, and not the case at all in totalitarian regimes. As long as it is known that the population is tightly controlled by police forces, and acts according to this constraint, its attitudes can hardly be invoked as an argument in favour of the existing order.

(c) Second-order observation is a component of the legitimacy experience, which acquires relevance through the nineteenth century, and it is intimately linked to the following mechanism: in the parliament, what happens out there can be used as an argument. Demonstrations of public dissatisfaction can be invoked as revealing errors in the government's action. The other way round, peace in the streets can be invoked as showing how successful this action is. Outside the parliament too, there is an increasing awareness of this mechanism. Riots once were in the first place forms of violent reactions against the armed forces of a regime, or a way for social tensions or suffering caused by misery to be relieved by aggression. Now the notion arises that parliamentary debates take place; that these debates matter for the life of the citizens, and that demonstrations are likely to be a topic of argument in them. This becomes a specific motive for organizing public demonstrations. The design of policies aiming at improving the life conditions of the lower classes is linked to this mechanism: their aim is to reduce the risk of riots and demonstrations, and to make it possible to invoke the happiness of the population as an argument in favour of the existing order.

The better politically organized the public demonstrations, and the more explicit their demands, the more elaborated are the governmental techniques for the prevention of such demonstrations. A remarkable episode in this societal learning process is this one: Bismarck was deeply impressed by the French civil war – the creation and the violent military repression of the *Commune de Paris* – taking place while the German forces were at the doors of Paris. The evaluation of this event was a strong motive of the efforts undertaken a few years later in setting up a new system of social insurance.[25] The aim was to improve the living standard of the working class, to foster cooperation between employers and workers, and thereby, obviously, to enhance the acceptance of the newly created German state.

---

25 On the relationship between the witnessing of the Commune and the later setting up of a social insurance system in Germany, see *Zöllner*, République fédérale d'Allemagne.

This is how what we learned to name techniques of legitimization of a political regime, emerged. These techniques experienced important evolutions over time. Firstly, new instruments of legitimization developed. In particular, the media played an increasing role, successively newspapers at the end of the nineteenth century, later the radio, from the 1920s onwards. Through the media, ideas acquired a new kind of impact, comparable in its structure to the impact of political power. On one hand, these techniques are likely rationally to convince the reader; on the other hand, they benefit from the appearance of adherence: as long as people buy the newspaper, or listen to the radio without expressing loud disagreement, they may be presumed as having accepted the message. And this force can be added to the force that ideas acquire when carried by a crowd in the form of slogans.

Secondly, the set of political regimes in competition, forming the material background of the legitimacy debate, also changed. The main opposition throughout the nineteenth century was between regimes identifying themselves by referring to liberal revolutions, and those claiming 'restauration' of the order challenged by these revolutions. As the memory of the *Ancien Regime* faded away, and historic experience revealed the difficulties in the implementation of democratic principles, it became an issue to find new alternatives to parliamentary democracy. The alternatives that acquired historical consistency in the 1930s are corporatism and comparable authoritarian political arrangements. The alternative between parliamentary democracy and authoritarianism remains until the end of World War II the background against which political regimes had to justify themselves. One explicit statement of the efforts of democracies to legitimate themselves, that is, to improve the conditions of their acceptance, was the joint declaration of the United States and the United Kingdom of 14th August 1941.[26] Democracy, according to this document, required 'freedom from want', which had to be, for that reason, one of the main purposes of public policies. The opposition between democracy and authoritarianism of the corporatist kind was replaced soon after the war by the opposition between West and East: that is, between liberal democracies on the one side and state socialism on the other side. Throughout this whole evolution, however, the basic structure of debates about legitimacy remained in the form of an opposition between two or more types of political order. The differentiated plurality of the states shaped the reality to be appreciated as a set of identifiable 'orders'; the stability that could be related to the current relations of forces in the different states obliged people to recognize the *validity* of each of these orders; the fact that there could be, here and now, different orders, an alternative made visible in the comparison between states, made it possible to question the justification – *legitimacy* – of existing – valid – orders.

A third evolution concerns the realities likely to be submitted to an evaluation of legitimacy. Up to now, we focused on debates about political orders considered as a whole. Technological, legal, and political evolutions may have contributed to the

---

26 See the Atlantic Charter, here quoted from the Resolution issued on 5 November 1941 by the ILO Conference, republished and commented in *Perrin*, La sécurité sociale, p. 221f.

fact that, not only political regimes, but also specific measures or commands, became objects of debates about legitimacy. This was favoured by the completion of the process of legal positivization, which made it possible to distinguish, in relation to every specific legal rule, the question of its validity from the question of its legitimacy. Furthermore, the process of technological rationalization led to the precise identification of operations, likely to be appreciated both under the aspect of their technical correctness, and form the viewpoint of their final outcome.[27] In the course of the nineteenth and twentieth centuries, states involved themselves to an increasing degree in the economy and in technological development. Many economic and technological operations become operations of the state. As a result of the parallel processes of positivization of the law and legalization of state activities, these differentiated operations were linked to legal rules describing them. Thus the legitimacy of single measures became an issue.

(d) The role of the social sciences in these processes changed over time, and these changes might be interpreted as revealing the differentiation of an observer's perspective of the third order. For decades, sociological scholarship and research played a role in what has been named here the second-order observer's perspective. This is most typically the case with surveys that aim to provide a precise picture of the population's attitude toward specific public issues.[28] This is also the case, arguably, with more theoretical, and earlier, efforts that aim to give an account of the mechanisms that favour the acceptance of rules in society. Remember the defence of professional structures, as a remedy against anomy, in Durkheim's foreword to the second edition of the *Social Division of Labour* (1902).

The position of sociology changes through the debate about its political role. This question had already been addressed by Max Weber. A broader reflection on the legitimatory impact of ideas, at a time in which the impact of the media and of the systems of public schooling and higher education was growing, took the form of a debate about ideologies; in Germany in relation to what was later named the *Streit um die Wissenssoziologie* [that is, the *controversy about the sociology of knowledge*].[29] The political role of the social sciences again became an issue of a broader discussion in the 1960s.[30] The main result of these debates was to convince many sociologists to withdraw form the business of normative evaluation and to specialize in the

---

27 The link between economic and technological differentiation, on the one hand, and differentiation processes within the legal order itself has been pointed out already by Max Weber: see *Coutu*, Le droit du travail comme ordre légitime, p. 335.
28 Examples are the surveys carried out in the 1940s in the United States by the Bureau of Applied Social Research run by Lazarsfeld and Merton; in France by the Institut français de l'opinion publique created 1938 by Jean Stoetzel. See *Cuin/Gresle*, Histoire de la sociologie, p. 57.
29 *Meja/Stehr*, Der Streit um die Wissenssoziologie.
30 It was during that period that the main works of the Frankfurt school were translated and became a focus of debate in Western social sciences.

production of objective pictures of social reality. One explicit reaction to this trend can be seen in Habermas's efforts to give new foundations to a normative approach of social reality.[31] And elements in the late work of Luhmann can also be interpreted in this sense.

Synthesis

Reality is always moving and it is certainly not limited by national borders. Nevertheless, it makes sense to focus the attention on a particular period, the first decades after the World War II, in which we find, stabilized for some time, at least in the Western developed world, a social reality where states played a central structuring role. They were in condition to play this role because populations expected them to play it, and accepted it, within certain limits. As a result of two centuries of institutional development, expectations were generated in multiple fora of debate and acquired force through democratic procedures of election, or referenda on constitutional or legislative proposals. Acceptance was revealed by the behaviour of the population, observed by the population itself, as well as by institutionalized actors, through media coverage, and through data gathered by professional research activity. Limits were the result, not only of these expectations and behaviours, but also of the fact that the states' agencies were neither the only organized players, nor the one sole homogeneous macro-actor.[32] A characteristic of this social reality that is more difficult to grasp is that positive law played a role on all its different levels and across them. Formulating expectations, differentiating behaviours, structuring the relations between organized players, and so on. Finally, this social reality was observed by cognitive devices linked to the states, but which, at least partly, developed according to their own logic: notably science and law.

The cohesion of this complex social reality was never an accomplished factum, but a problem to be solved, and, as a matter of fact, to some extent, successfully solved: it was a problem which existed as long as one considered this set of social institutions as worthy of preservation, but which appeared and had to be formulated in different terms, according to the place in which it was perceived. The recent destiny of the word 'legitimacy', as we have reconstructed it by analysing the works of Habermas and Luhmann, reveals precisely this phenomenon: a general concern with a certain kind of social coherence, symbolized by the use of one and the same word; experiences of that problem that vary according to social positions, and that lead to

---

31 *Habermas*, Faktizität und Geltung.
32 A more detailed discussion of this point should take into account the considerable differences that exist between continental and Anglo-American experiences of the state: see *Sciulli*, Societal Constitutionalism. This paper, however, pays little attention to the differences and tensions that exist between different state agencies. Tensions between central state agencies are one major topic in the later works of Bourdieu; see especially *Bourdieu*, La main gauche et la main droite de l'État.

different, even if somehow complementary, definitions of this same word. Despite these differences, one element remains, because it is relevant on all levels and for the relations between them: the law. By its formal definition, law suggests that it requires the addition of substantial motives, if the different elements to the constitution in which it participates are to form a coherent reality. So the use of the word 'legitimacy' in public debates, as opposed to 'legality', reveals the experience that societies characterized by quite specific features, at a certain historical time, had of their cohesion or lack of it.[33]

Legitimacy as a question in world society

The foregoing discussion confirms the tight relationship between the experience of the state and the notion of legitimacy. Recently, however, the question of legitimacy has insistently been raised in relation to issues that transcend national borders. The structures of social relations, in our times of globalization, at a global scale, are certainly quite different from those existing, some decades ago, within the borders of states. In consequence, in these new debates the word 'legitimacy' is likely to have a meaning quite different from the definition that has been proposed here. But, even in the discussion of international topics, the national state is still a reference, and this will probably preserve at least part of the relevance of former definitions. So it seems advisable to find ways explicitly to reconnect these different uses of the word. This could be done by taking the proposed definition as a starting point and analysing where, precisely, new contexts and thereby other meanings are to be considered.[34]

A first point to be emphasized is that, since the word has been applied for some decades in a given context, namely national public spaces and administrations, it can easily be 'transplanted' to other arenas of debate. The questions are: What conditions might favour such a transplant? And what will its impact be? We shall come back to the second question at the end of this essay. The first might help us to structure this section.

A first powerful reason for transplanting the word 'legitimacy' onto the international level is that there is international law. The modern question of legitimacy is a question complementary to the one of the legal validity. As soon as there are rules, produced on an international level, which are formally comparable to those enacted on a national level, so that they may be qualified as 'legal' in the same way

---

33   Luhmann, developing a reasoning that inspires the model here presented, qualifies 'legitimacy' as 'formula of contingency' (Kontingenzformel) of the political system: *Luhmann*, Die Politik der Gesellschaft, p. 125. On this concept, see *King/Thornhill*, Niklas Luhmann's Theory of Politics and Law, p. 73.
34   This is the method adopted, on precisely the same issue, but constructing a somehow different definition of 'legitimacy', by *Peters*, Public discourse, Identity, and the problem of democratic legitimacy.

as national legal rules, these international rules are, again like national legal rules, apt candidates for the question of legitimacy. A second reason is that this law is encountered under circumstances and in contexts that are comparable to those in which it is encountered on a national level. Applying the four perspectives of the model here proposed, the first reason is likely play a role on all levels. The second reason, on the other hand, deserves a more detailed discussion, reviewing separately the four perspectives already analysed on a national level.

Arguably, the transplanting of the term 'legitimacy' is more likely to occur on the fourth level, on the level of third-order observers, in particular if these observers are social scientists. Indeed, while their practice became increasingly international, social sciences have not undergone any radical transformation since their establishment during the nineteenth century. They were conceived, from the outset, as international: as disciplines producing knowledge claiming to be of universal validity. Organizational structures were originally mainly nationally based, but they were soon extended to include trans-national devices: that is, journals, learned societies, congresses, and so on. Only the scope of analysis was, for several decades, mainly national. In close relation, many legal scholars also started to work in international settings and devoted increasing attention to comparative and international law. Under these circumstances, quite naturally, questions formerly concentrated on national realities now began to be discussed on an international level. Among these was the question of the legitimacy of social structures – now observed on a global scale – that are legalized by rules belonging to international law: that is, the question of the capacity of the rules of international law to establish effective links between differentiated social instances in order to bring about some cohesion to a more comprehensive social reality. This is what Habermas undertakes, when outlining his three-level model of a world constitutional order.[35]

In this respect, however, social scientists and other analysts of our global world observe, on the other levels, realities that are quite different from those analysed at a national scale. The deeper the analysis goes, in consequence, the more they need to readjust their concepts and models. One very important difference lies in the law itself. On a national level, law applies, essentially, to the relations between persons, and between the persons and the state. On a global scale, it applies, in a similar way, to relations between persons, and between persons and states, but also to the relations between the states, between states and supranational entities, and between supranational entities and persons.[36] In the face of this more complex legal universe, it seems advisable to draw a distinction between two realms, even if there will be some overlap between them: on the one hand, these are rules that apply mainly to

---

35 *Habermas*, Zwischen Naturalismus und Religion, pp. 324-365. Quoting these reflections of Habermas and working with comparable purposes, *Brunkhorst*, Cosmopolitanism and Democratic Freedom.
36 To complete the picture, we should also consider the status of organized players other than the states: multinational corporations and non-governmental organizations.

relations between persons, or between persons and functionally specialized state agencies; on the other hand, these are rules that apply mainly to states considered as a whole, as international players, and the relations between them.

Supranational and international law applying mainly to persons

International law includes a considerable number of rules applying to persons – or private companies – when they engage in activities that extend beyond national borders. These rules concern mainly private persons involved in cross-border relations: for example, partners in commercial relations, members of the same family who live in different countries, and so on. They also address the activities of state agencies, as far as these agencies have a role to play in the processing of these private relations: for example, courts handling cases of international family law, or taxation offices entitled to receive taxes related to trans-national commercial transactions. A similar category of international rules applies to the relations between non-nationals and specialized state agencies: for example defining the status of foreign students in schools, or foreign patients in hospitals and health centers.

These rules form nowadays an increasingly wide and dense normative network. State agencies are, to an increasing degree, trained to, and ready to apply them effectively, and people – globally acting businessmen or scientists, as well as migrant workers – are learning to deal with them. Thus, in this domain, international law, given its effective application, can be analysed in terms similar to those applied to domestic law. It makes sense to recognize the validity of the rules, since there is a significant probability that they will be enforced, as resulting simply from their legality, legality supplied by international conventions or supranational regulation. This validity is thus comparable to the one of national legislation.[37] Under these circumstances, the question of their legitimacy may also be posed in the same fashion in which it has been raised in relation to national rules and measures.

But what are the contexts in which this question can be raised? To make it easy, let us start with the level of the first-order observers: that is, interested people looking at what other people say and do. Here, the first problem that we encounter is that there may be no common experience between the people to whom the rules apply, given the fact that they may live in different countries. To take one example: the Bologna Process in universities. The reforms are experienced at best as national processes, or even local. Students and faculties, if not personally involved in the implementation of the reform procedures, have a vague notion of what goes on around Europe in other universities. Even so, some shared experience of the practice of international rules might come about when such rules apply to a rather specific population. Migrant workers learn from each other what the existing rules are, how they

---

37 For a tentative assessment of the validity of this part of international law, see Gessner and Cem Budak (eds), Emerging Legal Certainty.

are applied, and what alternative uses are possible, alternative uses that may be legitimated by the experience of the behaviour of other people.[38]

On the other hand, when it comes to the level of the direct participation in discussion about the merits of such international rules, we encounter a picture completely different from the one suggested by the reconstruction of national legitimization processes. Indeed, such international rules are almost never subject to democratic procedures in which the people concerned would be entitled to participate in their approval according to their experiences and principles.[39] Definitely, leaving aside rare exceptions, persons are not participants in international legislative processes, and, because of this, they hardly consider themselves participants in any kind of international legitimization process.

What we encounter, however, is a situation that also exists on a national level but that has been neglected in the above presented reasoning. There are no discussions between citizens anticipating an effective democratic participation on the basis of effective experience of such participation. Yet there are discussions between persons regarding existing international rules as something that is out of their reach, a fact that does not prevent them talking about the way people and state agencies deal with them, and the way national and international entities try to promote, to legitimate them. This is precisely the kind of discussion we have in Europe, not only among specialists in European affairs, but to an increasing degree among ordinary citizens, commenting on – and often complaining about – our experience of European rules, and the way they are handled by our governments and by 'Brussels'. Strictly speaking: these are ordinary third-order observers.

Considering now the level of second-order observers, there are several differences compared to national settings. First of all, here we are dealing with two levels: the international entity in the framework of which the international rule was enacted, and the agencies of the states to which the rule applies. The entity presumably more directly interested in the implementation of the rule is the international organization. This entity, however, is not concerned by the opinion people have about the rule, at least not in the sense that a refusal could have direct political consequences. This opinion matters as far as it may hamper the effectiveness of the rule. And if there would be a will to enhance the recognition of the rule, it is questionable whether the international entity has means available to promote it on a national level. Conversely, the national states, which are responsible for implementing the rule, are not necessarily directly interested in its application. If the rule is rejected by interested people, this has no direct consequences for them; if it is accepted, it might be pre--

---

[38] Concrete examples of such alternative uses of European social security law, see *Guibentif*, Cross-Border Legal Issues Arising from International Migrations.

[39] Among the rare exceptions, popular votes in Switzerland ratifying international agreements, such as, to take a recent example, one that extends to nationals from Romania and Bulgaria the right to free circulation of workers between Switzerland and the European Union.

sented as a merit of the national government, with no impact, therefore, on the legitimacy of the international legal order.[40]

To appreciate this institutional setting, it is worth remembering a mechanism that works on the national level. There, the unity of the state and of the legal system connects the question of the legitimacy of single rules with the one of the whole social order. Broad refusal of many concrete rules would mean a challenge to the very authority of the state and to the validity of the law. This is actually a situation we meet in the periphery of the world system.[41] So it is possible to close a circle that obliges governments to commit to permanent efforts to obtain legitimacy for the legislation in force, and to take into account limitations of legitimization strategies and the actual state of the public opinion. In the current state of international – as well as of European – affairs, such a circle seems to be impossible to close. This is the case, first, because of the separation between the international level of rule production and the national level of rule implementation. This is the case, second, because there is no such a notion of unity of the international law as there has been in relation to national legal orders. It will not be possible, at least not for decades, to eliminate tensions between national and international orders, and between different international orders. This is the case, third, because the persons have no institutionalized ways to express their acceptance of the rules that apply to them, and they are not able to express their acceptance of the complex institutional order as a whole.[42] Here we have to add a crucial element to the picture: within such a framework, organized interests trying to influence institutional decision-making processes have a substantially more favourable position than is the case on national level. This explains the relevance of criteria belonging to the world of trans-national business in the policy guidelines issued by entities such as the European Commission or the OECD.[43]

Supranational and international law applying to states

When it comes to international rules applying to states, we encounter a legal reality that differs radically from national legal realities. Indeed, the addressees of these rules are at the same time the agents of their enforcement. There may be international organisations through which the production of rules and decisions is committed to a community of states, acting as a community. But when it comes to taking meas-

---

40 For a more detailed discussion of this mechanism, at a European level, see *Outhwaite*, Legitimacy in the European Union.
41 It is worth remembering here, applying systems theory to such settings, *Neves*, Verfassung und Positivität des Rechts in der peripheren Moderne.
42 This could have been the case in Europe, but has been avoided. For a critical appreciation of this process: Give Europe a say, The Economist.
43 This explains, in more prudent and abstract terms, the fact that law and politics withdrew from economic activity and from the scientific activity linked to it. In this sense, see *Sand*, Legitimacy in Global and International Law.

ures according to these rules and decisions, individual states have to act. This means that this enforcement is directly conditioned by the power relations between the states involved. And the historical experience is that there is no necessary link between the content of the international rules, and the purposes of those states that dominate these power relations. Consequently, in contrast to what happens in the domain of international rules addressing persons, or in the domain of national legal rules, the fact that a convention has been signed, or a decision taken, does not, in this domain of international law, have an implication of probable effectiveness.

Under these circumstances, the problem of legitimacy acquires a different shape, compared with the contexts discussed thus far. What is at stake here is not to question the justification of a rule whose validity we actually experience. The question here is to contribute to legal validity itself, since it is not convincingly demonstrated by the actual behaviour of the states. Legitimacy, here, is not externally related to validity; it contributes, as far as possible, to its formation. In other words: on the level of international rules applying to states, where legal validity is not factually supported by the global effectiveness of a legal order – let us say by factual validity – it has to be produced by the addition of legitimacy – let us say by a mixture of formal validity and substantial legitimacy.

This means that, in national settings and in the realm of international rules addressing persons, the question of legitimacy triggers debates and efforts that might strengthen existing orders, or otherwise, in the long run, bring about changes in them. In the realm of international rules addressing states, the question of legitimacy triggers debates and measures that might transform concrete measures or rules, from accidental events, into signs of an emerging order.

Now let us reconstruct the structures of these debates, using the four-perspective model outlined above. A first, strict application of this model leads to rather frustrating results. Considering that the addressees of the rules here are states, we have to locate states on the different levels: that is, as states participating in discussions about the justification of the rules applying to them; as states observing other states applying – or ignoring – such rules; as states trying to promote certain perceptions of their conduct on the part of other states. Such things exist, but for several reasons they have little to do with the processes we tried to reconstruct as legitimization processes. The difference between the third level and the other two is not so sharp as in the processes discussed up to now, because on all three levels we would have a world of states. And the relations between states are not comparable to the relations between individuals that we have considered so far. There are no direct discussions, but encounters between representatives, who will present interests and positions but are not so intent on persuasion. And states do not observe each other as people do, firstly because other means are used, which have to grasp an obviously more vast and complex reality; secondly because the structural differences between states are deeper than between individuals, so that any transposition of an interaction concept inspired by Mead or Parsons, as used up to now, would be absurd.

In fact, such a picture, which might perhaps have fitted the structures of international relations in early modernity, does not match the current reality. Now, even where we are dealing with rules addressing states, persons also have to be taken into account. On the one hand, this is because, they suffer – or benefit from – the consequences of what happens between states, or, in more general terms, from the way states behave themselves within the community of states. And these consequences are nowadays easy to witness thanks to media coverage. On the other hand, it is because sometimes, even if only under quite specific circumstances, these consequences might be taken into account at the moment persons have to participate in domestic democratic procedures.

Under these conditions, the four-level reality, suggested for national legitimization processes, also exists on an international level, even if the different spheres are far less clearly structured and the whole set of social spheres is more complex. It is more complex because the relations between states – negotiating with or observing each other – form specific realms, which are somehow duplicated by spheres formed by relations between persons, and persons and states. And it is less clearly structured, because no relations are established between what happens on the levels of what is discussed and practiced, by states as well as by people, and what happens on the other levels. So demonstrations might take place worldwide against the action of a state, demonstrations that reveal a universe of debates, and that are witnessed as a fact by participants and non-participants. But such demonstrations have no direct effect on the behaviour of the state in question. However – and here lies the crucial point – they have a diffuse effect, revealed in particular by the reactions that anticipate it, such as a tight control of the media coverage in war situations.

This brings us back to the third-order observers who ask the question of legitimacy in the face of international issues. What might be their role in such a context? One possible role is, having identified these – somehow fuzzy and quite complex – structures, to contribute to their strengthening. By reviewing the precise circumstances under which, and the ways in which, persons are able to participate in international dynamics; by making clear how this participation might effectively take place; by showing that this participation cannot be ignored because what happens here is, in the long run, linked to what happens in other parts of the world. This is actually what Habermas does in his recent papers on citizenship, in which he argues that citizenship needs to be conceived as participation in a state (among others, Germany), as well as, through this same process, as participation in a global player (in this case Europe), which involves active participation in the world's transformation. Such a concept, however, needs to be actually produced by an adequate institutional design, and by an appropriate management of the institutions by politicians.[44] This is what Mireille Delmas-Marty does, when locating in her model of a plural world order the role of experts and scientists, and their responsibility in sharing knowledge with oth-

---

44 *Habermas*, Europapolitik in der Sackgasse.

er citizens.[45] This is what Boaventura de Sousa Santos does, when theorizing counter-hegemonic globalization, and participating in efforts to give organizational structures to this trend.[46] These are all different ways of contributing to the differentiation of a world citizenry, the first level needed for a world order likely to be 'legitimized'; that is, where organizational structures are grounded on discussions between and practices of individual human beings.

What are such third-order observers doing – what are we doing – exactly? In general terms, one may say: they (we) are addressing a normative question to the reality of international relations. In more specific terms: they (we) are addressing it in a way that seeks to strengthen what could be elements of order in that reality, and that seeks to promote the differentiation and the interconnection of levels of individual discussions and interactions, and levels of organized decision making and action.

Here it is worth attempting to form a bridge between the two realms of international law here distinguished. Indeed, the effort of developing a trans-national citizenry could also have relevance for the future of international law applying to persons. The fact is that in contemporary society it seems easier to motivate people to participate in demonstrations against gross violations of human rights by states than in demonstrations regarding more technical issues of labour or commercial law, even if demonstrations about such issues do also take place. And it is not by chance that the question on 'legitimacy' is raised more frequently in relation to issues of the first type.[47] But any evolution in the public perception of international issues regarding, in the first place, the behaviour of states in respect of basic human rights issues is likely to favour the development of a trans-national citizenry able also to pick up more technical issues.

The role of sociology in the current context

To analyze the role of sociology, we first should come back to the national situation. As a point of fact, on a domestic level, legitimacy seems to have lost at least part of its relevance in the political discourse. In these conditions, the form of involvement of sociology in strategies of legitimization, in the sense defined above, changes.

As far as the socio-political context is concerned, there seems to be a trend toward less substantive argumentation in political discourse. Bauman, among others, speaks about growing relevance of the 'there is no alternative' argument.[48] This statement is confirmed by a cursory reading of contemporary official literature about, among other issues, social policies or higher education reform.[49] The main argument is the

---

45 *Delmas-Marty*, Les forces imaginantes du droit III, pp. 195-245.
46 *De Sousa Santos*, Beyond neoliberal governance.
47 See *Fine*, Political argument and the legitimacy of international law.
48 *Bauman*, Europe: An Unfinished Adventure, pp. 73, 128.
49 See for instance the Joint Report on Social Protection and Social Inclusion.

one of competitiveness, which submits the assessment of concrete policies to objective criteria of whether they are suited to the globalization process. The evidence gathered to validate these criteria does not result from the factual evaluation of the impact of concrete measures: it results from the fact that governments, in convergent ways, give priority to these criteria. There is no need to justify measures over against possible alternatives, but to recognize that the measures are the only possible measures, as response to a objective trend. The underlying motive of an objective economic trend might remind us the notions of 'forces of history' or 'forces of nature' that orients, according to Arendt, the working of totalitarian states.[50] Even if there are obvious and profound differences under other aspects between the current situation and the reality of totalitarian states, being two of these differences: the consensus on the priority to be given to human rights, and some equilibrium between states and players on the economic field.

Another change that has taken place in the socio-political environment is that, at least for the moment, the clear alternative between political models, which prevailed through successive opposition for two centuries, no longer exists. If there still exists an effective opposition between social models, it is that between Western societies and radical Muslim conceptions of human togetherness. But this opposition is not an opposition between conceptions of the state, where comparable effective states make it possible both to recognize the validity of political order, and at the same time, on a distinct level, to question their legitimacy.[51]

This new situation means that we are now challenged to discuss the question of political order, for the first time for two centuries, without any concrete alternatives likely to offer concrete experiences to support the concepts that we mobilize. This is a situation Luhmann somehow anticipated when he stated that legitimization was not an issue anymore.[52] Moreover, some recent trends could be interpreted as the result of strategies aimed at using the legitimacy issue against itself: that is, of strategies questioning the legitimacy of social movements questioning the legitimacy of certain public policies.[53]

This brings us back to the role of sociology and the social sciences in contemporary society. In a context where public discussion of our political arrangements seems to have lost its spaces and its references, the social sciences and sociology are still called to play a role in processes where they have to survey attitudes of the public and participate in communication strategies aiming at having some impact on

---

50 *Arendt*, Origins of Totalitarianism.
51 At least insofar as I am in condition to understand the claims of radical Muslims, the order they pretend to disseminate merges again the question of the validity and the question of the legitimacy in the sole notion of God's will. However, a better awareness of debates taking place within the Muslim world could allow us to identify common notions between them and our legitimacy debates. This could pave the way to an – even if remote – trans-cultural discussion of the possibilities of institutionalised togetherness.
52 *Luhmann*, Partizipation und Legitimation.
53 *Guibentif*, La légitimité des mouvements sociaux.

these attitudes. In fact, the social sciences are now heavily involved in the process leading to the design of public policies,[54] and their purpose is, on the one hand, to assess the probable acceptance of the measures, and, on the other hand and more principally, to show the objective and unavoidable facts that dictate the political options.[55] Significantly, in such a context, public discussion involving social scientists is organized after the political choices have been taken.[56]

Given the risks linked to the involvement of the social sciences in such endeavours, we could draw the conclusion: social sciences, and especially sociology, cannot limit themselves to participation in legitimization processes by carrying out research on behalf of other second-order observers: they must also take on the role of third-order observer. Among other third-order observers, in particular non-specialized citizens, their responsibility is to map the complex set of debates in which our comparatively simple national public spheres have broken up; to make this map understandable and to show what might be the impact of discussions taking place there; in particular, to demonstrate what it means when the discussion mobilizes the word 'legitimacy' in the sense it acquired through two centuries of hesitant but intense collective learning in democratic government. The responsibility of the social sciences, thus, is to promote the circulation of this word between these arenas, and so to contribute, at a moment where legitimacy has ceased to be an issue on the national level and only retains some social force in limited parts of international debates, to strengthen its semantic potentialities. To remember that this word embodies a – however disenchanted – experience of citizenry that invites people, on a national as well as on a trans-national level, not to remain at the distanced level of third-order observers, but, again, to participate.

Acknowledgements

I warmly thank Chris Thornhill for his extremely valuable suggestions for the final formulation of this paper.

---

54 On the role of social sciences in the design of European social policies, see some elements of the analysis in *Guibentif*, The Liquidity and Solidity of Contemporary Social Reality.
55 As examples see *Ambrósio*, A regulação social da educação'; *Baganha*, Política de imigração; *Ferreira*, De que falamos quando falamos em regulação na saúde?'. These views, however, show varying degrees of recognition of the autonomy of scientific analysis, and of openness in the practical recommendations.
56 On the example of Portugal, see *Santiago et al*, Tertiary Education for the Knowledge Society. The reform of Higher Education was discussed in a meeting that took place seven months after the coming into force of a new legislation on that issue, strongly inspired by OECD recommendations.

Bibliography

Ambrósio, Teresa, A regulação social da educação, Trajectos: Revista de comunicação, cultura e educação 4 (2004), pp. 71-79.
Arendt, Hannah, The Orgins of Totalitarianism, New York, 1973.
Baganha, Maria Ioannis, Política de imigração. A regulação dos fluxos, Revista Crítica de Ciências Sociais 73 (2004), pp. 29-44.
Bauman, Zygmunt, Europe: An Unfinished Adventure, Cambridge, 2004.
Bourdieu, Pierre, La main gauche et la main droite de l'État, in Le Monde 14 January 1992, republished in Contre-feux, Paris, 1998, pp. 9-17.
Brunkhorst, Hauke, Cosmopolitanism and democratic freedom, in this volume.
Coutu, Michel, Le droit du travail comme ordre légitime, in Coutu, Michel and Rocher, Guy (eds), La légitimité de l'État et du droit. Autour de Max Weber, Québec/Paris, 2005, pp. 333-353.
Delmas-Marty, Mireille, Les forces imaginantes du droit III: La refondation des pouvoirs, Paris, 2007.
Ferreira, Ana Sofia, De que falamos quando falamos em regulação na saúde?, Análise Social 171 (2004), pp. 313-337.
Fine, Robert, Political argument and the legitimacy of international law: A case of distorted modernisation, in this volume.
Foucault, Michel, La gouvernementalité, in Foucault, Michel, Dits et écrits, in 4 vols. Paris, 1994, III, pp. 635-657.
Foucault, Michel, Sécurité, territoire et population, Paris, 2004.
Gessner, Volmar and Cem Budak, Ali Cem (eds), Emerging Legal Certainty. Empirical Studies on the Globalization of Law, Aldershot, 1998.
Give Europe a say, *The Economist* (27 October 2007).
Guibentif, Pierre, La pratique du droit international et communautaire de la sécurité sociale – Étude de sociologie du droit de la coordination, à l'exemple du Portugal, Basel/Frankfurt am Main, 1997.
Guibentif, Pierre, Cross-Border Legal Issues Arising from International Migrations: The Case of Portugal, in Gessner, Volmar and Cem Budak, Ali (eds), Emerging Legal Certainty, Aldershot, 1998, pp. 241-282.
Guibentif, Pierre, La légitimité des mouvements sociaux. Un exercice conceptuel dans le prolongement de Habermas et Luhmann, in Coutu, Michel and Rocher, Guy (eds), La légitimité de l'État et du droit. Autour de Max Weber, Québec/Paris, 2005, pp. 259-298.
Guibentif, Pierre, The Liquidity and Solidity of Contemporary Social Reality: the Example of Social Inclusion Policies, in Přibáň, Jiri (ed), Liquid Society and its Law, Aldershot, 2007, pp. 173-197.
Habermas, Jürgen, Legitimationsprobleme im Spätkapitalismus, Frankfurt am Main, 1973.
Habermas, Jürgen, Moralbewusstsein und kommunikatives Handeln, Frankfurt am Main, 1983.
Habermas, Jürgen, Erläuterungen zur Diskursethik, Frankfurt am Main, 1991.
Habermas, Jürgen, Faktizität und Geltung, Frankfurt am Main, 1992.
Habermas, Jürgen, Zwischen Naturalismus und Religion, Frankfurt am Main, 2005.
Habermas, Jürgen, Europapolitik in der Sackgasse. Nicht die Bevölkerungen, die Regierungen sind der Hemmschuh. – Plädoyer für eine Politik der abgestuften Integration, in *Habermas, Jürgen/Steinmeier, Frank-Walter*, Essen, 2008, pp. 15-30.
Hess, Andreas, From Philadelphia to Vitoria via Bonn? Why there is no Constitutional Patriotism in the Basque Country, in this volume.

Annual Joint Report on Social Protection and Social Inclusion, by the European Council and the European Commission: http://ec.europa.eu/employment_social/spsi/joint_reports_en.htm#2008.
Kant, Immanuel, Metaphysik der Sitten, Stuttgart, 1990.
King, Michael/Thornhill, Chris, Niklas Luhmann's Theory of Politics and Law, Basingstoke/New York, 2003.
Luhmann, Niklas, Legitimation durch Verfahren, Neuwied, 1969.
Luhmann, Niklas, Rechtssoziologie, Reinbek bei Hamburg, 1972.
Luhmann, Niklas, Participation und Legitimation. Die Ideen und die Erfahrungen, in Luhmann, Niklas, Soziologische Aufklärung 4, Opladen, 1987, pp. 152-160.
Luhmann, Niklas, Das Recht der Gesellschaft, Frankfurt am Main, 1993.
Luhmann, Niklas, Globalization of World Society. How to Conceive of Modern Society ?', International Review of Sociology 7 (1997), pp. 67-79
Luhmann, Niklas, Die Politik der Gesellschaft, Frankfurt am Main, 2000.
Meja, Volker/Stehr, Nico, Der Streit um die Wissenssoziologie, Frankfurt am Main, 1982.
Neves, Marcelo, Verfassung und Positivität des Rechts in der peripheren Moderne: Eine theoretische Betrachtung und eine Interpretation des Falls Brasilien, Berlin, 1992.
Outhwaite, William, Legitimacy in the European Union, in this volume.
Perrin, Guy, La sécurité sociale. Son histoire à travers les textes. Tome V. Histoire du droit international de la sécurité sociale, Paris, 1993.
Peters, Bernhard, Public discourse, identity, and the problem of democratic legitimacy', in Eriksen, Erik O., (ed), Making the European Polity. Reflexive Integration in the EU London, 2005, pp. 84-123.
Rey, Alain (ed), Le grand Robert de la langue française, Paris, 2001.
Thornhill, Chris, Niklas Luhmann's Political Theory: Politics after Metaphysics?, in King, Michael and Thornhill, Chris (eds), Luhmann on Law and Politics. Critical Appraisals and Applications, Oxford, 2006, pp. 75-99.
Sand, Inger-Johanne, Legitimacy in Global and International Law: A Sociological Critique, in this volume.
Santiago, Paulo/Tremblay, Karine/Ester Basri, Ester/Arnal, Elena, Tertiary Education for the Knowledge Society, Paris, 2008.
Santos, Boaventura de Sousa, Beyond neoliberal governance: the World Social Forum as subaltern cosmopolitan politics and legality, in De Sousa Santos, Boaventura and Rodríguez-Garavito, César (eds), Law and Globalization From Below: Towards a Cosmopolitan Legality, New York, 2005, pp. 29-63.
Saunders, David, The Necessary Secularism of Legitimate Authority, in this volume.
Sciulli, David, Societal Constitutionalism: Procedural Legality and Legitimization in Global and Civil Society, in this volume.
Turnbull, Niklas, Legitimation in terms of questioning: Integrating political rhetoric and sociology of law, in this volume.
Zöllner, D., République fédérale d'Allemagne, in Köhler Peter-A., Zacher Hans-F., Hesse Philippe-Jean (eds), Un siècle de sécurité sociale 1881-1981, Lausanne, 1982, pp. 7-132.
Cuin, Charles-Henry/Gresle, François, Histoire de la sociologie , in 2 vols. Paris, 1992.

Societal constitutionalism: Procedural legality and legitimation in global and civil society

David Sciulli

Two idealized traditions of political, legal and constitutional discourse and theorizing, one Anglo-American, the other continental, are irrelevant empirically under contemporary conditions, those of post-industrialization, system complexity and globalization. Indeed, any lingering presuppositions based directly on these received, idealized approaches, whether in popular consciousness or in scholarship, are today inimical to democratic consolidation and democratic quality in advanced societies. They are even more harmful to the prospects for benign democratization in the South and East or, certainly, for advancing "social justice" in benign ways anywhere in the world. In exploring why this is the case for both traditions we bring into view the increasing salience of procedural legality and "societal constituents" in contemporary societies.

The idealized Anglo-American tradition is society-centered, thus viewing political, legal and constitutional institutions from the bottom up. It posits that an amorphous "constituent force" in civil society, a faction of the larger public, is capable (somehow) of being ever-vigilant in restraining the state short of arbitrariness or abuse. Jurgen Habermas conveyed this idealized tradition to continental readers in 1962 by exploring the rise and fall of what he called the "bourgeois public sphere," from the late seventeenth century to the mid-nineteenth century.[1] In turn, the idealized continental tradition is state-centered, thus viewing political, legal and constitutional institutions from the top down. It attributes quite literally an aura and majesty to the state, such that the state provides an exemplar of probity and leadership for all major organizations and institutions in civil society.

By contrast to both of these idealized traditions we propose that what accounts ultimately for limited government, lawfulness and constitutionalism under first modern conditions and then contemporary conditions are three factors. First, the constituent force or public realm has been *institutionalized* in identifiable positions in civil society, as opposed to remaining dispersed and amorphous. Thus, its effectiveness in restraining state arbitrariness no longer relies on dispersed citizens putatively sharing cultural understandings and social-psychological beliefs regarding state exercises of power. Nor does it rely, as we will see, on the putative self-restraint of mobilized partisan groups *of any kind*, whether left or right, informal or officially authorized. Yet, these institutionalized positions are as dispersed across civil society as were the coffee-houses, salons and table societies of Habermas' public realm: They

---

1 *Habermas*, The Structural Transformation of the Public Sphere.

are institutionalized within major intermediary associations in civil society, led by professions and publicly traded corporations.

Second, being structural and institutional rather than cultural and social-psychological, the social infrastructure of democratic social and political change today is comprised of what we can call *societal constituents*. These constituents, ultimately responsible structurally for limiting the state institutionally, are located *within positions of a certain kind* (discussed below). They are not located within any sets of freestanding or free-floating social influentials who putatively share institutionally salient cultural understandings and social-psychological beliefs.

Third, *what* societal constituents institutionalize within identifiable positions in major intermediary associations is a set of distinctively bright line, *procedural-normative* restraints on arbitrary exercises of collective power of any kind, public or private. These restraints are typically applied first to the state, but the presence of societal constituents structurally in civil society also increasingly extends them to powerful corporate actors in civil society, including the intermediary associations just noted.

Our point in emphasizing the importance of structural (positional) and procedural-normative restraints on arbitrariness is that there can no longer be found in *any* civil society today, or trans-nationally, any set of ultimate *substantive-normative* restraints on arbitrariness capable of securing shared cultural understandings, let alone shared social-psychological beliefs. Rather, what possibly can be found, at least in some civil societies, is a bright line, procedural-normative threshold standard of state arbitrariness or caprice. This is what can be institutionalized within civil society as more or less invariant restraints on state arbitrariness or caprice. Such a threshold standard is in fact available to sociologists and legal scholars, provided most notably by Lon Fuller's extra-statutory and extra-constitutional desiderata of lawfulness, of procedural-normative legal integrity.

I. Lawfulness, picket fences and epistemology

By Fuller's accounting, courts of any kind – whether criminal, civil, family, constitutional or corporate – can only enforce statutory laws or constitutional provisions with consistency over time and across cases – lawfully – when these positivist laws themselves incarnate eight procedural-normative qualities (irrespective of what they require in substance, whether from subjects *or enforcers*). Consistently enforced laws: apply generally to violators, do not contradict each other, and in addition are publicized, prospective, clear, relatively constant, possible to obey and congruent with the actual conduct of enforcement authorities.[2]

A shorthand way of characterizing this procedural normative threshold standard of lawfulness is to say that consistently enforced rules of any kind are by definition clear and possible to obey. They are clear at least to those trained in the law, and

---

2 *Fuller*, The Morality of Law, pp. 46-84.

they can be obeyed by citizens with modest or typical effort as opposed to demanding unusual or heroic effort. This shorthand description encompasses all of the other desiderata above because, as examples, retroactive rules, unpublicized rules, rules frequently changed and rules not applied to all violators are simultaneously unclear and, as a result, difficult or impossible to obey even with heroic effort.

At first glance, this procedural-normative threshold of rule clarity and consistency may seem trivial, self-evidently legitimating all modern legal systems without exception. However, quite the opposite is the case. In the first place, the legal systems of autocracies routinely encroach against this threshold. The same is true, for that matter, of the legal systems of many new democracies in the East and South. Moreover, even in the most established democracies we find not only periodic or one-shot encroachments, in specific legislation or judicial rulings. We also find systemic pressures of drift toward general or ongoing encroachments. The renowned American political scientist, Theodore Lowi, has been warning since 1969, with the publication of *The End of Liberalism*, about such a drift in the United States.[3]

Regardless, we may convey the institutional significance of procedural legality metaphorically: The procedural-normative integrity of law places a quite flimsy white picket fence around the Leviathan. Literally any untoward twitching of the whale's tail, fin or snout can obliterate great swaths of this fence. Moreover, the whale (state agencies) may twitch entirely nonchalantly, unthinkingly, rather than purposefully with malice of forethought. Likewise, some observers of the twitching (leaders of social movements) may acclaim the beast for "liberating" itself from "bourgeois" niceties or formalities. They thereby confuse state formalism, which is entirely negotiable, with procedural integrity, which is not. Whether done nonchalantly or purposefully, *any* destruction of the fence is always an unambiguous event on the ground, because the presence or absence of *any part* of the fence is bright line.[4]

Quite unlike state- and rights-formalism on the Continent, in short, procedural integrity introduces into organized interaction bright line, non-negotiable qualitative normative standards of behavior, of fidelity and encroachment - however minimalist

---

3 *Lowi*, The End of Liberalism.
4 One of the greatest threats to procedural legality today in all democracies, whether advanced or new, comes ironically from countries' highest courts. Rather than focusing first and foremost on whether existing law, and its enforcement, exhibits procedural integrity, courts instead engage directly in legislative (or executive) activities: substantive policy initiatives - from abortion to medical treatment, narcotics, gender, housing, wages and sexual preference. This is as true of the U.S. Supreme Court as it is of Constitutional Courts from Germany to Colombia. For instance, even liberal legal scholars who favor the substantive outcome of Roe v. Wade (such as Cass Sunstein), which legalized abortion nationally in the U.S., agree that Court reasoning here lacked procedural integrity. See *Sunstein*, Radicals in Robes and The Fate of Roe v. Wade and Choice. The Colombia Constitutional Court, established in 1991, is a literal archetype of legislative overreach and thus of procedural integrity breakdown. For favorable accountings of this Court which nonetheless demonstrate our point of criticism, see *Faundez*, Democratization Through Law; and *Uprimny/Garcia-Villegas*, The Constitutional Court and Social Emancipation in Colombia.

these standards may be. As many theorists note (from Amitai Etzioni to Jurgen Habermas and then Benjamin Gregg), procedural integrity contributes at best to a "thin" orderliness, of shared cognition and mutuality; the latter, in turn, may range from shared respect, to tolerance, to indifference. It does not yield a "thick" orderliness of affect and solidarity or shared purpose.[5]

For present purposes it is beyond the scope of this paper to explore further why Fuller's approach to lawfulness can credibly claim universality. We can only simply assert that the procedural-normative integrity of law is buttressed by Habermas' and Karl-Otto Apel's proceduralist consensus theory of truth as well as Talcott Parsons' references to what he called collegial formations (as found in professions).[6] This means that Fuller's desiderata can credibly claim grounding at an epistemological level, unlike any nation-state's standards of mere positivist legality. Given this, it can then also credibly claim universality, as opposed to conceding particularism or partisanship (as Anglo-American or "Northern" or "bourgeois"). No positivist approach to law – whether Hans Kelsen's or H.L.A Hart's and then Joseph Raz's – can claim this epistemological grounding and thus universality.[7]

II. From formalist "correctness" or "right" to procedural integrity: Three theses

Collective power which is exercised consistently with procedural-normative integrity, whether exercised by the state or by any intermediary association in civil society, differs fundamentally from formalistic standards of substantive "correctness" or "right," on one side, and from *any* directly substantive-normative (or culturalist) understanding of either basic individual rights or "social justice," on the other. This includes *any* such standards or understandings upheld by *any* putative constituent group or public realm. Just as Habermas, Apel, Gerard Radnitzky and others found it necessary to replace all ontologies, including all positivist copy theories of truth, with a proceduralist epistemology, a discourse theory of truth, so the state tradition of the Continent will be compelled to shift its categorical foundations - and for entirely comparable reasons. In both cases the shift is necessary simply to account analytically and empirically for facts on the ground: for the possibility of shared cognition over time by dispersed individuals and partisan groupings (including schools of

---

5 *Etzioni*, The New Golden Rule; *Habermas*, Between Facts and Norms; *Gregg*, Thick Moralities, Thin Politics.

6 See *Sciulli*, Theory of Societal Constitutionalism: Foundations of a Non-Marxist Critical Theory.

7 Fuller and Hart engaged in a famous debate from 1958 to 1969, which included major books by each: Hart's The Concept of Law and Fuller's (poorly titled) The Morality of Law (1964), with a long response to critics in the 1969 revised edition. In many respects Hart built upon Kelsen's earlier legal positivism, and then Joseph Raz's collected chapters in The Authority of Law can be read as the final rebuttal to Fuller on Hart's behalf. See *Fuller*, The Morality of Law; *Hart*, The Concept of Law; *Raz*, The Authority of Law.

thought) whose immediate interests (and understandings) are otherwise competing (or incommensurable) and always potentially conflictual.

Proceduralist discourse theories of truth are needed to account for shared cognition over time by dispersed scientists, their shared cognition of falsification and thus of the defensible scope of truth-claims. Likewise, proceduralist structural and institutional theories of legitimacy and authority are needed to account for shared cognition over time by dispersed citizens and partisan groupings of arbitrary exercises of collective power, whether public or private. Such theories are needed to account, that is, for the defensible scope of state-claims, or of association-claims or corporate-claims within civil society, regarding either bearing fiducial responsibility or wielding socio-cultural authority in the public interest, in the best interests of the larger society.

1. The baseline: System complexity

Our first thesis is that the fetishizing on the Continent of state-formalism and rights-substance is indeed already being displaced in practice, on both sides, due to contemporary systemic pressures of post-industrialization and globalization. Amidst these pressures, this fetishizing is giving way not only to what Niklas Luhmann calls system complexity and autopoiesis (self-referential steering and evolution). It is also giving way, by various routes, to the overriding, non-negotiable significance and salience, both structurally and institutionally, of lawfulness as procedural-normative legal integrity, not as formalistic state correctness or right as positivist legality. The problem is that major social theorists on the left, led by Habermas, appreciate this without appreciating that procedural-normative integrity spans not only the state but also readily identifiable, increasingly state-independent major intermediary associations in civil society.

Still, we must first note why the concession on the left to system complexity, again led by Habermas, is settled so conclusively today, as opposed to being neglected or disregarded – as in the past (from Marx through Lukacs and Gramsci and the entire first generation of the Frankfurt School). This issue has been settled by the literal mountain of social scientific research and theorizing which describes and explains the sheer system decentralization and global dynamism of contemporary advanced societies. Thus, on one side, the elaborate functionalist theories of Talcott Parsons and others clearly conveyed this, and the same is true, certainly, of Luhmann's systems theory. The latter revolves around the notion of dispersed social systems and subsystems being autopoietic or self-regulating, and thus beyond the capacity of any state-administrative hierarchy to direct in detail, through legal positivism.[8]

On the other side, what is remarkable about Jurgen Habermas' long-standing efforts to theorize the *Lebenswelt* (lifeworld) and to support his warnings about its

---

8   For example, see *Luhmann*, Social Systems.

"colonization" by intrusive systems - of state administration and market acquisitiveness – is how much Habermas simultaneously concedes to Parsons and Luhmann.[9] Moreover, he yields ground here not because he wishes to do so but precisely because he must: Habermas appreciates he cannot possibly otherwise be taken seriously as a disinterested social theorist. Any refusal to concede system complexity would marginalize him as some utopian or blind partisan, like the first generation of the Frankfurt School.

The problem, again, is that Habermas fails to see that lawfulness as procedural-normative legal integrity is being extended from the state to major intermediary associations in civil society of a certain kind.[10] He instead emphasizes the "emancipatory" potential of new social movements. Our alternative emphasis, however, establishes simultaneously the structural and institutional limits of both types of continental fetishizing noted above. It establishes the limits of:

- state socio-cultural authority over and fiducial responsibility for civil society; and of

- individual rights-exercise and self-interestedness (acquisitiveness and cupidity) in substance, at least within and around certain institutionalized venues in civil society.

More generally, the problem is that much of the debate in Germany (and elsewhere in continental Europe), first around *Rechtsstaat* historically and then around *Sozialstaat* and *Bundesstaat* today, still tends to collapse this distinction.[11] Procedural-normative integrity of any kind is disparaged as "bourgeois" because it is confused with structurally and institutionally pliable formalism. It is not appreciated as being entirely distinct from, and above and beyond, state correctness and rights-formalism, thus legal positivism.

Elevating lawfulness as procedural-normative legal integrity above the *Rechtsstaat* – and above *all* of the latter's later formalistic variations, including *Sozialstaat* – is necessary today because systemic pressures of post-industrialization and globalization are in fact transferring both socio-cultural authority and fiducial responsibility from the state to major intermediary associations within civil society *of a certain kind*. These pressures are transferring both of these formerly statist qualities to those intermediary associations which contain what we are calling *structured situations*. They are not transferring statist qualities to "neo-liberal" venues, to corporate

---

9   Pierre Bourdieu concedes just as much, but more indirectly: He concedes it by referring to literally dozens – scores - of distinct "fields," each of which privileges certain "positions" and "dispositions" over others. For example, see *Bourdieu*, The Social Structures of the Economy.
10   For instance, see *Habermas*, Between Facts and Norms.
11   The same is likely true of the French debate over etat de droit (state of right), the Spanish debate over estado de derecho or estado constitucional and the Italian debate over costituzionale dichiari (constitutional it declares).

bodies (or partisan groupings) which contain only *fluid sites* of commerce and recreation or *embedded exchanges* of information and expertise, or both.

Our point is that it is changes in (1) the independence of intermediary associations from the state and in (2) the internal governance of these state-independent intermediary associations (thus in private governance structures) which bear centrally on the structure and direction of institutional change of both the state and citizenship today. Thus, the difference between the "state" societies of the continent and the limited governments of the Anglo-American world cannot be traced today, if they ever could be, to differences in "civic cultures" or political participation rates or, certainly, "national character" (or *geistig* qualities).[12] The difference historically has been first structural and then institutional, and today this difference is steadily disappearing in practice under global systemic pressures.

More important for our purposes, the characteristics of this convergence are also now coming into view at a conceptual level. Structurally, the continent's statist tradition favors centralizing socio-cultural authority and fiducial responsibility in the state administration, and the result institutionally is the state-formalism of *Rechtsstaat* or *Sozialstaat*. This is then complimented by a formalistic fetishizing of substantive individual and group rights. The result, institutionally, is that such formalisms are readily compromised, on both sides, by *any* putative *Gerechtigkeitsstaat*, state of substantive justice or righteousness.

By contrast, the Anglo-American tradition of the constituent group favors, structurally, dispersing socio-cultural authority and fiducial responsibility to intermediary associations in civil society as well as to certain private governance structures, in particular those of publicly traded corporations. The result institutionally is limited government, the lawfulness (as opposed to positivist correctness or right) of public governance, and then societal constitutionalism, the lawfulness of private governance structures in civil society.

2. Systemic limitations of the state

Our second thesis is that today the received pattern on the continent, of ongoing state-administrative centralization of fiducial responsibility and socio-cultural authority, is simply no longer sustainable - whether on the continent or elsewhere. This is the case not only because of global systemic pressures. It is also the case for two other reasons. One is that old-style state-administrative centralization lacks legitimation regardless on its own terms. This is due to the worldwide discrediting of authoritarian "state" societies following the fascist experiences of the first half of the twentieth century. Everywhere, across all established democracies today, literally all influential groups agree on "the bankruptcy of the state as a liberalizing institution."[13]

---

12 *Almond*, Comparative Political Systems.
13 *Krieger*, The German Idea of Freedom, p. 469.

The other reason is that the state's *abilities* as an institution to exercise socio-cultural authority today are suspect. The state may well be capable of delivering welfare services, as an intrusive *Wolfarhtsstaat*. But it is hardly self-evidently capable today of occupying credibly the socio-cultural high ground, whether as a *Kulturstaat* or a *Sozialtaat*. Which state anywhere in the world today credibly provides *the* exemplar for the *entire* occupational order of corporate pre-eminence (socio-cultural authority), occupational upgrading and responsibility (professionalism) or employee or personnel cultivation (*Bildung*)? Does even the French state credibly claim this today? Lagging here at an institutional level, even high state officials in France no longer provide in their persons (habitus) *the* exemplars of "correct" socialization, motivation and expertise for everyone else in the occupational order and larger society. They are no longer trusted to be the sole source of and ultimate guarantor for all fiducial responsibilities borne by dispersed experts for the wellbeing of their patients, their clients or their other dependents. In what civil society today is such an encompassing trusteeship any longer expected of the state and its hierarchies of officials?[14]

In this light we need to rethink on broader, more sociological grounds, a *fuller range* of consequences of welfare-state retrenchment, of the rise of so-called "neo-liberal" socio-economic decentralization. It is simplistic and ideological to reduce these consequences to any unbridled "hegemony" of capitalist acquisitiveness and cupidity. The same is true of attributing these consequences exclusively or even primarily to American geopolitical leadership, as transferred to the continent unwittingly but perniciously through the "gateway" of Great Britain.[15]

To the contrary, "neo-liberal" socio-economic decentralization within established democracies revolves around and is being driven forward in some large part by a quite extra-economistic process, namely a dispersion of professionalism from the state to major intermediary associations in civil society. Put somewhat differently, the socio-cultural authority and fiducial responsibility once centralized in state-administrative hierarchies are now being dispersed to professions as well as to publicly traded corporations and other major intermediary associations of a certain kind. All of these are venues in civil society which contain structured situations as opposed to only fluid sites of commercialism or embedded exchanges yielding only emergent norms.

Put most succinctly, the continent and the rest of the world, including the new democracies of the South and East, are now accommodating in various ways, inadvertent and purposeful, a diffusion of professionalism more and more deeply into and broadly across civil society. This ongoing dispersion is proceeding apace under multidimensional systemic pressures, not as a result of any one-dimensional unleashing of "neo-liberal" acquisitiveness or of American "cultural imperialism."

---

14 On the absence of "statesmanship" in the private bar and public bench of the U.S., see *Kronman*, The Lost Lawyer.
15 *Bourdieu/Wacquant*, The Cunning of Imperialist Reason.

3. Structured situations and constituent positions in civil society

Our third thesis is that the venues of structured situations and professionalism in civil society just noted contain today what we can call positions of societal constituency. They contain identifiable positions which today are providing structurally the social infrastructure supporting lawfulness, first within and around the state and then within and around major intermediary associations in civil society. These positions are providing this social infrastructure in the complete absence of any constituent force or public realm. Indeed, because the social infrastructure they are providing is first and foremost structural, it is intrinsically depoliticizing. Success or failure here, that is, does not *hinge* on periodic *mass* mobilizations of political parties, social movements, voluntary associations or NGOs – although these can be beneficial at times (and sinister at others).

Today's positions of societal constituency in major intermediary associations provide bright line indicators of changes in the institutional design of the larger social order, that spanning the state and civil society. They provide these bright line indicators in the complete absence of any possible iteration of a constituent group or of formalistic state correctness or formalistic rights-guarantees. The key to identifying these positions of societal constituency is, in fact, to distinguish structured situations in civil society from fluid sites and embedded exchanges. Only structured situations, that is, contain *entrenched* positions of power, positions which are *capable* simultaneously of wielding socio-cultural authority within civil society and bearing fiducial responsibilities for dependents' wellbeing.

In this sense structured situations differ *fundamentally*, both analytically and empirically as well as both structurally and institutionally, from three other types of sites:

- Sites of simple commercial transacting and contracting; these are, of course, the arm's-length market relations idealized by neoclassical economists. There is little reason to dwell on these.

- Sites of elective diversion, of discretionary leisure and entertainment; these are similar structurally, and also need not be explored here.

A bit more complicated, both analytically and empirically, are:

- Sites of embedded commercial (and other) exchanges of information and services; these are the repetitive market (and other) relations typically studied by network analysts and economic sociologists.

These exchanges, even if rather short-term, typically yield ongoing social relationships and what Ralph Turner and others call emergent norms of interpersonal behavior and what Pierre Bourdieu calls "dispositions." But none of the three sites above contain entrenched positions at all, let alone those of power.

First and foremost, structured situations are distinct from all other sites or venues in that they alone revolve around two sets of positions which are *entrenched* rather than simply embedded – let alone fluid, and thus literally position-less. On one side, structured situations contain positions of power, discretionary judgment and trust. These are the entrenched positions professionals occupy in any ongoing professional-client relationship, whether applied or academic. These also happen to be the entrenched positions corporate officers occupy in any governance structure of publicly traded corporations. On the other side, structured situations also contain positions of dependence, vulnerability and apprehension. These are the entrenched positions clients *and patrons* of professional services occupy, and which stakeholders occupy in corporate governance structures.

Being structural and invariant in any structured situation, entrenched positions of dependence were in evidence in the Paris visual *Academie* during the *ancien regime* despite the fact that the patrons of visual *academiciens* occupying these positions were typically men of gentle birth and lofty status. Outside the occupational field of ambitious painting and sculpture, *gentilshomme* would rarely entertain, let alone defer to, the ceremonial and decorative judgment or taste of commoners.[16] Yet, even the king and court nobility (*noblesse d'epée*), to say nothing of royal administrators (*noblesse de robe*) and provincial gentry (*noblesse d'ancienne extraction*), had no alternative structurally, upon successfully retaining *academicien* visual services, other than to occupy entrenched positions of dependence. Irrespective of their superior status and putatively innate reason and taste, they could not avoid trusting socially lowly visual *academiciens* to advance their honor, their socio-cultural wellbeing, in one area of ambitious decoration and ceremony, that of narrative painting. Of course, this relationship of impersonal trust simultaneously confirmed *academiciens'* reputations as liberally-trained occupational practitioners, as prototype professionals.[17]

This same relationship of impersonal trust reappears today, albeit in quite different occupational fields. Upon successfully securing vital legal and medical services, for instance, even the wealthiest clients, individual or corporate, have no alternative structurally other than to trust, respectively, their freedom and physical wellbeing to the discretionary judgment of these liberally-trained practitioners.

Our point is that both sets of entrenched positions – those of power and those of dependence – are found only in situations which are structured. And both sets of positions are indeed fixed, and in two respects. First, neither positional power nor positional dependence is contingent upon quotidian social constructions of meaning. Neither is available, that is, for substantial renegotiation by participants or interested observers. Power and dependence accrue to these positions irrespective of what in-

---

16 *Shapin*, A Social History of Truth: Civility and Science in Seventeenth Century England, chap. 3. Indeed, such deference was not as evident even within this occupational field in Italy, for reasons we cannot explore here. See *Sciulli*, Structural and Institutional Invariance in Professions and Professionalism.

17 *Sciulli*, Paris Visual Academie as First Prototype Profession; *Sciulli*, Professions before Professionalism.

dividual participants or observers happen to believe social-psychologically or happen to understand culturally. For instance, the notion of professionalism was anachronistic in the seventeenth century, and thus unavailable culturally to *gentilshomme* and visual *academiciens*. Likewise, even today the notion of professionalism is alien to all continental languages.[18] Yet, always and everywhere, entrenched positions of power and dependence are nonetheless present within structured situations.[19]

In addition, the relationship between these positions is equally fixed, equally beyond social construction and renegotiation. Being entrenched on both sides, the relationship between these two sets of positions, of dependence and of power, is literally non-negotiable. The relationship between them is tactile, weighty, not merely some social construction or rhetorical posturing which participants can alter or adjust as they wish.

Thus, always and everywhere incumbents of the first set of positions in structured situations exercise *positional power* over dependents. This remains the case even when these incumbents are visual *academiciens* and their clients or patrons are *gentilshomme*, otherwise (in the views of contemporaries) superior ontologically as well as more prominent socially, more powerful, and wealthier. Related, always and everywhere incumbents of entrenched positions of power are oriented structurally by readily identifiable *positional interests*. These are distinguishable, both analytically and empirically, from incumbents' roles, statuses and self-interests as individuals, to say nothing of their vanity or idiosyncrasy as personalities.

In this respect, position differs fundamentally from both status and role – two of sociology's most basic concepts.[20] For instance, the status an individual has in the larger society, in the stratification system – whether based on wealth, power, influence or any other attribute – may well bear on whether an individual enters the *role* of accused or defendant in a legal setting. But, upon entering this role, irrespective of how or why this happens, no individual defendant, even of the loftiest social status, can avoid occupying an entrenched position of dependence. No individual defendant can avoid trusting his wellbeing impersonally to a stranger, defence counsel, relying on him or her to bear structurally a fiducial responsibility for his wellbeing.

Likewise, the clients and patrons of doctors, lawyers, engineers, research scientists and other professionals also cannot escape occupying, at some point, entrenched positions of dependence within ongoing (rather than momentary) professional-client relationships. To be sure, a client of professional services can seek and secure a second opinion and, for that matter, a third opinion - a tenth opinion. Indeed, a client of professional services might himself or herself be a fellow professional practitioner and, therefore, be entirely familiar with what is happening and will happen. But a client (or patron) of professional services, irrespective of their roles and statuses in the larger society, cannot avoid at some point trusting his wellbeing (or long-term stake) quite literally to a particular professional practitioner, typically a stranger.

18 *Sciulli*, Continental Sociology of Professions Today.
19 See *Sciulli*, Structural and Institutional Invariance in Professions and Professionalism.
20 *Sciulli*, Editor Observations: On Position.

In turn, no individual professional can avoid exercising positional power over dependents, and thereby avoid bearing fiducial responsibility structurally for their wellbeing. This responsibility far exceeds any norms of principal-agent relationships at other sites, venues or locales of interaction. As such, it brings into view how positional interests differ from individuals' self interests. For example, a lawyer or doctor may have a self interest in shirking or goldbricking, in failing to extend his most robust efforts and capacities on behalf of a client or patient. But the same lawyer or doctor has a positional interest, recognizable at law, in extending himself regardless. This is the case not only because advancing these positional interests benefits literally anyone occupying a lawyer or doctor position (and then, of course, anyone occupying a client or patient position). More important, should self-interest ever be seen unambiguously to trump positional interest, this in itself exposes a lawyer or doctor to challenges to his or her *positional power* over dependents. Such challenges can originate first with laymen (in informal and then formal complaints by clients, patients or their relatives), or with colleagues (in inquiries in various review committees), or finally with litigants (in malpractice cases and derivative suits in courts of law).[21]

This distinction, between variable statuses (and habituses), roles and self interests, on one side, and entrenched positions and fixed positional interests, on the other, cannot be drawn at all, let alone unambiguously, at fluid sites of interaction (whether commercial or recreational). Moreover, it is difficult, typically impossible to draw it within embedded exchanges. For instance, it is impossible to draw this distinction within patron-client networks. More generally, this is where Bourdieu's discussions of embeddedness within fields become deficient.

Our point is that within structured situations these distinctions are at once bright line and routinely recognized at law, first in common law countries but today increasingly on the Continent. This is why it is vital today, in moving beyond individuals' roles, statuses, and self-interests, to bring structured situations and positional interests into sociological analysis explicitly.[22]

We can further illustrate why this distinction is vital by turning briefly to a second major set of intermediary association in modern civil societies, in addition to professions, which quintessentially contains structured situations, not simply embedded exchanges: publicly traded corporations. In the private governance structures of these corporations, middle managers, long-term suppliers, bondholders and other "stakeholders" cannot escape occupying entrenched positions of dependence. The very term "governance *structure*" conveys this. Having invested careers, or altered manufacturing facilities, or dedicated capital long-term to a particular firm, it is either literally impossible for stakeholders to exit on short notice or they can exit only at considerable cost. By contrast, shareholders typically remain at entirely fluid sites of commercial contracting: they can sell their shares at any time, literally on a whim.

Thus, both ongoing professional-client relationships and corporate governance structures are quintessentially sites, venues or locales of impersonal trust. This is

---

21 *Rothman*, Strangers at the Bedside; *Shapiro*, Bushwacking the Ethical High Road.
22 For a philosophical rationale for this distinction, see *Sen*, Positional Objectivity.

why Anglo-American law (and increasingly continental and European Union law)[23] holds that those occupying entrenched positions of power within these relationships and structures bear fiducial responsibilities for the wellbeing of dependents. In corporate governance disputes these responsibilities are codified formally at law, as fiducial duties of care and loyalty.[24]

III. Implications for social justice

In modern societies, first private property and then the presence of structured situations in civil society, beyond those in particular agencies of the state itself are vital to *consolidating* limited government and then improving democratic quality. This consolidation, that is, is vital to seeking greater social justice, let alone realizing it.[25] By decentralizing and dispersing power into and across civil society, both of these institutions help to restrain the state short of autocracy and thereby provide basic institutional foundations for ongoing democratization. The strongest single argument that has ever been presented in favor of private property, never rebutted by Marx or, certainly, by any real world experience with Marxism, communism or socialism, is that every ounce of power left to markets to allocate is an ounce of power denied the state to exercise.

1. Some questions and options

We might consider, in this light, which social policies are most likely to advance "social justice," however defined (whether by Hayek, Rawls, Walzer or Sen):[26]

- An educational system in which only public schools are tolerated, or one in which private schools are also permitted to recruit and instruct students?

- A postal system in which only state agencies deliver mail and packages, or one in which private parcel services are also permitted to deliver materials?

- Related, an Internet system in which state agencies register and regulate all portals and all e-mail services, or one in which the state largely sits on the

---

23 *Teubner*, Expertise as Social Institution; *Teubner*, Societal Constitutionalism.
24 For elaboration, see *Sciulli*, Corporate Power in Civil Society.
25 For a cross-national comparison of the link between social justice and even basic democracy, electoral democracy, let alone limited government and greater democratic quality, see *Merkel/Kruck*, Social Justice and Democracy.
26 These are the four theorists whose discussions of social justice are considered in *Merkel/Kruck*, Social Justice and Democracy.

sidelines – intervening, at most, only into unambiguous instances of excess or endangerment?[27]

- A health care system in which all services are provided through mandatory state-based coverage or one in which employers, insurance carriers and wealthy individuals are also permitted to secure services – and precisely in order to stimulate private initiative and innovation in pharmaceutical research, surgery and other branches of the health care system?

Thinking about this listing more generally, we may pose additional questions:

- Is justice being served when the personnel of public agencies providing transportation, postal, medical and other "socialized" services – the ticket sellers, the station and office attendants – are lackadaisical in serving the public? Is it served when they are indifferent to long lines and shoddy service and thereby impose an entire range of qualitative costs upon the public?

Such costs include endless frustration, as well as anticipating such frustration prior to arriving on site. They also include being compelled to invest endless hours of discretionary time, which individuals could have devoted to leisure or, for that matter, to activities maximizing their own capacities and abilities (as Marxists originally defined *Gemeinwesen* beyond capitalism).

- Why is it that public services directed to the poor and working class, those parts of the public lacking large reserves of discretionary income but possibly possessing considerable reserves of discretionary time, provide *the* standard or criteria by which "social justice" is defined? Why is it not private services directed to the middle-class and higher, those parts of the public possessing discretionary income and willing to expend it in order to receive services with alacrity, and thus to transfer their discretionary time elsewhere?[28]

- As new democracies of the South and East develop larger, more established or secure middle-classes, will the public's standards or criteria of social justice shift accordingly? Will scholarly standards then also shift, or will scholars simply turn elsewhere in the world to identify with the poor and indigent?

---

27 *Teubner*, Expertise as Social Institution; *Teubner*, Societal Constitutionalism.
28 Why not compel haute couture restaurants to seat certain numbers of indigents for every hundred paying customers? Or compel homeowners to take in the indigent – as was done routinely in the American colonies across the seventeenth and eighteenth centuries?

Now it may be that some social scientists scanning this listing might well argue that social justice is clearly advanced by a top-down, state-based approach – or, looking in the opposite direction, that privatization invariably yields inegalitarian results and "alienation" of labor. However, it is clear today that the onus of proof is now on them to make the case for socializing goods and services. The onus is no longer on proponents of one or another degree of privatization. This is the case not only because of the contemporary anachronism of the "state" society tradition noted earlier but also because fiducial responsibility and socio-cultural authority are already being decentralized into civil society, not simply acquisitiveness and cupidity alone.

2. Social movements: The left alternative to societal constituents

Having been compelled to concede system complexity to Parsons and Luhman as the backdrop for his theorizing of "emancipation," Habermas appreciates he cannot avoid conceding another point, as a corollary. System complexity demands "self-discipline" by left social movements which advocate for an "alternative society," if they also wish to avoid a new autocracy. Any "alternative society" worthy of being lived in today, Habermas appreciates, must accommodate system complexity in one way or another.

Moreover, Habermas also appreciates that even members of left social movements, like everyone else in civil society today, is incapable of identifying "progress" or "regress" in common directly in substance, directly in describing curent policy proposals, ongoing policy implementation or unfolding shifts in trajectories of social change. Even committed leftists can only secure a common understanding of "progress" or "regress" through ongoing discursive activities which establish and maintain procedural-normative integrity. Short of this, any putative consensus is imposed: it is a product of manipulation or systematic distortion or, even more insidiously, of threats and strong-arm controls.

Among other left theorists, Jean Cohen and Andrew Arato have been among the most forthright in following Habermas in these concessions, as they explore the institutional and social-movement options available in theorizing "civil society" today.[29] By contrast, Immanuel Wallerstein's calls to return to standards of "substantive rationality" for guidance, as opposed to any notion of procedural integrity as a self-disciplining mediation, are at once utopian and irresponsible; Vittorio Olgiati is similar.[30] Such calls literally invite autocracy. Yet, other recent leftist critics of "bourgeois law" or "capitalist law" have done the same, as they promote quite different vision of "social justice," different from those articulated by Habermas or Wallerstein (or Hayek, Rawls, Walzer and Sen).

---

29 *Cohen/Arato*, Civil Society and Political Theory.
30 *Wallerstein*, Social Science and Contemporary Society; *Olgiati*, Shifting Heuristics.

The leftists we have in mind are those who seek a legal order which, on explicitly particularistic substantive-normative grounds, benefits the weak or poor *exclusively*, and thus abandons any pretense of lawfulness as procedural integrity because this would only place obstacles in the way of a new, quite literally hegemonic *Wohlfahrtsstaat* and *Sozialstaat*.[31] They then disregard, as an altogether secondary and unimportant concern, whether autocracy might result. That is, they fail to consider whether *any* such alternative could possibly be kept consistent with system complexity and *any* democratic-constitutional polity - or would instead invariably lapse into one version or another of autocracy.[32]

Boaventura de Sousa Santos, for instance, initially dismissed Habermas' efforts to reconcile Marxism or leftist progressivism on the basis of a proceduralist legal universalism. He considered the latter an "imperial universalism," invariably harming the weak and poor in the South (Latin America).[33] Today he is more deferential to Habermas.[34] Santos (with co-author Leonardo Avritzer) considers Habermas "the author within counter-hegemonic theories [...] who opened the discussion on proceduralism as a societal practice and not as a method of constituting governments." But Santos says this only because he takes seriously Habermas' emphasis on the importance of new social movements. Santos lauds this as a "societal and participatory proceduralism – as a principle of wide participation." He does not see proceduralism as incarnating a principle of non-negotiable restraints on arbitrary collective power, whether by the state or in civil society.[35]

Returning in this light to Habermas and Cohen and Arato, as they assess what is possible systemically today what does it mean, actually, for them to call upon leftist (and other) social movements to be "self-disciplining," and thus more mature than blindly partisan?[36] It means that they are extending qualities or characteristics central to professionalism – personal disinterestedness and a corporate commitment not to exercise their collective power irresponsibly – directly to social movements, in the absence of any institutional underpinning or structural-based rationale. The result is a bad fit, first at a conceptual level and then, even more, in empirical application. This way of thinking about social movements is in itself utterly utopian, and

31 *De Sousa Santos*, Toward a New Common Sense: Law, Science and Politics; *De Sousa Santos* (ed), Democratizing Democracy: Dezalay and Garth (eds), Global Prescriptions.
32 For example, see *De Sousa Santos*, Toward a New Common Sense: Law, Science and Politics, p. 517.
33 *De Sousa Santos*, Toward a New Common Sense: Law, Science and Politics pp. 507-8.
34 This calls to mind a similar U-turn by Robert Summers, in his assessment of Fuller's legal theory. Critical of Fuller during the 1970s, by 1984 he conceded the salience of his procedural-normative approach to lawfulness: *Summers*, Lon L. Fuller.
35 *De Sousa Santos/Avritzer*, Introduction: Opening up the Canon of Democracy, p. xliv. Andrew Arato is similar: 'Constitutionalism is the major modern mechanism guaranteeing popular sovereignty in the sense of including beyond the representatives an expanding circle of participants who are responsible for fundamental law making and revision.' See *Arato*, Accountability and Civil Society, p. 309.
36 A recent confessional by America's greatest living playwright brings this call to an individual level: *Mamet*, Why I am No Longer a "Brain-Dead Liberal"'.

naïve. On what basis can anyone expect leftist (and other) social movements to be mature and self-restraining in policy advocacy, and particularly over time, in the heat of political battle?

Going beyond this, we propose that what accounts structurally for democratic consolidation under contemporary conditions is the presence of societal constituents in civil society and in selected state agencies. These are the participants in any structured situation who, in simply advancing *their own immediate positional and corporate interests*, simultaneously establish and then maintain the integrity of a collegial (or deliberative) form of organization and of the threshold standard of procedural integrity. That is, societal constituents have an immediate positional and corporate interest in establishing and maintaining lawfulness. In turn, this then permits everyone else – including social movement leaders and members – to identify bright line thresholds of "progress" or "regress" in the direction of policy proposals and social change.

These same bright line thresholds, that is, are what can facilitate an ongoing maturation of social movements, which Habermas and Cohen and Arato are wrongly seeking more directly at either a cultural level or a social-psychological. But this also means that, absent these markers, *everything* does indeed become politicized. Everything becomes subjected to blind (immature) partisanship. Then, at best, such partisanship can be restrained only in substance, and always only temporarily, by periodic elite pacts and electoral bribery (through transfer payments) in substance.[37] That is, the structural limitations imposed by system complexity as well as by a limited government or lawful state no longer appear truly structural, thus non-negotiable. They instead appear ever-available for elite and electoral renegotiation, and thus for partisan mobilization. Why exactly should leftist movements exhibit self-restraint within such a structural and institutional setting?

With two notable exceptions, all great radical social movements *of putative substantive rationality*, right and left, have turned autocratic under modern conditions. This was clearly displayed in Europe and Asia from the 1920s to the 1940s, and it was displayed no less in the American South or subsequently during the McCarthy era. One exception is the postwar evolution on the Continent from a *Rechtsstaat* to a *Sozialstaat*. Yet, this exception is precarious even today because it rests on shaky structural and institutional grounds; nowhere is it truly consolidated either structurally or institutionally, as a truly limited government and lawful democratic society. Everywhere in Europe, as well as elsewhere, a *Sozialstaat* remains vulnerable structurally to autocratic turns, particularly those leftward.

The other exception is that provided by Ghandi and then King, Walesa and Aquino: they stimulated and led nonviolent, mass social movements - self-limiting, thus auto-lawful, substantive-normative revolutions.[38] Karol Edward Soltan calls this "a [second] stage in the constitutionalization of protest and revolt." The first stage was

---

37   Karl/Schmitter, Modes of Transition in Latin America, Southern and Eastern Europe.
38   The relative pacifity following the fall of Communism is not relevant here because much more was involved than simply a clash between sets of substantive-normative standards of social justice.

the revolutionary tradition of open revolt, from the random and aimless violence of peasant rebellions and early worker protests forward. "Revolutions" today tend to be more limited in their socially significant powers. They also tend to be restrained by self-imposed rules. With this in mind Soltan advocates what he calls "generic constitutionalism," in an effort to push forward on a scholarly front this broadening of constitutionalist tradition. A self-limiting, constitutionalist social movement does not simply refrain from violence. It also limits itself to *obviously just goals* ("self-evident truths"), about which *moral* disagreement is so minimal that manipulative politics cannot hide behind any more ambitious smokescreen.[39]

The problem is that on directly substantive-normative grounds the only way to distinguish legitimate self-discipline from corruption (the excluding of social-movement competitors) is to know a great deal about each particular community of practice at issue.[40] But here is where the ambiguity and vagueness of all substantive-normative standards of "social justice" come home to roost, in the absence of the concepts of structured situation, positional interest and procedural-normative lawfulness. Here is also where Habermas and Cohen and Arato recapitulate the traditional continental call for self-restraint, simply transferring the latter from the "moral" *Sozialstaat* to "moral" social movements in civil society, not to any intermediary associations, let alone those of a particular kind.

These calls are consistent with a notion of "calling," of unquestioned personal commitment to correctness or right. But they are utterly inconsistent with lawfulness and professionalism proper, which are less culturalist, and not strictly and immediately personalist or social-psychological. They are instead structural and institutional. This is precisely why professional behavior is far more amenable to (collegial) deliberation and disinterestedness, the latter understood as upholding a lawful (responsible) positional (impersonal) interest, not as simply subduing naked self-interestedness and commercial acquisitiveness.[41]

Once again, the heart of a constitutional regime according to continental thinking is *some* self-limiting popular sovereign, some self-limiting constituent group. And under modern conditions this is intrinsically precarious – indeed perilous - both structurally and institutionally. Moreover, this way of thinking can only continue to seem to make sense when the state remains the font of all major power resources. As the "state" society tradition ends, however, a diffusion of socio-cultural authority

---

39   *Soltan*, Generic Constitutionalism, pp. 79, 92. The issue is not that Ghandi and King were eventually killed. The issue is why reactions against their movements, in India and in the American South, were not more violent – dramatically more violent? They were not more violent because these reactions could not credibly be cast in moral terms. To the contrary, Ghandi in fact shared culturalist, substantive normative (geistig) understandings with fellow Indians (of all religions), which were not present earlier when he was in South Africa. Likewise, King shared such understandings with fellow Southerners (of all "races" or ethnicities), which were not present whenever he traveled North, particularly to Chicago.
40   *Anderson*, Pragmatic Liberalism, the Rule of Law, and the Pluralist Regime, p. 112.
41   See Susan Shapiro on American law firms routinely turning away new business opportunities when the latter conflict with the interests of either current clients or past clients: *Shapiro*, Bushwacking the Ethical High Road.

and fiducial responsibility to dispersed intermediary associations becomes a possibility. To be sure, this diffusion is depoliticizing – as are elite pacts, consociational accommodations, or patron-client networks. But, unlike them, this diffusion is also simultaneously more protective institutionally against state abuse. It is also more cleansing institutionally of any manifestations of corruption or one-sidedness within the pacts, accommodations and networks just mentioned.

We can conclude with the following quite accurate observation by Sousa Santos and Avritzer: "[R]epresentative democracy tends to be low-intensity democracy, a tendency that has deepened in recent times." One reason for this tendency, they go on to say, is that this sort of democracy confines itself to the "citizen-space." Another is that in today's "post-welfare state, neo-liberal world," the state is an active agent of a "mercantilization of social relations." They conclude, now inaccurately, that this means "the tension between democracy and capitalism has thereby disappeared and democracy has in fact become a conditionality of neoliberal globalization. With the increase of social inequalities came the increase of social despotisms."[42]

We can now see that Sousa Santos and Avritzer always see these – and all other political and social changes – directly in substantive-normative terms, which means their views cannot on reasoned grounds rebut the quite opposite views of others. Everything is politicized. More important, the issue today is not at all whether democracy and "capitalism" are compatible. Much water has passed under this bridge since Marx's day, and Weber's.

The issue today is whether democracy, as limited government and lawful exercises of positional power in civil society, as institutionalized procedural-normative restraints on all arbitrary exercises of collective power, is compatible with *any* directly substantive-normative way of identifying inequality – except for the most abject material conditions or other morally unproblematic conditions? All such extreme conditions, certainly, *are* incompatible with democracy in the sense just noted. But this is a point upon which modernization theory insisted during the 1950s and early 1960s. It is hardly a challenge to North "hegemony." It is also hardly any indication that democracy in the sense above is particularist rather than universal.

Simply to note that limited government originated in England and the United States, first as an unwritten constitution and then as written one, does not somehow demonstrate that either constitutionalism or limited government is particularist rather than universal today, under contemporary systemic conditions. In the first place, this line of criticism does not establish that *any* modern society, existing or possible, can attain social justice more readily or over time in the absence of constitutionalism and limited government.[43] More generally, any types or standards of social, political or economic behavior which *are* universalist – as opposed to types or standards of somatic or psychosomatic behavior – will have *originated* at some place and some time in particular. Pointing this out hardly disqualifies them as what Parsons once called "evolutionary universals."

---

42 *De Sousa Santos/Avritzer*, Introduction: Opening up the Canon of Democracy', p. lxv.
43 *Merkel/Kruck*, Social Justice and Democracy:

For instance, the modern research university surfaced first in Germany, not elsewhere, during the middle third of the nineteenth century. Does pointing this out somehow establish that this institution (or some functional equivalent) is not universal today, as compared to the medieval exegetical university? Likewise, Johns Hopkins University in Baltimore introduced admission examinations to American medical schools, in 1893. Does this fact disqualify the institution of entrance examinations to advanced instruction as a literal universal today, and not only in the field of medicine? Finally, political parties originated in the early American Republic (during the 1820s and 1830s); is this a particularist institution today, or universalist?

Bibliography

Almond, Gabriel A., Comparative Political Systems, Journal of Politics 18 (1956), pp. 391-409.
Anderson, Charles W., Pragmatic Liberalism, the Rule of Law, and the Pluralist Regime, in Elkin, Stephen L. and Soltan, Karol Edward (eds), A New Constitutionalism: Designing Political Institutions for a Good Society, Chicago, 1993, pp. 96-116.
Arato, Andrew, Accountability and Civil Society, in Peruzzotti, Enrique and Smulovitz, Catalina (eds), Enforcing the Rule of Law: Social Accountability in the New Latin American Democracies, Pittsburgh, 2006, pp. 307-322.
Bourdieu, Pierre, The Social Structures of the Economy, Cambridge, 2005.
Bourdieu, Pierre/Wacquant, Loïc, The Cunning of Imperialist Reason, in Wacquant, Loïc (ed), Pierre Bourdieu and Democratic Politics: The Mystery of Ministry, Cambridge UK, 2005, pp. 178-198.
Cohen, Jean-Louis/Arato Andrew, Civil Society and Political Theory, Cambridge MA, 1992.
De Sousa Santos, Boaventura, Toward a New Common Sense: Law, Science and Politics in the Paradigmatic Transition, New York, 1995.
De Sousa Santos, Boaventura (ed), Democratizing Democracy: Beyond the Liberal Democratic Canon, London, 2005.
De Sousa Santos, Boaventura/Avritzer, Leonardo, Introduction: Opening up the Canon of Democracy, in de Sousa Santos, Boaventura (ed), Democratizing Democracy: Beyond the Liberal Democratic Canon, London, 2005.
Dezalay, Yves and Garth, Bryant G. (eds), Global Prescriptions: The Production, Exportation and Importation of a New Legal Orthodoxy, Ann Arbor MI, 2002.
Etzioni, Amitai, The New Golden Rule: Community and Morality in a Democratic Society, New York, 1996.
Faundez, Julio, Democratization Through Law: Perspectives from Latin America, Democratization 12 (2005), pp. 749-765.
Fuller, Lon L, The Morality of Law, rev. ed., New Haven, 1974.
Gregg, Benjamin, Thick Moralities, Thin Politics: Social Integration AcrossCommunities of Belief, Durham NC, 2003.
Habermas, Jürgen, The Structural Transformation of the Public Sphere: An Inquiry Into a Category of Bourgeois Society, translated by Thomas Burger, Cambridge MA, 1989.
Habermas, Jürgen, Between Facts and Norms: Contributions to a Discourse Theory of Law and Democracy, translated by W. Rehg, Cambridge MA, 1998.
Hart, H.L.A, The Concept of Law, Oxford, 1961.
Karl, Terry Lynn/Schmitter, Philippe, Modes of Transition in Latin America, Southern and Eastern Europe, International Social Science Journal 128 (1991), pp. 269-84.
Krieger, Leonard, The German Idea of Freedom: History of a Political Tradition, Chicago, 1972.
Kronman, Anthony, The Lost Lawyer, Cambridge MA, 1993.
Lowi, Theodore J., The End of Liberalism: Ideology, Policy and the Crisis of Public Authority, New York, 1969.
Luhmann, Niklas, Social Systems, Stanford, 1995.
Mamet, David, Why I am No Longer a "Brain-Dead Liberal"', Village Voice (11 March 2008).
Merkel, Wolfgang/Kruck, Mirko, Social Justice and Democracy: Investigating the Link, Internationale Politik und Gesellschaft 7 (2004), pp. 134-58.
Olgiati, Vittorio, Shifting Heuristics in the Sociological Approach to Professional Trustworthiness: The Sociology of Science, Current Sociology 54 (2006), pp. 533-547.

Raz, Joseph, The Authority of Law: Essays on Law and Morality, Oxford, 1979.
Rothman, David J., Strangers at the Bedside: A History of How Law and Bioethics Transformed Medical Decision Making, New York, 1972.
Sciulli, David, Theory of Societal Constitutionalism: Foundations of a Non-Marxist Critical Theory, New York, 1992.
Sciulli, David, Corporate Power in Civil Society: An Application of Societal Constitutionalism, New York, 2001.
Sciulli, David, Continental Sociology of Professions Today: Conceptual Contributions, Current Sociology 53 (2005), pp. 915-942.
Sciulli, David, Paris Visual Academie as First Prototype Profession: Rethinking the Sociology of Professions, Theory, Culture and Society 24 (2007), pp. 35-59.
Sciulli, David, Professions before Professionalism, Archives européennes de sociologie 48 (2007), pp. 121-147.
Sciulli, David, Editor Observations: On Position, Comparative Sociology 7 (2008), pp. 1-9.
Sciulli, David, Structural and Institutional Invariance in Professions and Professionalism, Oslo, Norway, Centre for the Study of Professions, 2008.
Sen, Amartya, Positional Objectivity, Philosophy and Public Affairs 22 (1993), pp. 126-145.
Shapin, Steven, A Social History of Truth: Civility and Science in Seventeenth Century England, Chicago, 1994.
Shapiro, Susan P., Bushwacking the Ethical High Road: Conflict of Interest in the Practice of Law and Real Life, Law and Social Inquiry 28 (2003), pp. 87-268.
Soltan, Karol Edward, Generic Constitutionalism, in Elkin, Stephen L. and Soltan, Karol Edward (eds), A New Constitutionalism: Designing Political Institutions for a Good Society, Chicago, 1993, pp. 70-95.
Summers, Robert S., Lon L. Fuller, Stanford, 1984.
Sunstein, Cass, Radicals in Robes, New York, 2005.
Sunstein, Cass, The Fate of Roe v. Wade and Choice, Boston Globe, September 14 2008.
Teubner, Gunther, Expertise as Social Institution: Internalizing Third Parties into the Contract, in Campbell, David, Collins, Hugh and Wightman, John (eds), Implicit Dimensions of Contract: Discrete, Relational and Network Contracts, Oxford, 2003, pp. 333-363
Teubner, Gunther, Societal Constitutionalism: Alternatives to State-Centred Constitutional Theory?', in Joerges, Christian, Sand, Inger-Johanne and Teubner, Gunther (eds), Constitutionalism and Transnational Governance, Oxford, 2004, pp. 3-28.
Uprimny, Rodrigo/Garcia-Villegas, Mauricio, The Constitutional Court and Social Emancipation in Colombia, in Santos, Boaventura de Sousa (ed), Democratizing Democracy: Beyond the Liberal Democratic Canon, London, 2005, pp. 66-100.
Wallerstein, Immanuel, Social Science and Contemporary Society: The Vanishing Guarantees of Rationality, International Sociology 11 (1996), pp.7-25.

The critique of instrumental reason: Between normative and sociological approaches to legitimate law

Darrow Schecter

The critique of instrumental reason is normally associated with Weber, Lukács, and the critical theory of the Frankfurt School. In many ways it appears to be exclusively bound up with questions of philosophy, aesthetics, and sociological theory, such that one might ask what relevance the critique has for questions concerning legality and legitimacy. The short answer can be formulated as follows: ever since Plato's *Republic*, the possibility of rational political authority and legitimacy based on knowledge rather than power or interest has exercised the political imagination of philosophers, legal theorists and activists. If one accepts that law and force are coterminous, lest one posit the existence of a divine source of juridical rationality, it is clear just how utopian the idea of rational political authority really is. But this utopianism is to some extent offset by the concrete reality that power is never directly exercised. The exercise of power is juridically mediated, which means that critical legal theory may well be in a position to enhance our understanding of domination beyond generic, a-historical and naturalist notions of power. To the extent that this is achieved, it may be eventually possible in theory and in reformed practice to distinguish between rational political authority and illegitimate exercises of knowledge-distorting power. The practical capacity to make such a distinction would constitute an important contribution to redeeming the promise of Enlightenment.

There will be a number of things to say about this below. For now it is worth noting that for thinkers such as Kant and Hegel modern legality holds out the promise of a rational alternative to arbitrary command, tradition, and functional requirements for order, and indeed, critical theory begins its search for the bases of what Habermas calls a rational society by examining the processes and events which seem to undermine the idealist philosophers' notion that law and history are real as well as rational.[1] Adorno, for example, who with Hegel is the key thinker in this paper, does not so much reject the ideal of rational authority, as question the plausibility of its possible existence in the light of some of the catastrophic events of the twentieth century. But the *Dialectic of Enlightenment* is not a romantic rejection of reason and Enlightenment. It is a convincing argument suggesting why those who defend rational law and non-populist legitimacy must grapple with the terrain staked out by Kant and Hegel (section 1 to follow), but cannot, for obvious historical reasons (National Socialism, Stalinism, Auschwitz, Hiroshima, et cetera) simply re-articulate the trajectory that goes from Kant and Hegel to Marx and communism, where the latter can be taken as the realisation of reason in history and the socio-economic and ma-

---

1   *Habermas*, Towards a Rational Society.

terial basis for the withering away of the state and conflict. Despite his doubts Adorno does not abandon the possibility that reason might be more than a strategic instrument in the struggle for mastery and domination, but he is also adamant that conditions enabling reason to play this role are at present discernible in terms of their absence, that is, they are not embodied by existing collective social subjects such as the industrial working class. What becomes, then, of the project of a rational alternative to arbitrary command, tradition, and functional requirements for order, if Kant, Hegel and Marx's ideas on the matter seem to have been discredited to a significant extent by actual events? This paper attempts to explore that question by looking at Hegel, Adorno, Habermas and Luhmann on legality, legitimacy and the critique of instrumental reason.

If in a modern context legality is often associated with reason and individual liberty (institutionalised in private property, rights of assembly, freedom of expression in the media and public sphere, et cetera), legitimacy is more often linked with authority and collective needs (stability and order, national territorial security and acceptable levels of redistribution and welfare provision). In reality, legality and legitimacy each have an individual as well as a collective dimension, which implies that it is misleading categorically to separate them into rational legality with an epistemological valence and functional legitimacy with a security/welfare valence. Moreover, this tendency to separate legality and legitimacy in terms of their epistemological and functional valences prevents social and normative theorists from understanding the specific modalities of power at work in modern societies. This may well seem counter-intuitive to those who assume that whatever rational and epistemological qualities one may ascribe to legality, political legitimacy is simply a functionalist concept devoid of epistemological content, and relevant only in terms of justifications for order and national unity. Yet to separate them into normative-rational and non-normative/functionalist components in this way amounts to a major concession to the idea that the egoistic citizen is a rational, individual, juridical subject, whilst the unified nation is a potentially irrational, collective subject whose needs can be arbitrarily defined by the requirements of the situation (perceived internal and external threats, et cetera). It will be suggested in what follows that this separation amounts to what one may designate as instrumental legitimacy, and it will be argued further that it is possible to develop Adorno's critique of instrumental reason into the beginnings of a critique of instrumental legitimacy. The immense difficulties involved in this project are illuminating to the extent that they illustrate how the specific crisis of philosophical idealism registered in obvious ways in Adorno's work is also indicative of a more general crisis of legitimacy in much less obvious ways if, that is, legitimacy is to be understood as something more rationally substantial than systemic stability and functional order. It might be the case that Adorno's ideas on the knowledge–content and truth–content of non-instrumental rationality can open up possibilities for new ideas concerning the existence of a non-instrumental juridical rationality with important implications for a reformed, non-populist understanding and practice of legitimacy. In attempting to make this argument, it must not be forgotten, in normative carelessness, that law and force are coterminous, and that the reformed practice in question is still anticipated rather than institutionally established.

In what follows it is suggested that it is possible to re-formulate the critique of instrumental reason and re-affirm its political relevance by developing the critique of instrumental reason into a critique of instrumental legitimacy, that is, the critique of a form of legitimacy which is intended to provide a stable framework for what are assumed to be more fundamental, inviolable liberties codified in liberal democratic law, such as private property and negative liberty more generally.[2] It will be seen that Adorno is of particular interest, in that he acknowledges the implausibility of any easy reconstitution of idealism and legal anthropology, on the one hand, but does not settle for the systems-theoretical recourse to notions of complexity and contingency as an answer, on the other. The question remains as to whether Adorno can contribute to re-thinking the question of legitimacy outside the anthropological and systems-theoretical frameworks. Whilst it is Habermas who wishes to occupy precisely this position beyond idealism and systems theory, there is evidence to suggest that the theory of communicative action offers an unsatisfactory response to some of the epistemological problems raised by negative dialectical philosophy and the empirical existence of self-referential systems. The inadequacies of the theory of communicative action are touched upon toward the end of the paper.

Adorno and Idealism

In his essay of 1958 on Georg Lukács entitled *Erpresste Versöhnung* [usually translated in English as *Reconciliation under Duress*], Adorno criticises Lukács's attempt to identify the conditions of a reconciled world as being already present in the collective subjectivity of the modern industrial proletariat. Although Adorno does not use the term *erpresste Versöhnung* in his book *Hegel: Three Studies* of 1963, it is probably fair to say that Adorno regards Hegel's theory of the modern state as another case where a philosopher unwittingly (or perhaps wittingly) serves the interests of illegitimate power by identifying the conditions of a reconciled world as already being present.[3] In Hegel's case it is of course not the presence of the modern industrial proletariat, but rather the institutions of the modern state that testify to the rationality of the real and the reality of the rational. In the *Phenomenology of Spirit* of 1807 and in a more explicitly political sense in the *Philosophy of Right* of 1821, Hegel explains that in its changing relationship with nature, humanity moves from unmediated unity with nature (in a hypothetical distant past) to mediated disunity, and from there to mediated unity with nature. The final result of this process is the

2   For a discussion of the differences between negative and positive liberty and their respective political implications, see *Berlin*, Two Concepts of Liberty. The essay is Berlin's inaugural lecture as Chichele Professor of Social and Political Theory at Oxford University, delivered on 31 October 1958, and originally published by Clarendon Press in the same year.
3   *Adorno*, Erpresste Versöhnung; *Adorno*, Drei Studien zu Hegel.

reconciliation (not identity) of humanity and nature, subject and object, and most importantly for this discussion, the reconciliation of individuals and the state. In time, Hegel suggests, collective humanity is able to apprehend reality as an intelligible process, and the individual members of humanity are able to accept the modern state as the condition of a rational will. Hence for Hegel there is an intimate relation between the state's rationality and its legitimacy.

From Adorno's perspective, and however much he seems to sympathise with a Marxist analysis of capitalism, it is clear that in many ways Lukács's theory of the unity of theory and practice in the collective subjectivity of the proletariat constitutes a significant theoretical regress with respect to Hegel. This is because Hegel already moves philosophy and social theory beyond the subjectivism of thinkers like Lukács, and, one might add in this context, beyond the subjectivism of Heidegger and Heidegger's notion of the collective subjectivity of *Das Volk*, by demonstrating that all subjectivity is mediated by social and historical objectivity.[4] What Hegel means by this in the *Philosophy of Right* is that subjectivity is mediated by the law and the other objectivations of *Geist* (mind, spirit) that assume institutional form in the family, civil society and the state. In what follows I will very briefly look at Hegel's notion that the mediated unity of humanity and nature assumes rational form in institutions, that is, what Hegel refers to as objective spirit, and then move on to examine why and how Adorno opposes Hegel's notion of historicised truth as *mediated unity* with his own notion of hermeneutic truth as *mediated non-identity*. The theory of non-identity, also presented as a critique of what Adorno sometimes calls identity thinking, runs throughout Adorno's entire oeuvre, including his lectures, and is systematically developed in *Negative Dialectics* of 1966.

Hegel's theory of the mediated unity of humanity and nature, from which he derives a theory of knowledge as well as a theory of the state, takes shape as a series of responses to what he takes to be the a-historical and insufficiently dialectical character of Kant's critical philosophy. It is perhaps worth recalling that at the core of Kant's critical philosophy is an attempt to rescue epistemological enquiry from a cul-de-sac. Kant holds that the attempt to explain the knowledge process by relying on the primacy of the mind or human consciousness variously defended by rationalists such as Descartes, is as questionable as the empiricist primacy of nature espoused in different ways by Berkeley, Locke and Hume. The impasse reached by these diametrically opposed positions, whether knowledge is to be sought in the mind or in nature, leads Kant to say that the question as to whether knowledge is exclusively and un-dialectically to be sought in humanity, or in an equally one-sided fashion in nature, is falsely posed. The real question is not whether we have dogmat-

---

4   Adorno's critique of what he takes to be Heidegger's subjectivism is developed in Part I of Negative Dialektik. In his comments on this paper Thomas Häussler points out that for Adorno, Lukács foregrounds agency and actors whilst taking the structural features of capitalism and institutions for granted. Hegel foregrounds the rationalising function of institutions, thereby neglecting the effect they have on individual actors. If both approaches are inadequate in different ways, Hegel has the merit of separating structure and agency much more clearly than Lukács, who has a tendency to combine and even fuse the two together.

ic, certain knowledge or merely random sensations and opinions, nor whether knowledge is to be sought in consciousness or in nature. The more pertinent question is: under what conditions is knowledge possible?

All of this is well-known, but what is of interest here is the parallel between the thesis that *knowledge* is only possible if there is a mediated unity between humanity and nature (instead of separation or identity), on the one hand, and the thesis that *political representation* can only be juridical and rational if there is a mediated unity between citizens and the state (again, instead of hermetic separation or organic fusion). For Kant, the condition that enables nature to be an object of human knowledge is a transcendental subject that can reflexively unify itself with reason, and thereby have *formal* knowledge of the phenomena that present themselves to the 12 categories of the understanding (causality, unity, plurality, possibility, necessity, substance, et cetera) in time and space. This last statement sheds a certain amount of light on the parallel just cited, for it suggests that the epistemological reality positing limits to human knowledge finds a significant complement in the political reality that political representation can only be rational if it is formal and juridical, lest, that is, it become arbitrary, authoritarian and irrational. Kant insists that there can be no pure, un-mediated objectivity, since all objectivity is mediated by human subjectivity in the guise of the 12 forms of the understanding and time and space as the two forms of sensible intuition. Conversely, he implies, there can be no pure, un-mediated unity between citizens and the state or theory and practice that is not metaphysical and authoritarian.[5] It must now be explained why Hegel thinks that political authority need not be either formal or metaphysical, since from his standpoint, merely formal state authority or authoritarian state authority is not really legitimate or rational authority.

The dialectic between humanity and nature becomes historicised when Hegel discovers that the forms of human reason and subjectivity mediating between humanity and nature are in a process of constant unfolding. For Hegel, Kant's great achievement vis-à-vis his predecessors is that he shows that all objectivity is mediated by subjectivity. But Hegel takes this dialectical argument considerably further by demonstrating that all subjectivity is mediated by socio-historical objectivity, that is, subjectivity is historically created, superseded and re-created as a result of the developing conditions of objectivity as these assume changing forms in ever new socio-economic and political institutions which produce qualitatively new, more perfectly knowing subjects at every stage of the historical process and its inexorable march toward more perfect forms of knowledge and freedom. Thus Hegel attempts to show that all subjectivity in the guise of consciousness is mediated by objectivity in the guises of history and society, such that consciousness is always historical and juridical consciousness rather than merely static, natural consciousness.

From the moment that this epistemological and historical reality has been laid bare, so to speak, one cannot convincingly rely on the Kantian notion of 12 fixed categories of the understanding, any more than one can rely on some timeless con-

---

5 *Kant*, Zum ewigen Frieden; *Kant*, Über den Gemeinspruch. These and other of Kant's political writings are available in English in Reiss (ed), Kant: Political Writings.

ception of human nature or essence. Another way of saying this is that humans are products of history and reason to an even greater extent than they are products of nature, and, what is more, reason is itself historically dynamic rather than anthropologically constant. Like reason, history has a dynamic structure that tends towards overcoming the limits of knowledge at the same time that it tends towards overcoming the limits of freedom. This is important for Adorno, since it implies that the rationality and legitimacy of the modern state might one day be *aufgehoben* [transcended] in its national-populist formulation.[6] In the *Philosophy of Right* Hegel suggests that the relation between humanity and nature can be characterised as a mediated totality in which the structure of the mediations is knowable. Accordingly, the humanity/nature totality is best understood as a rational configuration of mediating concepts that is gradually uniting mind, that is, *subjective spirit*, with institutions – i.e. *objective spirit* – over the course of the historical process. He defends an epistemological and sociological argument that articulates the dynamism of the knowledge process in relation to the dynamism of the historical process as a movement from unmediated unity to mediated disunity, and from there to mediated unity. Hence in terms of his project to overcome the epistemological limits of Kantianism, which posits a barrier between the phenomena and the things in themselves, whilst also overcoming the political limits of Kantianism, which cannot think beyond formal juridical unity between citizens and the state, Hegel is deeply dependent on a theory of history culminating in the resolution of antinomies in higher syntheses.[7]

Anticipating Adorno's argument for a moment, one can say that Adorno intimates that *mediated unity* in theory turns out to be, in what he sees as the administered society of ubiquitous exchange, *mediated identity* in practice, which is reflected in institutionalised identity thinking. For Adorno, real freedom lies with the institutionalisation of mediated non-identity rather than with the institutionalisation of mediated unity. It seems that what he means by mediated non-identity is a form of reconciliation between humanity and nature which is no longer achieved under duress, but is arrived at instead through mediating instances that recognise that each person is an instance of human, historicised nature, or rather, that there is no human nature as such, but as many human natures as there are human beings, and that these distinct natures are also historically generated. This is the crux: an epistemologically and politically legitimate political order would have somehow to respect this pluralism without breaking down into chaos. But it would be genuinely plural, and would be no longer based on the commercial variety of different manufacturing brands, or the electoral tactics of competing parties in their bid for officially recognised power. This indicates the enormous difficulties inherent in institutionalising mediated non-identity, and foreshadows Habermas's project to theorise its feasibility outside of Adorno's negative idealist framework, as will be seen. Adorno maintains that con-

---

6 *Adorno*, Minima Moralia, aphorism 20, pp. 43-5; *Jaeggi*, Kein Einzelner vermag etwas dagegen: Adornos Minima Moralia als Kritik von Lebensformen, pp. 115-141.
7 This is what separates Hegel's response to Kant from those of Fichte (self-positing ego) and Gentile (absolute unity of theory and practice and the unity of citizen and the state). See *Bellamy*, Modern Italian Social Theory, ch. 6.

trary to the claims Hegel makes for the pluralism and institutionalised freedom he deems to be characteristic of the modern state, what we actually have is a competitive, antagonistic variety of the same commodities and parties rather than real pluralism or authentic difference, where the term 'variety of the same' might sound sociologically simplistic, and in any case contradictory.[8]

Where Marx is a theorist of the mechanisms of exploitation and inequality in modern industrial societies, Adorno, following Nietzsche, sheds light on the institutions of coerced integration and conformist behaviour patterns in them. One of the tasks of critical social theory and critical legal theory is to illuminate the dynamics that produce exploitation and marginalisation, whilst simultaneously engendering authoritarian integration. It is perhaps possible to comprehend this simultaneity as a sociological paradox which can be unravelled, rather than as a logical contradiction that should simply be 'solved' or dismissed as insoluble. Whilst Adorno's approach to paradox is to relate it to the dialectical one discussed above demonstrating that humanity is a part of nature but not identical to nature, and that it is indeed possible to be in two (socio-historical) places at the same time, Niklas Luhmann stresses what one might call the reality of form, that is, the notion there is no metaphysical essence or content 'behind' form, that form is at once form and content. He suggests that instead of juxtaposing form (appearance) and content (essence), one should keep in mind that form has an inside and an outside.[9] Although Marx goes some of the way by explaining the dynamics of exploitation with his critique of political economy, and the Frankfurt School ably supplies a critique of instrumental reason to expose the institutional dynamics of coerced reconciliation and integration, an approach which effectively combines the critique of political economy with the critique of instrumental reason has not yet been fully elaborated. It is suggested in this paper that a promising way of going about this is by re-examining the relations be-

---

8   It is also apparent that much of Adorno's sociological theory often does not get much further than an intuitive appreciation of the merely formal plurality of 'capitalist society', if one might call it that for the moment. Whether one is speaking of commodities or of political parties, he observes, this is a plurality that is for the most part limited to commercial and political varieties of substantially similar 'products'. But he often seems to imply that this homogenisation can be explained as a direct result of a society that is based on an exchange of equivalents which marginalises real difference, i.e., the non-identical. If one compares Adorno's notion of the exchange society with Georg Simmel's analysis of the dynamics of reciprocal exchange and money in Philosophie des Geldes (The Philosophy of Money, 1907), it becomes clear that if Adorno is a distinguished philosopher and aesthetic theorist, he is somewhat of a poor sociologist. Axel Honneth argues that far from being a problem peculiar to Adorno, there is a fundamental sociological deficit in virtually all of critical theory. See *Honneth*, Kritik der Macht, chapter 1. It is interesting to note that relatively late in life (1965), Adorno wrote an essay which shows much greater sociological sophistication and nuance than was evident in his previous work. See *Adorno*, Gesellschaft.
9   *Luhmann*, Die Paradoxie der Form; *Clam*, Die Grundparadoxie des Rechts und ihre Ausfaltung. The point in relation to Adorno and Luhmann is that it is misleading categorically to contrast the former as an idealist without sociological relevance with the latter as a sociologist who has transcended philosophy through post-anthropological enquiry. See the concluding pages of this article.

tween reason, legality and legitimacy, and that one can do this by examining the relations between knowledge and political form. This remains the challenge of Enlightenment, and raises a series of questions which I will very briefly return to below in relation to Habermas and Luhmann, but which can be summarised as follows: can there be a juridical practice of mediated non-identity in which the price for overcoming natural scarcity is not, as in existing forms of late-democratic populist liberalism and state socialist collectivism, reconciliation under duress which subjugates historicised subjectivity to historically and socially entrenched mechanisms of coerced integration? For the purposes of sketching the beginning of an answer, Adorno's notion of mediated non-identity as *reconciliation* can be contrasted with Hegel's notion of mediated unity as nationally-rooted ethical life and *recognition*. This somewhat subtle but noteworthy difference between historicised dialectics and negative dialectics is indicative of their related yet distinct approaches to theorising epistemological questions in conjunction with socio-economic, ethical, and political questions.

For both thinkers, legitimacy contains a marked rational and epistemological dimension which goes well beyond the usual categories of interest aggregation and power sharing. But whilst Hegel stresses the importance of recognition through struggle, as in the now very famous pages in the *Phenomenology* on the master/slave dialectic, or through private property, as in the *Philosophy of Right*, Adorno is more interested in the rational content of aesthetic experience, and in the ways in which non-instrumental reason and experience occasionally explode the boundaries of antagonistic subjectivity.[10] If for Hegel reason becomes objectively realised in institutions when people recognise something of themselves in the seemingly opposed wills of other people, through love, property, and collective deliberation, Adorno is much more reluctant to see reason at work in existing institutions. Adorno seems to be thinking about a form of reason that at present is only discernible in terms of its manifest absence from existing, actual institutions. It is a form of affirmative reason that unexpectedly illuminates ways of living and knowing rather than a form of means-oriented reason derivative of struggles for survival and recognition. Hence for the author of *Negative Dialectics*, however much Hegel moves epistemology and social theory beyond Kant's critical philosophy, Hegel's philosophy is deeply indebted to the logic of capitalist forms of exchange, ownership, and, ultimately, to the logic of antagonistic subjectivity. This should not be surprising, Adorno adds, since Kant and Hegel are ultimately bourgeois philosophers who say something true about a world that is false and exploitative; as such, their thinking offers a non-apologetic

---

10 There can be little doubt that Adorno's sensitivity to the dynamics of coerced integration and reconciliation under duress are inspired by his understanding of Nietzsche's critique of the rampant conformity institutionalised in modern society (by contrast, he seems never to have read Tocqueville). Scholarship on the Frankfurt School has paid relatively little attention to the links between Nietzsche and Adorno. Hence in most works on critical theory one often finds an overemphasis on the influence of Marx and the centrality of the question of exploitation, at the expense of the importance of Nietzsche and the sociological dimension of coerced integration.

conceptualisation of life and knowledge in the era in which the bourgeoisie revolutionises the mode of production and modes of consciousness as well.[11]

From mediated unity to mediated non-identity

This raises two questions. Why, for Adorno, does mediated unity in practice tend not to resemble Hegel's harmonious vision of pluralistic diversity within elastic unity, but instead to take institutional shape as mediated identity, something Adorno understands as reconciliation under duress and coerced integration of individual natures in the name of economic efficiency and authoritarian order? Why does Adorno nonetheless wish to retain Hegel's epistemological reliance on dialectics and mediations? For the first question there is an obvious and a less obvious answer. The obvious answer to the first question is that Hegel's theory about the rationality of objective spirit is very convincing until history 'runs off course', so to speak, and indeed, the events of the twentieth century made Adorno and many others reflect on the ways in which history had obviously ceased 'automatically' to produce richer forms of knowledge and freedom, and, in a parallel development, Enlightenment *reason* had evolved towards industrial and technological *rationalisation*. From Adorno's standpoint, the twentieth century world is not a rational world of enlightened, rational individuals or legitimate, democratic states. It is rather a world in which, as he somewhat indelicately puts it in *Negative Dialectics*, individuals perish in concentration camps according to a rationalised plan that reduces them to *Exemplare* (specimens or samples). That is, in the disenchanted, rationalised world as opposed to the rational world, they are not really individual human beings, but rather commodified samples or generic types condemned to removal and elimination. In his *Notes on Beckett's Endgame* he presents a more nuanced analysis, though it is also one that comes to basically similar conclusions.[12]

Adorno of course does not place the blame for this on Hegel. But he does have an objection to Hegel, which is part of the less obvious answer to the first question above. Although Hegel points the way beyond the voluntarist subjectivism of thinkers like Fichte, Lukács, and Gentile, he is nonetheless a philosopher of reconciliation under duress and an advocate, in *Phenomenology of Spirit* (paragraphs 20 and 23, to cite but two) and elsewhere, of the notion that the whole is real, and that the subject (rather than Aristotle's substance) is the absolute.[13] A partial explanation as to why pluralist mediated unity in theory tends toward authoritarian mediated identity in practice can be found in Hegel's idealist version of identity thinking, which posits the ultimate *identity* of A and Non-A; this is what Luhmann re-designates in an anti-idealist vein instead as the *difference* between identity and difference. This raises the

---

11   *Adorno*, Vorlesung über Negative Dialektik, pp. 25-32, 227-37; and *Adorno*, Kants Kritik der reinen Vernunft, pp. 307-320, p. 411.
12   *Adorno*, Negative Dialektik, p. 355; and *Adorno*, Versuch, das Endspiel zu verstehen.
13   *Hegel*, Die Phänomenologie, pp. 20-25; *Adorno*, Vorlesung über Negative Dialektik, pp. 93-5; and *Adorno*, Ontologie und Dialektik, pp. 12-14, 155-58, 326-28.

question of possible compatibilities between negative dialectics and certain strands of post-metaphysical sociological thinking, such as systems theory.[14] Hegel's dialectical method says something true about a world that is antagonistic, un-reconciled and ultimately false precisely because historically realised dialectics engender social processes that suppress rather than preserve what is not identical to conceptual thought – at least to date.[15] This leads to the second question raised above concerning the reasons why Adorno wants to retain mediations and dialectics despite his misgivings about Hegel's methodology.

Adorno intimates that Hegel is a theorist and practitioner of thinking as mastery, which for Adorno is a problem closely related to thinking as the defining feature of antagonistic subjectivity. The institutional corollaries of antagonistic subjectivity are oppressive states based on the tautological idea of naturally national unity (which is likely to produce racism not because people are naturally racist, but because they have been juridically constituted as such) and other botched, instrumental mediations between humanity and nature that perpetuate scarcity ethics and politics under conditions of objective post-scarcity. By studying the actual functioning of liberal democratic forms of justice, law, freedom, and punishment in practice, one can observe these epistemologically and sociologically flawed mediations at work as they marginalise and exploit at the same time that they homogenise and integrate coercively. Hence Adorno insists that dialectical processes are indeed at work in modern industrial democracies, and that we do have Hegel to thank for analysing why this is so. But in the last analysis it is not Hegelian or even Marxist dialectics that structure the mediated relations between economy, knowledge, experience and political form. Hegel regards the mediated unity of subject/object, nature/humanity, and citizen/state to be achieved in *Geist*, whilst Marx sees these mediating syntheses at work in the labour process (however imperfect and authoritarian this is under capitalism, capitalism nonetheless represents a great step beyond feudal-agrarianism, and points the way forward to a genuine synthesis of humanity and nature in communism). Adorno wants to retain Hegel's emphasis on mediations and dialectics, which is able to say something true about a world that is false, whilst jettisoning the models of consciousness and subjectivity that Kant and Hegel bequeath to Marx and Lukács. Adorno does not want to jettison knowledge and reason. He also does not want to abandon the possibilities of consciousness altogether, which, *pace* Habermas, does not make him an avowed philosopher of consciousness (see below). Instead of asking under what conditions knowledge is possible, as Kant does, Adorno asks, under what conditions is non-instrumental reason possible? The further ques-

---

14 *Luhmann*, Soziale Systeme, p. 26. This qualified compatibility is highlighted by *Jahraus*, Martin Heidegger: Eine Einführung, pp. 229-30, and *Gripp*, Theodor W. Adorno, ch. 5. As regards the Jahraus reference, Heidegger's ambiguity is noteworthy. Although Heidegger is characterised as a subjectivist thinker in this paragraph as well as earlier in this paper, he is also the author of Identität und Differenz, an implicitly post-metaphysical work which will certainly have influenced Luhmann's notion of the difference (as opposed to the identity) of identity and difference.
15 *Hegel*, Die Phänomenologie, p. 19; *Adorno*, Wozu noch Philosophie?

tion which Adorno does not ask, but which is of great potential interest here, is: how might non-instrumental reason reform existing forms of legal rationality, and, what are the implications in terms of the theory and practice of non-instrumental legitimacy?

In *Negative Dialectics*, Adorno remarks that utopia is perhaps best conceived of as a knowledge utopia in which it is paradoxically possible to make use of concepts to attain access to sensuous, mimetic, non-conceptual knowledge.[16] The juridical-political corollary of this utopian epistemological paradox is possible access to extra-legal legitimacy by way of legal reform. It is the ideal of legitimacy institutionalised as a realised principle of knowledge rather than as a principle of functional order, where knowledge is spontaneous, cerebral-sensuous, *individual as well as collective* (like legality and legitimacy), informal yet systematic, and all-embracing in a way which is both casual and comprehensive. Knowledge of this kind is unthinkable in abstraction from legal systems, politics, and the societies in which individuals live, which is why Adorno's thinking is implicitly juridical and explicitly political despite his own emphasis on philosophy and aesthetics. His critics might argue that Adorno is a philosopher without political relevance, or that what is remotely relevant in political terms has been *aufgehoben* [overcome or transcended] in Habermas's theory of communicative action and discourse ethics. Indeed, Habermas seems the obvious mediator between Hegel's historical reason, which, it may be claimed, has a critical deficit, and Adorno's aesthetic reason, which, although critical, undoubtedly has a practical and a sociological deficit. It is also arguable that with his ideas on communicative action, discourse ethics, and the life-world/civil society, Habermas does offer proposals concerning the institutionalisation of mediated non-identity which address some of the limits of the philosophy of consciousness of which Adorno remains a highly unorthodox and ambivalent exponent, despite his professed materialism and respect for the 'primacy of the object'.[17] The argument sketched here avoids the in some ways plausible but nonetheless too easy solution of settling on Habermas as representative of the perfect middle position between Hegel and Adorno. This has become an almost standard position among the considerable number of theorists who wish to eschew Kant and Rawls's moral theories of justice and legality, which are deeply anthropological, naïve on power, and lack a sociological dimension, without embracing the implicit conservatism of Luhmann's sociological systems theory, which indicates few if any normative guidelines on the questions of legality and legitimacy. Hence however briefly, Habermas and Luhmann must be looked at in order to explain why it is perhaps more promising to see if some of Adorno's ideas can be examined with an eye to their practical and juridical relevance beyond the frameworks established by the theories of communicative action and autopoietic systems.

---

16   *Adorno*, Negative Dialektik, p. 21.
17   *Adorno*, Negative Dialektik, p. 187.

Ethical life and communicative action, or negative dialectics and systems theory?

The departure from a substantively rational account of legal legitimacy to Luhmann's notion of legitimation through procedure is foreshadowed by the transition from Hegel's theory of the state as mind objectified to Weber's insistence that whatever politics in its various instantiations might be, the state is the monopoly on the legitimate use of force within a given territory.[18] In the course of thinking about the state from Machiavelli to Weber, one notes a growing sensitivity to the distinction between the government, which has the authority to make laws, and the state, which by comparison is a much broader and far more elastic concept with wide-ranging sociological implications that go well beyond the scope - if not the jurisdiction – of government.[19] There are several possible conclusions to be drawn from the fact that governments are juridically authorised but not practically empowered to 'normatise' social relations with legislative means. For the methodological positivist, the most obvious one is the need to distinguish between norms and laws, and therewith, by implication, between rationality and legitimacy. For the republican, it is Rousseau's warning that democracy is only possible in small communities with high levels of interpersonal contact and minimal levels of social equality. For the anarchist, it could be Proudhon's belief that only de-centralised and federal decision-making structures can reverse the tendency of governments to compensate for their empowerment deficits with more and more cumbersome and inappropriate statutes that end up oppressing producers and consumers. Hegel's approach is to acknowledge the reality of corporate pluralism and the qualified autonomy of the system of needs, whilst ensuring that civil society remains subordinate to the higher rationality of the state. This is a solution to the question of legitimacy, which Marx rejects for reasons related to the extra-legal power of capital as well as the legalised power of property: indeed, Marx understands capital and property in terms of social relations rather than juridical norms. However discredited Marxism may be in some respects, in historical terms it can be argued that sociology really begins here.[20]

By the time Weber grapples with both the profundity and inadequacy of Marx, he suggests that there is a corollary to the fact that the state is a monopoly on the legitimate use of force within a given territory: it is erroneous to suppose that what is actual is rational and what is rational is actual, since rationality is itself different de-

---

18 *Weber*, Politik als Beruf, pp. 505-6; *Luhmann*, Legitimation durch Verfahren, pp. 27-53.
19 A longer discussion might examine how this distinction between government and state has been modified by the increasing use of the term governance, largely as a result of Foucault's impact on social and political theory. See *Foucault*, La vérité et les formes juridiques. Some may argue that the epistemological approach to legitimacy only makes sense within the government-state model, which has been undermined by the bio-political and systems-theoretical paradigms.
20 It is in this sense that Hannah Arendt remarks that "Our tradition of political thought had its definite beginning in the teachings of Plato and Aristotle. I believe it came to a no less definite end in the theories of Karl Marx", *Arendt,* Tradition and the Modern World, p. 17.

pending on the context in which reason is operative. In *Economy and Society* he distinguishes between value-rationality and means-rationality, and distinguishes further between value-oriented, means-oriented, tradition-oriented and affect-oriented social action. Hence from Weber's perspective there is no plausible way to consolidate legitimate state authority with a substantive, value-rational concept of legality, since consolidation is synonymous with concentration, and concentration contradicts the plural and contingent character of social life and action. In a market situation, actors are driven by an interest in gain rather than by the pursuit of truth or mutual understanding, and as such, it is rational for them to act competitively, bearing in mind their class, status and, where relevant, party affiliation. In another situation, where tradition or affect are more important motivating factors, rational action means something else to social actors than the pursuit of material gain. Complexity and contingency dictate that there is no way to concentrate normative reason and juridical authority in the state, and, in anticipated critique of Lukács, there is also no way to consolidate social action and social subject in the proletariat or any other strategically-rational and unified class. A political party may claim to re-present or even build such unity, but that is of course a very different matter.[21]

In his early writings Habermas analyses the role of means-oriented, instrumental reason in the modern world, and expands on Weber's notion of the plurality of rationalities just discussed in the introduction to the final section of this paper. In *Knowledge and Human Interests* (1968) he submits that modern societies are differentiated to such an extent that one must distinguish between systemic imperatives in the economy and state, which demand and reproduce technologically, financially and bureaucratically-mediated forms of instrumental action, on the one hand, and cognitive imperatives anchored in the life-world, which demand and develop linguistically-mediated forms of understanding and agreement that aspire to juridical codification, on the other. That is to say that without denying the significant presence of means-oriented action and systemic imperatives in modern industrial societies, he suggests that social relations are nonetheless also characterised by the rational autonomy of actors as well as their mutual interest in transforming speech claims into instances of communication which might eventually become the basis of legal norms. Hence whilst accepting the gist of Weber's complexity and differentiation theses, Habermas is also confident that reason and legitimacy can be re-coupled through the mediating instances of communication in the life-world, and through the normative dimension of law in the state.[22] This is one of the arguments developed in great detail years later in the *Theory of Communicative Action* (1981) and *Between Facts and Norms* (1992).

In these later works, and especially in the latter, Habermas submits that the *Rechtsstaat* [*state of law*] cannot be institutionalised without some form of radical democracy in which normative ideals and sociological realities are brought into a substantial degree of harmony, which in fact does happen because regulative ideas are also constitutive ideas. Just as Hegel distinguishes between family, civil society

21 *Weber*, Wirtschaft und Gesellschaft, Part I.
22 *Habermas,* Erkenntnis und Interesse, parts 2-3.

and state and then re-articulates their mediated unity as a "philosophy of right", that is, as a theory of institutionalised objective spirit of which the real basis is law, Habermas maintains that rights discourses originate in speech acts in the life-world, where they proliferate in communicative channels that establish and consolidate ties between everyday life, scientific research, citizens, the public sphere and the state. It is in these instances of social and communicative action, he suggests, that Adorno's mediated non-identity of particular individuals is preserved in ways that the author of *Negative Dialectics* cannot imagine because of his embittered resolution to see identity thinking at work almost everywhere in what he mistakenly takes to be the totally administered society. Mediated non-identity is preserved by respecting and protecting individual autonomy, and transcended by giving collective form to understanding and then consensus, in the guise of legitimate law. Although the danger of colonisation of the life-world by systemic imperatives does exist, the life-world is also insulated and protected from total administration and rampant instrumental rationality by the very mechanisms that Weber discusses. In other words, modern societies are divided into spheres of differentiated rationality and simultaneously unified to varying extents by overlapping life-worlds.[23]

This prevents them from collapsing into (a) imaginary all-encompassing centres governed by a single principle or (b) unravelling into an equally implausible series of disconnected peripheries, language games, and private semi-realities. In making this argument Habermas sets his position off from Horkheimer and Adorno (imaginary centres), since in his estimation they dismiss rather than redeem the as yet unfulfilled promise of modernity with their *Dialectic of Enlightenment*, on the one hand, and from Luhmann (disconnected peripheries), who fundamentally misunderstands the capacity of modern societies to sustain and regenerate their normative bases by way of communicative action, on the other. If in the first instance cul-de-sacs are an immediate consequence of disenchanted, negative idealism, in the second instance confusion is caused by a methodology that is cybernetic and meta-biological rather than properly normative and sociological. He suggests that it is one thing to move beyond idealism and the philosophy of consciousness. But it is quite another to abandon crucial anthropological categories such as language, communication, autonomy and other categories without which the state can be nothing more than a legitimate monopoly on the use of force, and reason must be instrumental. Since Rawls's ahistorical moral abstraction is unsatisfactory on other, equally obvious grounds, Habermas's theory of communicative action appears to redress the critical deficit in Hegel, salvage what there is to be salvaged in Adorno, move theory beyond idealism and the philosophy of consciousness, and at the same time, avoid the pernicious normative implications of post-structuralism and systems theory.[24]

This carefully elaborated argument would seem to be resistant to theoretical incursions from all sides. But Habermas's ability to anticipate his critics' attacks, absorb-

---

23 *Habermas*, Faktizität und Geltung, pp. 13, 22, 61, 89, 108, 240, 451-6.
24 See Habermas's contribution in *Habermas/Luhmann*, Theorie der Gesellschaft oder Sozialtechnologie: Was leistet die Systemforschung?, also *Habermas*, Der philosophische Diskurs der Moderne, chaps. 5, 7, 9, 11-12, and *Habermas*, Wahrheit und Rechtfertigung, Part II.

ing what he needs and discarding what he rejects, sometimes produces the unexpected effect of strengthening the critique of communicative action. It looks like he sets out to transcend the philosophy of consciousness whilst retaining selected bits of its anthropological foundations, for to abandon these altogether would place him uncomfortably close to what he will not accept in Heidegger, Foucault, Wittgenstein, Derrida and Luhmann. Luhmann looms as the key opponent within the terms set out in this paper, since he too discusses issues that are central to Habermas's concerns with legality, legitimacy, democracy, knowledge and reason. At this stage one may ask: (1) if one is going to retain some aspects of the anthropological-humanist tradition according to the implicit thesis that the legitimacy of the *Rechtsstaat* as a *rational* institution is endangered without them, then why not re-elaborate those aspects that push that tradition to its limit, as Adorno does, without which the success of the proposed transcendence has to be considered doubtful, and, (2) does the combination of residual humanism, universal speech pragmatics and the system/life-world distinction really suffice to qualify a theory as post-idealist and/or properly sociological?

Luhmann explains why the issues raised by distinctions such as subject/object and life-world actors/systemic structures are more effectively conceptualised in terms of inside/outside (reality of form) and system/environment (reality of complexity and contingency). He draws on Husserl's first steps beyond the subject/object dichotomy and Parsons's incipient systems theory to show that instead of theorising the rationality of actors and the domination of systems, one can discern the rationality of systems and the contingency of the environments that separate discrete systems from each other. In other words, if one is really serious about transcending idealism one should be prepared to accept the end of humanism and juridical rationality as well. This entails accepting that rationality is a property of systems rather than of actors, that actor autonomy, like reason, has more to do with adjusting to uncertainty than it does with the realisation of political or communicative essences, and that communication can and does take place independently of humans. On this account communication takes place between social systems and not, emphatically, between social systems and the non-social, of which speech is an example. Hence there is no direct communication between individuals, state and society. The implication is that legitimacy is based on a precarious and ongoing series of adjustments between systems and environments, and is patently not the result of a rational agreement between citizens and states.[25] Luhmann abandons the theory of overlapping life-worlds for the *observation* of the diverse environments that form the outer boundaries of systems.[26] This approach and its implications for legality and legitimacy casts major doubt on the thesis that rights discourses originate in speech acts in the life-world, where they proliferate in communicative channels that establish and consolidate ties between everyday life, scientific research, citizens, the public sphere and the state. Moreover,

---

25   *Luhmann*, Erkenntnis als Konstruktion, pp. 237-8.
26   *Luhmann*, Soziale Systeme, ch. 5.

it also casts doubts too on the belief that the *Rechtsstaat* is only feasible on the basis of a radical democracy with stable life-worlds and a vibrant public sphere of informed, active citizens.[27]

According to the apparently anti-theoretical postulates of autopoiesis, laws and rights are the products of a juridical social system which operates as a series of closed, self-referential processes in conjunction with social systems of value (economy), truth (science), power (politics), intimacy (family), belief (church), et cetera.[28] In subtle contrast with Weber's *Economy and Society*, Luhmann writes in terms of *The Economy of Society*, and instead of the *Philosophy of Right*, Luhmann offers *The Law of Society*, *The Politics of Society*, and so on, such that society can be studied as a series of systems without a centre (legal, political, religious or otherwise) which communicate with each other through codes. This project culminates in *The Society of Society*, published a year before Luhmann's death in 1998, which completes the work started with *Social Systems* in 1984. Both works indicate how systems generate sense to the extent that they can define their respective boundaries, reduce complexity, meet expectations in varying degrees, and react to contingency. To this extent it is more appropriate to speak of system rationality than value rationality or inter-subjectivity; he describes the modalities of speechless communication between systems through which they perform a kind of sociological equivalent of Husserl's *époché* [bracketing] in order to reproduce the conditions necessary to stabilise their functioning. Interesting in this context is Luhmann's contention in *Social Systems* that systemic differentiation makes the question of reason all the more urgent at the same time that it makes it all the more resistant to an overarching solution.[29]

Habermas regards Luhmann's methodology as tantamount to the liquidation of reason.[30] This is a somewhat odd reaction given that since his early distinction between interaction and labour in *Knowledge and Human Interests*, Habermas repeatedly confines the scope of non-instrumental reason to a relatively small dimension of socio-economic and political reality which purportedly exists in the midst of sys-

---

27 Luhmann, Autopoiesis als soziologischer Begriff, pp. 146-7. In this essay Luhmann discusses the processes of observation-description-cognition (p. 142) in a manner which is somewhat reminiscent of Dilthey's theory of experience-expression-understanding. Luhmann might be inclined to say that understanding, like social action, is longer tenable in its humanistic usage.
28 Is Luhmann's autopoietic model anti-theoretical? Is it conservative? If in this context conservative means determined to shore up theoretical tradition, then it is certainly not, since Luhmann is effectively de-constructing core concepts of Western anthropological and juridical understandings of legitimacy and other issues. If there is a conservative here it might actually be Habermas, and indeed, in terms of analysing the ways in which what passes for reason actually functions in existing institutions, there are several points of convergence between Adorno's critique of instrumental reason and Luhmann's outright dismissal of reason, both of which have little in common with Habermas's theory of communicative rationality.
29 Luhmann, Soziale Systeme, p. 645 (chs 11-12 discuss the issue in detail); Luhmann, Die Gesellschaft der Gesellschaft. By the time of the writing of the latter, Luhmann abandons this residually normative use of the term reason.
30 Habermas, Der philosophische Diskurs der Moderne, p. 431.

temic operations, whilst at the same time dedicating great energy to the critique of what he considers to be the metaphysics of the philosophy of consciousness. This paper suggests that despite the problems raised by the systems-theoretical approach to legality and legitimacy, which cannot be discussed in the necessary detail here, it is in many respects more consistent than the communicative-action approach, especially as regards the deconstruction of what have become untenable anthropological assumptions about human agency and the teleology of agreement. In its most stringent formulations, systems theory challenges these assumptions in crucial instances of speech, communication, understanding and social action. These are precisely the instances in which the communicative action approach wants to cling to the humanistic ideal of rational legitimacy even after dismissing or ignoring the claim that there can be rationally legitimate control of the economy.[31] If there can be no rationally legitimate control of the economy beyond the instrumental requirements necessary to secure modest levels of redistribution, which are technical and administrative rather than cognitive and substantially rational, why should there be rationally legitimate law, not to mention a legitimate state in the broader sense? In terms of the attempt to answer this question within a communicative action framework, it is clear that the claims variously made for the life-world, public sphere, communicative action and civil society are forced to carry far more weight than they can possibly bear. This leaves the issue of power under-theorised from both normative and sociological standpoints. Hegel, Adorno, Luhmann, and Habermas all agree in different ways that legitimacy is based on knowledge rather than on merely more and less stable configurations of interest aggregation and welfare distribution. Admittedly, one is usually talking about non-normative and instrumental knowledge, to very different degrees, depending on the thinker in question. Luhmann convincingly shows that it is the tentative knowledge systems have of each other - at least for the time being – and not the understandings generated between individual speakers with mutually compatible truth claims. Does the stand-off find its conclusion here, or might the Hegel/Adorno comparison sketched earlier be able to make an unsuspected contribution to this debate?

If it is worth bearing in mind the distinction between the state and government, it is undoubtedly advisable not to conflate legitimacy in a broad, sociologically and normatively ambitious sense, with the institutional practices that generate law at present. It is hard to imagine that non-instrumental legitimacy can somehow co-exist with an otherwise legitimacy-neutral legal order, unless, that is, one reduces the criteria defining legitimate law to adequate regard for procedure. Against the undoubted rigour of systems theory one may ask, provided that one does not do so in defence of naïvely normative anthropology, if this does not amount to a pyrrhic victory over the problems of existing varieties of humanism. Hence the kind of knowledge that defines legitimate law and legitimacy more generally (if it can be sup-

---

31 Habermas dismisses the claim in Marx, who is taken to task as an inconclusive renegade from the philosophy of consciousness, and largely ignores it as it is formulated in the works of Franz Neumann and especially Otto Kirchheimer. See *Schecter*, The History of the Left from Marx to the Present, ch. 3.

posed for the moment that the latter might exist) is of great importance. Although there are very substantial divergences between Hegel, Adorno, Habermas and Luhmann about the structure of the knowledge which informs the institutional practices of legitimacy, it is suggested above that for each thinker it is nonetheless a form of genuine knowledge, and not mere interest aggregation combined with surveillance and policing. The subtle convergences between non-identity thinking and systems theory noted at various points in this paper attempt to create an epistemological opening in which Adorno's post-metaphysical thought might encounter Luhmann's post-humanist legitimacy beyond the frameworks offered by the theories of *Sittlichkeit* [ethical life] and communicative action. If fruitful at some point in the future, that encounter could produce knowledge regarding the dialectics of legality and legitimacy, especially if it can succeed in formulating an approach which combines Adorno's dialectical sensitivity to the reality of mediation with Luhmann's analysis of the reality of social form. It may be able to anticipate the moment when power ceases to be under-theorised, and thereby glimpse the institutional contours of a society in which knowledge and legitimacy cease to be instrumental.

Bibliography

Adorno, Theodor W, Drei Studien zu Hegel: Aspekte Erfahrungsgehalt Skoteinos, oder Wie zu lesen sei, Frankfurt, 1963.
Adorno, Theodor W, Wozu noch Philosophie?, in Eingriffe: Neun kritische Modelle, Frankfurt, 1963.
Adorno, Theodor W, Negative Dialektik, Frankfurt, 1966.
Adorno, Theodor W, Gesellschaft, in Soziologische Schriften I, Frankfurt, 1979. pp. 9-19.
Adorno, Theodor W, Erpresste Versöhnung, in Noten zur Literatur, Frankfurt, 1981, pp. 251-280.
Adorno, Theodor W, Versuch, das Endspiel zu verstehen, in *Adorno*, Noten zur Literatur, Frankfurt, 1981, pp. 281-321.
Adorno, Theodor W, Kants Kritik der reinen Vernunft, Frankfurt, 1995.
Adorno, Theodor W, Minima Moralia: Reflexionen aus dem beschädigten Leben, Frankfurt, 1997.
Adorno, Theodor W, Ontologie und Dialektik, Frankfurt, 2002.
Adorno, Theodor W, Vorlesung über Negative Dialektik, Frankfurt, 2003.
Arendt, Hannah, Tradition and the Modern World, in Between Past and Future: Eight Exercises in Political Thought, New York, 1954.
Bellamy, Richard, Modern Italian Social Theory: Ideology and Politics from Pareto to the Present, Stanford, 1987.
Berlin, Isaiah, Two Concepts of Liberty [1958], in Hardy, Henry and Hausheer, Roger (eds), Isaiah Berlin: The Proper Study of Mankind, London, 1998.
Clam, Jean, Die Grundparadoxie des Rechts und ihre Ausfaltung: Ein Beitrag zu einer Analytik des Parodoxen in Teubner, Gunther (ed), Die Rückgabe des zwölften Kamels: Niklas Luhmann in der Diskussion über Gerechtigkeit, Stuttgart, 2000, pp. 109-45.
Foucault, Michel, La vérité et les formes juridiques, in Dits et écrits I, 1954-1975, Paris, 2001, pp. 1406-1514.
Gripp, Helga, Theodor W. Adorno, Paderborn, 1986.
Habermas, Jürgen, Erkenntnis und Interesse, Frankfurt, 1968.
Habermas, Jürgen, Towards a Rational Society, Boston, 1970.
Habermas, Jürgen/Luhmann, Niklas, Theorie der Gesellschaft oder Sozialtechnologie: Was leistet die Systemforshung?, Frankfurt, 1974.
Habermas, Jürgen, Der philosophische Diskurs der Moderne, Frankfurt, 1985.
Habermas, Jürgen, Faktizität und Geltung: Beiträge zur Diskurstheorie des Rechts und des demokratischen Rechtsstaats, Frankfurt, 1992.
Habermas, Jürgen, Wahrheit und Rechtfertigung: philosophische Aufsätze, Frankfurt, 1999.
Hegel, Georg Wilhelm Friedrich, Die Phänomenologie des Geistes, Stuttgart, 1987.
Heidegger, Martin, Identität und Differenz, Stuttgart, 1957.
Honneth, Axel, Kritik der Macht: Reflexionsstufen einer kritischen Gesellschaftstheorie, Frankfurt, 1989.
Jaeggi, Rahel, Kein Einzelner vermag etwas dagegen: Adornos *Minima Moralia* als Kritik von Lebensformen, in Honneth, Axel (ed), Dialektik der Freiheit: Frankfurter Adorno-Konferenz 2003, Frankfurt, Suhrkamp, 2005, pp. 115-141.
Jahraus, Oliver, Martin Heidegger: Eine Einführung, Stuttgart, 2004.
Kant, Immanuel, Zum ewigen Frieden: Ein philosophischer Entwurf and Über den Gemeinspruch: Das mag in der Theorie richtig sein, taugt aber nicht für die Praxis, in Schriften zur Anthropologie, Geschichtsphilosophie, Politik und Pädagogik I, Frankfurt, 1977, pp. 223-4, 150-154.
Luhmann, Niklas, Legitimation durch Verfahren, Frankfurt, 1969.

Luhmann, Niklas, Soziale Systeme, Frankfurt, 1984.
Luhmann, Niklas, Die Gesellschaft der Gesellschaft, Frankfurt, 1997.
Luhmann, Niklas, Die Paradoxie der Form, in Jahraus, Oliver (ed), Niklas Luhmann: Aufsätze und Reden, Stuttgart, 2001, pp. 243-261.
Luhmann, Niklas, Erkenntnis als Konstruktion, in Jahraus, Oliver (ed), Niklas Luhmann: Aufsätze und Reden, Stuttgart, 2001, pp. 218-242.
Luhmann, Niklas, Autopoiesis als soziologischer Begriff, in Jahraus, Oliver (ed), Niklas Luhmann: Aufsätze und Reden, Stuttgart, 2001, pp. 137-158.
Reiss, Hans (ed), Kant: Political Writings, Cambridge, 1970.
Schecter, Darrow, The History of the Left from Marx to the Present: Theoretical Perspectives, London, 2007.
Simmel, Georg, Philosophie des Geldes, Leipzig, 1907.
Weber, Max, Wirtschaft und Gesellschaft, Tübingen, 1980.
Weber, Max, Politik als Beruf, in Gesammelte politische Schriften, Tübingen, 1988, pp. 505-560.

Section II:
Legitimacy as a problem in international law:
Critical and cosmopolitan approaches

Legitimacy in global and international law: A sociological critique

Inger-Johanne Sand

The conditions of legitimacy in modern and complex societies

Legal and political communication, and their institutions and their trajectories, have been vital parts of the dynamics and the infrastructure of modern and democratic societies. They have produced generalized legal norms and collectively binding decisions concerning a multiplicity of vital social themes in forms and processes, which have been perceived of as generally legitimate. Law and politics have been differentiated as autonomous communicative systems with the specific tasks of making decisions and creating legal norms across social boundaries. However, they have accomplished this without having any direct knowledge of the themes on which they decide. Niklas Luhmann has analyzed this in the following terms:

> The impossibility for the political system effectively to control other systems with an adequate grasp of consequences and limited risk is inversely proportional to the facility with which such decisions can be put into force [...]. The astonishing expansion of competence in the welfare state begets a gigantic and uncontrollable machinery for increasing risk.[1]

Law and politics can thus be seen as paradoxical communicative systems, which, on one hand, combine a high degree of abstraction and differentiation and which, on the other hand, contribute significantly to social cohesion and effective and legitimate decision-making. For this reason, they have been labelled the immune-systems of modern societies.[2]

Social problems are dealt with by political and legal decisions, but they are not solved in any direct material sense. Law and politics disseminate social meaning and semantics throughout society. Their function is to create norms and a normative infrastructure, and to make decisions. They are highly operative, but they always possess insufficient knowledge and so they also entail significant elements of risk. In modern and democratic societies, law and politics are highly dependent on the fact that they are perceived as legitimate in their operations: this is due partly to the significant power that they exert and partly to the relative uncertainty and complexity of the situation in which their decisions are made. Being recognized as legitimate becomes crucial both for political and for legal operations. However, legitimacy is also a quality that seems to escape definition. Clearly it has to do with acceptability

---

1 *Luhmann*, Risk, p. 145.
2 *Luhmann*, Law as a Social System, p. 475.

and some kind of transparency, but what this exactly means is more unclear. Martti Koskenniemi writes that legitimacy becomes the defining third value between law and morality: a value that, on the one hand, is undefinable and that, on the other hand, is a quality that combines law and morality, yet that is also different from each of these elements.[3]

On the one hand, many theories attach legitimacy to vital principles such as democracy, division of powers, fundamental rights and the rule of law. However, this does not explain the great variations of the applications, practices and evaluations of these principles in time and place. These principles also fail to account for the paradoxical character of the function of law. On the other hand, legitimacy may be explained and attached to a combination of accepted procedures and commonly accepted frames of reference or contexts. The legal and political institutions and procedures of nation states have, to different degrees, presupposed common frames of references in terms of common language(s), historical accounts and descriptions of cultural, social and economic conditions. These have created a background for understanding what legitimacy is. Even if there have been strong ideological polarizations within nation states there have usually existed common frames of reference, which have created some kind of basis for notions of legitimacy and for rendering political and legal processes and decisions acceptable.

In a globalized society and in a society with continuously changing and qualitatively new technologies such frames of reference seem more difficult to establish. Decision-making processes are often conducted from a distance, under complex conditions or in a polycontextual or heterogeneous setting. There is often uncertainty and a lack of common background from which to evaluate whether a procedure or a decision is legitimate. The context and the preconditions of legal and political decision-making are significantly changed by the increasing differentiation and specialization of the function systems of modern society, including the systems of economics and science.[4] Law and politics as generalized decision-making systems often operate under highly specialized conditions on the areas they regulate. In order to stabilize the highly differentiated communicative systems a variety of complex structural and organizational couplings have evolved between the legal and the political systems and other communicative systems.[5] The increasing complexity of the areas of politico-legal regulation has also made it more complicated to understand the conditions of legitimacy for legal and political decision making.

I will propose that any analysis of the legitimacy of law and politics in modernity needs to take its point of departure from an analysis of *the functions* of law and politics and of the ways in which they can realistically be performed. Several recent changes in the general social conditions of legal and political decision-making may be seen as potentially vital influences of the capacity of law for performing its function of normative and predictable decision making. Arguably, these may change, and

---

3   *Koskenniemi*, Legitimacy, Rights and Ideology, p. 371.
4   *Luhmann*, Risk, p. 145; *Habermas*, Between Facts and Norms, p. 448.
5   *Luhmann*, Law as a Social System, p. 476.

even challenge, the legitimacy, or the conditions of legitimacy, of law. These include changes in *the factual, the social and relational and the temporal* conditions of law and legal decision making.[6]

First, we can observe that there is a change *in the factual dimension* of the social processes or objects to be regulated by law. These processes and objects are increasingly differentiated, specialized and continuously in flux, and they are influenced by new knowledge and technologies. The relations between the different fields to be regulated become increasingly complex due to their extreme specialization. In the regulation of highly specialized areas, legal semantics become increasingly dependent on the semantics of the areas to be regulated. Close structural couplings are often created which also influence the more precise functioning of normative expectations and legal norms.[7] Complex relations are created between law and the objects and areas to be regulated.

Second, in *the social dimension* legal norms are increasingly created and stabilized both in legislation and in adjudication by *an increasing number of different actors and institutions*. Legal regimes overlap each other. National, international and transnational levels of regulation interact and become interdependent at times without clear legal relations.[8] Public, private and civil society actors interact in new ways. Different courts overlap and compete for jurisdiction and legal influence. Law is consequently both observed and operated by an increasing number of actors, who also possess different types of public authority, and who operate in different contexts. Normative expectations are thus created in an increasingly polycontextual and polycentric space. Actors belong to extremely different contexts have to communicate on the formation of legal norms.

Third, we can observe that social semantics in general and law in particular experience a change in their *temporal modality*: this change leads from a past-present, via a present-future, to a future-future orientation. Social communication, including legal communication, is increasingly oriented towards the future, relying less on past experiences and traditions. New technologies and knowledge contribute to a change from normative to cognitive expectations.[9] Vital values and principles are increasingly unstable. Normative predictability is clearly influenced by this. Despite this, however, legal norms and communications cover an increasing number of social fields and seem to be increasingly vital in society. This may affect the forms of norms and normative expectations, and it may affect what we understand by normativity.

All changes referred to above may challenge *the conditions and the possibilities for the normative function of law* in modern society.[10] Legal communication is in-

---

6 *Luhmann*, Soziale Systeme, ch. 2.
7 See *Clam*, What is Modern Power?
8 *Koskenniemi*, Global Legal Pluralism.
9 *Luhmann*, Law as a Social System, p. 468; *Luhmann*, Modern Sciences and Phenomenology.
10 *Luhmann*, Soziale Systeme, ch. 2; *Luhmann*, Law as A Social System, chapters 11-12; *Sassen*, Territories, Authorities, Rights; *Fischer-Lescano/Teubner*, Regime-Collisions; *Sand*, Polycontextuality as an Alternative to Constitutionalism.

creasingly polycontextual and heterarchical and decreasingly hierarchical in its organization. The close relations between law and politics are supplemented by close interactions between legal and scientific, and legal and economic communications. Ambitious and comprehensive forms of legal regulation have also contributed to close interactions and conflicts between legal and ethical communications. The changing context and preconditions of law and politics in respect of instability, complexity and polycontextuality make it more difficult to find a basis from which to evaluate institutions, procedures and decisions as legitimate. To the extent that securing normative expectations is the core function of law, the legitimacy of law will also be linked to how this functions.[11]

Luhmann has raised the question of whether this has the consequence that normative expectations decrease in importance next to cognitive expectations.[12] However, there are no signs of a decrease in the significance of legal communication and regulation in modern society. If anything, the opposite is the case, and the importance of law in society seems to be increasing rather than diminishing. Legal regulations now cover an increasing number of social areas, and they do this in increasingly specialized and ambitious ways. Law has become a body of institutions that are as much social facts as mere normative expectations.[13] Legitimacy in law, as far as this can be observed, is not less important than was previously the case. Paradoxically, in fact, legitimacy may have become a more indefinable and at the same time an increasingly crucial quality of law in a global and complex society.

Habermas maintains that democratic procedural qualities of legislation are the only way to guarantee legitimate law in a post-metaphysical society. He states as a precondition for this that we live in "pluralistic societies in which comprehensive world-views and collectively binding ethics have disintegrated".[14] As a result of this, he claimed that there is thus no longer the possibility of basing legitimacy on more substantive values or principles. We have to live with disagreements. Democratic procedures enable information, arguments and reason to "float freely", and they are the only means to enable legitimacy to be constituted across boundaries in society. Modern law is fundamentally Janus-faced in the sense that both basic human freedom rights and nation-state legislation and the coercive protection of rights are equally and interdependent vital parts. The core structure of law relies upon this fundamental contradiction. The implication of this is also that there is a deep interdependence between the opening of politics and the closing of law and between legislation and adjudication.

Luhmann's theories of modern society as functionally and communicatively differentiated are, not specifically legal or political, but primarily sociological. His objective is to show how society functions, not to make normative predicaments about

---

11 *Thornhill*, Towards a historical sociology of constitutional legitimacy.
12 *Luhmann*, Law as a Social System, p. 470.
13 *MacCormick*, Institutions of Law, chapters 2, 7 and 16.
14 *Habermas*, Between Facts and Norms, p. 448.

it.[15] Legal and political communications perform certain functions in society, and their legitimacy must be seen in relation to these functions, and to the manner in which they are performed.[16] For Luhmann, legitimacy can only be produced as an internal part of the processes of law and politics, and it can only be evaluated on the basis of and as an internal aspect of these processes. There is no privileged external viewpoint from which it may be judged.[17] Legitimacy is unavoidably self-referential, although it may also be used as a set of external criteria to be settled by second-order observation.[18] It can only be understood and analyzed as already part of something, and always on the basis of that relevant context.

Both Habermas and Luhmann argue from a position that sees political and legal institutions as vital for the functioning of modern society. Habermas's primary interest is in the procedures and institutions, but he realizes the significance of their social preconditions. Luhmann is primarily interested in "the social", and in how society functions, but he also emphasizes the precariousness of the connections between the social qualities of modernity and its organization in legal and political institutions. They both then emphasize the vital and unavoidable interdependencies between the many social functions and communications of modernity and the functioning of the legal and political institutions. Legitimacy may then be seen as a coupling between the social and the politico-legal communications.

Challenges for legitimacy I: The factual dimension

An increasingly functionally differentiated and complex society

Legitimacy is a term that is most often used in relation to *politico-legal orders* – both to their formal definitions and their practices – as well as to the social practices surrounding them. It usually presupposes a social or an institutional context or an institutional pattern, which is in some way delimited and which offers a more or less given context for reflection on what legitimacy is. Values such as basic individual freedom rights, democracy and rule –of law are presumed to be self-explanatory and vital parts of a concept of legitimacy to such an extent that the boundaries between these concepts and values are blurred. Legitimacy thus becomes part of certain specific discourses or languages of political and legal orders. This is not necessarily a problem. It does not imply a critique of these values. But it reminds us that we must be conscious of our prejudices and pre-understandings of these values, of the exclusion of others, and of the embeddedness of concepts, including that of legitimacy.

---

15 *Luhmann*, Law as a Social System, chapters 1, 3 and 11.
16 *King/Thornhill*, Niklas Luhmanns Theory of Politics and Law, p. 73.
17 *Luhmann*, Risk, p. 145.
18 *Luhmann*, Legitimation durch Verfahren, p. 27; *Luhmann*, Die Politik der Gesellschaft, pp. 122, 162 and 358; *Thornhill*, German Political Philosophy: The Metaphysics of Law, p. 333.

The theories of modern society as *functionally and communicatively differentiated* that have been developed by Luhmann and others, as well as the theories of governmentality by Foucault, describe modern societies as polycontextual and as consisting of many forms of social communications, dynamics or power.[19] The political and legal orders and institutions are not marginalized in such analysis, but they are placed in parallel to other social and communicative systems such as the economic, the scientific, the mass-medial, the artistic, and the religious systems. There is no hierarchical order between these: instead, there is heterarchical interaction and interdependence. The political and legal forms of communication are still vital in that they are able both to convey and process meaning across social and sectoral boundaries and to make decisions. As discussed, for this reason they are defined in some theories as the *immune-systems of society* and they possess the ability to intervene in the problems and contradictions of other systems, and, without actually solving the problems involved, to increase systemic complexity and so to produce instruments for dealing with these problems.[20] The constant processes of differentiation and specialization within the different social systems increase both the possibilities and the complexity of communication within each system and between different systems. The non-communication between the different systems and their logics continue to exist. Society becomes increasingly dependent on the many structural couplings and linkage institutions created or evolving between the systems. Other systems apart from the political and the legal systems may in this process gain increasing complexity, and they may also become increasingly complex in relation to the interventions of the legal and the political systems.

Both the economic and the scientific systems specialize increasingly in ways which make political and legal interventions increasingly indirect, complex and even highly improbable. To illuminate, Luhmann, Gunther Teubner, Duncan Kennedy and others have contributed to describing the *evolutionary processes* of modern society and its communication. To this end, they have proceeded from an analysis of the differentiation of and between the communications of economics, science, law and politics, and they have built on this by examining the processes in which, in increasingly complex ways, *structural and organizational couplings* have been created between these communications.[21] In the era of the comprehensive welfare state the general goals of social welfare, education, industrial production etc prevailed as separate and general goals, and they were designed to lead to a more *affluent, industrial and welfare society*. The economy and the state, with its law and politics, were intensively coupled, but politics and law were perceived as the media of generalized decision making. The economy was seen more as a tool. Against the background of

---

19 *Luhmann*, The Differentiation of Society, pp. 229-254; *Luhmann*, Soziale Systeme, chapters 1 and 5; *Foucault*, The Essential Works, vol. 3: Power, pp. 201-223.
20 *Luhmann*, Soziale Systeme, p. 369.
21 *Luhmann*, The Differentiation of Society, pp. 229-254; *Teubner*, Reflexives Recht; *Kennedy*, Three Globalizations of Law and Legal Thought: 1850 – 2000; *Wiethölter*, Materialization and Proceduralization in Modern Law; *Willke*, Die Ironie des Staate, pp. 175-210.

the post-Keynesian era, emerging globalism and the risk-society, the different function systems continued their processes of differentiation and specialization.[22] The economic and scientific systems have differentiated, specialized and expanded in ways that have increasingly challenged the political and legal forms of communication and regulation. The economic semantics have changed from a strong emphasis on Keynesian macro-economics and couplings with political institutions to a stronger emphasis on the market and micro-economics. Science has created an enormous number of new, complex and experimental technologies which also are being applied, at times with a substantial lack of knowledge regarding their outcomes.[23] Luhmann has argued that the economic and scientific systems and their dynamics seem to expand more easily on a global level than the *legal* and political systems.[24] The latter are more dependent on specific social, cultural and linguistic contexts for their frame of reference whereas the former expand more easily across such frames of reference. The dynamics of change in legal and political communication is then different from and more sensitive to context than the dynamics of science and economics. When law and politics are strongly influenced by the latter, this may create an asymmetry in the conditions of legitimacy. The more contextually sensitive legal and political communications can easily be substantively or discursively dominated by scientific and economic communication.

I will argue that *the economic and scientific functions* of communication are developing degrees and forms of differentiation, which make them increasingly specialized and autonomous in their formation of meaning and thus difficult to regulate politically and legally. The economic communications differentiate in the direction of an increasingly efficient and effective economy. An increasing number of social areas are included in an economic program that is oriented towards cost-efficiency. Even in public budgets standard demands for return on investments, comparable to market rates, are generalized across the board. In the financial market increasingly creative and economically specialized instruments have been created in order to increase market efficiency. The economic crisis that began in 2008 can partly be explained as a condition in which creative, complex and untransparent financial tools spiralled out of control. The international financial market has been very insufficiently regulated, and the same is true for some of the financial institutions, even in the most developed states. There have been serious gaps between the dynamics of financial markets and political and legal regulation.[25] One of the reasons for this is probably the degree of differentiation and specialization and the increasing future-orientation of economic strategic communications resulting from this. Scientific communications are also increasingly highly differentiated and specialized and expanding into an increasing number of social areas and programs. In some areas such as biotechnology and information technology new technological innovations create

---

22 *Clam*, What is Modern Power?
23 *Luhmann*, Risiko und Gefahr.
24 *Luhmann*, Modern Sciences and Phenomenology, p. 34.
25 *Luhmann*, Modern Sciences and Phenomenology, p. 34

highly specialized communications that may be widely applied and powerful yet at one and the same time too complex and untransparent for anyone outside small circles of highly trained specialists to understand. The result of this is partly that political and legal regulation and decisions will have to rely heavily on applying semantics and discursive patterns borrowed from highly specialized fields without creating specific political or legal versions of these patterns. Legal and political communication will become blind to the meaning that is transmitted. Their autonomy is then challenged. One further implication of this is also that the weighing and balancing of values or considerations between these and other fields will seem illusory or highly complex because the different values are closed into their highly specialized semantics.

Structural and institutional couplings are continuously created to deal with the differences and the lack of communication between the different communicative rationalities, but they diversify and multiply and create increasingly complex interactions.[26] Coupling institutions are at times created on regional and global levels, and they involve highly specialized scientific and economic communications. The new structural couplings may seem to be *highly improbably structures*: that is, they contain linkages between highly specialized and abstract communications compared to the more locally and socially embedded institutions of the welfare-state era. The linkages between organization systems may be effective, but they may also be highly abstract in terms of meaning.[27] Even the structural couplings that evolve between, on the one hand, highly specialized economic and scientific systems and, on the other hand, political and legal systems seem to be increasingly complex, abstract and improbable: this both underlines the incommunicability between the different communications and, paradoxically, it allows for effectively functioning couplings and organizations.

As legal and political communication is highly dependent on specialized and complex semantics obtained from other communicative rationalities, legitimacy can easily become a seriously challenged quality. At a substantive level, vital parts of social discourses tend to be exclusively based on scientific, economic or other specialized rationalities, and they are in effect closed to other considerations. Procedurally the semantic closure will have the same consequences. It may be quite difficult to develop a sense of legitimacy based on particular political or legal procedures, principles and forms if the social and factual semantics of the objects to be regulated also become normatively dominant.

The functions of law and politics reside in the fact that they create normative expectations of normative expectations, and that they produce collectively binding decisions concerning most social themes, even in situations where they lack direct knowledge of the objects about which they make the decisions. These functions are not only specialized in their operations, but they also contribute to the transmission

---

26 *Luhmann*, Law as a Social System, p. 476.
27 *Sand*, Hybrid law – law in a global society of differentiation and change; *Teubner*, Dealing with Paradoxes of Law.

of meaning in society, across social boundaries, and through their various subsystems, institutions, and programs they generate forms of legitimacy reaching beyond specialized communications.[28] In doing this law and politics have performed general and integrative functions in the evolution of modern society.[29] Claims for *legitimacy* have been part of their semantics. If, however, the semantics of law and politics become too dominated by and dependent on the social semantics of the objects of regulation, their particular functions and the basis for their legitimacy may suffer.

In the present state of functionally differentiated modernity *the general and integrative functions* of law and politics are subject to challenge. The liberal markets have strengthened their position vis-à-vis other economic programs and vis-à-vis the political system. Markets are clearly still regulated, but the arguments of economic efficiency and the expansion of a market economy have clearly won a prioritized place in relation to other political programs.[30] The economic argument that liberal markets are the most efficient and thus indirectly produce the most welfare, seems to have triumphed over the more mixed-economy arguments. In the same vein, many scientific and technological programs seem to have gained a certain degree of autonomy, or they are protected from intervention by political programs. The WTO treaties and their many sub-agreements illustrate the arguments regarding the relative position of the liberal economic programs concerning trade and the position of certain forms of scientific communication and new technologies.[31] More specifically, the WTO panel and AB decisions in several cases such as Meat Hormones, Biotech etc further illustrate these points.[32] Many of the same arguments could be made in relation to the EU and the ECJ. The WTO treaties and the WTO institutions appear to have assumed a position of considerable communicative autonomy in relation to politics and law. Certain communicative programs seem unsusceptible to the regulatory programs of politics and law.

What implications, then, does this have for the application of legitimacy in political and legal programs and as a more general point of reference for governance? I will argue that legitimacy is a relational concept applied primarily in social and political settings. Legitimacy is a quality of a certain program in relation to other programs. I will also argue that it is primarily a social, legal or political concept. It is not an instrumental or exact concept. With the increasing autonomy of the economic and scientific systems and programs in relation to politics and law, and thus with the growing intervention of the former in the spheres of government and governance, it may become increasingly difficult to employ legitimacy as a reflexive concept in

---

28 *Luhmann*, Law as a Social System, chapters 1 and 9; *Luhmann*, Risk, ch. 8.
29 *Luhmann*, Law as a Social System, chapters 3 and 11.
30 *Stiglitz*, Globalization and its Discontents, London, 2002; *Howse*, From Politics to Technocracy – and back again, pp. 102-108
31 *Howse*, From Politics to Technocracy – and back again, pp. 102-108; *Godard*, Social Decision-making under Conditions of Scientific Controversy; *Sand*, The Legal Regulation of the Environment and New Technologies.
32 WT/DS 26, AB 1997/4, WT/DS 291, 292, Panel report 2006.

relation to some of the arrangements that we would normally see as parts of government and governance.[33] I will argue that the forms of communicative autonomy seen in the communicative programs of liberal economics and science and new technologies seem to escape or to be rather incompatible with general and normative concepts and semantics such as legitimacy, proportionality, justifiability etc. Liberal economic and scientific communicative programs have strong internal dynamics and logics, which are generally closed to evaluative or normative concepts related to other systems.

Integrating economic and scientific programs into more comprehensive programs of governance and legal and political regulation may be described as the construction of *structural or organizational couplings*. Some of the current programs of the economic and scientific systems, however, are increasingly specialized and highly complex in their internal constructions, and in consequence they are not easily susceptible to political or legal regulation. The result of this might be highly complex couplings with highly specialized communications on both the substantive and the politico-legal procedural sides. It may become close to impossible for political and legal communications to intervene in the social discourses involved. Legal and political procedures may easily become purely technical and socially blind, losing their ability to apply more substantive balancing concepts such as justifiability, proportionality and legitimacy.

Example: The WTO, liberal trade, scientific evidence and social regulation.

The WTO for example is clearly an organizational coupling between politics, law, economics and science. When observing some of the main mechanisms of the treaties (for instance, GATT art. XI and XX, the SPS and TBT Agreements, TRIPS etc.), it seems that the coupling is primarily organizational and of a rather indirect character. The main goal of the WTO treaties is to create and stabilize a construction supporting an increasingly international market place that is structured by programs of liberal economics (art. XI and the application of this). The exceptions and adaptations to the logic of the liberal market in GATT art. XX and in SPS are formulated and have been applied in such a way that they take second place to the latter. Environmental and health protection must be supported by scientific evidence. Mere politics or administrative discretion is not enough. There is a trace of precaution in the SPS agreement, but only as a possibility to postpone for a short interval, not to hinder. Liberal market structures and scientific arguments demand relative forms of autonomy in the texts and implementation of the treaties. They are not part of a balancing or discretionary scheme. Economic and scientific communications may then be described as having in a certain sense invaded or become dominant to parts of previous political and legal schemes. One possible explanation for this may be that

---

33 *Teubner*, Autopoietic Law; *Teubner*, De collisione Discursum.

economic and scientific semantics may be more easily applied across cultural and linguistic boundaries than political and legal semantics.[34] There has been a pre-argumentation that precedes the structure of the treaties. Applying demands for legitimacy to the implementation and interpretation of the treaties as such seems difficult in so far as they have an internal logic, which does not recognize such arguments. When a political program includes references to other systemic programs that – for example – consist of highly complex economic or scientific rationality, then evaluative standards such as legitimacy or proportionality may be difficult to apply: that is, because the economic or scientific programs involved will have self-referential dynamics not easily compatible with politico-legal evaluative standards. These may of course be applied to the general political programs and the processes through which the treaties are made, but they will appear as external to the sub-programs and their other logics. It is generally difficult to relate concepts such as legitimacy to organizational or structural couplings which comprise different and mutually incompatible elements: this is because an evaluation or an argument directed at one of the elements or at the results of decision making may be denied relevance for other. The form of politics that is included in the WTO treaties may then reduce the scope of politics and exclude some of its arguments.

Challenges for legitimacy II: The social dimension

Legitimacy and globalization: The context of politics, law and legitimacy

Law and politics have played a vital role in the evolution of modern societies because they have facilitated collective decision making and stabilized normative expectations institutionally. In democratic societies legal and political communication has to a large extent occurred within the boundaries and the institutions of nation states and thus within specific and more or less collectively known contexts. There may have been vital political schisms and disagreements, but at the same time there have usually existed common historical, social, and economic frames of reference. Political and legal semantics have used these common frames of reference. Their functions and rationalities are also to a very large degree connected with and sensitive to the historical, social and communicative contexts of which they are a part, and these are used in the creation of communication, decisions and norms.[35] In democratic nation-states such common frames of reference have been vital for the creation of common forms of meaning and acceptance and legitimacy.

Over time, and particularly in recent years, there has however been a significant increase in the *factual interdependencies* and *the exchange* of technologies, knowledge and experience between states and regions across their boundaries. This has

---

34 *Luhmann*, Risiko und Gefahr, pp. 131-169.
35 *Luhmann*, Risiko und Gefahr, pp. 131-169.

led to equally significant increases in political and legal co-operation on regional and international levels. Climate and environmental change is probably the most obvious and indisputable example of factual interdependence and serious problems to be solved across state boundaries. Places of origin of the problems and of their effects do not coincide. In such areas international co-operation and regulations are necessary and of the greatest significance. International trade has surged and created a variety of forms of cooperation and inter-dependence: economic, industrial, cultural, environmental, scientific, etc, and also political and legal.[36] The production of Western consumer goods in Asia means that aspects of the environmental problems and of the problems related to the working environment of the affluent Western world are now located in other territories. States and regions with very different levels of development of the economy are connected via trade and thus influence each other significantly, although usually in *ad hoc* ways. Environmental problems and climate change do not respect state boundaries. Human-rights ideals and discourses are both local and universal, and they thus almost by definition cross over state boundaries. The internet and the various technologies that make it possible are in fact global and non-boundaried networks. Also other new technologies and knowledge are developed and applied inter- and trans-nationally, in difference to social and cultural contexts.

A variety of *transnational situations* have then thus been established. Dilemmas and problems arise for which there often are no clear procedural and institutional models of resolutions. Saskia Sassen has described some of these situations as *frontier zones and as analytic borderlands*.[37] "New" territories are defined by the factual problems emerging across previous institutional and territorial boundaries. Nation states and international organizations interact, overlap, cooperate and compete in new ways due to new challenges. International organizations have in some instances evolved beyond what has previously been their normative pattern.[38] Despite this, however, the factual problem trajectories do not coincide with the political and legal institutions and with the procedures for decision making and norm construction or with our cultural and normative patterns that we use to describe them.[39]

An increasing number of *international treaties, organizations and courts* have been set up in order to attempt to deal with the needs of international and regional political and legal coordination and regulation. The treaties and the legislation are increasingly comprehensive, and the courts and dispute-settlement bodies are increasingly judicially organized and operatively effective.[40] However, they are still different from similar nation-state institutions in a number of ways. The treaties and the

---

36 *Scholte*, Globalization: A Critical Introduction.
37 *Sassen*, Territory, Authority, Rights, p. 380.
38 *Weiler*, The Constitution of Europe, chapters 1, 8 and 9; *Howse*, From Politics to Technocracy, pp. 95-117; *Slaughter*, A New World Order, ch. 6; *Held*, A Global Covenant, pp. 73-88, 137-143.
39 *Habermas*, The Postnational Constellation and the Future of Democracy, pp. 58-112
40 *Koskenniemi*, Global Legal Pluralism; *Koskenniemi/Leino*, Fragmentation of International Law?; *Fischer-Lescano/Teubner*, Regime-Collisions; *Slaughter*, A New World Order, ch. 6.

international legislation are comprehensive – but they are also fragmented and asymmetrical.[41] Each treaty addresses one set of problems or purposes, often without the ability to see the different and conflicting types of problems in relation to each other. The organizations are not directly democratic in relation to citizens, and thus they differ from nation-state institutions.[42] They are generally based on states as members, and many of them are dominated by internal secretariats and experts. They are set up as top-down tools for dealing with separate issues and areas of problems. They are dominated by different elites. Their democratic qualities are indirect, via the member states. The problems they deal with may be acute and serious. International organizations may perhaps constitute relative improvements in terms of international politics and law, but they are still often fragmented and sectoral. The citizens and groups of peoples in the member states are often notably heterogeneous in their composition in respect of social, cultural and economic background more than what is today represented in the compromises of international negotiations and treaties. The citizens may represent extremely different socio-economic interests behind the common interests of solving international problems: for example, problems relating to climate or environmental change. The frames of reference in which international organizations make political and normative judgements are different from nation-states. They will often depend on compromises and narrow consensus, they often refer to singular objectives, and they have a more indirect relation to the citizenry. The requirements for dealing with or coordinating an increasing variety of problems on a regional or international level have, however, become acute and increasingly important. Nonetheless, creating democratic political institutions and the preconditions for a common civil society takes time, and in view of the social and cultural heterogeneity involved, it is a complex process. It is still uncertain how it may be possible to create sufficiently democratic and accountable institutions at regional and international levels, which are also able to deal with more heterogeneous and socially complex purposes.

The problem I want to focus on here is the very basic problem of *what the contexts of such international institutions are,* and the problems that the complexity, fluidity and fragmentation of such contexts create for any normative evaluation of them in respect of their legitimacy. In addition to this there is the problem of multilayered organizations and procedures whose relation to each other is not sufficiently clarified. International organizations are usually set up in order to solve specific problem areas or to coordinate an area in a more general way. Many of the most influential international organizations are organized by nation-states and refer to their legitimacy without having a specific legitimacy of their own. In many instances, however, the actual effects of the decision-making power of international organiza-

---

41 *Koskenniemi/Leino*, Fragmentation of International Law; *Fischer-Lescano/Teubner*, Regime-Collisions.
42 *Weiler*, The Constitution of Europe, pp. 324-357. Here Weiler describes how the citizens may have quite different, but also legitimate, relations and forms of belonging to different institutional levels.

tions appear to exceed their formal mandates or the intentions of their creators. This may also include some of the most influential international courts, such as the European Court of Justice, the European Court of Human Rights, the WTO Dispute Settlement Bodies. On the other hand, it is arguable that some of the most influential international organizations and courts have "risen to the occasion" in responding to the challenges of solving cross-boundary problems. They may then lack elements of formal legitimacy, but may have gained effective legitimacy by being able to make operative decisions across boundaries. The legitimacy of influential and comprehensive international organizations and courts may, consequently, be viewed from a greater variety of perspectives than their national counterparts: that is to say, they may be assessed from political, legal, territorial, economic perspectives, and they also be assessed in light of different principles of organization.

I have argued above, however, that the quality of legitimacy is closely connected to the semantics and the contexts of political and legal organizations. The semantics of an organisation may encourage or discourage different conceptions of legitimacy. Both internal and external evaluations of legitimacy, however, will also rely very heavily on the way in which the context, in all its dimensions, of the organization or the decision-making situation is perceived. As discussed above, nation-state politico-legal institutions possess certain collectively accepted frames of reference. For international organizations and particularly for international courts, this is much more complex. They have a given mandate, but they operate in international and thus in more multi-dimensional and multi-perspectival contexts. They usually have a shorter history and a more controversial one. Apart from their particular mandate, their international or regional social or political contexts are less well defined. The different participants or observers may also more easily interpret both the contexts and the organisations themselves in different ways. There is often no consensus outside of the wordings of the text of the mandate. The communication of international organisations and courts will then often lack commonly accepted and more complex frames of reference, which may be used by the organizations themselves, their members and their observers, as a context for reflection on or evaluation of possible legitimacy.

Another vital aspect of the social dimension of law in a globalized society is the interaction between the many layers of political and legal institutions. National, regional, inter- and trans-national institutions interact closely, but also in a variety of ways which, in view of the increasingly intensive forms of cooperation and interaction, are not always formally fully clarified. As mentioned above, the demands for regulatory and normative institutions to coordinate social, economic and other factual processes across national boundaries have exceeded the technologies and the theories that we actually posses for ordering and explaining such institutions on a legitimate basis. The institutions on the different levels exist, but their competencies, organisation and potentials for legitimacy differ substantially.

Such organizations are today at times given very comprehensive political or legal competences while at the same time being based on relatively quite narrow texts or purposes. There exists today, in several cases, an asymmetry between the instrumental political or legal competences of an organization and the lack of definition and of recognition of the wider context to which they pertain.[43] When the WTO, the ECJ or the ECHR make their decisions or judgements it may be difficult to define the wider social or other contexts within which they make their decisions. This makes it inherently difficult to make any evaluation of their legitimacy. Legitimacy is a normative and relational concept. When the context of the object in question is unclear and uncertain, it is also difficult to make any meaningful statement of the degree of legitimacy, which it may or may not possess.

I will argue that with the increasingly global and regional factual mutual *interdependencies* across nation-state borders and the emerging regional and international politico-legal organizations possessing increasingly *effective* law-making and adjudicative competences there emerge new challenges to the functioning of the legal and the political systems and to the ways in which they may be perceived as legitimate.[44] To be able to decide whether a specific form of governing or decision making is legitimate, there must first be some kind of common description of what is to be governed, and of the conditions under which governance is conducted etc, to serve as a frame of reference for reflection on legitimacy. An excessively heterogeneous and conflictual context, or a context which is unclear and too uncertain, cannot easily be used as a basis for reflection on legitimacy. An analysis and a discussion of the legitimacy of the WTO or the UN, therefore, would have to be produced from a great variety of different perspectives, and it would then result in a variety of conclusions – none of which would have the legitimacy to represent the whole.

Example: The international war on terrorism as an example of multiple and uncertain contexts

The so-called "international war on terror" was declared, first by the US president, after the 9/11 attack on the Twin Towers in New York. This was followed by UN declarations for national legislation against terrorism, and over time such legislation has been enacted in many UN member states. As part of the war on terror, the invasions and wars in Iraq and Afghanistan were started. New legal vocabularies were initiated primarily by the US: the result of this was Guantanamo, new definitions of torture, and also the concept itself of an international war on terror as an indefinite and open adventure. The international war on terror is obviously a comprehensive theme, and it involves, addresses and incorporates a variety of very different social and political contexts and different normative orders at the same time, while also

---

43 Joerges and Petersmann (eds), Constitutionalism, Multi-Level Governance and Social Regulation.
44 Joerges, Sand and Teubner (eds), Transnational Governance and Constitutionalism.

simultaneously attempting to construct a common new legal framework and vocabulary. In the case of the war on terror, I will argue that, both at a cognitive and at a normative level, this involves integrating drastically different contexts and situations.[45] Owing to the pretence that there is "one" international war on terror with the same normative goals the social and political differences in the states and territories involved are hidden.

The particular feature of this case is that direct war is waged by states far away from the war scenario and on a quite indirect basis. The suffering of war is then too distant for those waging the war to see. The local interactions of war are complex, and it is conducted by a variety of groups rather than by two distinct parties. The arguments regarding the war are also untransparent: they include both the claim that it is necessary to fight terrorism in the Western states and to seek to establish more stable regimes in the territories of the war itself. The legality of the situation is complex for many reasons. One reason why this is so is that some of the vital concepts being used are vague and indeterminate; another reason is that comprehensive delegations are used in sensitive areas. The legitimacy of the situation is more complex. The differences of the various contexts and territories involved are obscured by a uniform and "morally correct" ideological presentation of the legislation on the war-on-terror.[46]

The legal implications of *some of the aspects concerning the aftermaths of 9/11 and the "war on terror"* are examples or illustrations of increasingly global dynamics, of legal disagreement and uncertainty and of what may be labeled as *analytic borderlands or frontier zones*.[47] Several classifications of such general global dynamics and incidents could be made, and at least three different types can be determined. First, there are *dynamics which are global, but which are marked by extremely different configurations* and have very different consequences in various territories. Global trade, the increasingly multi-cultural society, human-rights discourse, climate change may serve as examples. Second, there are *incidents which have occurred in one place/space, but which have repercussions in other places* so that a global discourse is created from very specific incidents. The primary example of this is 9/11, the ensuing "war on terror", and the concept of international terrorism. Third, there are *local and specific incidents, which become trans- or international themes* for political and legal decision making. The wars in Afghanistan and Iraq are examples of this. The wars have very local and specific configurations. At the same time, however, some of the primary decisions regarding the wars have been taken at a great distance, in other regions of the world.

---

45 *Sands*, Lawless world: Making and Breaking of Global Rules; *Kennedy*, Of War and Law, p. 83. On the history of the conflicts within humanitarian law, see *Kennedy*, The Dark Sides of Virtue, ch. 8.
46 *Borradori/Derrida*, Fundamentalism and terror – A dialogue with Jacques Derrida, pp. 85-94.
47 *Sassen*, Territories, Authorities, Rights, pp. 378-390.

Two vital questions concerning legal norms which emerge in multi-level trajectories and in analytic borderlands might be formulated as follows: *What are the contexts in which they emerge? What are the contexts in which they are practiced?* The function of law is continually to produce and stabilize normative expectations and over time to produce a more comprehensive system of legal norms, which can be applied in relation to each other and thus form a more general system of law. Normative expectations and legal norms are usually presumed to emerge from, to be part of and to *reflect on* specific social contexts. Legal norms are presumed to be in some sort of relation to a social, economic, or cultural context out of which they have emerged. One question that arises from this, then, concerns the relevant social context or frame of reference, both for international organizations or dispute-settlement bodies and for the relevant institutional actors in nation states applying and interpreting international legal texts. Another question that arises from this is whether it is possible to define legitimacy in such poly-contextual settings. Polycontextuality is not necessarily new to law, but its dimensions have been extended. In some areas of international regulation, such as the war –on terror, uniform reality descriptions, reasons and goals are not only presumed, but also emphasized as the essence of the project. The distinct differences between the contexts of the participants are not disclosed and are not thematized.

Challenges for legitimacy III: The modality of time and legitimacy

The third element which renders the meaning of the concept of legitimacy increasingly complex and precarious is the change in our use of the modality of time. The use of normative expectations implies a complex interaction between cognitive and normative expectations. There must be cognitive expectations before there can be normative expectations. Normative expectations are used to create stabilizing structures across differences in the cognitive expectations. With the increasingly comprehensive, rapid and continuous changes in the sciences, in new technologies, in the economy and also in most other areas of social and cultural relations, cognitive expectations may tend to assume primacy over normative expectations. This is especially the case as the former have the ability continually to learn and change, whereas the latter act counterfactually to stabilize norms against specific temporal occurrences.[48] As an increasing number of areas tend to rely on knowledge and technologies to organize society, legal regulations and norms will have to apply or connect to the semantics of these areas and their continuous change and reflexivity. Knowledge and technologies are today continuously produced, re-invented and reflected. In some areas experimental technologies are applied.[49] There is, consequently, an increasing future-orientation in the manner in which we organize society and also in

---

48 *Luhmann*, Law as a Social System, p. 468.
49 *Luhmann*, Risiko und Gefahr, pp. 131-169; *Luhmann*, Modern Sciences and Phenomenology; *Giddens*, Consequences of Modernity.

the way in which we structure legal norms and make decisions. As discussed above, we might discern a change in the modality of time from a present-past orientation, through a present-future, to a future-present orientation. Even in law we reflect more on the future and the possible consequences of legal rulings and less on the past and traditions. Obviously this affects the functioning of law, both internally and in its relations to other communicative systems.

Despite this, however, to reiterate a point made above, there is no suggestion that the change towards cognitive expectations and future-orientation as the main temporal mode has made law and legal norms less vital in the communication and organization of society. Normative expectations are just as in demand as previously, if not more. Legal norms are expanding into an increasing number of social areas. Domestic legislation, the uses of contracts, the uses and the relevance of rights, the number of international treaties and the numbers and relevance of courts and other forms of dispute resolution are all increasing significantly. An international project on "International Courts and Tribunals" has recently identified 125 international courts and other dispute settlement institutions.[50] There is clearly some form of legalization or juridification of many social spheres. At the same time, however, the forms and the semantics of law seem in many areas to be strongly influenced by and coupled with the semantics of other communicative systems. Cognitive and normative expectations seem to merge. The normativity and predictability of law are required to operate in closer connection with rapid and constant cognitive changes, including scientific and technological changes. Instability in the cognitive structures seems to generate a demand for normative expectations. Normativity and predictability must then be balanced in the attempt to combine normative structures with constant and quite complex factual changes.

Legal norms are today increasingly regulating areas where we do not operate on the basis of experience or stabilized knowledge. Increasingly, we apply new knowledge and new technologies, about whose consequences we know little. New technologies are increasingly developed in an experimental manner. The increasingly complex structure of new technologies will mean that it may be increasingly difficult to know the consequences of the application of new technologies, in biotech and telecommunications, and also elsewhere.[51] The consequences may be uncertain, unpredictable, irreversible and possibly significant. The decisions to apply and implement the new technologies are often made by people who do not know their implications or by people who have knowledge of consequences yet are willing to defy them. Uncertain consequences are accepted as part of a technological society, of risk society and as the price of economic growth.[52] The decisions to regulate uncertainty may be taken as elements of political communication, but legal communication also necessarily contributes because of the range of interpretation and the delegations

---

50 *Fischer-Lescano/Teubner*, Regime-Collisions; *Koskenniemi/Leino*, Fragmentation of International Law, pp. 553-579.
51 *Luhmann*, Modern Sciences and Phenomenology, pp. 34-37.
52 *Godard*, Social Decision-Making, 39-73.

implied by the decisions. Law then increasingly regulates matters in the future, and it is based on anticipatory knowledge, often very uncertain, of probable consequences.[53] Legal decision making in areas of environmental and health protection and the regulation of new technologies is today unavoidably challenged by the tasks of dealing with unpredictable, and very significant risks, which can quite possibly have irreversible consequences. The uses of chemicals in the environment and in food, the increasing use of genetically modified plants in agriculture, carbon dioxide emissions, and climate change are only some examples of a comprehensive use of experimental technologies. Law is applied to regulate the application of some of these technologies: in this, however, it is more useful as a regulatory technique than as a normative resource associated with justifiability and substantive predictability. Or, to express this in different terns, law's predictability becomes part of the unstable and changing areas of regulation, and this supplants the predictability of law in the more classical sense. The taken-for-grantedness of such uncertainties makes legitimacy a problematic concept. Significant parts of the basis for decision making are unknown. Politics and law are drawing on the future, and in so dong they base themselves on an interest-balanced argumentation (in the present). Law has become an inherent part of risk-society, but as yet there has not been sufficient reflection on and elaboration of the consequences of this. There may be good reasons for constructing decision making in this way, but deciding on its legitimacy may be highly complex.

Increasingly uncertain and comprehensive consequences are also seen in many other areas of society, in particular in the rapid development of international financial markets, the uses of information technologies for surveillance, international migration, increasingly multi-cultural communities, and new family patterns.[54]

Example: The new biotechnologies: Regulating life and death, and exceeding the boundaries of law and politics.

The new evolutionary steps of biological and genetic technologies and of their application present qualitatively new innovations in bio-politics and thus in the potential relations between the population and public authorities. Human beings now have the capacities for creating life, for manipulating it in many senses, and for causing death through the application of widespread technologies, and thus through administrative decisions with potentially extremely comprehensive and significant consequences.[55] When vital questions of life and death – with implications for many people – can be decided politically, administratively and legally, these communicative and governing media assume a new character. Decision making is then not only about justice, the distribution of goods or about balancing different social interests. It also deals, both directly and symbolically, with issues of the most extreme impor-

---

53 *Luhmann*, Risiko und Gefahr, pp. 131-169.
54 *Luhmann*, Risk, pp. 145-174; *Luhmann*, The Modern Sciences and Phenomenology.
55 *Agamben*, Homo Sacer, p. 3; *Fukuyama*, Our Posthuman Future, chapters 3, 4 and 12.

tance for humanity, whose consequences are highly variable. The themes and the possible consequences are of a different order from other types of social and economic regulation. In cases of doubt, such decisions cannot, be taken simply through the balancing of various interests. Simply referring to liberal rights is also insufficient. These are at times decisions on a different level. Human beings have taken on powers that are difficult fully to comprehend or survey. *Ultimately there is a different type of responsibility involved.* The relative position of legitimacy in such dilemmas is complex, and it is not always the most appropriate concept.

In the regulation of biological and genetic technologies law and politics become dependent on highly specialized scientific knowledge and on the manner in which this is presented by scientists. Lawyers and politicians may of course overrule the experts, but they cannot replace their knowledge with their own. Ethics will also be part of the theme. When regulating on the application of biological and genetic technology there will be an unavoidable complex interaction and interdependence of the roles and functions of scientists, medical doctors, administrators, politicians, lawyers and ethics. Law and politics will then unavoidably overstep the limits assigned to them from the point of view of a liberal government.

Summary and conclusion

In the above I have pointed to three types of social change that may contribute to a change in the conditions and the forms of political and legal decision making, and in their relations to other communicative functions.

First, political and legal decision-making are becoming more dependent on and entrenched in other forms of communication, such as scientific, economic and ethical communications. The different functions of communication and the different organizations as parts of which they emerge have become increasingly differentiated and specialized, which makes any communication between them more improbable. Structural and organizational couplings are used to create interdependencies between highly specialized semantics. Also, the coordination between different legal goals and the balancing of different values have become extremely complex and abstract. The functions of law and politics in generating collectively binding decisions and legal norms which can be applied across society have become increasingly challenged and at many points improbable.

Second, law is today developed by an increasing number of authoritative actors and institutions. Different legal regimes in different territories and on different levels of governance interact with each other. The different actors, institutions and regimes emerge in different social contexts and thus with different frames of reference. The co-ordination of these politico-legal regimes and their forms of law is complex because they emerge from different social and communicative preconditions including different normative structures and values.

Third, law is increasingly regulating on the future and operating without certain knowledge of the consequences of its regulatory acts. Law is increasingly oriented towards the future and not the past. Legislation is increasingly intertwined with and interdependent upon other communicative functions, such as politics, economics, science and ethics. Political and legal communications are then part of quite complex structures of interdependent communication and decision making. Both the social and the factual sense-dimensions of politics and law are multi-dimensional, referring to a variety of other functions. Political and legal communications do not today always refer to a given and recognizable context. They may refer to multiple contexts with unclear relations between them, and there may be a very unclear context.

The concepts of legality and legitimacy have become fluid and adaptable, but they are also part of certain preconceptions of what politics and law and their institutions are. The current conditions of legal and political decision making seem to break with some of these preconceptions: this places political and legal decision making in a more complex and multi-dimensional context, to which it is difficult to accommodate the idea and the practice of legitimacy in a consistent manner. Normative and evaluative standards such as legitimacy are elements with which it is difficult to negotiate or to which it is difficult to give meaning in contexts that, even if observed in a procedural perspective, are more complex and future-oriented contexts. This may be the price of a more complex and global society with unclear frames of reference. At the same time, however, we need to be clear that law and legitimacy appear to be increasingly crucial concepts, and some of the decision-making themes and scenarios mentioned above address problems in which there is an urgent requirement for a normative standard such as legitimacy. A new way of thinking about legitimacy may have to deal more profoundly with multiple and more complex and conflictual meanings and situations. Appraisals of legitimacy will in the future have to deal with and accept situations of highly increased complexity, polycontextuality and risk.

Acknowledgements

I am indebted to Chris Thornhill for valuable and constructive comments.

Bibliography

Agamben, Giorgio, Homo Sacer, Stanford, 1998.

Borradori, Giovanna/Derrida, Jacques, Fundamentalism and terror – A dialogue with Jacques Derrida, in Borradori, Giovanna (ed), Philosophy in a Time of Terror, Chicago, 2003, pp. 85-94.

Clam, Jean, What is Modern Power?, in King, Michael and Thornhill, Chris (eds), Luhmann on Law and Politics: Critical Appraisals and Applications, Oxford, 2006, pp. 145-162.

Fischer-Lescano, Andreas/Teubner, Gunther, Regime-Collisions: The Vain Search for Legal Unity in the Fragmentation of International Law, Michigan Journal of International Law 25 (2004), pp. 999-1046.

Foucault, Michel, The Essential Works, vol. 3: Power, London, 2001.

Fukuyama, Francis, Our Posthuman Future, New York, 2002.

Giddens, Anthony, Consequences of Modernity, Stanford, 1990.

Godard, Olivier, Social Decision-making under Conditions of Scientific Controversy, in Joerges, Christian, Ladeur, Karl-Heinz, and Vos, Ellen (eds), Integrating Scientific Expertise into Regulatory Decision-making, Baden-Baden, 1997, pp. 39-73.

Habermas, Jürgen, Between Facts and Norms, Cambridge, 1996.

Habermas, Jürgen, The Postnational Constellation and the Future of Democracy, in The Postnational Constellation: Political Essays, Cambridge, MA, 2001, pp. 58-112.

Held, David, A Global Covenant, Cambridge, 2004.

Howse, Robert, From Politics to Technocracy – and back again. The Fate of the Multilateral Trading Regime, American Journal of International Law 96 (2002), pp. 95-117.

Joerges, Christian and Petersmann, Ernst-Ulrich (eds), Constitutionalism, Multi-Level Governance and Social Regulation, Oxford, 2006.

Kennedy, Duncan, The Dark Sides of Virtue, Princeton, 2004.

Kennedy, Duncan, Three Globalizations of Law and Legal Thought: 1850 – 2000, in Trubek, David and Santos, Alvaro (eds), The New Law and Legal Development, Cambridge, 2006.

Kennedy, Duncan, Of War and Law, Princeton, 2006.

King, Michael/Thornhill, Chris, Niklas Luhmanns Theory of Politics and Law, Basingstoke, 2003.

Koskenniemi, Martti, Legitimacy, Rights and Ideology, Associations 7 (2003), pp. 349-373.

Koskenniemi, Martti, Global Legal Pluralism. Multiple Regimes and Multiple Modes of Thought, lecture presented at Harvard University in 2005: www.helsinki.fi/eci/Publications/MKPluralism-Harvard-05d%5B1%5D.pdf.

Luhmann, Niklas, The Differentiation of Society, New York, 1981.

Luhmann, Niklas, Soziale Systeme, Frankfurt, 1984.

Luhmann, Niklas, Risiko und Gefahr in, Luhmann, Niklas (ed), Soziologische Aufklärung, vol. 5: Konstruktivistische Perspektiven, Opladen, 1990, pp. 131-169.

Luhmann, Niklas, Risk: A Sociological Theory, Berlin, de Gruyter, 1993.

Luhmann, Niklas, Law as a Social System, Oxford, 2005.

Luhmann, Niklas, Modern Sciences and Phenomenology, in Rasch, William (ed), Theories of Distinction: Redescribing the Descriptions of Modernity, Stanford, 2002, pp. 34-37.
Luhmann, Niklas, Legitimation durch Verfahren, Frankfurt, 1983.
Luhmann, Niklas, Die Politik der Gesellschaft, Frankfurt, 2000.
MacCormick, Neil, Institutions of Law, Oxford, 2007.
Sand, Inger-Johanne, The Legal Regulation of the Environment and New Technologies, Zeitschrift für Rechtssoziologie 22 (2001), pp. 1-38.
Sand, Inger-Johanne, Polycontextuality as an Alternative to Constitutionalism, in: Joerges, Christian, Sand, Inger-Johanne and Teubner, Gunther (eds), Transnational Governance and Constitutionalism, Oxford, 2004, pp. 41-65.
Sand, Inger-Johanne, Hybrid law – law in a global society of differentiation and change, in Calliess, Gralf-Peter, Fischer-Lescano, Andreas, Wielsch, Dan, and Zumbansen, Peer (eds), Soziologische Jurisprudenz. Festschrift für Gunther Teubner, Berlin, 2009, pp. 705-720.
Sassen, Saskia, Territories, Authorities, Rights. From Medieval to Global Assemblages, Princeton, 2006.
Sands, Philippe, Lawless world: Making and Breaking of Global Rules, London, 2006.
Scholte, Jan-Aart, Globalization: A Critical Introduction, Basingstoke, 2000.
Slaughter, Anne-Marie, A New World Order, Princeton, 2004.
Stiglitz, Joseph E., Globalization and its Discontents, London, 2002.
Teubner, Gunther, Reflexives Recht, Archiv für Rechts- und Sozialphilosophie 68 (1982), pp. 13-59
Teubner, Gunther, Autopoietic Law, Oxford, Blackwell, 1993.
Teubner, Gunther, De collisione Discursum, Cardozo Law Review 17 (1996), pp. 901-918.
Teubner, Gunther, Dealing with Paradoxes of Law: Derrida, Luhmann, Wiethölter, in Perez, Oren and Teubner, Gunther (eds), On Paradoxes and Inconsistencies in Law, Oxford, 2006, pp. 41-64.
Thornhill, Chris, German Political Philosophy: The Metaphysics of Law, London, 2007.
Thornhill, Chris, Towards a Historical Sociology of Constitutional Legitimacy, Theory and Society 37 (2008), pp. 161-197.
Weiler, Joseph, The Constitution of Europe, Cambridge, 1999.
Wiethölter, Rudolf, Materialization and Proceduralization in Modern Law, in: Teubner, Gunther (ed), Dilemmas of Law in the Welfare State, Berlin, 1986, pp. 221-249;
Willke, Helmut, Die Ironie des Staates, Frankfurt, 1992.
WT/DS 26, AB 1997/4, WT/DS 291, 292, Panel report 2006.

Cosmopolitanism and democratic freedom

Hauke Brunkhorst

Section I

Cosmopolitanism can be defined as the global extension of the *polis* or *res publica* (Cicero, Seneca), the construction of a *civitas maxima* (Wolff, Kelsen), the constitution of a cosmopolitan citizenship or *Weltbürgerschaft* (Kant, Parsons), or the unlimited inclusion of the other (Dewey, Habermas). In ancient political theory this idea was based on a universal idea of man as a rational and political animal (*zoon politicon*). In this context, this idea was 'universal', not only in the sense that it extended the human *res publica* to a *human* cosmopolis, but also in the sense that it reunited human *civil society* and *civic law* with *nature* and *natural* (and *divine*) *law*. This idea of a unification of the *polis* with the whole *cosmos* in a single *cosmopolis* was at least the reason why Kant called it a *sublime* idea.[1]

Yet, in contrast to Kant, in classical political philosophy (Plato, Aristotle, Cicero) all men are seen as designed with the *potential* to perform a *rational life-plan within a political community*. Kant himself only presupposed that all men are born with *equal rights of freedom*, and that everybody, at any time, and without exception, *can* only form a *good will* if he or she wants to do so, and if he or she tries to *act* in accordance with morally universal claims.[2] The crucial difference between classical and modern political philosophy, between Aristotle and Kant, Plato and Hegel, Cicero and Marx is that in classical (or old-European) theory only the human *potentia* or capacity to perform a rational and political life is universal and so a capacity of *all* men (including women, children, slaves, strangers, peasants etc). Its *actual* performance, however, is not. Some are born without the ability to actualise their *potentia*, others prove in the course of their life that they cannot realize it (this may be because they live in the countryside in small villages, because they have lost their leadership over a household or *oikos*, because they are not virtuous and rich enough, or because they are barbarians from the East etc).[3]

The *realization* of the universal capacity of all men was always *logically* (or conceptually) restricted to the happy few. Although everybody *can be* perfect, only a few *can realize* this potential because only a few *are* – by birth or socialization – perfect enough for true citizenship or nobility. It belongs to the *meaning* of words

---

1 Kant, Die Religion innerhalb der Grenzen der bloßen Vernunft, p. 873. Kant here calls the 'Vereinigung aller Menschen' – that is, the unification of all men, which is the very meaning of the ritual of public addresses to God – a 'erhabene Idee': that is, a sublime idea.
2 *Kant*, Grundlegung zur Metaphysik der Sitten, p. 345.
3 *Fine*, Cosmopolitanism, p. 110.

like 'perfection' or 'virtue' that they are related to a hierarchy of more or less perfect, more or less virtuous persons, groups, classes, people(s), cities, kingdoms etc. The *Gattungswesen* (or idea) that *potentially* exists within *any* individual *actually* comes to existence if *some* perform it with perfection, and only the most perfect ones come close enough to the ideal form of the *zoon politikon*. If (for sake of argument) all others were kept as slaves, this would change nothing because the *Gattungswesen* cannot be damaged by its bad (slavish) performance. Consequently, the *conceptual dualism* of essence and appearance, *Gattungswesen* and its performance, is deeply committed to preserving *social stratification* and *class rule*.[4]

The universal idea of a political and rational man functioned as an *ideology* for the self-justification of class-rule that was reinforced and stabilized by the *societal structure* of stratified societies. Even if we counterfactually suppose that the ruling classes originally came to power through virtue and perfection, once they were in power they tried – and *had* to try if they did not want to lose their power – to preserve it for themselves and their families and children by *any* means that served the self-preservation of the power of the new ruling class, whether these were virtuous means or not. If they wished to avoid decline, they were bound to a logic of the *symbolically differentiated medium of power*, for which perfection and virtue were matters of indifference.[5] Consequently, virtue became an ideology, and the intellectuals of the ruling classes experimented with the teleology of happiness that became, in its most sophisticated variants, a philosophy of *eudaemonia* and the good life.[6]

The structurally stabilized aristocratic ideology of *virtue and perfection* was closely related to the idea of *representation*.[7] Only the most perfect political animals were considered able to represent the true rational and political essence of all people of a polity, and the even more universal principle of the political and rational essence of all men. As a result, *Representation was structurally coupled with perfection, stratification and centralization*. Only the best at the *top* (kings/nobles/highly ranked citizens) of the societal hierarchy and in the (*urban*) *centre* of the world (Rome as the one and only city: *urbs*) or a specific world region were held fit to represent, not only the essence of their subjects, but also the substantial essence (or the universal ideas) of the whole cosmos. In this, and only in this elitist and ideological way, classical political thinking was already inherently cosmopolitan. Classical cosmopolitanism was thus a 'cosmopolitanism of the few'.[8]

---

4   This criticism originally goes back to John Dewey and Max Horkheimer. On this, see *Brunkhorst*, Rorty, Putnam and the Frankfurt School; *Brunkhorst*, Dialectical Positivism of Happiness.
5   Paradigmatic for is Macchiavelli's The Prince. For a reiteration of this from a modern functionalist perspective, see *Luhmann*, Macht.
6   *Weber*, Gesammelte Aufsätze zur Religionssoziologie, II: p. 246.
7   On the history of the idea of representation, see *Hoffmann*, Repräsentation. Excellent in particular on the changes in representation in the turn to modernity is *Mansfield*, Modern and Medieval Representation.
8   *Calhoun*, The Class Consciousness of Frequent Travelers. See also *Calhoun*, "Belonging"; *Calhoun*, Nations Matter, and my critical review in *Brunkhorst*, Review of Nations Matter.

The social structure of old-European stratified societies like the Roman Empire consisted in a tremendous number of social, political, economic and cultural inequalities, not only *between* classes, but also *within* the social classes and sub-classes, and this was a kind of inequality which today has become almost incomprehensible.[9] Even the idea of a political *isonomia* (of the best!) was conceived, not as an order of equal rights, but as an order of competition (*agonia*) for *privileges*. A good and stable political or civil society (*koinia politike, societas civile*) was conceived as a system of asymmetric and hierarchical social relations, and symmetric relations between equals (*inter pares*) were regarded as deviant or unstable, even among lovers and friends.[10] The same was true of 'international' relations between cities or between princes. Equal legal sovereignty of princes or states was a late invention, and it did not occur before the sixteenth century, the time of the first Protestant revolution.[11]

If Roman cosmopolitanism was much more universal and individualized than Greek cosmopolitanism, the price of this double progress was a complete depoliticization of the cosmopolis into a mere *bios theoreticos*: a fictious global community of philosophers that hardly represented anything more than an ideological glorification of a superstructure suitable for the Roman Empire.[12] Roman cosmopolitanism transformed all human beings into free members of the cosmopolitan order of nature, and Roman *ius naturale* for the first time described all men as born free and equal. This is evident in the formulae: '...everyone would be born free by the natural law...' (Ulpian, Dig I, 1,4) and '...with regard to the natural law, all men are equal...' (Dig 50, 17, 32). However, the free and equal nature of all men (including all animals) was not at all in contradiction with slavery (or eating animals), and all the other social inequalities, regulated by *ius gentium* and *ius civile* in all its brutal

---

9   *Stolleis*, Diebstahl an sich selbst. Speaking of the Roman Empire, Stolleis states: 'If we take the half-free farmers with hereditary land rights, the serfs, the salaried farmers and the emancipated slaves into consideration, we observe a diversely stratified society. *Its defining feature was inequality,* even amongst slaves' (Emphasis is my own, HB). For more comprehensive treatment, see Stolleis, Historische und ideengeschichtliche Entwicklung des Gleichheitssatzes.
10 *Foucault*, Der Gebrauch der Lüste; Veyne (ed), History of Private Life.
11 On the Protestant revolution, see *Berman*, Law and Revolution II, and *Witte*, Law and Protestantism.
12 Women certainly fared better under the Roman Stoics than under the Greeks. But even there the real value of the new ideals of the loving couple were hardly higher than the 'edifying style' of its philosophical and poetic champions: 'When Seneca and Pliny speak of their married lives, they do so in a sentimental style that exudes virtue and deliberately aims to be exemplary. One consequence was that the place of the wife ceased to be what it had been. Under the old moral code she had been classed among the servants, who were placed in her charge by delegation of her husband's authority. Under the new code she was raised to the same status as her husband's friends [...] For Seneca the marriage bond was comparable in every way to the pact of friendship. What were the practical consequences of this? I doubt there were many. What changed was more than likely the manner in which husbands spoke of their wives in general conversation or addressed them in the presence of others' (*Veyne*, The Roman Empire, p. 42).

details. Natural law acted as the final justification for treating slaves like animals, pets or – as in Roman law – things (*res*).[13]

Classical Roman cosmopolitanism only functioned as a method of ruling through agreement in the fictitious cosmopolis. In the real *Imperium Romanum* the usual methods of *leges pacis imponere* prevailed: that is, execution, deportation, mass enslavement.[14] On the other hand, however, it must be admitted that even these natural laws, which were designed as a *description* of nature (and not as a prescriptive legal rule) and had no *normative* meaning within the Roman Empires positive law, did give rise to an extraordinarily progressive 'effective history' [*Wirkungsgeschichte*]. In particular, in the course of a long history of *legal and political revolutions* and *radical reinterpretations* the *symbolic* meaning of these laws was transformed into normative constitutional meaning. This culminated in the Enlightenment and the constitutional revolutions of the eighteenth and nineteenth centuries.[15]

Section II

For Kant the 'cosmopolitan right' (*Weltbürgerrecht*) 'of universal hospitality' was intended to constitute a world citizenship and a rudimentary international legal subjectivity of individual human beings. Kant's *supranational* universal hospitality is a matter, not of 'philanthropy', but of 'right'. Kant's point is strictly anti-hierarchical and egalitarian. The 'right to visit' is an equal entitlement to unhindered and free movement of citizens, and *not of their rulers and the armies they commanded*. This right enabled people to enter into a 'possible commerce [*Verkehr*]' with any human being at all, and, consequently, it gave 'no-one more right than another to be on a place on the earth'.[16] The right to hospitality for Kant is a basic right that legally constitutes a (rudimentary) *global civil society* and *cosmopolitan citizenship*. It is no longer only a human right, but it becomes, as it is exercised, a civic right.

This idea was very familiar in the philosophy of European Enlightenment. Francois Quesnay had already advocated, in order to bring to completion the new and border-transcending freedom of markets, the freedom of *laissez-faire*, which complemented the other border-transcending freedom of *laissez-passer*.[17] A similar radical move was taken in the famous French *Declaration of Human and Civic Rights* from August 1789. In contrast to the later constitutional textbooks the *Declaration* refers to the universal idea of an original social contract, and, consequently, it does not distinguish between the universal extension of men as bearers of human rights and citizens as bearers of civic rights. As they are transformed from the state of na-

---

13   For a different view of Ulpian's account of the natural right of freedom in the more narrowed context of lex mercatoria, see *Höffe*, Demokratie im Zeitalter der Globalisierung, p. 236.
14   See also *Demandt*, Der ideale Staat, p. 263; *Canfora*, Der Bürger; *Flaig*, Europa begann bei Salamis; *Finley*, Das politische Leben in der antiken Welt.
15   See *Nussbaum*, Kant and Cosmopolitanism.
16   *Kant*, Toward Perpetual Peace.
17   Quoted from *Streeten*, Globalisation, p. 25.

ture into the state of society, only the *meaning*, not the *extension* of rights, is modified. Men are becoming citizens and human rights are replaced by civic rights. The idealism of the *Declaration*, which Hannah Arendt strikingly called the 'Jacobin patriotism of human rights',[18] was not only an ideology.

From the time of the democratic revolutions of the eighteenth century we can observe an impressive process of social and institutional learning, which has regularly led to the inclusion of formerly excluded voices, persons, groups, classes, sexes, races, countries, regions etc. In the words of Rawls: 'The same equality of the Declaration of Independence which Lincoln invoked to condemn slavery can be invoked to condemn the inequality and oppression of women.'[19] The experience of a successful learning process of social inclusion can be, and has been, extended to incorporate former silenced voices of Western societies as well as the oppressed voices of non-Western cultures. Despite this, however, the reality of Western democracies often looks different. The story of impressive normative learning is not the whole story. If we tell the whole story then we have to accept that in many cases (and, in some perspectives, in all cases) the *expansion of social inclusion was acquired at the price of new exclusion*, or of new forms of latent or manifest oppression. The history of Western civilization and Western democracy is not only a Rawlsian success story of *expansion through the inclusion of the other*. It is at the same time a Foucaultian or Anghien story of *expansion through imperialism*, a story from the 'heart of darkness'.[20] Since the first European division of the world in the Treaty of Tordesillas 1494 between Spain and Portugal imperialism has vanished and reappeared in constantly changing fashion, and with constantly changing subterfuges and labels – some of which in fact were even anti-imperialist.[21] Even the present state of inclusion of the other within an emerging cosmopolitan civil society sometimes appears to be nothing else than the expression of a highly exclusive 'class consciousness of frequent travelers.'[22]

---

18   *Arendt*, Elemente und Ursprünge totaler Herrschaft, p. 170.
19   *Rawls*, Political Liberalism, p. 29.
20   *Conrad*, Heart of Darkness.
21   *Anghie*, Imperialism.
22   *Calhoun*, The Class Consciousness of Frequent Travelers; *Calhoun*, "Belonging"; *Calhoun*, Cosmopolitism and Belonging. Yet as true as it is, in many other cases one must be very careful in criticizing cosmopolitanism. Hegel once wrote that the 'hatred of law is the shibboleth whereby fanaticism, imbecility and hypocritical good intentions manifestly reveals themselves': *Hegel*, Grundlinien der Philosophie des Rechts, § 258, note. This is even truer of the hatred of the idea of cosmopolitan law (from which Hegel himself was not completely free). In the twentieth century this hatred was related closely to the disastrous ideologies of fascism and other totalitarian (e. g. Stalinist) movements. It was the 'rootless cosmopolitan Jew' who inflamed the murderous fantasies of all right-wing nationalists. Anti-Semitic criticism of cosmopolitanism, at least until the end of the Second World War, had a strong backing in nearly all kinds of conservative and neoconservative thinking. See on this, *Fine*, Cosmopolitanism, p. 21.

Section III

But the reproduction of social structures of class rule and relations of domination, exclusion and silencing does not change the *normative facticity* (Joerges) that resides in the fact that all modern democratic constitutions since the eighteenth century are reliant on the universal legal principles of the *inclusion of all human beings* and the *exclusion of inequality*.[23] The normative meaning of these two principles becomes manifest when communicative power appears as the (albeit deeply ambivalent) 'power of revenge' (that is: *rächende Gewalt*, to use the words of Habermas). We can give two relatively harmless examples of this. One is – Woken up in Seattle:[24] 'Voi G8, Noi 6 000 000 000'. Another, with less noise, is: People, who, on highly dubious legal grounds, were listed as terrorists by the Security Council, and were deprived of nearly all their rights and powers of legal redress, yet who some years later tried, and succeeded, to petition before the European Court in Luxemburg, and so experienced a change in fortune. Even the Supreme Court now seems susceptible to legal pressure.[25] Legal textbooks, and in particular constitutional textbooks are not only talk: they are in fact 'objective spirit' (Hegel), and they 'can strike back'.[26]

If there is anything specifically characteristic of the 'Western legal tradition',[27] it is this dialectical dual structure of law, which is on the one hand a *medium of repression* and *stabilization of* (counterfactual) *expectations* (Luhmann), yet which on the other hand is an instrument able to *change the world*, and to 'begin with the establishment of the *civitas dei* on earth' (Berman). Or, expressed in more secular terms: Law is a *medium of emancipation*, which is why Kant and Hegel even identified law with egalitarian freedom, or defined law as the 'existence of freedom' (*Dasein der Freiheit*).[28] What is now so specifically characteristic of Western constitutional law is the fact that the deep tensions, and even the contradictions, between these two faces of repression and emancipation (Habermas speaks here of a *Janus*-face) have been 'reconciled' by legal institutions which have learned to *coordinate conflicting powers*. Harold Berman speaks in this regard of a *dialectical reconciliation of opposites*,[29] but we could also add that it is a dialectical (and procedural) reconciliation of *lasting* opposites, of *lasting* conflicts, differences and contradictions.[30]

---

23 *Marshall*, Citizenship and Social Class; *Stichweh*, Die Weltgesellschaft, p. 52.
24 *Byers*, Woken up in Seattle, pp. 16-17.
25 *v. Bernstorf*, Procedures of Decision-Making; *Warbrick*, The European Response to Terrorism in an Age of Human Rights; *Cameron*, European Union Anti-Terrorist Blacklisting.
26 *Müller*, Wer ist das Volk?, p. 54.
27 *Berman*, Law and Revolution.
28 *Kant*, Metaphysik der Sitten, pp. 345, 434, 464; *Hegel*, Grundlinien der Philosophie des Rechts, § 4; close to this, see *Marx*, Verhandlungen des 6. Rheinischen Landtags.
29 *Berman*, Law and Revolution, p. 5.
30 Law of collision or 'Kollisionsrecht' (as discussed by Joerges, Teubner, and Fischer-Lescano) has deep roots in Western constitutional law. One can join Chantal Mouffe in describing this

The constitutional *spirit* of the revolutions of the eighteenth century became *objective* for the first time within the borders of the modern nation state. This state always had many faces. These include the Arendtian face of violence, the Habermasian face of administrative power, the Foucauldian face of surveillance and punishment, the faces of imperialism, colonialism, war on terror and so on. However, the nation state, once it became democratic, possessed, not only the *administrative power of oppression and control*, but at the same time the *administrative power to exclude inequality* with respect to *individual rights, political participation* and *equal access to social welfare and opportunities*.[31] Only the modern nation state possessed, not only the normative *idea*, but also the administrative *power* to achieve that. From the very beginning this was the hard core of the utopia of the Enlightenment. Up to the present all advances in the reluctant *inclusion of the other*, and so also all advances of cosmopolitanism, are, to a greater or lesser degree, advances that have been accomplished by the modern nation state. National constitutional regimes have solved the *three basic conflicts* of the modern capitalist and functionally differentiated society. Stated in very rough historical terms, which leave a number of empirical questions open, we can say that the formation and the democratic development of the nation state has provided a series of solutions that are constitutive of modern societies.

First, the nation state has solved the (motivational) *crises of religious civil war* (Protestant Revolutions) of the sixteenth and seventeenth centuries. It has achieved this through the *constitutional reconciliation of lasting conflicts* between religious, agnostic and anti-religious belief systems.[32] This was – very schematically – the result of a two-step-development, accomplished in a manner that was both *functionally* and *normatively* universal. That is to say, on one hand, that the *functional* effect of the formation of a territorial system of states consisted in the transformation of the uncontrolled atomic explosion of religious freedom into a controlled chain reaction that kept the productive forces of religious fundamentalism alive and its destructive forces (to some degree) under control. This was initially the repressive effect of the *confessionalization* of the territorial state.[33] Furthermore, on the other hand, during the long and reluctant process of *democratization* of the nation state, repressive confessionalization was replaced by *emancipatory legislation* which, ultimately led to the implementation both of the equal freedom *of* religion and the equal freedom *from* religious and other belief systems.[34]

    too as a transformation of antagonism into agonism – if one keeps in mind (against Mouffe) the constitutive role of constitutional law in this transformational process.

31   *Marshall*, Citizenship and Social Class, p. 33.
32   This was the very specific achievement and the specific advance of the Western legal tradition since the papal revolution of the eleventh and twelfth century. See generally *Berman*, Law and Revolution, I. On the distinction of different types of crises (motivational, legitimatory etc) see *Habermas*, Legitimationsprobleme im Spätkapitalismus.
33   *Reinhard*, Geschichte der Staatsgewalt; *Schilling*, Die neue Zeit; *Dreier*, Kanonistik und Konfessionalisierung: *Stolleis*, Konfessionalisierung oder Säkularisierung; Reinhard and Schilling (eds), Die katholische Konfessionalisierung.
34   *Parsons*, The System of Modern Societies.

Second, the emerging nation state also has solved the (legitimisation and) *constitutional crisis* of the public sphere, of public law and public power, which marked the old European *Ancien Régime* and culminated in the constitutional revolutions of the eighteenth and nineteenth centuries. Constitutions have transformed *antagonistic class struggles into agonistic political struggles between political parties, unions and entrepreneurs, civic associations etc.*[35] Bloody constitutional revolutions became in the (more successful) process(es) of (Western) history *permanent and legal revolutions*.[36] Once again, the effect of this was twofold. It led, on one hand, to a *functional* transformation of the destructive and oppressive potential of a highly specialized politics of accumulation of power for power's sake into a (more or less) controlled explosion of all the productive forces of public *and* administrative power.[37] This, in turn, was accompanied by *democratic emancipatory legislation*, which finally brought about the implementation of the freedom *of* public power together with the freedom *from* public power.

Third, moreover, the nation state has even solved the *social class conflicts* (social revolutions)[38] of the nineteenth and twentieth centuries. It accomplished this through the emergence of a regulatory social welfare state, which transformed the elitist bourgeois parliamentarianism of the nineteenth century into egalitarian mass-democracy. The social class struggle was institutionalized,[39] and the violent social revolution became a legally organized 'educational revolution'.[40] In this respect, it was the great *functional* advance of social democracy that it kept most of the productive, and (to some degree) got rid of the destructive, forces of the exploding free markets of money, real estate and labour.[41] It achieved this by overcoming the fundamentalist bourgeois dualism of private and public law.[42] In the first decades of social welfare regimes, this was more or less an achievement of *administrative law* and *bureaucratic rule* in a regime of *low-intensity democracy*.[43] Further, in this respect, the ongoing *democratic* Rights Revolution,[44] which was directed against low-intensity democracy, finally led to the implementation of the freedom *of* markets in

35 Mouffe states: 'We could say that the task of democracy is to transform antagonism into agonism': *Mouffe*, On the Political, p. 20.
36 See *Habermas*, Ist der Herzschlag der Revolution zum Stillstand gekommen?.
37 In this respect three very different approaches, one of which is historical, one of which is power-theoretical, and the third of which is derived from systems theory, illuminate this. See *Lüdtke*, Genesis und Durchsetzung des modernen Staates'; *Foucault*, Überwachen und Strafen; *Luhmann*, Verfassung als evolutionäre Errungenschaft.
38 Usually the narrative of the social revolutions is told as a gradual transformation of the nation state. See *Marshall*, Citizenship and Social Class; *Parsons*, The System of Modern Societies. This seems quite plausible. However, the story can also be told as part of the global legal revolution of the twentieth century (see below).
39 *Hoss*, Der institutionalisierte Klassenkampf.
40 *Parsons*, The System of Modern Societies.
41 *Polanyi*, The Great Transformation.
42 *Kelsen*, Das Problem der Souveränität und die Theorie des Völkerrechts; *Kelsen*, Reine Rechtslehre); *Kelsen*, Demokratie und Sozialismus.
43 On low-intensity democracy, see *Marks*, The Riddle of all Constitutions.
44 *Sunstein*, After the Rights Revolution.

conjunction with the freedom *from* markets. This transformed the system of individual rights, which was based on the freedom of property, into a comprehensive system of welfare *and* anti-discrimination norms.

Despite this, however, the impressive normative *and* functional advances of the Western democratic nation state were obtained at the price of its original cosmopolitan claims.

Section IV

The modern nation state up to 1945 was the state of the regional societies of Europe, America and Japan, and the rest of the world was either under their imperial control or kept outside. Until the mid of the twentieth century, the *exclusion of inequality* meant internal equity for the citizens of the state, and external inequality for those who did not belong to the regional system of states. There was not even a serious or legal demand for a *global* exclusion of inequality.

When Kant proposed the 'cosmopolitan condition' of linking nations together on the grounds that in modern times 'a violation of rights in one part of the world is felt everywhere',[45] his notion of the (political) *world* (as distinct from the *globe*) was more or less restricted to Europe and the European system of states.[46] When Hegel wrote of the 'infinite importance' of the fact that 'a human being counts as such because he is a human being, not because he is a Jew, Catholic, Protestant, German, Italian, etc.', Hegel also, and in fact in these very words, restricted the legal meaning of human rights to male citizens, biblical religions and European nations.[47] He further explicitly limited human rights to national civic law (of the *bürgerliche Gesellschaft* and its *lex mercatoria*) that forfeits its validity in questions regarding the essential concerns of the executive administration of the state (*der Staat*) and its particular relations of power and extra-legal acts of sovereignty (*besondere Gewaltverhältnisse, justizfreie Hoheitsakte*). Consequently, Hegel condemned any '*cosmopolitanism*' that opposed the concrete *Sittlichkeit* [ethical life] of the state.[48] Some decades later, when one of the 'gentle civilizers of nations' (to use the phrase of Koskenniemi), Johann Caspar Bluntschli, declared that the implementation of a 'humane world order' (*menschliche Weltordnung*) was the main end of international law,[49] he did not see any contradiction between this noble aim and his (and his col-

---

45 This is Kant's argument in Towards Perpetual Peace.
46 Whereas the Globe for Kant was not much more than a logical or transcendental category that limited in particular our practical reason (See *Brandt*, Das Erlaubnisgesetz), he saw the world (mundus) as the historically existing world order. In political terms that meant for Kant the world of European states and the European ruling class. See *Höffe*, Gerechtigkeit, p. 53.
47 *Hegel*, Philosophie des Rechts, § 209.
48 *Hegel*, Philosophie des Rechts, § 209. For a more differentiated reading in particular of Hegel, see *Fine*, Kant's theory of cosmopolitanism and Hegel's critique.
49 *Bluntschli*, Das moderne Völkerrecht der civilisierten Staaten, p. 59. Compare with this *Fischer-Lescano/Liste*, Völkerrechtspolitik.

leagues') identification of the modern state with a male-dominated civilization. He stated: '*Der Staat ist der Mann*',[50] and he also saw no contradiction with his latently racist thesis that all law is Aryan.[51] The liberal cosmopolitanism of the 'men of 1873' who founded in the same year the *Institut de droit international* and invented a cosmopolitan international law, was completely Eurocentric, relying on the basic distinction between (Christian) *civilized nations* and *barbarian people*, the rough states of the nineteenth and early twentieth century.[52] The generous tolerance of the men of 1873 was from the very beginning paternalistic and repressive.[53] It is therefore no surprise that the liberal cosmopolitan humanists who wanted to found a humane world order soon became apologists of Imperialism,[54] and they defended King Leopold's private prerogative state [*Maßnahmenstaat*] in the heart of darkness by drawing a strict legal distinction between *club-members* on the one side and *outlaws* (Bluntschli) on the other.[55] Following this line of argumentation Article 35 of the Berlin Conference on the future of Africa (1884-85) offers 'jurisdiction' for *us* civilized nations of Europe, 'authority' for *them* in the heart of darkness.[56] Guantámano, in short, has a long Western pre-history.

However, during the time from 1945 to the present day, classical imperialism (not a more and more de-territorialized and flexible kind of hegemony) vanished,[57] Eurocentrism was completely decentred, state sovereignty was legally equalized, and the state went global. In conjunction with the globalization of the modern constitutional nation state, therefore, all functional subsystems, which – from the sixteenth century until 1945 – were bound to state power and to the international order of the regional societies of Europe, America and Japan, became *global systems*. The last square meter of the globe became state-territory (at least legally),[58] and even the moon became an object of international treaties between states.[59] The rational and secular *regional culture*, which originally was the specific *occidental rationality* (Weber) of Europe and North America, became a rational and secular *culture of the world*, and it constitutes the basic orientations of all main actors of the global society: that is, of states, organizations and human individuals.[60] The consequence of this, which has not yet been sufficiently understood, is that now Western rationalism, functional differentia-

---

50 Quoted from *Koskenniemi*, The Gentle Civilizer of Nations, p. 80.
51 *Koskenniemi*, The Gentle Civilizer of Nations, p. 77
52 *Bermann*, Bosnien, Spanien und das Völkerrecht.
53 *Koskenniemi*, The Gentle Civilizer of Nations, p. 69. On repressive tolerance, see Marcuse, Repressive Toleranz.
54 *Koskenniemi*, The Gentle Civilizer of Nations, p. 168
55 *Koskenniemi*, The Gentle Civilizer of Nations, p. 83.
56 *Koskenniemi*, The Gentle Civilizer of Nations, p. 126.
57 This is the best point in a poor book: *Hardt/Negri*, Empire. For a much better account the systemic transformation of hegemony, see *Fischer-Lescano/Teubner*, Regime-Kollisionen; *Buckel*, Subjektivierung und Kohäsion.
58 *Oeter*, Prekäre Staatlichkeit.
59 *Dobner*, Konstitutionalismus als Politikform.
60 On global culture, see *Meyer*, World Society and the Nation-State; *Meyer*, Weltkultur.

tion, legal formalism and moral universalism are *no longer something specifically Western*: Eurocentrism has been *completely decentred.*[61]

At the end of the twentieth century human rights violations, social exclusion of global and local regions and tremendous inequalities, hegemony and imperialism (that still divide the North West from the rest of the world) did not disappear. But now (and this is a major difference between the beginning of the twentieth century and the beginning of the twenty-first century) these matters are perceived as *our own* problems, and they are perceived, not only politically and economically, but also from the point of view of *universal equal rights*, as a problem that concerns every citizen of the world. Before the middle of the twentieth century these rights never existed as a *global system of positive legal norms*. We now *have* serious and legally binding claims for a *global exclusion of inequality*.

We ought perhaps to describe this development, and at the same time re-describe the history of the twentieth century – the age of extremes (Hobsbawn) – as the result of a great and successful *legal revolution*, which began at the end of the First World War with the American intervention in the war (and not to forget the tragic Russian Revolution) in 1917.[62] President Wilson forced the Western allies to claim revolutionary war objectives, and from this moment on the war (and later the Second World War, again as a result of American intervention) was fought, not only for self-preservation and national interest, but also for global democracy and global legal peace: 'To make the world safe for democracy' (Wilson). The legal revolution ended in 1945 with the constitution of the United Nations in San Francisco. A new system of basic human rights norms, coupled with a completely new system of at once inter-, trans- and supranational institutions and organisations, was created during the short period from 1941 to 1951. This system in fact included international welfarism, which was invented *before* the great triumph of national welfare states.[63]

The development of international law has changed deeply since the founding of the United Nations. It has witnessed a turn from a law of coordination to a law of cooperation (Art. 1 par. 2, 3 UN),[64] the founding of the European Union, the Human Rights Treaties from the 1960s, the Vienna convention on the law of the Treaties, and the emergence of international *ius cogens*, etc. The old rule of equal sovereignty of states became the 'sovereign equality' *under* international law (Art. 2 par. 1 UN); individual human beings became subject to International Law; democracy became an emerging right or a legal principle that can also be made valid against sovereign states; the right to have rights, whose absence Arendt lamented in the 1940s, is now a legal norm that binds the international community.[65] All these legal rules are of course broken again and again. However, this is not a specific feature of international law: it happens with national law as well. What is new today is *that international*

---

61 *Brunkhorst*, Solidarity.
62 For a first account of this thesis, see *Brunkhorst*, Die Globale Rechtsrevolution; *Brunkhorst*, Kritik am Dualismus des internationalen Rechts.
63 *Leisering*, Gibt es einen Weltwohlfahrtsstaat?
64 *Bast*, Das Demokratiedefizit.
65 For a more comprehensive overview *Brunkhorst*, Die Globale Rechtsrevolution.

and cosmopolitan equal rights have become binding legal norms, and they can thus be taken seriously. There is no longer any space for any actions outside the law or outside the legal system.[66] In consequence, if there once was any difference in principle between national and international law, there is no longer any such difference. This is in fact what Hans Kelsen, Alfred Verdross and other cosmopolitan international lawyers had already claimed during the First World War.

Section V

Nonetheless, the international (and national) legal and revolutionary progress is as deeply ambivalent and fragile as all other things in a highly accelerated and complex modern society.[67] There exist now, on the one hand, the basic legal principles of the *global inclusion of the other* and the *global exclusion of inequality*. Yet on the other hand there exist global functional systems, a global public, and global spheres of value, which emerge with great rapidity, and which *tear themselves off from the constitutional bonds of the nation state*. This is a double-edged process that has caused a *new dialectic of Enlightenment*. The most dramatic effect of this process that has formed the global society is the decline of the ability of the nation state to exclude inequalities effectively – even within the highly privileged OECD-world. This has three very significant consequences.

These consequences are observable, first of all, in the *economic system*. In this respect, we can observe the complete transformation of the *state-embedded markets of regional late capitalism* into the *market-embedded states of global turbo-capitalism*.[68] The negative effect of economic globalization on our rights is that the freedom *of* markets explodes globally, and it is often combined with heavy, sometimes war-like competition: *There will be Blood*.[69] At the same time, then, the freedom *from* the negative externalities of markets declines rapidly.

Surprisingly enough, in questions regarding the religious sphere of values we can make a similar observation and identify similar consequences. Global society makes the proposition that is true for the capitalist economy equally true for the autonomous development of the religious sphere of values. In consequence, second, we are now confronted with the transformation of the *state-embedded religions of Western regional society* into the *religion-embedded states of the global society*.[70] Since the

---

66   *Byers*, Preemptive Self-defense, p. 189.
67   *Rosa*, The universal underneath the multiple.
68   *Streek*, Sectoral Specialization. As we now can see, the discussion of late capitalism was not wrong, but it has to be restricted to state-embedded capitalism, and state-embedded capitalism indeed is over. But what then came was not socialism but globally disembedded capitalism, which seems to be as far from the state-embedded capitalism of the old days as it is from socialism.
69   One-sided, but striking in this regard is the neo-Pashukanian analysis of international law in *Mieville*, Between Equal Rights.
70   *Brunkhorst*, Globalizing Solidarity.

1970s, religious communities have crossed borders and have been able to escape from state control. Again the negative effect of this on our rights is that the freedom *of* religions explodes, even to such a degree that it sometimes leads to religious war: *There will be Blood*. Yet, at the same time the freedom *from* religion comes under pressure everywhere from religious fundamentalism and from (neo-conservative) public and administrative power.

Last but not least the (internally fragmented) executive bodies of the state have decoupled themselves from the state-based separation, coordination and unification of powers under the democratic rule of law, and they too have gone global.[71] The more they are decoupled from national control and judicial review, the more they are coordinated and associated on regional and global levels, where they constitute a group of loosely connected transnational executive bodies. Post-national ('good' or 'bad') governance without (democratic) government is performed at one and the same time through a partly formal and egalitarian *rule of law*, through an elitist *rule through law*, and through an informal *bypassing of (constitutional) law and democratic public* by means of a new regime of soft-law legislation. This law, as things stand, has no normatively binding force. Empirically, however, it has a strong binding effect.[72] It therefore resembles the old Roman *senatus consultum*, which had no legally binding force, but every official was well advised to follow it.[73] As a result of this, the executive power seems to be undergoing the same transformation as markets and religious belief systems, and it is thus transformed, third, from *state-embedded power to power-embedded states*. This leads to a new *privileging of the globally more flexible second branch of power vis-à-vis the first and third one*, which jeopardizes the achievements of the modern constitutional state.[74] The effect of this is an accelerating process of a global *original accumulation of power beyond national and representative government*. Some examples of this are the following: the Basel-Bank-Committee,[75] the so-called Bologna process of the European reform of the university system,[76] the work of the Council of Europe's Presidents, Prime Ministers and Foreign Ministers, who (with the sole exception of the voice of the president of the *European Commission*) only have a clear democratic mandate for

---

71 During the last few years a whole industry of research emerged on transnational administration. For a selection, see *Tietje*, Die Staatsrechtslehre und die Veränderung ihres Gegenstandes; *Möllers*, Transnationale Behördenkooperation; *Kingsbury/Krisch/Steward*, The Emergence of Global Administrative Law; Möllers, Voßkuhle and Walter (eds), Internationalisierung des Verwaltungsrechts; *Fischer-Lescano*, Transnationales Verwaltungsecht. On the globalization of executive power, see *Wolf*, Die neue Staatsräson; *Dobner*, Did the state fail?; *Lübbe-Wolf*, Die Internationalisierung der Politik.
72 *Bernstorf*, Procedures of Decision-Making, p. 22; *Möllers*, Transnationale Behördenkooperation.
73 *Wesel*, Geschichte des Rechts, p. 163.
74 *Wolf*, Die neue Staatsräson.
75 *Möllers*, Transnationale Behördenkooperation.
76 *Brunkhorst*, Unbezähmbare Öffentlichkeit.

national foreign policies, but not for what they are primarily doing: namely, European domestic politics.[77]

The three great transformations of the world society have turned the democratically elected and legally organized political power within the nation state into the power of a *transnational politico-economic-professional ruling class* – including high ranked journalists working on TV and for *Bild-Zeitung* or *The Sun* and media stars who function as a system of *bypasses*, which are implemented to remove the core of political decision-making from *any spontaneous formation of communicative power through an untamed and anarchic public sphere*. It seems now as if the Habermasian filters, supposed to transform public opinion into political decision-making,[78] are working the other way round, and are closing the doors on public opinion. White-Paper-Democracy is the outcome of this. The new transnational ruling class hardly relies on egalitarian will-formation anymore. This class is (not so unlike the *national* bourgeoisie of the nineteenth century) highly heterogeneous and characterized by multiple conflicts of interest. Yet it has a certain number of *common class interests*: for instance, it seeks to increase its room for maneuver by withdrawing from itself democratic control, and, as a comfortable side-effect of this, it aims to preserve and increase its enormously enlarged, individual and collective opportunities for private profit generation.[79] This is the new *cosmopolitism of the few*. Instead of global *democratic government* we now are approaching some kind of directorial global *Bonapartist governance*: that is, soft Bonapartist governance for *us* of the North West, and hard Bonapartist governance for *them* of the South East, the failed and outlaw states and regions of the globe.[80]

The deep division of the contemporary world into two classes of people – that is, into people with good passports and people with bad passports – is mirrored by the constitutional structure of the world society. Today there already exist a certain kind of global constitutionalism, which is one of the lasting results of the revolutionary change that began in the 1940. However, the existing global constitution(s) is (are) far removed from being democratic.[81] All post-national constitutional regimes are characterized by a *disproportion between legal declarations of egalitarian rights and democracy* and *its legal implementation by the international constitutional law of check and balances*. Hence, the legal revolution of the twentieth century was successful, but it was unfinished. The one or many global constitutions are in bad shape, and they are based on a constitutional compromise (Franz Neumann) that

---

77 *Dann*, Looking through the federal lens.
78 *Peters*, Öffentlichkeit.
79 *Wolf*, Die neue Staatsräson.
80 *Anghie*, Imperialism.
81 For the thesis that the UN-Charter is the one and only constitution of the global legal and political order, see Fassbender, The United Nations Charter as Constitution of the International Community. See different approaches in *v. Bogdandy*, Europäisches Verfassungsrecht; Albert and Stichweh, Weltstaat und Weltstaatlichkeit; *v. Bogdandy*, Constitutionalism in International Law; *Brunkhorst*, Globalising Democracy without a State; *Brunkhorst*, Demokratie in der globalen Rechtsgenossenschaft. For the thesis of constitutional pluralism, see *Teubner*, Globale Zivilverfassungen.

mirrors the hegemonic power structure and the new relations of domination in the world society. As Inger-Johanne Sand has recently described this situation:

> The treaties and the legislation are increasingly comprehensive, and the courts and dispute-settlement bodies are increasingly judicially organized and operatively effective. However, they are still different from similar nation-state institutions in a number of ways. The treaties and the legislation are comprehensive – but they are also fragmented and asymmetrical. Each treaty addresses one set of problems or purposes, without the ability to see the different and conflicting types of problems in relation to each other. The organizations are not democratic in relation to citizens, and thus they differ from nation-state institutions. They are generally based on states as members, and many of them are dominated by internal secretariats and experts. They are set up as top-down tools for dealing with separate issues and areas of problems. They are dominated by different elites.[82]

Scientific and technical expertise has again become an ideology,[83] and it obscures the social fact that 'most regulatory decisions involve normative assumptions and trigger redistributive outcomes that cannot be reduced to seemingly objective scientific inquiries; each time someone wins and someone looses.'[84] Because of this, what seems to be necessary and out of reach in the present situation of (pessimistically speaking) post-, or (optimistically speaking) pre-democratic global constitutionalism is a Kantian *Reform nach Prinzipien*,[85] or a 'radical reformism' (Habermas), as well as a new 'democratic experimentalism' (Dewey/Möllers), which operates on the same level as the power of the emerging transnational ruling class: Beyond representative government and national government.[86]

Section VI

What could radical reformism or *Reform nach Prinzipien* mean today? It is not easy to answer this question. But before posing the hard questions of constitutional change and institutional design, which often fail because they are not conceptually adequate to the level of complexity of modern society, we should start again with concepts and principles, and that means with a critique of *dualism* and *representation* in legal and political theory.

Dualistic and representational thinking has already been completely deconstructed by the revolutionary philosophy (and scientific praxis) of the twentieth century, in particular by philosophers like John Dewey, Ernst Cassirer (after his sym-

---

82   *Sand*, Legitimacy in global and international law: A sociological critique, in this volume.
83   See *Marcuse*, On Science and Phenomenology; *Habermas*, Technik und Wissenschaft als 'Ideologie'.
84   *Bernstorf*, Procedures of Decision-Making, p. 8.
85   *Langer*, Reform nach Prinzipien.
86   *Marks*, Riddle of all Constitutions, p. 2.

bolic turn), the early Heidegger, the late Wittgenstein, or W. v. O. Quine.[87] Nonetheless, representational thinking that is deeply based on dualism still prevails in political and legal theory. In particular in International Law and International Relations, dualism covers a broad mainstream of opposing paradigms. From realism in International Relations to critical legal studies, from German *Staatsrecht* to critical theory, from liberalism to neo-conservatism the state-centred dualism is founded in tacit consent: this is seen in the conceptual dualism between *Staatenbund* [confederation of states] and *Bundesstaat* [federal state], between international and national law, between constitution and treaty, between public law and private contract, between state and society, between politics (or '*the* political') and law, between law-making and law-application, between sovereign and subject, between people and representatives, between (action-free) legislative will-formation and (weak-willed) executive action, between legitimacy and legality, between heterogenous population and (relatively) homogenous people, between *pouvoir constituant* and *pouvoir constitué* etc. All these dualisms prevent us from conceptually constructing European and global democracy in adequate fashion, and so, finally, from joining the *civitas maxima*.

However, what Dewey and the pragmatists did with classical idealistic and metaphysical dualisms in philosophy, Kelsen and his students did with the dualisms in political, legal and constitutional theory. They replaced each of them by a *continuum*. Kelsen's and Merkl's paradigm case was the legal hierarchy of norms [*Stufenbau des Rechts*].[88] The doctrine of *Stufenbau* [legal hierarchy] transforms the dualisms of legislative will and executive performance, of political generation and professional application of legal norms, of general law and specific judgment, and last but not least of international and national law into a *continuum of concretization*.[89] Therefore, if on all levels of the continuum of concretization, legal norms are (politically) created, the principle of democracy is only fulfilled if those who are affected by these norms are included in fair and equal manner on all levels of their creation (albeit in what, in all probability, will be very different ways).

Moreover, if we go (following Jochen von Bernstorff) one step further than Kelsen,[90] and abandon the transcendental foundation of a legal hierarchy and the *Grundnorm*, then we are left with an enlarging or contracting circle of legal and political communication, which has no beginning and no end *outside* positive law *and* democratic will formation.[91] Only on that condition could democracy supersede the last (highly transcendentalized and formalized) remains of the old-European *legeshierarchy* and *natural law*, which is higher than democratic legitimization, and only

---

87 A paradigmatic account of this is *Rorty*, Philosophy and the Mirror of Nature. For recent developments, see *Brandom*, Making It Explicit; *Habermas*, Wahrheit und Rechtfertigung.
88 *Merkl*, Allgemeines Verwaltungsrecht, pp. 160, 169; *Merkl*, Prolegomena zu einer Theorie des rechtlichen Stufenbaus.
89 *v. Bernstorff*, Kelsen und das Völkerrecht, p. 181.
90 *v. Bernstorff*, Der Glaube an das universale Recht.
91 This comes close to Habermas's normatively strong or Luhmann's normatively neutralized idea of cycles of communication without a subject (subjektlose Kommunikationskreiläufe). See *Habermas*, Faktizität und Geltung; *Luhmann*, Legitimation durch Verfahren. For comparative commentary, see *Neves*, Zwischen Themis und Leviathan.

then could the last inherited burden of dualism, which 'weighs heavily like a nightmare on our brains' (Marx), be supplanted. Furthermore, we can read Kelsens theory, no longer primarily as a scientific theory of pure legal doctrine, but also as a practically oriented theory (and anticipation) of the global legal revolution of the twentieth century: that is, as a hopeful message, and as an attempt to change our worldview and our vocabulary in a way that is adapted to a praxis that emancipates us from ideological blindness, and helps us to rid ourselves of the old international law of 'sorry comforters' (Kant).[92]

After the mirror of nature, and the mirror of the true nature of the people, are broken, and, consequently, after *representation*, democratic institutions in general should be designed to enable the *expression* of political and individual self-determination in a great variety of different organs or legal bodies, such as parliaments, courts, governments, administrations, federal, inter-, trans- and supranational regimes, and also in different forms and procedures of egalitarian will-formation, including 'participatory', 'deliberative' 'representational' or 'direct' democracy, which can be combined with, or replaced by, one another. Even if Kelsen today sometimes is read as a strong defender of representational democracy and parliamentary supremacy (or at least priority), this reading is wrong. Like Dewey, Kelsen set out a strong and compelling criticism of the whole idea of representation, and he replaced it with the idea of a continuum of different *practical methods* to express political opinions and to make decisions that are egalitarian.[93] To avoid an obstinate misunderstanding, therefore: Radical criticism of *representational* democracy must not necessarily be critical of *parliamentary* democracy. Instead, it can also lead, first, to a re-interpretation of parliamentary democracy as one (possible)[94] *part* of a comprehensive (procedural) *method* of egalitarian will formation, deliberation and decision-making.[95] It can lead, second, to a relativization of parliamentary legislation. Parliaments can no longer be interpreted as the highest organs of the state, as the one and only true representative of the general will of the people, or as even the essential, higher or refined will of the better self of the people (the one that is better adapted to the ideas of intellectuals), or as the representation of the *Gemeinwohl* or commonwealth (whatever that is). Consequently, for pragmatic reasons parliaments may be the best method of democratic will formation in a given historical situation, but this depends on circumstance and is subject to change.

To conclude: The double criticism of dualism *and* representation has far-reaching implications for theories of democracy and constitutional design. These implications have a Kelsenian origin, but they extend far beyond Kelsen's partisanship with parliamentary democracy. The implications of this criticism are:

---

92 *Brunkhorst*, Dualismus des internationalen Rechts.
93 *Kelsen*, Vom Wesen und Wert der Demokratie; *Kelsen*, Allgemeine Staatslehre; *Kelsen*, Reine Rechtslehre.
94 Nothing is neccessary in a democratic legal regime except the normative idea of equal freedom: *Kant*, Metaphysik der Sitten, p. 345; *Maus*, Zur Aufklärung der Demokratietheorie; *Brunkhorst*, Solidarity, pp. 67-77; *Möllers*, Demokratie, pp. 13, 16.
95 *Kelsen*, Wesen und Wert.

(1) If on all levels of a continuum of concretization, legal norms are (politically) created, then the principle of democracy is only fulfilled if those who are affected by these norms are included in fair and equal manner

- on all levels of their creation – local, national, regional and global levels (albeit in what, in all probability, will be very different ways)

- in courts as well as in administrations and parliaments, in state organs and political associations as well as in the societal community, in cultural institutions and economic enterprises (the whole Parsonian AGIL-schema is thus open for democratization,[96] as long as it does not destroy either private or public autonomy).[97]

(2) The different (public and private) organs, forms and procedures of legislation, administration and jurisdiction are *all possess an equal distance to the people*, and no organ, and no procedure is left to represent the people as a whole: 'No branch of power is closer to the people than the other. All are in equal distance. It is meaningless to take one organ of democratic order and confront it as the *representative* organ to all others. There exists no democratic priority (or supremacy) of the legislative branch.'[98] Instead of any substantial sovereign, democracy only allows procedural sovereignty, which must express itself in '*subjektlosen Kommunikationskreisläufen*' (cycles of communication without a subject).[99]

(3) Whereas the concept of the (higher) *legitimacy* of a ruling substantial subject (the king or the state as '*Staatswillenssubjekt*')[100] is as fundamental for *power-limiting constitutionalism* as it was for medieval Christian, papal or later absolutist regimes with their guiding idea of the 'two bodies of the king'[101] – *democratic and power-founding constitutionalism* completely replaces *legitimacy* completely with a legally organized procedure of egalitarian and inclusive *legitimization*.[102] The procedures of legitimization no longer have any higher legitimacy. They are nothing other than products of democratic legislation, and legitimization is consequently circular – not inthe sense of a closed and vicious

---

96 *Möllers*, Staat als Argument, p. 423. Möllers argues that the dualistic distinction of Staat vs. Gesellschaft [that is, the state conceived in opposition to society] excludes democracy. This applies in particular to the order of the Grundgesetz [Basic Law]: 'Democracy is also possible beyond the state' because 'Article 20, Section 2, Clause 1 of the Basic Law treats the state that is committed to democracy as a determinable part of society' (424).
97 *Maus*, Aufklärung der Demokratietheorie; *Habermas*, Faktizität und Geltung.
98 *Möllers*, Expressive vs. repräsentative Demokratie.
99 *Habermas*, Faktizität und Geltung, pp. 170, 492.
100 *Brunkhorst*, Der lange Schatten des Staatswillenspositivismus.
101 *Kantorowicz*, The King's Two Bodies.
102 *Habermas*, Faktizität und Geltung; *Möllers*, Gewaltengliederung.

circle but in the sense of an open, socially inclusive hermeneutic circle or loop of *legitimization without legitimacy.*[103]

(4) Democracy is not, as the young Marx once wrote, the 'solved riddle of all constitutions'. Instead, as Susan Marks has objected, democracy is the 'unsolved riddle of all constitutions'[104] In consequence of this, a constitution that is democratic, has to keep the riddle open. It belongs to the *necessary meaning of specifically modern democracy* that the 'meaning' of 'democratic self-rule and equity' can never be 'reduced to any particular set of institutions and practices'.[105] Without the 'normative surplus'[106] of *democratic meaning* or the *meaning of democracy* which always already transcends any set of *legal procedures of democratic legitimization*, the people, or the 'subject' of democracy, would no longer be a self-determined group of citizens, or a self-determined group of all men,[107] who are affected by a given set of binding decisions. If they are not able to exhaust the meaning of democracy, and to experiment within an unlimited meaning-variance of keywords such as equality, equity, freedom, constitution, rights or rule of law, if we the people are not able to determine, discover, construct or disclose new meanings of democracy (input-legitimization), then there is no democracy. There is only a heteronomous people of – possibly happy – slaves (output-legitimization).

---

103 Democratic legitimization is inclusive because it governed by the one and only constitutional principle of democracy, and that is the principle of self-legislation or autonomy. This principle is socially inclusive because it presupposes that a procedure of legitimization that is democratic has to include everybody who is concerned by legislation and jurisdiction, therefore all exceptions (e. g. babies) have to be justified publicly and need compensation through human rights. See *Müller*, Wer ist das Volk?; *Brunkhorst*, Solidarity, Chap. 3; *Marks*, Riddle of all Constitutions.
104 *Marks*, Riddle of all Constitutions, p. 103.
105 *Marks*, Riddle of all Constitutions, pp. 103, 149.
106 *McCarthy*, Philosophy and Critical Theory, p. 21.
107 'All men' can mean a lot of things. It can, for example, mean all men in a bus, all men on German territory, all men with US passports (that is far less than all US citizens), all men on the globe, all men in the universe, all men who are French citizens, all men who are addressed by a certain legal norm. Democracy and democratic legitimization is only concerned with the last two meanings (and the possible tension between them).

Bibliography

Anghie, Antony, Imperialism, Sovereignty and the Making of International Law, Cambridge, Mass, 2004.

Arendt, Hannah, Elemente und Ursprünge totaler Herrschaft, Munich, 1991

Bast, Jürgen, Das Demokratiedefizit fragmentierter Internationalisierung, in Brunkhorst, Hauke (ed), Demokratie in der Weltgesellschaft, Soziale Welt Sonderheft, 2009.

Berman, Harold, Law and Revolution: The Formation of the Western Legal Tradition, Cambridge, Mass, 1984.

Berman, Harold, Law and Revolution II: The Impact of the Protestant Reformation on the Western Legal Tradition, Cambridge, Mass, 2006.

Bermann, Nathanial, Bosnien, Spanien und das Völkerrecht – Zwischen Allianz und Lokalisierung in Brunkhorst, Hauke (ed), Einmischung erwünscht? Menschenrechte und bewaffnete Intervention, Frankfurt, 1998, pp. 117-140.

v. Bernstorf, Jochen, Procedures of Decision-Making and the Role of Law in International Organizations' (draft paper)

v. Bernstorff, Jochen, Der Glaube an das universale Recht: Zur Völkerrechtstheorie Hans Kelsens und seiner Schüler, Baden-Baden, 2001.

v. Bernstorff, Jochen, Kelsen und das Völkerrecht, in Brunkhorst, Hauke and Voigt, Rüdiger (eds), Rechts-Staat, Baden-Baden, 2008.

v. Bogdandy, Arnim, Europäisches Verfassungsrecht, Berlin, 2003.

v. Bogdandy, Arnim, Constitutionalism in International Law, Harvard International Law Journal 47 (2006), pp. 223-242.

Bluntschli, Johann Caspar, Das moderne Völkerrecht der civilisierten Staaten, 3rd edition, Beck, 1878.

Brandom, Robert, Making It Explicit. Reasoning, Representing and Discursive Commitment, Cambridge, Mass, 1994.

Brandt, Reinhard, Das Erlaubnisgesetz, oder: Vernunft und Geschichte in Kants Rechtslehre, in Brandt, Reinhard (ed), Rechtsphilosophie der Aufklärung, Berlin, 1982.

Brunkhorst, Hauke, Dialectical Positivism of Happiness: Horkheimer's Materialist Deconstruction of Philosophy, in Benhabib, Seyla, Bonß, Wolfgang and McCole, John (eds), On Max Horkheimer. New Perspectives, Cambridge, Mass, 1993, pp. 67-99.

Brunkhorst, Hauke, Rorty, Putnam and the Frankfurt School, Philosophy and Social Criticism 22 (1996), 1-16

Brunkhorst, Hauke, Der lange Schatten des Staatswillenspositivismus, Leviathan 31 (2003), pp. 362-381.

Brunkhorst, Hauke, Solidarity. From Civic Friendship to a Global Legal Community, Cambridge, Mass, 2005, pp. 107-113.

Brunkhorst, Hauke, Globalising Democracy without a State: Weak Public, Strong Public, Global Constitutionalism, Millenium: Journal of International Studies 31 (2002), pp. 675-690.

Brunkhorst, Hauke, Solidarity: From Civic Fiendship to a Global Legal Community, translated by J. Flynn, Cambridge, MA, 2005.

Brunkhorst, Hauke, Demokratie in der globalen Rechtsgenossenschaft, Zeitschrift für Soziologie. Sonderheft (2005), pp. 330-348.

Brunkhorst, Hauke, Unbezähmbare Öffentlichkeit. Europa zwischen transnationaler Klassenherrschaft und egalitärer Konstitutionalisierung' (2007) 35 Leviathan, pp. 12-29.

Brunkhorst, Hauke, Globalizing Solidarity: The Destiny of Democratic Solidarity in the Times of Global Capitalism, Global Religion, and the Global Public, Journal of Social Philosophy 38 (2007), pp. 93-111.

Brunkhorst, Hauke, Die Globale Rechtsrevolution. Von der Evolution der Verfassungsrevolution zur Revolution der Verfassungsevolution?, in Christensen, Ralph and Pieroth, Bodo (eds), Rechtstheorie in rechtspraktischer Absicht, Berlin, 2008, pp. 9-34.

Brunkhorst, Hauke, Kritik am Dualismus des internationalen Rechts – Hans Kelsen und die Völkerrechtsrevolution des 20. Jahrhunderts' in Kreide, Regina and Niederberger, Andreas (eds), Verrechtlichung internationaler Politik. Ende oder Neubeginn der Demokratie?, Frankfurt am Main, 2008, pp. 90-114.

Brunkhorst, Hauke, Review of Nations Matter: Culture, History, and the Cosmopolitan Dream. By Craig Calhoun. London: Routledge, 2007, American Sociological Review 73 (2008), pp. 284-286.

Buckel, Sonja, Subjektivierung und Kohäsion. Zur Rekonstruktion einer materialistischen Theorie des Rechts, Weilerswist, 2007.

Byers, Michael, Woken up in Seattle, London Review of Books 22 (2000), pp. 16-17.

Byers, Michael, Preemptive Self-defense: Hegemony, Equality and Strategies of Legal Change, The Journal of Political Philosophy 11 (2003), pp. 171-190.

Calhoun, Craig, The Class Consciousness of Frequent Travelers: Toward a Critique of Actually existing Cosmopolitanism, The South Atlantic Quarterly 101 (2002), pp. 869-897.

Calhoun, Craig, "Belonging" in the Cosmopolitan Imaginary (2003) 3 Ethnicities 3 (2003), pp. 531-553.

Calhoun, Craig, Cosmopolitism and Belonging (Paper presented at the World Congress of the International Institute of Sociology, Stockholm 2005).

Calhoun, Craig, Nations Matter. Culture, History, and the Cosmopolitan Dream, London, 2007

Cameron, Iain, European Union Anti-Terrorist Blacklisting, Human Rights Law Review 2 (2003), pp. 225-256.

Canfora, Luciano, Der Bürger, in Vernant, Jean-Pierre (ed), Der Mensch der griechischen Antike, Frankfurt, 1993.

Conrad, Joseph, Heart of Darkness, New York, 2005.

Dann, Phillip, Looking through the federal lens: The Semi-parliamentary Democracy of the EU, Jean-Monnet working paper: www.jeanmonnetprogram.org/papers/02/020501.pdf.

Demandt, Alexander, Der ideale Staat, Cologne, 1993.

Dobner, Ptera, Did the state fail? Zur Transnationalisierung und Privatisierung der öffentlichen Daseinsvorsorge: Die Reform der globalen Trinkwasserpolitik (2006) at:

http://www.dvpw.de/dummy/fileadmin/docs/2006xDobner.pdf

Dobner, Petra, Konstitutionalismus als Politikform, Baden-Baden, 2002.

Dreier, Horst, Kanonistik und Konfessionalisierung. Marksteine auf dem Weg zum Staat, in Siebeck, Georg (ed), Artibus ingenius. Beiträge zu Theologie, Philosophie, Jurisprudenz, und Ökonomik, Tübingen, 2001, pp. 133-169.

Fassbender, Bardo, The United Nations Charter as Constitution of the International Community, Columbia Journal of Transnational Law 36 (1998), pp. 529-619.

Fine, Robert, Kant's theory of cosmopolitanism and Hegel's critique, Philosophy and Social Criticism 29 (2003), pp. 611-632.

Fine, Robert, Cosmopolitanism, London, 2007.

Finley, Moses I., Das politische Leben in der antiken Welt, Munich, 1991.

Fischer-Lescano, Andreas, Transnationales Verwaltungsecht, Juristen-Zeitung 63 (2008), pp. 373-383.

Fischer-Lescano, Andreas/Liste, Philip, Völkerrechtspolitik: Zur Trennung und Verknüpfung von Recht und. Politik in der Weltgesellschaft, Zeitschrift für Internationale Beziehungen 27 (2005), pp. 209-249.

Fischer-Lescano, Andreas/Teubner, Gunther, Regime-Kollisionen, Frankfurt am Main, 2005.

Flaig, Egon, Europa begann bei Salamis, Rechtshistorisches Journal 13 (1994), pp. 411-432.

Foucault, Michel, Der Gebrauch der Lüste. Sexualität und Wahrheit, vol 2, Frankfurt am Main, 1986.

Foucault, Michel, Überwachen und Strafen. Die Geburt des Gefängnisses, Frankfurt am Main, 1994.

Habermas, Jürgen, Technik und Wissenschaft als 'Ideologie', Frankfurt am Main, 1968.

Habermas, Jürgen, Legitimationsprobleme im Spätkapitalismus, Frankfurt am Main, 1973.

Habermas, Jürgen, Die Ideen von 1789, Frankfurt am Main, 1989.

Habermas, Jürgen, Faktizität und Geltung: Beiträge zur Diskurstheorie des Rechts und des demokratischen Rechtsstaats, Frankfurt am Main, 1992.

Habermas, Jürgen, Wahrheit und Rechtfertigung, Frankfurt am Main, 1997.

Hardt, Michael/Negri, Antonio, Empire, Cambridge, Mass, 2000.

Hegel, G. W. F., Grundlinien der Philosophie des Rechts, in Werke, edited by Moldenhauer, E. and Michel, K.M. in 20 vols. Frankfurt am Main, 1969), VII.

Höffe, Ottfried, Demokratie im Zeitalter der Globalisierung, Munich, 1999.

Höffe, Ottfried, Gerechtigkeit – Eine philosophische Einführung, Munich, 2001.

Hoffmann, Hasso, Repräsentation, fourth edition, with a new introduction, Berlin, 2003.

Hoss, Dietrich, Der institutionalisierte Klassenkampf, Frankfurt am Main, 1972.

Kant, Immanuel, Die Religion innerhalb der Grenzen der bloßen Vernunft in Werkausgabe, edited by Weischedel, Wilhelm, in 12 vols., Frankfurt am Main, 1976, VIII.

Kant, Immanuel, Grundlegung zur Metaphysik der Sitten in Werkausgabe, edited by Weischedel, Wilhelm, in 12 vols., Frankfurt am Main, 1976) VII.

Kant, Immanuel, Metaphysik der Sitten in Werkausgabe, edited by Weischedel, Wilhelm, in 12 vols., 1976, VIII.

Kant, Immanuel, Toward Perpetual Peace, in The Cambridge Edition of the Works of Immanuel Kant: Practical Philosophy, edited by Wood, Allen and Gregor, Mary, Cambridge, 1996, pp. 311-352

Kantorowicz, Ernst H., The King's Two Bodies, Princeton, 1957.

Kelsen, Hans, Das Problem der Souveränität und die Theorie des Völkerrechts, Tübingen, 1920.

Kelsen, Hans, Allgemeine Staatslehre, Berlin, 1925.

Kelsen, Hans, Vom Wesen und Wert der Demokratie, Tübingen, 1929.

Kelsen, Hans, Reine Rechtslehre, Vienna, 1934.

Kelsen, Hans, Demokratie und Sozialismus, Vienna, 1967.

Kingsbury, Benedict/Krisch, Nico/Steward, Richard B., The Emergence of Global Administrative Law: http://law.duke.edu/journals/lcp.

Koskenniemi, Martti, The Gentle Civilizer of Nations: The Rise and Fall of Internataionl Law, 1870-1960, Cambridge, 2001.

Langer, Claudia, Reform nach Prinzipien. Untersuchungen zur politischen Theorie. Immanuel Kants, Stuttgart, 1986.

Leisering, Lutz, Gibt es einen Weltwohlfahrtsstaat?, in Albert, Matthias and Stichweh, Rudolf (eds), Weltstaat und Weltstaatlichkeit, Wiesbaden, 2007, pp. 185-205.

Lübbe-Wolf, Gertrude, Die Internationalisierung der Politik und der Machtverlust der Parlamente', forthcoming in Brunkhorst, Hauke (ed), Demokratie in der Weltgesellschaft, Soziale Welt Sonderheft, 2009.

Lüdtke, Alf, Genesis und Durchsetzung des modernen Staates, Archiv für Sozialgeschichte 20 (1980), pp. 470-491.

Luhmann, Niklas, Legitimation durch Verfahren, Frankfurt am Main, 1983.

Luhmann, Niklas, Macht, Stuttgart, 1988.

Luhmann, Niklas, Verfassung als evolutionäre Errungenschaft, Rechtshistorisches Journal 9 (1990), pp. 176-220.

Mansfield, Harvey C., Modern and Medieval Representation, in Pennock, J. Roland and Chapman, John W. (eds), Representation, New York, 1968.

Marcuse, Herbert, On Science and Phenomenology, in Cohen, Robert S. and Wartofsky, Marx W. (eds), Boston Colloquium for the Philosophy of Science (1962-1964): Proceedings, Boston Studies in the Philosophy of Science, volume 2, New York, 1965, pp. 279-291.

Marcuse, Herbert, Repressive Toleranz, in Wolf, Robert Paul, Moore, Barrington and Marcuse, Herbert (eds), Kritik der reinen Toleranz, Frankfurt am Main, 1973.

Marks, Susan, The Riddle of all Constitutions, Oxford, 2000.

Marshall, T. H., Citizenship and Social Class, London, 1992.

Marx, Karl, Verhandlungen des 6. Rheinischen Landtags. Debatten über das Holzdiebstahlsgesetz in Marx, Karl/Engels, Friedrich, Werke, in 43 vols, Berlin, 1958-68, I: 109-147.

McCarthy, Thomas, Philosophy and Critical Theory, in Hoy, David C. and McCarthy, Thomas (eds), Critical Theory, Oxford, 1994.

Maus, Ingeborg, Zur Aufklärung der Demokratietheorie, Frankfurt am Main, 1992.

Merkl, Adolf, Allgemeines Verwaltungsrecht, Vienna/Berlin, 1927.

Merkl, Adolf, Prolegomena zu einer Theorie des rechtlichen Stufenbaus, in Klecatsky, Hans, Marcic, René and Schambeck, Herbert (eds), Die Wiener rechtstheoretische Schule, Vienna, 1968.

Meyer, John W., World Society and the Nation-State, American Journal of Sociology 103 (2005), pp. 144-181.

Meyer, John W., Weltkultur, Frankfurt am Main, 2005.

Mieville, China, Between Equal Rights: A Marxist Theory Of International Law, London, 2005.

Möllers, Christoph, Staat als Argument, Munich, 2001.

Möllers, Christoph, Gewaltengliederung, Tübingen, 2005.

Möllers, Christoph, Demokratie, Berlin, 2008.

Möllers, Christoph, Expressive vs. repräsentative Demokratie, in Kreide, Regina and Niederberger, Andreas (eds), Transnationale Verrechtlichung. Nationale Demokratien im Kontext globaler Politik, Frankfurt am Main, 2008.

Möllers, Christoph, Transnationale Behördenkooperation, Zeitschrift für ausländisches öffentliches Recht und Völkerrecht 65 (2005), pp. 351-389.

Möllers, Christoph, Voßkuhle, Andreas, and Walter, Christian (eds), Internationalisierung des Verwaltungsrechts, Tübingen, 2007.

Mouffe, Chantal, On the Political, London, 2005.

Müller, Friedrich, Wer ist das Volk? Eine Grundfrage der Demokratie, Elemente einer Verfassungstheorie, VI, Berlin, 1997.

Neves, Marcelo, Zwischen Themis und Leviathan, Baden-Baden, 2000.

Nussbaum, Martha, Kant and Cosmopolitanism, in Bohman, James and Lutz-Bachmann, Matthias (eds), Perpetual Peace: Essays on Kant's Cosmopolitan Ideal, Cambridge, Mass, 1997.

Oeter, Stefan, Prekäre Staatlichkeit und die Grenzen internationaler Verrechtlichung, in Kreide, Regina and Niederberger, Andreas (eds), Verrechtlichung internationaler Politik. Ende oder Neubeginn der Demokratie?, Frankfurt am Main, 2008, 90-114.

Parsons, Talcott, The System of Modern Societies, Englewood Cliffs, 1972.

Peters, Bernhard, Öffentlichkeit, Frankfurt am Main, 2008.

Polanyi, Karl, The Great Transformation: The Political and Economic Origins of our Time, New York, 1944.

Rawls, John, Political Liberalism, New York, 1993.

Reinhard, Wolfgang and Schilling, Heinz (eds), Die katholische Konfessionalisierung, Gütersloh, 1995.

Reinhard, Wolfgang, Geschichte der Staatsgewalt, Munich, 1999.

Rorty, Richard, Philosophy and the Mirror of Nature, Princeton, 1979.

Rosa, Hartmut, The universal underneath the multiple: Social acceleration as the key to understanding modernity, in Costa, Sergio, Domingues, J. Maurcio, Knöbel, Wolfgang, and da Silva, Josué (eds), The Plurality of Modernity: Decentering Sociology, Munich, 2006, pp. 22-42.

Sand, Inger-Johanne, Legitimacy in global and international law: A sociological critique, in this volume.

Schilling, Heinz, Die neue Zeit. Vom Christenheitseuropa zum Europa der Staaten 1250 bis 1750, Berlin, 1999.

Stichweh, Rudolf, Die Weltgesellschaft, Frankfurt, 2000.

Stolleis, Michael, Konfessionalisierung oder Säkularisierung bei der Entstehung des frühmodernen Staates, Ius Commune 20 (1993), pp. 1-24.

Stolleis, Michael, Historische und ideengeschichtliche Entwicklung des Gleichheitssatzes, in Wolfrum, Rüdiger (ed), Gleichheit und Nichtdiskriminierung im nationalen und internationalen Menschenrechtsschutz: Beiträge zum ausländischen öffentlichen Recht und Völkerrecht 165 (2003), pp. 7-22.

Stolleis, Michael, Diebstahl an sich selbst, Frankfurter Allgemeine Zeitung (24th May 2006).

Streek, Wolfgang, Sectoral Specialization: Politics and the Nation State in a Global Economy, Paper presented at the 37th World Congress of the International Institute of Sociology, Stockholm 2005.

Streeten, Paul, Globalisation – Threat or Opportunity?, Copenhagen, 2001.

Sunstein, Cass, After the Rights Revolution, Cambridge, Mass, 1993.

Teubner, Gunther, Globale Zivilverfassungen, Zeitschrift für ausländisches öffentliches Recht und Völkerrecht 63 (2003), pp. 1-28.

Tietje, Christian, Die Staatsrechtslehre und die Veränderung ihres Gegenstandes Deutsches Verwaltungsblatt 17 (2003), pp. 1081-1164.

Veyne, Paul (ed), History of Private Life: From Pagan Rome to Byzantium, Cambridge, Mass, 1992).

Veyne, Paul, The Roman Empire, in Veyne, Paul (ed), History of Private Life: From Pagan Rome to Byzantium, Cambridge, Mass, 1992.

Warbrick, Colin, The European Response to Terrorism in an Age of Human Rights' (2004) 15 European Journal of International Law 15(5) (2004), pp. 989-1018

Weber, Max, Gesammelte Aufsätze zur Religionssoziologie, in 3 vols., Tübingen, 1978, II.

Wesel, Uwe, Geschichte des Rechts, Munich, 1997.

Witte, John, Law and Protestantism: The Legal Teachings of the Lutheran Reformation, Cambridge, 2002.

Wolf, Klaus-Dieter, Die neue Staatsräson – Zwischenstaatliche Kooperation als Demokratieproblem der Weltgesellschaft, Baden-Baden, 2000.

Political argument and the legitimacy of international law: A case of distorted modernisation

Robert Fine

Introduction

The springboard for this paper is the observation that the terminology of international law, and especially the terminology of international humanitarian and human rights law, has assumed a radically enhanced role in public deliberation and political argument. The tendency to treat humanitarian and human rights legal norms as a standard against which to measure the legitimacy of acts of state has become increasingly marked. This phenomenon, if correctly observed, raises a number of intriguing sociological issues around the origins, meaning and desirability of this development.

I shall argue that there are good reasons to support the enlarged scope of international law in public life. These have to do with the need for a higher law to inhibit the otherwise overweening power of states to exercise coercive violence; to protect the rights and welfare of minorities, non-nationals and other vulnerable groups within nation states; to prevent aggressive wars, colonial conquests, occupations and inhuman methods of warfare; to compensate for the deficits of exclusively national forms of governmental decision-making; to generalise norms of democratic legitimacy; and not least to remove the 'halo effect' that once endowed heads of state with a sense of their own impunity.[1]

My more qualified contention, however, is that the current tendency to construe international law as an ideal synthesis creates as many problems as it solves and should be resisted. A tendency toward idealisation is evident in a jurisprudence which treats the 'constitutionalisation of international law' as the marker of the transformation of law from an instrument of power into the crucible in which all power relations are dissolved; in a legal history which defines the transition from classical international law to contemporary cosmopolitan law as one in which *realpolitik* and state sovereignty finally give way to the authority of human rights and international law itself; and in a political theory which imagines a world order in which the role of political judgment is replaced by procedures of a wholly legalised international order still to come. My own intuition is that the answer to the distortion of political argument by power is not to be sought in the creation of a wholly legalised international order-to-come but in the enhancement of political argument. To

---

1   The phrase 'halo effect' is drawn from *Jaspers*, The Question of German Guilt.

use Durkheimian terminology, I shall argue that certain social pathologies are associated with the idealisation of international law and I shall focus on the construction of outlaw states and peoples. Working through John Rawls's *Law of Peoples*, I maintain that the tendency to idealise international law is related to the propensity to criminalise not just individuals and states but whole peoples. While it has been widely argued that the concept of 'outlaw' states introduces a hierarchical outlook into international law, the concern I explore is that the slippage from condemning a *state* for human rights abuses to condemning a *people* as unworthy of recognition within the Society of Peoples is internal to Rawls's conception of the Law of Peoples and introduces a potentially damaging logic of stigma. If the legitimacy of international law lies in its capacity to humanise political conflicts, so that even the perpetrator of crimes against humanity or genocide is treated as a responsible and rational human being, then it is imperative that we should resist the temptation to label those who commit such crimes as inhuman monsters, that is, to dehumanize the dehumanisers. Those who commit crimes of this nature typically dehumanize the people against whom their crimes are committed. The legitimacy of international law suffers to the extent that it is put into the service of reproducing the cycles of demonisation that preceded it.

In conclusion I raise the question of what my analysis of the legitimacy problems of international law suggests for the development of a politics of human rights. I maintain that the interpretation and application of human rights and humanitarian norms take place on a contested terrain where rival political interests and claims are argued out. Human rights and humanitarian norms are not and cannot become definitive of politics; rather they stand in need of a politics able to resist the 'Schmittian' temptation to use international law as a means by which the ancient practice of demonising others can once again be institutionalised in an apparently universalistic and legal guise. I suggest that the best chance of developing such a politics lies in recognising that the enhanced scope of international law does not provide the content for an abstract cosmopolitan ideal against which to measure the actual world, but rather represents the necessary legal form of contemporary capitalist society and its global reach. International law offers a major resource for combating illegitimate power but it is relative to other norms and always contains the possibility of conflict between what it is and what it ought to be.

International law and the legitimacy of state action

The starting point of this paper, then, is the observation that whether a particular act on the part of a state or group of states or non-state actors is deemed in accordance with or in violation of international law, is now regularly advanced as a basis for deciding on the legitimacy of the act in question or in some cases of the actor itself. Appeal is regularly made not only to international legal norms but also to the general *values* and *principles* of international law to defend or reject the legitimacy of a state action, even if these values and principles require the reform of actually existing international laws for their realisation. The claim that an act of state accords with or violates international law is rarely tested in court, but the opinions of international lawyers, political theorists and political actors are regularly invoked. In major international conflicts (for example, genocide in Cambodia and Rwanda, the first Gulf War, the NATO intervention in Kosovo, the US-UK invasion of Iraq, the US occupation of Afghanistan, the US detention of 'unlawful enemy combatants' in Guantanamo, and Israel's invasions of Lebanon and Gaza) it is a common rhetoric to appeal to some notion of international law or to some notions within international law to authorise a particular political argument. Labels drawn from the lexicon of international criminal law (crimes of aggression, war crimes, crimes against humanity, genocide, torture) or from the Geneva Conventions ('disproportionate response' and 'collective punishment') are now employed to depict perpetrators, not just as morally wrong or politically imprudent, but as offenders against international law. Judgments of this sort may be based on legal definition of the offences in question but also on common usage, which may substantially differ in form and content from legal definitions. There are cases of military action of which we may morally or politically disapprove, not least for the hardship they impose on civilians, but which may not be criminal according to existing norms of international law. We cannot assume that international law is necessarily on the side of what we consider right.[2]

Public engagement with international law on this scale appears to be a fairly recent phenomenon. International lawyers, political actors and academic observers have maintained that international law became the stuff of public debate mainly since 1989 and that its present public status contrasts with its relative invisibility in the post-1945 period when international law was widely regarded as ineffective or narrowly technocratic in its concerns and citizens were inclined to rely either on the resources of domestic legal systems or on their own moral and political judgments unmediated by law.[3]

---

2   This tendency is illustrated in debates in *The Guardian* over the legality as well as legitimacy of the Israeli invasion of Gaza in January 2009. One letter to the Guardian runs as follows: 'As international lawyers, we remind the UK government that it has a duty under international law to exert its influence to stop violations of international humanitarian law in the current conflict between Israel and Hamas. A fundamental principle of international humanitarian law is that the parties to a conflict must distinguish between civilians and those who participate directly in hostilities' (14/01/09). This even-handed approach to the crucial distinction between civilians and combatants was matched by numerous attempts to place this aspect of international law on one side or the other of the conflict. Thus the British Committee for the Universities of Palestine wrote in their Declaration of 'Gaza's Guernica': 'We say enough is enough. As long as the state of Israel continues to defy humanity and international law, we, the citizens of the world, commit ourselves to boycotting Israel' (28/12/08). On the other side, in response to the UNHCR Report on Gaza Robbie Sabel argued that 'Hamas knowingly and deliberately targeted civilians and civilian targets in Israel and based itself in civilian areas' whilst there was no evidence that the phosphorous shells Israel used in civilian areas had been used 'in an illegal way' (7/05/09).

3   Hamid Ansari, Vice-President of India, inaugurating the International Conference on International Law in the Contemporary World organized by the Indian Society of International Law (ISIL), commented that the last three decades have witnessed the metamorphosis of interna-

In the field of legal theory the authority of international law in determining the legitimacy of state action is invoked from a surprising number of perspectives – even from within the field of critical legal studies which is not renowned for upholding any positive law as a standard against which to measure the legitimacy of political action. The elevation of international law, in whole or in part, into a standard for determining the legitimacy of state actions may be not as new as it appears, but my argument is that today the idea of international humanitarian and human rights law performs functions not unlike those performed in the past by the idea of a universal law of nature: it serves as the measure against which the positive actions of nation states can be critically assessed and as a trump card for concluding political argument.

Justifying the expanded scope of international law

The Marxist international lawyer, Bill Bowring, makes a totally compelling case for 'the blatantly unlawful behaviour of the US and UK in the invasion and occupation of Iraq'. He situates the invasion and occupation of Iraq in relation to the normative decline of international law since the halcyon days of the period of decolonisation when its focus was on the 'firm establishment of the right of peoples to self-determination'.[4] In nostalgic mode Bowring describes the right of nations to self-determination as the 'revolutionary kernel of international law' and follows Alasdair MacIntyre in presenting the development of human rights as a regrettable displacement of the supremacy of the right of self-determination.[5] This perspective is rooted in the normative requirements of decolonisation movements but does not address the normative dysfunctions of the right of nations to self-determination that gave rise to the expansion of human rights and humanitarian law in the first place.[6] Good rea-

---

tional law from a tool for the regulation of formal diplomacy between states and coordination of international intercourse to an elaborate canvas covering complex areas of transnational concerns such as trade, economy and development, nuclear energy, outer space, human rights and environment. He opined that the problems created by the dramatic expansion of the scope and instrumentalities of international law should not blind us to the significant success achieved in ameliorating the welfare of mankind. He maintained that international human rights and humanitarian law have 'expanded their scope and application to become one of the most comprehensively regulated branches of international law' and that this is in the final analysis 'for the good of humanity': http://indiaedunews.net/Law/VicePresident_inaugurates_ Conference_on_International_Law_7337/print.asp.

4 See the introduction to *Bowring*, The Degradation of the International Legal Order. Antony Anghie emphasises the enduring imperial character of the discipline of international law in *Anghie*, Imperialism, Sovereignty and the Making of International Law.

5 Alasdair MacIntyre characterises human rights as 'the idiom alike of the good, the bad and the ugly' in *MacIntyre*, Community, law and the idiom and rhetoric of rights, p. 7.

6 Hannah Arendt comments that 'at precisely the moment when the right to national self-determination was recognised for all of Europe and when its essential conviction, the supremacy of the will of the nation over all legal and "abstract" institutions was universally accepted'. It indicated 'the transformation of the state from an instrument of the law into an in-

sons have been advanced to support the enlarged scope of international law beyond, though not in place of, the right of nations to self-determination.⁷

What has changed? Today, international law not only claims a 'soft' influence over states to take human rights into account but in some instances demands compliance and declares a duty to obey. The norms of international law increasingly function as a higher law vis-à-vis that of states and there is an increasing number of treaty-based norms that obligate all states whether or not they have signed the treaty in question. These include prohibitions on torture, genocide, crimes against humanity, disappearances and the like. The dependence of international law on state consent has declined, as has the state's degree of freedom in interpreting and enforcing international law. The involvement of the UN not only in conflicts *between* states but also in conflicts *within* states affords international law a pivotal role in responding to events such as civil wars, the breakdown of government, major human rights abuses and in some cases the promotion of democracy. Non-state or quasi-state actors (such as international courts and tribunals as well as transnational executives, non-governmental organisations as well as multi-national companies) have emerged as major players in international legal processes. International lawyers are now heard to say that the subject matter of international law has expanded to such an extent that there is no clear nucleus of sovereignty states can invoke against it.⁸

The case for the expanded role of international law may be historically grounded, Jürgen Habermas does, in 'the monstrous mass crimes of the twentieth century' as a result of which 'states as the subjects of international law forfeited the presumption of innocence that underlies the prohibition on intervention and immunity against criminal prosecution under international law'. ⁹ The principles of equal sovereignty, human rights and the authority of international law itself are defended on the grounds that, even if different emphases and interpretations are given to these prin-

---

strument of the nation'. Henceforth, she writes, 'only nationals could be citizens, only people of the same national origin could enjoy the full protection of legal institutions'. See *Arendt*, Origins of Totalitarianism, p. 275. See also the critique of the right of nations to self-determination in *Kedourie*, Nationalism.

7   Hannah Arendt comments: 'We became aware of the existence of a right to have rights [...] only when millions of people emerged who had lost and could not regain these rights because of the new global situation. [...] This calamity arose not from any lack of civilization [...] but on the contrary [...] because there was no longer any "uncivilised" spot on earth, because whether we like it or not we have really started to live in One World', in *Arendt*, Origins of Totalitarianism, pp. 296-7.

8   The relativisation of sovereignty in international law is reflected in the recent sociological literature on cosmopolitanism. For example, Daniel Levy and Natan Sznaider write that 'an increasingly de-nationalized conception of legitimacy is contributing to a reconfiguration of sovereignty itself'. They suggest that whilst 'states retain most of their sovereign functions, their legitimacy is no longer exclusively conditioned by a contract with the nation, but also by their adherence to a set of nation-transcending human rights ideals'. This becomes consequential for states as 'adherence to global human rights norms confers legitimacy': *Levy/Sznaider*, Sovereignty transformed.

9   *Habermas*, The Constitutionalization of International Law and the Legitimation Problems of a Constitution for World Society, p. 444.

ciples, they enable co-operation and trust between nations, foster civil and welfare rights of citizens and non-citizens alike, protect minorities, curtail the abuse of power by states and ensure freedom from domination by other states.[10] They can generalise norms of democratic legitimacy and compensate for the structural deficits of national processes of decision-making when they lead to outcomes (like water shortages or pollution) that are unacceptable from a more regional or global point of view. They can provide principles on which to appeal against oppressive actions of the state even in the absence of or in opposition to the positive laws of the international community.

There are good reasons to think that the expanded scope of international law is not merely a facade or empty utopia notwithstanding the neglect of or contempt for international law sometimes shown by big and small powers alike. The non-participation or non-compliance of big powers is well known, witness the reluctance of the US government (most marked under George W Bush) to sign up to international treaties, such as those on torture, global warming and the international criminal court. However, the relation of big powers to international law has not generally been one of unilateralism alone but rather one of ambivalence between commitment to international law on the one hand (which may be more or less verbal) and isolationism, unilateral action, indifference and cynicism on the other. In the past the US played a major role in important developments of international law: the formation of the League of Nations, the Kellogg-Briand Pact (proscribing wars of aggression), the establishment of the Nuremberg Tribunal, the formation of the UN, the Declaration of Human Rights, etc. Today the election of Obama might be understood as pronouncing the long-term rational interests the US has in binding emerging major powers (like China, Russia, Brazil and India) to the rules of a politically constituted international community.[11]

Powerful states have their own interests in supporting international law. These are for reasons to do with regulation (it sets rules), pacification (it reduces resistance), stabilisation (it preserves the current order) and legitimation (it justifies power). To be sure, powerful states also encounter restraints on the exercise of their power imposed by international law. The norms of international law restrict their freedom of action, prevent the rapid reshaping of international norms, and make it difficult for big powers to apply rules only to others and not to themselves. Powerful states can respond to these restraints with a multiplicity of strategies: they may try to manipulate international law to suit their own interests; they may try to reshape the concepts

---

10 For the role played by the appeal to human rights in defending the welfare rights of asylum seekers see *Morris*, An emergent cosmopolitan paradigm?.
11 During this presidential election, in an interview given to the American Society of International Law, Barack Obama articulated his view on the role of international law in foreign policy and contrasted it with that of President Bush: 'Promoting strong international norms helps us advance many interests, including non-proliferation, free and fair trade, a clean environment, and protecting our troops in wartime. Respect for international legal norms also plays a vital role in fighting terrorism. Because the [Bush] administration cast aside international norms that reflect American values, such as the Geneva Conventions, we are less able to promote those values abroad'.

and rules of international law to exempt themselves from its provisions or carve out space for the pursuit of their own interests; they may create zones of exclusion where the norms of international law have no purchase (as in Guantanamo Bay); they may substitute domestic law over which they retain more complete control for the less certain authority of international law; or they may withdraw altogether from international law and simply bring military superiority to bear. All these strategies involve trade-offs but they point to the equivocations of power in relation to international law, not to a simple opposition.[12]

From the other side of the state-civil society divide, it has been argued that international law suffers from a deficit of democratic legitimacy and that the expanded role of international law simply aggravates this deficit. One response to this lack of democratic legitimacy is to appeal to the liberal tradition of natural right theory (from Locke to Dworkin and Rawls) that draws its resources from the natural order of things and conceives of human rights largely as an external barrier imposed on the sovereign legislator. While this liberal conception of international law cannot satisfy the principle of the co-originality of rights and democracy that we may wish to defend, Jürgen Habermas points out that we do not have to sever international law altogether from channels of democratic legitimation institutionalised within the nation state and to a lesser degree within transnational federations. The normative substance of international law rest on rights, legal principles and criminal codes tried and tested within democratic constitutions and the application and enforcement of international laws receive indirect backing from democratic processes instituted within nation states. Public interest groups in global civil society can confer a supplementary level of democratic legitimacy on human rights, even if their influence does not translate directly into political power.[13] Whilst international law does not and arguably cannot satisfy the standards of democratic legitimation that underwrite national law making and enforcement, some defensible reasons may be given for this – for example, that international law performs limited and generally supplementary functions compared with those performed by nation states and therefore does not need the same level of democratic legitimacy.[14] The argument that international law is invalidated by its lack of democratic legitimacy may be no less one sided than the argument that the legitimacy of international law can be exclusively based on the substantive ground of its protection of human rights. It neglects the role that international human rights and humanitarian law can play in initiating or securing democracy at the national level.[15]

---

12 I am indebted here to *Kumm*, The legitimacy of international law.
13 Seyla Benhabib looks to the human rights activism of civil society organisations to underwrite the democratic normativity of international law and applies the concept of 'democratic iterations' in this context. She explores, for instance, women's rights movements in predominantly Moslem countries and their struggles for women's equality: *Benhabib*, Another Cosmopolitanism. See also Stammers, Social movements and the social construction of human rights; and *Morris*, Welfare, asylum and civil society.
14 Jürgen Habermas argues along these lines in *Habermas*, The Divided West, pp. 139-143.
15 Hauke Brunkhorst offers a critical view of the legitimacy problems caused by the democratic deficit in human rights: 'While human rights are becoming stronger, democracy is becoming

One of the problems confronting the enhanced role of international law is that different parties tend to pick and choose those aspects of international law which in some way favour their interests. Imperialists may be well disposed to those bits of international law which outlaw terrorism but not the bits which relate to the mistreatment of prisoners of war. Anti-imperialists may be better disposed to the bits of international law that uphold a right of resistance against occupation but less keen on international law's injunctions against harming civilians. Both parties may be disdainful of actually existing international law on the grounds that it is controlled by their opponents but still use the rhetoric of international law to accuse the other of hypocrisy as well as of violating international law itself. From both points of view it can appear that it is not just because the other party commits worse crimes that it deserves to be prosecuted but also because it is the biggest hypocrite – appealing to international law in theory but disregarding it in practice.[16] The predisposition toward selectivity may cast doubt on the legitimacy of expanding the scope of international law. The argument, for example, that international criminal courts are selective in whom they choose to prosecute for war crimes, a selectivity based not on the nature of the crimes that have been committed or on the harm they have caused but on who the accused are and whether they are deemed allies or enemies of those who authorise the court, raises thorny problems that can serve to devalue the legitimacy of international criminal law.[17] Once again, the selectivity issue does not invalidate the expanded role of international law, even if the legitimacy problems that flow from it cannot be wished away. It is no more convincing an argument that one war criminal should not be prosecuted because another equally heinous war criminal has not been prosecuted than it would be in relation to speeding offences.

The appeal to international humanitarian and human rights law as an authoritative ground of political argument reflects the expanding scope of international law in general. The normatively equivocal development offers an essential response to escalating dangers that were inherent in the structure of the nation state from its beginning and came to the fore with the advent of imperialism and post-imperial nationalisms. At the end of a century which has known unprecedented levels of organised terror and mass misery alongside the equally unprecedented development of material wealth and democratic forms, I would say that the expanded role of international law in society meets urgent humanising requirements.

---

weaker. Each and every person everywhere has rights [...] but at the same time the political right of citizens to the legislative, parliamentary elaboration of these rights [...] is declining [...]. The weak public sphere [...] has to leave the creation, modification, elaboration and implementation of these rights to the springing up of many different sources of law and are not (sufficiently) democratically legitimate': *Brunkhorst*, Solidarity, pp. 149-150.

16 I am indebted to David Hirsh for this observation. See *Hirsh*, Law against Genocide: Cosmopolitan Trials, pp. 151-160.
17 The issue is investigated in more depth and with a different conclusion in the work of David Chandler. See for instance: *Chandler*, International justice, in Archibugi (ed) Debating Cosmopolitics, pp. 27-39.

The idealising of international law

My more critical argument is targeted at the tendency to rationalise cosmopolitan law – by which I refer to the human rights and humanitarian aspects of international law – as an ideal synthesis of all prior conflicts. I maintained in the introduction that a tendency toward idealisation is to be found in a jurisprudence that treats the 'constitutionalisation of international law' as the marker of the transformation of law from an instrument of power into the 'crucible in which power is dissolved'; in a historiography which treats the transition from 'classical international law' to 'cosmopolitan law' as a transition from *realpolitik* and state sovereignty to human rights and the authority of international law itself; and in a political philosophy which imagines a utopian world order in which the role of political judgment is displaced in the idea of a wholly legalised international order to come.[18]

Jürgen Habermas represents the constitutionalisation of international law as an alternative to both realist and ethical conceptions of the primacy of power over law: the former rooted in the *realpolitik* of 'classical' international relations, the latter in the projected benevolence of imperial domination. Habermas sees the constitutionalisation of international law as a resource for confronting the power both of nation states and of the nation state writ large as the world state. For Habermas the constitutionalisation of international law is sometimes presented not just as a marker of legal and social change but of the transubstantiation of law from instrument of power to the crucible of its dissolution: 'constitutionalisation reverses the initial situation in which law serves as an instrument of power'.[19] The historical narrative Habermas constructs is that within the framework of the nation state law was at first a means by which power was organised. Then with the advent of constitutional government a reversal was effected when power began to serve as the instrument of law, but this reversal was limited by the fact that the universal principles of the constitution and the power of the state were fused in one and the same institution. At the international level, however, where legitimate authority is no longer based on the formation of a world state but on the universal principles of the constitution itself, the effect of constitutionalisation is a legal order in which the supremacy of law over power can finally be actualised. According to this narrative the constitutionalisation of international law suggests nothing less than the inversion of the primacy of power over law into the primacy of law over power.[20] This metamorphosis of law lies in tension with

---

18 See *Rosas*, State sovereignty and human rights; Teubner, Societal constitutionalism; Kumm, The Legitimacy of International Law: A Constitutionalist Framework of Analysis; *Goldstein/Kahler/Keohane/Slaughter*, Introduction: Legalization and World Politics; *Schilling*, On the Constitutionalization of General International Law. See also my own discussion in *Fine*, Cosmopolitanism, pp. 59-77.
19 *Habermas*, Divided West, pp. 130-132 and 149.
20 As Carl Schmitt put it, classical international law was not a 'lawless chaos of egoistic wills to power […] egoistic power structures existed side-by-side in the same space of one European order, wherein they mutually recognised each other as sovereigns. Each was the equal of the other, because each constituted a moment of the system of equilibrium': *Schmitt*, The Nomos

Habermas' own sociological writings where he emphasises that the problems and tasks we inherit today are symmetrical to the challenges our predecessors faced in the past. [21]

Jean Cohen has persuasively argued that the idea that international law *already* has a constitution, either written in the UN Charter or unwritten, to which the power of states has already been reduced to the status of servant, is vulnerable to the charge that it dresses up the strategic power-plays of strong states in the universalistic rhetoric of law and human rights.[22] However, the idea of a constitutionalised international order-to-come also has its problems. It attributes current abuses of international law to the incompleteness of the transition from the old order of nation states and to the restricted reach of existing global remedies: the International Court of Justice lacks compulsory jurisdiction; the International Criminal Court lacks adequate definition of war crimes; the Security Council is in urgent need of reform; the UN does not yet have its own army or juridical mechanisms for deciding when to use it. We are led to believe that if and when these restrictions are overcome, law will finally emancipate itself from the control of power. But how much credibility can we grant to this juridical narrative?

Consider the contentious case of humanitarian military intervention. It is evident that moral and political judgements have in the past played a pivotal role in its justification and authorisation.[23] However, if we declare that moral and political judgments are necessary only because the constitutionalisation of international law is not yet complete, then they must appear as a stop-gap measure to be surpassed when the constitutionalisation of international law is complete.[24] The move to situate humanitarian military intervention strictly within the framework of international law stems from a justified desire to put an end to merely moral justifications of the use of force and confront the danger that human rights rhetoric provides a justification for military aggression or imperial conquest. [25] It promises to overcome the ambivalences caused by having to choose between, say, endorsing *illegal* action by a coalition of states designed to protect people from serious violation of their human rights or adhering to an international legal framework incapable of offering an effective regime of rights enforcement. It does so by transferring responsibility for difficult judgments from the sphere of political deliberation to the legal system.[26] A court of law is to have the authority to make binding decisions on issues of intervention; perpetrators are to be prosecuted for criminal acts; a UN army is to be organised as an effective intervening force. The spectre of a new figure of universal sovereignty, international law with a fighting force at its disposal, haunts this cosmopolitan out-

of the Earth in the International Law of the Jus Publicum Europaeum, p. 167. See also *Scheuerman*, Carl Schmitt: The End of Law, esp. chapter 6.
21 See *Johnson*, Globalising democracy: reflections on Habermas's radicalism.
22 *Cohen*, Whose Sovereignty?, p. 10.
23 *Krisch*, Legality, morality and the dilemma of humanitarian interventions after Kosovo.
24 *Smith*, Anticipating a cosmopolitan future: the case of humanitarian military intervention.
25 *Fine/Smith*, Cosmopolitanism and humanitarian military intervention.
26 See the case for an international court to make such decisions put forward in *Archibugi*, Cosmopolitan Guidelines for Humanitarian Intervention.

look. In answer to the question posed by Jacques Derrida, whether it represents poison or remedy or both, it would be an interesting thought-experiment to imagine what the constitutionalisation of international law might actually look like in this sphere of operations.[27] Would the same rulers now in power go to war against atrocity-committing regimes because judges say they should? Would the 'responsibility to protect' focus exclusively on military intervention or would it also include support for civil rights movements, free trade unions, women's equality movements and democratic political parties in atrocity-committing regimes? Would it grant rights of asylum for those fleeing from atrocity-committing regimes? Would military action against atrocity-committing regimes be conceived exclusively in terms of exogenous state intervention or would it include support for endogenous liberation forces seeking to overthrow a genocidal regime – as was the case in Rwanda where genocide was brought to an end not by the international community but by the Rwanda Patriotic Front and Rwanda Patriotic Army?

I wonder whether the constitutionalisation of international law cannot to my mind do the work demanded of it. An alternative perspective might look for an answer to the distortion of political argument not in the creation of a wholly legalised international order but in the nurturing of less distorted forms of political argument. Rather than treat international law as the ultimate authority capable of transcending political power, we should come to terms with the fact that we live in a world without transcendent authority in which all standard of behaviour are questionable. Whilst in the past belief in transcendent authority relied on religious trust in a sacred beginning or on unquestioned standards of behaviour, my 'Arendtian' contention is that in our world international law should not be elevated into a reconstituted form of transcendent authority but be treated in a strictly secular fashion as a material resource 'we' have to hand in confronting anew the problems of living together and indeed in constituting ourselves as a collectivity in the first place.[28]

International law and pariah peoples

Let me now turn to what I call, following Durkheim, the social pathologies that derive from the idealisation of international law. I can illustrate the problem I wish to highlight by reference to the *Law of Peoples* advanced by John Rawls. The principles Rawls outlines for the *Law of Peoples* are for the most part philosophical reformulations of well-established principles of international law. They emphasise the

---

27 Derrida, Philosophy in a Time of Terror, pp. 123-133.
28 That my contention is 'Arendtian' may be illustrated through the following quotation: 'History and nature have become equally alien to us […]. [By contrast] humanity, which for the 18th century in Kantian terminology was no more than a regulative idea, has today become an inescapable fact. This new situation, in which "humanity" has in effect assumed the role formerly ascribed to nature or history, would mean in this context that the right to have rights, or the right of every individual to belong to humanity, should be guaranteed by humanity itself. It is by no means certain whether this is possible': *Arendt*, Origins of Totalitarianism, p. 297.

self-determination of peoples, respect for treaties and other agreements between peoples, non-intervention in the internal affairs of other peoples, and norms regulating the conduct of war between peoples. In line with more recent developments in international law they also advance more interventionist themes: peoples are bound to honour human rights, the principle of non-intervention may be suspended in the case of major human rights abuses, and the authority of international organisations such as the United Nations must be upheld.

Rawls maintains that those Peoples who acknowledge and uphold human rights should be recognised as equal members of a Society of Peoples. He has a liberal view of membership in the sense that he includes within the Society of Peoples *non-liberal* regimes insofar as they are 'reasonable' or 'decent', that is, insofar as they do not have aggressive international aims, respect some basic human rights, have some idea of consulting their citizens, and to some extent acknowledge the authority of the Law of Peoples itself. However, Rawls excludes 'outlaw states' from the Society of Peoples, that is, those states which fail to meet these minimum standards. Outlaw states lies at the bottom of a threefold hierarchy of states Rawls sets up: liberal, decent and outlaw. It is characteristic of Rawls to say little about the institutional dynamics of classification and exclusion. How serious would a rights-violation have to be to exclude a state from the Society of Peoples? Which international body has the authority to determine exclusion and on what basis? Rawls' ideal theory is designed to clarify the goals of reform and identify the wrongs that are most urgent to correct, but the politics of labelling outlaw states remains outside his purview.[29]

The concept of 'outlaw states' has been accused of introducing a 'fundamentalist' outlook into international law. For example, Nico Krish argues that since the mid-1980s the US has developed a category of outlaw states under varying titles – 'terrorist states', 'state sponsors of terrorism', 'rogue states', 'states of concern', 'axis of evil' and even 'the evil ones'.[30] He maintains that those states labelled 'outlaw states' have been treated as second-class states which no longer enjoy the full protection of international law. He also maintains that individual members of 'outlaw states' have been stripped of some of the rights they would otherwise enjoy under human rights and humanitarian law – for instance, through their designation as 'unlawful combatants'. The further issue I want to raise stems from Rawls's preference for the category of 'peoples' over that of 'states'. This move is designed to break from the assumption said to underpin classical international law that allows for unrestricted state sovereignty in the pursuit of national interests. The concept of Peoples, Rawls argues, emphasises membership of a legal order in which sovereignty is mediated through law and can never be conceived as absolute.

This choice of terminology, however, has its downside inasmuch as the concept of a 'people' collapses a vital distinction within political thought – that between the state and the people over whom the state rules. Rawls would doubtless agree that to

---

29 Although I do not share the author's conclusions, the difficulties of labelling are well rehearsed in *Mandani*, Saviors and Survivors: Darfur, Politics and the War on Terror. This discussion is picked up in *Carter/Virdee*, Racism and the sociological imagination.
30 *Krisch*, Imperial international law.

exclude a *people* from the *Society of Peoples* on the grounds that their *state* fails to observe basic human rights is an open door to injustice – whether or not the majority of the people support the state in question. The slippage from condemning a *state* for human rights abuses (whether against its own people or other people) to condemning a *people* as unworthy of recognition within the Society of Peoples introduces a dangerous principle into the idea of international law. In Rawls himself, there is a tension between on the one hand his notion of 'outlaw states' and on the other his preference for the concept of 'peoples' over that of 'states'. In everyday political argument this confusion can be especially damaging if a 'people' is condemned and excluded from the society of peoples on account of acts committed by the state which rules the people in question. It is damaging because it threatens to pathologise a 'people' because of the actions of the state that acts in their name.

If one of the functions of international law is to humanise human conflicts and this is one of the sources of its legitimacy, then even individual perpetrators of war crimes, crimes against humanity, genocide and so on must be treated as responsible and rational human beings. [31] The aim of international criminal or humanitarian law is not to demonise perpetrators in the same way as perpetrators typically demonise those against whom they commit their crimes. It is rather to break such old cycles of hatred. If perpetrators are prone to dehumanize their victims, the legitimacy of international human rights and humanitarian law rests on its ability not to repeat these cycles of hatred but on the contrary to reveal the humanity even of those individuals who played their part in the collective endeavor to destroy the idea of humanity. However, the demonisation even of individuals, that is, the willingness to treat them as inhuman monsters, is a potential internal to international law.[32] Some critical lawyers argue that hegemonic powers in the West have at times used the idea of human rights to degrade non-Western peoples and cultures.[33] Others have pointed out that human rights activists may be tempted to reproduce old colonial ways of thinking by pathologising non-Western cultures as inimical to the human rights of

---

31   See, for example, the much misunderstood account in *Arendt*, Eichmann in Jerusalem. Arendt emphasises the proclivity of the prosecution to treat the accused as an inhuman antisemitic monster and argues that such de-humanisation detracts from the purpose of a trial: 'the question of individual guilt or innocence, the act of meting out justice to both the defendant and the victim, are the only things at stake in a criminal court' (p. 298).

32   Alain Finkielkraut maintains in relation to the Barbie Trial that though 'the Holocaust was from Eichmann to the engineers on the trains [...] a crime of employees [...]. [I]t was precisely to remove from crime the excuse of service [...] that the category of crimes against humanity was formulated.' On the other hand, he warned against the temptation to reduce the prosecution to 'an exultant face to face confrontation between Innocence and the Unspeakable Beast'. Finkielkraut argues that this would rewrite the Holocaust as a 'meaningless idiot's tale' which leaves only a 'gaping black hole': *Finkielkraut*, Remembering in Vain, pp. 3-4 and 60-61.

33   Costas Douzinas makes this case forcibly in *Douzinas*, Human Rights and Empire: The Political Philosophy of Cosmopolitanism. He decries the 'American' assertion that the Guantanamo Bay prisoners have no rights because, in Bush's words, they are 'evil murderers'. Douzinas comments that 'human rights with their principles and counter-principles [...] are much easier to manipulate than clear proscriptions of state action' (p. 59).

women.[34] Others argue that the idea of human rights has been used in a prejudicial way to criminalise 'Israel' alone among nations – and not just the state but also the people.[35] This is not the place to establish in which particular instances international human rights and humanitarian law has been most instrumentalised in the service of 'othering' individuals, states or peoples, but it is to suggest that this potentiality exists within international law and is brought to the surface through the idealisation of international law as a transcendent standard of judgment and category of understanding. It has to do with the casting of international law as a trump card in political argument that saves us the work of making our own case or as a new device for reproducing the imperial human-inhuman duality.

Conclusion: international law and the critique of distorted modernisation

David Kennedy's comment that the international human rights movement might be 'more part of the problem in today's world than part of the solution' goes much further down the road of cynicism than I would. It seems to me that he is right, however, when he observes that 'promoting human rights can sometimes have bad consequences' and highlights the danger that 'well-intentioned people can end up supporting the very things they earlier wished to denounce'.[36] The transformation of international law since 1989 into 'cosmopolitan law' is a barometer of our times. It is a distinctive legal expression of the current stage of development of capitalist society or to use Hegelian language of the modern system of right as a whole. Today the expanded scope of international law proceeds on the basis of many pre-existing forms of right: rights of property, contract, exchange and punishment; rights of moral judgment and family life; rights of welfare, free association and political participation; rights of national self-determination, sovereignty and non-intervention. The rise of human rights and humanitarian law is beset by the same kinds of social conflict and conceptual abuse that enter into these preceding forms of right. In facing up to the violence of modern capitalist society it is now as tempting to idealise human rights and humanitarian law as it was in the past to idealise the state (or parts of the state such as the executive or representative assembly) or to idealise civil society (or parts of civil society such as its civic associations). This temptation is understandable enough but it is liable to feed the disillusionment we observe when the

---

34 'The gratuitous connection between culture and violence is almost invariably brought up in relation to the Third World': *Kapur*, The tragedy of victimisation rhetoric, p. 8. Kapur is perceptively critical, for instance, of those who would depict 'dowry murder' as an Indian 'cultural practice' rather than as a form of domestic violence.
35 'Year after year, the UN Commission on Human Rights spent far more time specifically criticizing Israel than any other country. Genocide in Cambodia, Indonesia, Rwanda, Congo, Algeria, Lebanon, and Sudan; slavery in Saudi Arabia, Mauritania, Western Sahara, Mali, and Sudan; and, starvation in North Korea, Burundi, Liberia, Ethiopia, Niger, Angola, and Sudan, did not merit much attention in comparison': *Habibi*, Human Rights and Politicized Human Rights.
36 *Kennedy*, The Dark Side of Virtue, pp. 124-125.

practice of human rights and humanitarianism falls short of the ideal it can never reach. If we expect too much of human rights, we prepare the ground for a politics of disillusionment. The politics of disillusionment threatens to turn genuine legitimation problems into a full-blown crisis of legitimation.

To my mind it is immeasurably valuable that the vocabulary of human rights and humanitarian law has entered into political argument. How in the modern world can we be responsible political actors if we don't have available to us linguistic terms like 'genocide', 'crimes against humanity', 'disproportionate response', 'collective punishment', 'torture' and 'terrorism' or on the other side terms like 'responsibility to protect', 'international criminal law' and 'humanitarian intervention'? The difficult task we face, however, is to learn how to use these terms, to make distinctions between them, to make judgments about their appropriate and inappropriate applications, to develop our understanding of what it is that they refer to. The difficult task, as I see it, is in short to develop a human rights culture. Making distinctions is the stuff of politics as well as law. It requires, to cite the instances provided by Gilbert Achcar, that we recognise the 'magnifying effect of TV broadcasts' on our perception of certain crimes (like the deliberate targeting of civilians in the twin towers) and not others, the potentially dehumanising effect of simply labelling an amorphously defined enemy as 'evil', and the importance of distinguishing between a 'pretty ordinary massacre' in which 3300 lives are taken and major massacres in which hundreds of thousands or even millions of civilians are targeted.[37] I would add that we add the importance of observing a consistency of judgment between those instances of human rights violation in which we have sympathy or at least understanding of the motives that lie behind it and those instances in which we have less sympathy and resist understanding. The particular temptation I have sought to confront in this paper is that which places international law in the service of dehumanising the collectivities we hold especially or uniquely responsible for the violence we abhor whilst at the same time promoting the image of the merely helpless or merely resistant 'victim subject' for the collectivities against whom the violence is committed.[38]

The question of what factors motivate the displacement of international law from a form of political and legal coordination of a global community subject to norms of political contestation into an ideal standard akin to natural law is a difficult one to address. The observation I wish to end with is only that this displacement may be related, paradoxically, to the delegitimation of the institutions that embody the principles of international law. The more institutions like the UN or the International Criminal Court or the UN Human Rights Council are questioned in their practical capacity to mediate or solve disputes, the more the abstract ideal of international law may be invoked. If this is so, it might indicate that it is in the failure of international institutions that the idealisation of international law finds its ground.[39] Be this as it

---

37 *Achcar*, The Clash of Barbarisms, pp. 27-33.
38 *Kapur*, The tragedy of victimisation rhetoric, p.1
39 'As a citizen, one would be more secure in knowing that international law is not about "infinite justice," but instead about the legally secured restoration of a legal peace that has been

may, the deformation of international law in the public sphere may be understood as a distorted form of modernisation that results from the separation of law and politics. It is an expression of the uneven development of the legal form of human rights and the human rights culture in which this form is set.

Acknowledgements

My thanks are due to the Oñati conference participants and especially to Gurminder Bhambra, Daniel Chernilo, Rodrigo Cordero, Costas Douzinas, David Hirsh, Lydia Morris, William Outhwaite, David Seymour and Chris Thornhill.

---

disrupted.' *Brunkhorst*, Solidarity, p. 150. Thanks to Rodrigo Cordero for alerting me to this possibility and the connection between my argument here and that put forward by Brunkhorst.

Bibliography

Achcar, Gilbert, The Clash of Barbarisms: The Making of the New World Disorder, London, 2006.
Anghie, Antony, Imperialism, Sovereignty and the Making of International Law (Cambridge, Cambridge University Press, 2005).
Ansari, Hamid, Inauguration speech at the International Conference on International Law in the Contemporary World organized by the Indian Society of International Law (ISIL): http://indiaedunews.net/Law/VicePresident_inaugurates_Conference_on_International_Law_73 37/print.asp
Archibugi, Daniel (ed), Debating Cosmopolitics, London, 2003.
Archibugi, Daniel, Cosmopolitan Guidelines for Humanitarian Intervention, Alternatives: Global, Local, Political 29 (2004), pp. 1-22.
Arendt, Hannah, Eichmann in Jerusalem: A Report on the Banality of Evil, Harmondsworth, 1977.
Arendt, Hannah, Origins of Totalitarianism, New York, 1979.
Benhabib, Seyla, Another Cosmopolitanism, Tanner Lectures, Oxford, 2006.
Bowring, Bill, The Degradation of the International Legal Order: The Rehabilitation of Law and the Possibility of Politics, London, 2008.
Brunkhorst, Hauke, Solidarity: From Civic Friendship to a Global Legal Community, Cambridge, Mass., 2005.
Carter, Bob/Virdee, Satnam, Racism and the sociological imagination, British Journal of Sociology 59 (2008), pp. 661-679.
Chandler, David, International justice, in Archibugi, Daniel (ed), Debating Cosmopolitics, London, 2003, pp. 27-39.
Cohen, Jean, Whose Sovereignty? Empire Versus International Law, Ethics and International Affairs 18 (2004), pp. 1-24.
Derrida, Jacques/Borradori, Giovanna, Philosophy in a Time of Terror: Dialogues with Jürgen Habermas and Jacques Derrida, Chicago, 2003.
Douzinas, Costas, Human Rights and Empire: The Political Philosophy of Cosmopolitanism, London, 2007.
Fine, Robert, Cosmopolitanism, London, 2007.
Fine, Robert/Smith, Will, Cosmopolitanism and humanitarian military intervention', in Hughes, Christopher and Devetak, Richard (eds), The Globalisation of Political Violence: Globalisation's Shadow, London, 2008, pp. 46-66.
Finkielkraut, Alain, Remembering in Vain, New York, 1992.
Goldstein, Judith/Kahler, Miles/Keohane, Robert O./Slaughter, Anne-Marie, Introduction: Legalization and World Politics', in Goldstein, Judith, Kahler, Miles, Keohane, Robert O., Slaughter, Anne-Marie (eds), Legalisation and World Politics, Cambridge, Mass, 2001. Habermas, Jürgen, The Divided West, Cambridge, 2006.
Habermas, Jürgen, The Constitutionalization of International Law and the Legitimation Problems of a Constitution For World Society, Constellations 15 (2008), pp. 444-455
Habibi, Don, Human Rights and Politicized Human Rights: A Utilitarian Critique, Journal of Human Rights 6 (2007), pp. 3-35.
Hirsh, David, Law against Genocide: Cosmopolitan Trials, London, 2003.
Jaspers, Karl, The Question of German Guilt, New York, 2000.
Johnson, Pauline, Globalising democracy: reflections on Habermas's radicalism, European Journal of Social Theory 11 (2008), pp. 71-86.

Kapur, Ratna, The tragedy of victimisation rhetoric: resurrecting the "native" subject in international / postcolonial feminist legal politics, Harvard Human Rights Journal 15 (2002), pp. 1-31.

Kennedy, Duncan, The Dark Side of Virtue: Re-assessing International Humanitarianism, Princeton, 2005.

Kedourie, Elie, Nationalism, Oxford, 1993.

Krisch, Nico, Legality, morality and the dilemma of humanitarian interventions after Kosovo, European Journal of International Law 13 (2002), pp. 323-335

Krisch, Nico, Imperial international law, Global Law Working Paper (2004), Hauser Global Law School Program.

Kumm, Mattias, The legitimacy of international law: A constitutionalist framework of analysis', European journal of International Law 15 (2004), pp. 907-931.

Levy, Daniel/Sznaider, Natan, Sovereignty transformed: A sociology of human rights. British Journal of Sociology 57 (2006), pp. 657-676,

Mandani, Mahmood, Saviors and Survivors: Darfur, Politics and the War on Terror, New York: 2009.

Morris, Lydia, An emergent cosmopolitan paradigm? Asylum, welfare and human rights, British Journal of Sociology 60 (2009), pp. 215-235.

Morris, Lydia, Welfare, asylum and civil society: a case study in civil repair, Citizenship Studies 13 (2009), pp. 365-379.

Obama, Barack, Obama to Promote International Law and Diplomacy: Suite 101.com November 2008:
http://internationalpolitics.suite101.com/article.cfm/obama_to_promote_international_law_and_diplomacy

Rosas, Allan, State sovereignty and human rights: Toward a global constitutional project, Political Studies (1995) (special issue on politics and human rights), pp. 61-78.

Stammers, Neil, Social movements and the social construction of human rights, Human Rights Quarterly 214 (1999), pp. 980-1008

Scheuerman, William, Carl Schmitt: The End of Law, London, 1999.

Schilling, Theodor, On the Constitutionalization of General International Law', Global Law Working Paper 05/05, Hauser Global Law Working Paper, New York University.

Schmitt, Carl, The Nomos of the Earth in the International Law of the Jus Publicum Europaeum, trans. G.L. Ulmen, New York, 2003.

Smith, Will, Anticipating a cosmopolitan future: the case of humanitarian military intervention, International Politics 44 (2007), pp. 72-89.

Teubner, Gunther, Societal constitutionalism: alternatives to state-centred constitutional theory', in Joerges, Christian, Sand, Inger-Johanne and Teubner, Gunther (eds), Transnational Governance and Constitutionalism, Oxford and Portland, 2004

Saving cosmopolitanism? Legality without Legitimacy

Costas Douzinas

Over the last few months, the neo-liberal model of capitalism, deregulated, free-market, greedy, based on financial gambling and disregard for any value other than profit has come to a crashing end. Unregulated free market political economy has received a huge blow, from which may not recover in the near future. The rise of neo-liberalism coincided with what sociologists call globalisation, political theorists cosmopolitanism and lawyers emerging 'humanity's law'.[1] In the absence of a political blueprint, cosmopolitanism, an ancient philosophical idea, has been resurrected and become the latest fashion of social and political theory. According to its apologists, when the twin projects of international and cosmopolitan law have been fully implemented across the globe (and for some they are well on the way), the Kantian promise of perpetual peace will come close to fulfilment.

Neo-liberalism is not just a pernicious economic model but an integrated worldview. It became the way we live, the institutional framework of our society, how we understand and imagine our relations with others and the world. Neoliberal capitalism formed the real, its institutions the symbolic and its ideology the imaginary orders of our societies in the last forty years. This essay argues that a deeper affinity exists between the global penetration of neo-liberalism and political and legal moralisation. Cosmopolitan capitalism is presented as globalisation with a human face: cosmopolitanism humanises inequalities, softens the side-effects of globalisation, limits oppressive and totalitarian regimes.

But is it possible that the whole world has accepted human rights, humanitarianism and international law as a global panacea, despite radically differing political, religious and cultural interests and beliefs? Have conflicts of class, ideological oppositions and national enmities ceased? Has the North and the South, the left and the right, the minister and the rebel accepted the same worldview? Obviously not. The best time to demystify ideology is when it enters into crisis. At this point, its taken-for-granted, natural, invisible premises come to the surface become de-naturalized, objectified and can be understood for that first time for what they are: ideological constructs. The crisis of neo-liberal capitalism questions the wider combination of economic, political, legal and cultural practices that dominated the recent period, and it offers an opportunity for imagining a different world.

This essay uses a recent contribution to the cosmopolitan debate by Robert Fine to organise the critique of cosmopolitanism in respect of its philosophy of history

---

1 *Teitel*, "Humanity's Law", p. 355.

and its views on law and rights.[2] It will conclude by arguing for a different radical cosmopolitanism.

A Fine cosmopolitanism

Robert Fine's *Cosmopolitanism* is the most sophisticated attempt to gather the different trends in the rapidly expanding cosmopolitan literature, arrange them thematically and save cosmopolitanism from idealisations and excesses. For Fine, cosmopolitanism is primarily an approach to social theory and secondarily to political practice. We will concentrate on three main directions in Fine's project: the methodological, philosophical and normative.

Fine signposts the epistemological and methodological stakes of the debate through a friendly critique of 'new' cosmopolitan theory, especially that of Jürgen Habermas, John Rawls and Ulrich Beck. For Fine, cosmopolitan social theory examines social relations through universalistic analytical tools and procedures in the service of a universal conception of humanity. But the cosmopolitan authors wrongly emphasise the national character of social theory in order to present cosmopolitanism as a radical break and innovation. As a result, these authors are not cosmopolitan enough. They return to Kant and natural law, link cosmopolitanism to existing communities and loyalties (national or European) and try to expand them to the globe. More specifically, Habermas's constitutional patriotism globalises German obsessions with constitutionalism, the *Rechtsstaat* and Europe. Rawls's 'law of peoples' turns American preoccupations with limited rights to world dispensation. Beck develops a 'cosmopolitan nationalism', a kind of higher, gentler nationalism or second Enlightenment, which breaks with the modernist edifice by globalising it. Finally, Martha Nussbaum impossibly conceives cosmopolitanism as the universalization of reason against the parochial claims of nation and community. 'New' cosmopolitanisms enlarge nationalism, patriotism, the constitution, juridification and European interests but neglect and idealise rather than confront universalism's exclusions.

In contrast to this, Fine argues, the best social theory has always been non-national and cosmopolitan. Cosmopolitanism is the outcome of historical evolution. It has emerged, in best Hegelian fashion, out of the advances, contradictions and impasses of modernity. In this sense, cosmopolitanism is a fact in the world. It is a form of right and institutional arrangement, manifest in laws, norms and practices such as human rights, expanded international law and international criminal justice, global civil society, international governmental and non-governmental organisations and the like. Cosmopolitan right is not something new. It presupposes a pre-existing variety of forms and contents, and it emerges through the internal contradictions and conflicts of previous right-forms. The form of right itself with its many divisions

2   *Fine*, Cosmopolitanism.

(morality, ethics, family and private life, civil society, the nation state) is assumed and 'sublated' in cosmopolitan right. Cosmopolitanism is neither the apex of modernity nor the culmination of the idea of right. It incorporates conflicts and contradictions and turns them into its own constituent 'moments'. After its emergence, all pre-existing forms of right change.[3]

Repeating Hegel's critique of Kant, Fine argues that we cannot just add cosmopolitan laws and institutions onto the form of modern state and expect the coming of perpetual peace. Kant's abstract universalism and its contemporary imitators can lead to the devaluation of values. Abstraction from determination, autonomy without concrete contents, and detached legalism can become sheer restless activity and end up in a fury of destruction, as was the case in the French revolution and, one suspects, the Iraq war. Fine is generous but sharp towards his targets. Despite his approval of the occasional humanitarian intervention, he curtly observes that the term 'outlaw states' has been used to launch pre-emptive strikes, deprive citizens of basic rights and demonise whole people. Fine's liking of (international) law is tempered by the 'unkindest image': the vision of a legal cosmopolitanism in which the same politicians are in power and we 'go to war for humanitarian reasons because a group of judges say we should.'[4]

This approach leads to the conclusion that we do not live in a 'cosmopolitan age', but that 'we do live in an age of cosmopolitanism'. Cosmopolitanism is the 'rational direction of humankind'. Unlike for Kant, no law of nature guarantees it behind our backs. However, if no artificial measures are taken to stop it 'the way is cleared for a cosmopolitan future.'[5] To this extent, while reality is not cosmopolitan, as Beck claims, cosmopolitanism is the most defensible philosophical project of the age.

Fortunately, global changes in communications and culture are moving in the right direction. However, something more radical is needed. The constitutional and legal designs are still too abstract, idealistic and too close to current national arrangements. Politics must be injected into cosmopolitanism. In particular, Fine argues, paying tribute to his other great inspiration, Hannah Arendt, that political judgments by ordinary citizens should be added to philosophical and legal idealisations.

This critique of 'new' cosmopolitanism is important, but limited. Fine's theoretical trajectory repeats his substantial Hegelian gesture. In the same way that cosmopolitan right is presented as the contemporary expression of all right, 'new' cosmopolitanisms become 'moments' in Fine's cosmopolitan theory, and they are both rejected and assumed in his wider canvas. This makes Fine's cosmopolitanism partly a descriptive project, which can subsume all current developments. The tendency towards a pragmatic Hegelianism is checked however. Certain aspects of 'new' cosmopolitanism are categorically rejected thus giving a clearer idea into the ideological bearings of cosmopolitan social theory.

---

3   *Fine,* Cosmopolitanism, pp. xii-xiii.
4   *Fine,* Cosmopolitanism, p. 95.
5   *Fine,* Cosmopolitanism, p. 19.

Fine rejects most emphatically the idea of belonging (to community, nation or state). Local, national or communal ties must be abandoned. We know the catastrophes that nationalism and racism visited the world. What is the alternative? Humans can belong anywhere, Fine believes. We face serious global predicaments, which must be confronted in common; we therefore have a great incentive to abandon particular ties for universal humanity.

Things, however, are not that simple. The political implications of abandoning national territoriality in favour of universal humanity are problematic. Democracy as political form and citizenship as the specifically modern subjectivity could only develop through a strong link between power and space. Modern politics has always operated within a limited territory controlled by a single authority; modern legitimacy has depended on spatial ordering. All major political forms, dynastic royalty (the principles of inheritance and personification of populations), nationalism (common characteristics of a people co-habiting in a particular territory) and representative democracy (the will of nation) combine power and place. Territorial nationalism was the precondition for the rise of democracy. For a simple majority to become an acceptable form of rule, people must feel that similarities with their neighbours are greater than their obvious economic, class or cultural differences. Nationalism provided the basic cultural homogeneity necessary for the rise of democracy. When such initial homogeneity does not exist, the introduction of democracy may explode the wider social conflicts of society and lead to atrocious wars. Arguably, this is what happened after the collapse of Yugoslavia.[6]

For humanity to replace nation, it should be able to perform a nation's functions. First, a new global spatial arrangement must develop and become the new terrain of political action. The idea of global democracy may be a favourite of political theorists trying to devise appropriate political procedures and electoral systems for the whole world.[7] Such mental experiments belong however to science fiction and not the tradition of utopia. Secondly, humanity as a universal normative concept should be able to replace national identities and help build a new type of cosmopolitan subjectivity. The current dominant cosmopolitan subjectivity, is according to Craig Calhoun's felicitous phrase the 'class consciousness of the frequent traveller.'[8] But Fine's suggestions are not convincing. If the European Union has been unable to organise politics of space to replace the democracies of place and territory, the globe cannot succeed either. Furthermore, humanity is far too abstract and indeterminate a concept, as will be argued below, to become the normative horizon for cosmopolitan identity.

Let us finally turn to the normative component of cosmopolitanism. Fine rejects a strong philosophy of history, identified with Kant, according to which humanity moves inexorably to the cosmopolitan stage and perpetual peace. This does not mean however that the advent of cosmopolitanism was a random occurrence. A po-

---

6   See *Hirst*, Space and Power.
7   *Archibugi*, The Global Commonwealth of Citizens.
8   *Calhoun*, Nations Matter.

werful normative urge, already part of reality, pushes towards cosmopolitanism. Its clearest formulation appears again in the figure of 'humanity'. Rejecting Beck's claim that liberal cosmopolitanism sacrifices particularity for an 'assumed universal equality',[9] Fine argues that 'humankind despite our differences is effectively one and must be understood as such.'[10] Humanity is not just an expression of formal universalization; it has substantive unity. All types of difference can be reconciled with humanity's dignity and become its constituent parts. Cosmopolitanism is therefore real and rational, methodological and normative: it is a cognitive strategy, an emerging fact in the world and a principle or ideal for action.

The universal humanity of differences, a kind of philosophical multi-culturalism, is also the basis of Fine's attitude towards radical critics of cosmopolitanism. Consistent with his Hegelianism, Fine adopts some critiques while rejecting 'one-sided' attacks. Critics, including the present scribbler, allegedly see cosmopolitanism as the latest version of imperialism, domination and violence. They believe that power can explain politics better than universal ideals and supranational bodies. Hegemonic states impose their interests under the mantle of universality, and they moralize wars and demonize their enemies. The critic 'sees in world history nothing but power, self-interest and contingency.'[11] Specifically addressing the present scribbler, Fine argues that my alleged 'top-down' approach to human rights sees them as instruments of control by the state, forgetting and devaluing their redemptive and emancipatory uses.

Cosmopolitanism is a fine example of the theoretical and political centre ground. It promises to save cosmopolitanism from exaggerations and extremes. Has it succeeded?

Cosmopolitan impasses

A common response by targets of critique is to claim that the critic has misunderstood their position or created a straw man. This approach, which ends up in detailed textual apologetics, is unnecessary in responding to such generous a critic as Robert Fine, from whom I have learned and with whom share a lot.[12] Instead, I will organize my comments along four theses critical of cosmopolitanism *tout court*.

---

9   *Fine*, Cosmopolitanism, pp. 13-14.
10 *Fine*, Cosmopolitanism, p. xvii.
11 *Fine*, Cosmopolitanism, p. 21.
12 Let me just quote the last sentences of my book The End of Human Rights: 'If human rights have become the "realized myth of postmodern societies this is a myth realized only in the energies of those who suffer grave and petty violations in the hands of the powers that have proclaimed their triumph. [...] When the apologists of pragmatism pronounce the end of ideology, of history or utopia, they do not mark the triumph of human rights. The end of human rights comes when they lose their utopian end', *Douzinas*, The End of Human Rights, p. 380; and from my Human Rights and Empire: 'Every time a poor, oppressed, tortured person uses the language of rights – because no other is currently available – to protest, resist, fight, she

These theses are as follows:

i. Humanity acts both as a normative universality and as a strategy for ontological classification between the rulers, the ruled and the excluded.

ii. Whether Kantian or Hegelian, a philosophy of history is both necessary and impossible for cosmopolitanism.

iii. The moralization and legalization of (international) politics results in the depoliticization of politics.

iv. The 'cosmopolitanism to come' confronts the catastrophes of neo-liberalism.

i. Humanity as ontological classification

If a common humanity of differences is the normative source of cosmopolitanism, its meaning and action should be generally agreed. But what is 'humanity'? How did we arrive at the concept and what does it entail?

The idea of 'humanity' is modern. Athens and Rome had Athenians or Romans but not 'men', in the sense of members of the human species. The word *humanitas* first appeared in the Roman Republic, and it meant *eruditio et institutio in bonas artes.* The Romans used it to distinguish between the *homo humanus,* the educated Roman who was subjected to the *jus civile,* and the *homines barbari,* the rest. Humanity enters the Western lexicon, not as a common quality, but as an attribute of *homo.* For Cicero as well as the younger Scipio, *humanitas* implies generosity, politeness, civilisation and is opposed to barbarism.[13] 'Only those who conform to certain standards are really men in the full sense, and fully merit the adjective "human" or the attribute "humanity"'.[14]

Christianity undermined the classical hierarchies. St Paul's statement (in Epistle to the Galatians 3:28) that there is no Greek or Jew, man or woman, free man or slave introduced the first universal conception of humanity into Western history. All people are equally part of humanity because they can be saved in God's plan. In Christian metaphysics, the immortal soul marks the human. People will be saved only if they accept the faith, since non-Christians have no place in the providential plan. Christian humanity was therefore empirically split between the faithful and the heathen. The second coming or *parousia* will unify the two parts in the kingdom of God. This radical divide became the basis of an eschatological philosophy of histo-

---

draws from and connects with the most honourable metaphysics, morality and politics of the Western world. Human rights have only paradoxes to offer', *Douzinas*, Human Rights and Empire, p. 33.

13 *Ullman,* What are the Humanities? p. 302.
14 *Baldry,* The Unity of Mankind in Greek Thought, p. 201.

ry. It founded the ecumenical mission and proselytizing drive of Church and Empire. In the Christian empire, the frontier between Greeks and barbarians was internalized, and divided the known globe diagonally between the faithful and the heathen, who should be corrected or eliminated if they stubbornly refused spiritual or secular salvation.

The Christian meaning of humanity was vigorously contested in one of the most important debates in history. In 1550, Emperor Charles V of Spain called a council of state in Valladolid to discuss the conquerors' attitude towards the Indians of Mexico. The Aristotelian philosopher Gines de Sepulveda and the cleric Bartholomé de las Casas debated on opposite sides. Sepulveda, who had just translated into Spanish Aristotle's *Politics*, argued that 'the Spaniards rule with perfect right over the barbarians who, in prudence, talent, virtue, humanity are as inferior to the Spaniards as children to adults, women to men, the savage and cruel to the mild and gentle, I might say as monkey to men.'[15] The Indians could be enslaved and treated as barbarian and savages in order to be civilized and proselytized.

Las Casas disagreed. The Indians have well-established customs and settled ways of life, he argued. They are 'unwitting' Christians, like Adam before the Fall. Respecting local customs is good morality but also good politics: the Indians would convert to Christianity, and also accept the Spanish authority if the conquerors respected their traditions, laws and culture. Las Casas combined theology and political utility in an early example of multiculturalism. But the Christian universalism of Las Casas was exclusive. He repeatedly condemned 'Turks and Moors, the veritable barbarian outcasts of the nations' since they cannot be seen as 'unwitting' Christians. As Tzvetan Todorov pithily remarks: there is 'violence in the conviction that one possesses the truth oneself, whereas this is not the case for others, and that one must furthermore impose that truth on those others.'[16]

The conflicting interpretations of humanity by Sepulveda and las Casas capture the dominant ideologies of Western empires, imperialisms and colonialisms. Against the universalist input of divine providence, the (religious or racial) other is inhuman or subhuman. This justifies enslavement and atrocities as strategies of the civilizing mission. At the other end, conquest, occupation and forceful conversion are strategies of spiritual or material development, of progress and integration of the innocent, naïve, undeveloped others into the main body of humanity.

The religious grounding of humanity was undermined by the liberal political philosophies of early modernity. The foundation of humanity was transferred from God to rational human nature. Legal and political innovations turned humanity, man as species existence, into the common and absolute value of the world while introducing new exclusions. The French Declaration of the Rights of Man and Citizen is typical. Article 1 introduces Enlightenment universalism. It states that 'men are born

---

15 *de Sepulveda*, Democrates Segundo of De las Justas Causa de la Guerra contra los Indios, p. 33, quoted in *Todorov*, The Conquest of America, p. 153.
16 *Todorov*, The Conquest of America, pp. 166, 168.

and remain free and equal of right'. Articles 2 and 3 however make clear that only national citizens enjoy legal and political rights.

Modern humanism secularized Christian spiritual equality. 'Man' is united with all others in the abstract traits or free will, reason and soul — the essence of humanity. This minimal humanity endows 'man' with autonomy, moral responsibility and legal personality. Individual dignity and (self-)respect follow the universalization of humanity. But at the same time, a gap opens between universal 'man', the ontological principle of modernity, and national citizen, its political instantiation and real beneficiary of rights. The modern subject reaches her humanity by acquiring political rights of citizenship. The alien does not have rights because she is not part of the state and as a result she is a lesser human being. One is human to greater or lesser degree because one is a citizen to a greater or lesser degree. In our globalized world not to have citizenship, to be stateless or a refugee is the worst fate. If human rights are given to people on account of their humanity and not some narrower membership, Arendt's inter-war stateless people, today refugees, economic migrants and prisoners in Guatanamo Bay, who have little if any national protection, should be their main beneficiaries. But as we know they have very few legal protections. They are legally abandoned, bare life, the *homines sacri* of our world.

ii. Cosmopolitanism and the philosophy of history

Secular universalism replaced religious eschatology with a historical teleology, which promised the future suturing of humanity and nation, man and citizen. This teleology has two possible variants: either the nation imposes its rule on humanity or universalism undermines parochial divides and identities. Both were evident in France. Imperialism, in the Napoleonic wars which spread the civilising influence through conquest and occupation (according to Hegel, Napoleon was the world spirit on horseback); or, the beginnings of a modern cosmopolitanism, in which slavery was abolished and colonials were given political rights for a limited period after the Revolution. In fact, it was left to the Haitian revolution, which extended political rights to all Haitians, including slaves, to uphold universalism against its inventors, the French.

Kant's philosophical cosmopolitanism was precisely the attempt to heal this split through the regulative action of humanity upon national differences and brutalities. As Fine rightly points out, Kant's philosophy of history was backed by a strong belief in rational natural law.[17] Kant placed a safe wager on the future unification of humanity and nation. It is guaranteed by nature, he believed, which acts behind history to bring it to the promised perpetual peace. Hegel's rejoinder carries an even stronger philosophy of history. The real is rational; world spirit is incarnate in history, cosmopolitan right does not overcome but emerges through historical conflicts,

---

17   *Fine*, Cosmopolitanism, pp. 27, 40-1, 138 and passim.

contradictions and tribulations. If for Hegel the coincidence appeared in the ethical state of the nineteenth century, for Fine the promise of humanity is emerging in contemporary cosmopolitanism.

Modern humanism was accompanied, however, by another series of divisions and exclusions, which have a much greater staying power than that between 'man' and citizen. The subject of the classical Declarations was an empty vessel, someone without gender, colour, history or tradition, as Hegel and Marx, Burke and de Maistre agreed. Legal personality guarantees the abstract similarity of dignity behind the manifold differences of identity. But the empirical man who enjoyed real, legal and political, rights was a man, all too man: a well-off, heterosexual, white, urban male who condenses in his person the abstract dignity of humanity and the real prerogatives of the community of the powerful. Women, people of colour, people of no property are 'improper' humans. They are given the consolation of dignity and respect but few legal and political rights. Class, gender, race, sexuality have acted as the material and cultural determinations against which the modern human is constructed. The normative ideal of a universal humanity was contaminated from the beginning by the various material and cultural exclusions that still form the ground of empirical life.[18] As Hegel explained, while the poor have a formal right to property, the lack of basic material means destroys not only their chances of survival but also their (self-)respect. It splits their identity between the abstract dignity of right and the concrete degradation of a life of dependency.[19] This split still characterises the many minorities, which, while they are given the abstract consolations of humanity, are subjected to systematic domination and oppression.

The concept of 'humanity' has acted both as the promise of liberation and as a strategy of ontological classification between rulers, ruled and excluded. One could object that the human rights movement has been the ongoing struggle to close the gap between the abstract man and the concrete citizen; to add flesh, blood and sex to the pale outline of the 'human' and extend the dignities and privileges of the powerful (the characteristics of normative humanity) to empirical humanity. This has not happened, however, and it is unlikely to do so through the action of cosmopolitan right. Today the inferior or threatening others are called the 'axis of evil', 'rogue' or 'indecent' states, 'bogus refugees', 'illegal immigrants', 'religious fundamentalists'. They are contemporary heirs of Sepulveda's 'monkeys', epochal representatives of inhumanity. Becoming human is possible only against this impenetrable inhuman background. Split into two, according to a simple moral calculus, the Other has a tormented and a tormenting part, both radical evil and radical passivity. He represents both our narcissistic self in its infancy (civilisation as *potentia*, possibility or risk) and what is most frightening and horrific in us: the death drive, the evil persona that lurks in the midst of psyche and society. In this project, empirical and normative humanity (humanity as quality shared or as a project to be achieved) will eventually coincide through the West's surgical intervention. Either the deceased,

---

18 *Cheah*, Inhuman Conditions, chs 1 and 7.
19 *Douzinas*, Identity, Recognition, Rights.

unworthy, inferior members will be cut off or they will be 'humanized' and integrated once they accept the wrong of their ways and agree to be 'civilized': severing or prosthesis, these are the ways of 'making human'.

History has an uncanny way of giving the lie to philosophies of history. For Kant cosmopolitanism was guaranteed, metaphysically, by the 'great artist Nature' and, historically, by the spread of trade. The spreading of trade, however, led to colonialism and Napoleon brought the pious hopes of the Master to an end. The 'new' cosmopolitans turn globalisation into an inexorable historical march. Human rights and international law become regulative ideas, a horizon, which promises the normative unification of split humanity. The neoliberal disaster undermines the historical process however and Iraq (Fine's Hegelian 'fury of destruction of the abstract') the normative claims.

A philosophy of history is equally necessary and impossible for the Hegelian alternative. In Fine's version, globalized world is pregnant with cosmopolitan right. The universalism of humanity, evident in human rights, humanitarianism and international criminal justice, is already incarnate in historical reality and moves existing arrangements towards their cosmopolitan transcendence. Humanity's 'cunning' is busy transforming the 'contingencies' of political domination, capitalist neoliberalism and unequal globalisation. It is a comforting thought daily refuted in the news. The fine attempt to save cosmopolitanism is caught in what we could call the 'dialectics of cosmopolitanism': it is caught, on one side, in the promise of a 'humanity which despite our differences is effectively one' and, on the other, in dominant and persistent practices, which do not welcome differences but use them to exclude the different.

iii. The de-politicization of politics

Cosmopolitanism has become the latest fad in political theory and international relations, and it has launched a thousand books and articles. Constitutional and legal arrangements are central to the various cosmopolitan designs. One has the impression that law has become a *deus ex machina* answering the intractable problems of social and political theory.[20] With a few exceptions however cosmopolitan discussion has stayed away from the legal aspects of the promised utopia. A rather banal positivist and journalistic approach has coloured the cosmopolitan image of the law. Let us briefly examine the legal aspects of the most complete cosmopolitan theory: that of Jürgen Habermas.

For Habermas, legal form democratically legitimated and morally validated constitutes the scaffold of cosmopolitanism. His post-national constellation promises the

---

20 Tom Osborne has argued that that the moralism of human rights should be extended towards an 'ethical judicialism' which would expand the legalisation of culture. See *Osborne*, What is Neo-Enlightenment, p. 523. For David Hirsch cosmopolitan trials express a 'worldliness as practical wisdom'. See *Hirsch*, Law Against Genocide, p. 154.

extension of Enlightenment republicanism to the world. A number of steps are necessary and are already happening. First, the autonomy of politics from capitalist interventions and state interference should be secured. Political decisions and values should become the object of rational deliberation and will-formation by citizens. Individual identities should be detached from nationalist or 'thick cultural' belonging and anchored on constitutional loyalty and political commitment (the famous 'constitutional patriotism'). Law is crucial in this respect. Its legitimacy is bifurcated, partly Rousseauian and partly (reformed) Kantian. Law and rights are outcomes of the democratic process while their form guarantees normative/moral validity.[21]

Modern cosmopolitanism is a German invention. Following Robert Kagan's thesis, cosmopolitanism can be seen as a sign of weakness and, one could add, *ressentiment*. A state or ideology tends to promote a strict legal/moral regulation of politics. once its aspirations to dominate militarily or economically have been defeated.[22] But the German tradition includes other voices. For Hegel, Kantian cosmopolitanism forgets the ethical status of the state, the struggle of states for recognition in international relations, the associated morality of war, as well as the centrality of national culture in the creation of identity.[23] For Nietzsche, morality is the absolutization and eternalization of a temporary balance of forces. Carl Schmitt attacked the moralization of politics: he argued that cosmopolitanism would lead to the world hegemony of a single power which, based on some version of morality, would destroy politics and the pluralism that characterized the pre-War international scene. Habermas accepts partly the legitimacy of Schmitt's critique and introduces a crucial distinction between human rights and morality. Human rights are creations of law, juridical concepts originating in the tradition of individual liberties. Morality on the other hand derives from the Kantian moral canon.

When cosmopolitans promote human rights, politics bends the knee, not to a single morality, but to law. The genealogies of human rights and morality differ, but they share a common foundation, which precedes their separation. Their common validity structure is the 'fundamental discourse principle', an elaboration of the Kantian categorical imperative with a Rawlsian inflection: 'just those action-norms are valid to which all possible affected persons could agree as participants in a rational discourse.'[24] While basic rights are historically and institutionally different, they are 'equipped with such universal validity claims precisely because they can be justified *exclusively* from the moral point of view'.[25]

These nuanced attempts to distinguish between rights and morality, which nonetheless share a common validity structure, are bizarre, but understandable. According to the standard jurisprudential narrative, the great achievement of legal moderni-

---

21 *Habermas*, The Postnational Constellation, ch. 3; *Habermas*, Between Facts and Norms, ch. 3.
22 *Kagan*, Paradise and Power. Kant, Kelsen and Habermas, the major exponents of cosmopolitanism, have followed frustrated German aspirations.
23 *Kochi*, The Other's War.
24 *Habermas*, Between Facts and Norms, p. 107.
25 *Habermas*, Between Facts and Norms, p.138.

ty was precisely the exclusion of ethics from law. Disenchanted modernity experiencing relativism and value pluralism and fearing nihilism, banished subjective values from legal operations. Law is presented fact-like as the answer to the irreconcilability of values. Its operation should not be contaminated by non-legal considerations. This is Habermas's gambit. By bifurcating rights into institutional-historical and moral aspects, he can claim both the 'objectivity' of law and the validity of (post-metaphysical) morality. But as the realist and critical legal traditions have argued for a long time, morals, ideology or political preferences cannot be kept out of law. 'Subjective' considerations are an integral part of legal operations while morality has commonly taken the form of a legal code.

We can see the artificiality and contortions of the dividing line between law and morality in the debate on Kosovo, the most important recent examination of the extension of international law towards a cosmopolitan phase. Three eminent international lawyers Professors Antonio Cassesse, Bruno Simma and Michael Glennon writing after the war, agreed that the use of force was illegal under international law and contrary to the United Nations Charter.[26] While the illegality perpetrated by NATO was grave, respect for the rule of law should be sacrificed, they agreed, at the altar of human compassion and the 'ethical viewpoint'. Michael Glennon went furthest. He stated: 'The higher, grander goal that has eluded humanity for centuries – the ideal of justice backed by power – should not be abandoned. If power is used to do justice, law will follow.'[27] Indeed. For lawyers, law is amoral, justice is extraneous to legal operations: it is the business of 'power'. Legal rules have replaced the ethical choices and when they run out, law has to turn to external moral sources. The lawyers assume that morality is like law: it has one dominant code-like conception whose demands are self-evident. Other types of ethics such as virtue ethics, the ethics of care, the ethics of alterity or even some various brands of utilitarianism are not even considered as potential ways of addressing moral dilemmas.

Habermas's on the other hand presents Kosovo as an attempt to push international law towards its cosmopolitan phase by violently upholding universal citizenship rights. If we compare his position with that of the lawyers, bedfellows on the Kosovo issue, a strange conclusion emerges. For the lawyers, moral considerations must be introduced because amoral international law runs out and declares the war illegal. The law on its own is inadequate to the task of saving humanity. For Habermas, politics should not be subjected to morality, a prospect that raises the spectre of Carl Schmitt. To avoid this, the law is called in as the universal but disinterested arbiter. Human rights save the day. But since lawyers have shown the law to be inadequate, human rights are bifurcated, into a juridical component and its moral foundation.

---

26 *Cassesse, Ex Injuria Jus Oritur*: Are We Moving Towards International Legitimation of Forcible Humanitarian Countermeasures in the World Community? p. 23; *Simma*, NATO, the UN and the Use of Force: Legal Aspects, p. 1; *Glennon*, The New Interventionism: the search for a just international law, p. 1.
27 *Glennon*, The New Interventionism: the search for a just international law, p. 7.

Habermas poses the problem and its answer in exactly the reverse terms from the lawyers. For the lawyers, morality saves politics from (inadequate) law, for Habermas, law saves politics from (potentially problematic) moralization. The sleight of hand is evident: morality and human rights are identified in their form and content but separated in respect to their action. But Schmitt's ghost cannot be exorcized. Whether moral or legal, a particular must legislate the universal, Stoic cosmopolitanism becomes Roman imperialism. Habermas had to admit as much after the Iraq war. Writing in 2003, he accused the United States of violating international law. America had been the 'pacemaker of progress on the cosmopolitan plan' but Iraq meant that it has 'given up its role as guarantor of international rights […] its normative authority lies in ruins.' There is not much difference between classical imperialism and American hegemonism. Imperial campaigns spread 'the universal values of their own liberal order, with military force if necessary, throughout the entire world. This arrogance doesn't become any more tolerable when it is transfers from nation-state to a single hegemonic state.'[28] This is the closest Habermas comes to a genuine *mea culpa* and an admission that despite the brutal attacks, Carl Schmitt may have carried the day.

Law like foreign priorities, economic arguments and military logistics is only one consideration governments take into account before deciding how to act. Rwanda, Darfur and Gaza indicate that humanitarian action and inaction are determined by the strategic interests of hegemonic powers. Similar considerations apply to international institutions when they act as a committee of governments. Before the Iraq war right and left insisted that a Security Council resolution would weaken objections. Three members of the Council, however, China, Russia and the United States, consistently violate the rights of their own citizens. No liberal would support the treatment of Tibetans or Chechens, or the death penalty so generously meted out in China and the US. Yet they were happy to accept these governments as the final arbiters of international legality. A few months before the war, I asked a high-ranking Chinese official if China would exercise its veto. He replied that his country has no interests in Iraq and by supporting the US it expects to be rewarded in trade relations and its own human rights difficulties. A few days later China joined the WTO. When in March 2009, Hilary Clinton pleaded with the Chinese authorities to continue their support of the American economy without mentioning human rights, she was not diverging from standard foreign policy. Morality and human rights are wheeled out when they support state interests, and they are easily discarded if they create real or imaginary constraints.

Robert Fine wishes to add politics to the cosmopolitan mix. However the claim that law can give right answers to hard political problems is a façade for depoliticizing politics. Nothing links the starving of the developing world and the 'illegal' immigrants of the metropolis with the Western middle classes claiming their human rights. Humanity is split between those benefiting and those suffering from cosmo-

---

28 *Habermas*, Interpreting the Fall of a Monument, p. 7. The essay originally appeared in the Frankfurt Allgemeine Zeitung on April 17, 2003.

politan neo-liberalism. If anything brings humanity together, it is not multicultural differences but the struggles in each state and region against the exclusions perpetrated by capitalist globalisation and the palliatives served by humanitarianism. Human rights are the latest expression of the eternal human urge to resist domination and oppression, the only 'natural law' identifiable throughout history. Natural and human rights were conceived in the eighteenth and twentieth centuries, and still remain defences against the abuses of public and private power. When they become tools of Western universalism or communitarian localism their purpose is undermined.

iv. The cosmopolitanism to come

Cosmopolitanism, human rights and humanitarianism are not results of the liberal or charitable disposition of the West. They are deeply linked with neo-liberal capitalism. When it became clear that the West could not compete in manufacturing because of its labour costs, it turned to the financial markets and the cheapest way of making money creating a phoney economic bubble: speculating on currency and credit by offering loans not for investment but to consumers using their homes as guarantee. The World Bank, the WTO and the IMF imposed this so-called 'Washington consensus' globally: they put pressure on developing states to deregulate their financial sector, remove all measures protecting local production and reduce welfare spending. The consumer boom that followed created super-rich elites but increased inequality and undermined development. The strict intellectual property rules imposed by the WTO further contributed to the imbalance between North and South by creating 'knowledge rich' and 'knowledge poor' countries. As a result, the gap between the North and the South and between rich and poor has never been greater. According to Oxfam, more than a billion people live on less than $1 a day. The difference in life expectancy between the European North and the sub-Saharan South approaches fifty years. An estimated thirty-five per cent of child mortality across the world is attributable to poor nutrition.[29] These catastrophic consequences had started destabilising the world order before the recent economic implosion.

Global moral and civic rules are the necessary companion of the globalisation of neo-liberal capitalism. Robert Cooper has called this 'toxic' combination the voluntary imperialism of the global economy. He states: 'It is operated by an international consortium of financial Institutions such as the IMF and the World Bank. [...] These institutions [...] make demands, which increasingly emphasize good governance. If states wish to benefit, they must open themselves up to the interference of international organisations and foreign states.' Cooper concludes that 'what is needed then is a new kind of imperialism, one acceptable to a world of human rights and cosmopolitan values.'[30]

29 www.guardian.co.uk/katine/2009/apr/01/malnutrition-threat-uganda
30 *Cooper*, The New Liberal Imperialism, p. 3

This is the dominant view of political and economic elites. But the historical sequence must be reversed, as the emergence of early capitalism indicates. The legal system first developed the rules necessary for the regulation of capitalist production, including rules for the protection of property and contract and the development of legal and corporate personality. Only later did civic rules emerge, mainly with the creation of civil and political rights, which led to the creation of the modern subject and citizen. Similarly today, the globalisation of the *sui generis* morality of human rights follows the gradual unification of world markets. As Upendra Baxi has put it, while human rights are devised for the protection of vulnerable people, 'the emergent paradigm insists upon the promotion and protection of the collective human rights of global capital in ways that "justify" corporate well-being and dignity even when it entails gross and flagrant violation of human rights of actually existing human beings and communities. [...] The power of human rights discourse has [...] been critically appropriated by global capital.'[31]

As economic practices, legal rules and governance are standardized, a unified ethics, semiotics and law become the international *lingua franca*. This common language promises perpetual peace but forgets its own founding violence. The extreme injustice of global distribution is invisible to cosmopolitan law and is reduced to the sphere of the private, natural inevitable and humanitarian intervention will not confront the regime of intellectual property that condemns millions of people to death by disease. Poverty, disease, lack of food and clean water, violence against minorities and women, HIV/Aids are the main causes of misery and death in the world. But they are not seen as worthy of 'humanitarian' intervention. They are demoted to the private and domestic, they become an invisible and normalized part of the contingencies of life for which not much can be done. They are left to the magnanimity of philanthropists and the good will of pop stars. Despite the rhetoric of universal international law only a tiny part of the world comes under its purview and only a few problems of interest to the West are defined as crises.[32]

Against imperial arrogance and cosmopolitan naivety, we must insist that global neo-liberal capitalism and cosmopolitanism are part of the same project. The two must be uncoupled; cosmopolitanism can contribute little to the struggle against capitalist exploitation and political domination. Rawls exempts social justice from his manifesto of the 'law of peoples'. Fine mentions peripherally only the political economy. Habermas wants to export European social and economic rights to the cosmopolitan globe. But this is counter-intuitive; it goes against economic and political priorities. The Western promise to the developing world is that the violent or voluntary adoption of the market-led, neo-liberal model, of good governance and limited rights will inexorably lead to Western economic standards is fraudulent. Historically, the Western ability to turn the protection of formal rights into a limited guarantee of material, economic and social, rights was based on huge transfers from the colonies to the metropolis. While cosmopolitan morality militates in favour of

---

31 *Baxi*, The Future of Human Rights, pp. 132, 146.
32 *Charlesworth*, International Law: A discipline in Crisis, p. 377.

reverse flows, Western policies on development aid and Third World debt indicate that this is not politically feasible. Indeed, the successive crises and re-arrangements of neoliberal capitalism lead to continuous dispossession of family farming by agribusiness and to displacement, urbanisation and forced migration. These processes expand the number of people without skills, status or the basics for existence. They become the human debris, the waste-life, the 'one-use humans', the bottom billion. But as Immanuel Wallerstein put it, 'if all humans have equal rights, and all the peoples have equal rights, then we cannot maintain the kind of inegalitarian system that the capitalist world-economy has always been and always will be.'[33]

The abandonment of the economics of inequality turns cosmopolitanism and human rights into a palliative at best, and it renders it counter-productive at worst. They are useful for a limited protection of individuals but they can blunt political and group resistance. The cosmopolitanism of legalists and pragmatists expands the imperial writ further. Human rights can re-claim their redemptive role in the hands and imagination of those who return them to the tradition of resistance and struggle against the advice of the preachers of moralism, suffering humanity and humanitarian philanthropy. How could we imagine this?

In our thoroughly secular era, cosmopolitan justice must be discovered in history, the *cosmopolis* immanent to the *polis*. This is the promise of what we could call the *cosmopolitanism to come*.[34] Phenomenology explains that I have no immediate access to the consciousness of the other, no perception of otherness; the other is never fully present to me. I can approach her only by analogy of the perceptions, intentions and actions available to me. But I am always with the other, being together, exposed to the singularity of the other and to otherness. In cosmopolitan ontology, each singular being is a cosmos, the point of intertwining and condensation of past events and stories, people and encounters, fantasies, desires and dreams, a universe of unique meanings and values. Each cosmos is a point of *ekstasis*, of opening up and moving away, of being outside ourselves in our exposure to and sharing with others, immortals in our mortality, symbolically finite but imaginatively infinite; existence, our only essence.

Cosmopolitan community is not the common belonging of communitarianism, a common essence given by history, tradition, the spirit of the nation. Cosmos is being together with one another, ourselves as others, being selves through otherness. The *cosmopolis* is the coming together of multiple and singular worlds, each exposed to each other in the sharing of the cosmos. The axiom of cosmopolitan justice is: respect the singularity of the other. We must invent or discover in the European genealogy of cosmopolitanism whatever goes beyond and against its institutionalisation: the principle of its excess. The cosmopolitanism to come extends beyond nations and states, beyond the nation-state. The questioning of sovereignty is philosophically necessary and has already started. But the attack on sovereignty does not take place in the name of non-sovereignty but in that of another sovereign, the individual.

33 *Wallerstein*, The Insurmountable Contradictions of Liberalism, p. 176-7.
34 *Douzinas*, Human Rights and Empire, ch. 7.

The principle of sovereignty remains intact even though some sovereigns have been weakened and some frontiers breached.

What must be attacked is the theological mask of sovereignty, represented today by the hegemonic powers. We cannot fight sovereignty and the nation-state in general without risking giving up the principles of equality and self-determination inaugurated by, with and against national sovereignty. In the current conjuncture, they may be an indispensable barrier against ideological, religious, ethnic or capitalist hegemonies which, masquerading as universalism or cosmopolitanism, claim the dignity of a cosmos that is nothing more than a market-place or the moral rationalisation of particular interests.

Dissatisfaction with nation, state, and the international comes from a bond between singularities. What binds me to an Iraqi or a Palestinian, to a Guatanamo detainee or a 'bogus refugee' is not membership of humanity, citizenship or community but a protest against citizenship, nationality and thick community. What binds my world to that of others is our absolute singularity and total responsibility beyond citizen and human, beyond national and international. The cosmopolitanism to come is neither the achievement of humanity nor a federation of nations; neither a form or right nor a constitutional arrangement. The cosmos to come is the world of each unique one, of whoever or anyone; the polis, the infinite number of encounters of singularities. This is a non-pragmatic cosmopolitanism worth fighting for.

Bibliography

Archibugi, Daniele, The Global Commonwealth of Citizens. Towards Cosmopolitan Democracy, Princeton, 2008.

Baldry, H C., The Unity of Mankind in Greek Thought, Cambridge, 1965.

Baxi, Upendra, The Future of Human Rights, Oxford, 2002.

Calhoun, Craig, Nations Matter. Culture, History, and the Cosmopolitan Dream, Abingdon, 2007.

Cassesse, Antonio, Ex Injuria Jus Oritur: Are We Moving Towards International Legitimation of Forcible Humanitarian Countermeasures in the World Community?, European Journal of International Law 10 91) (1999), pp. 23-30.

Charlesworth, Hilary, International Law: A discipline of Crisis, Modern Law Review 65 (2004), pp. 377-392.

Cheah, Pheng, Inhuman Conditions. On Cosmopolitanism and Human Rights, Cambridge MASS., 2006.

Cooper, Robert, The New Liberal Imperialism, The Observer 7 April 2002, p. 3.

Douzinas, Costas, The End of Human Rights, Oxford, 2000.

Douzinas, Costas, Identity, Recognition, Rights: What can Hegel Teach us about Human Rights, Journal of Law and Society 29 (2002), pp. 379-405.

Douzinas, Costas, Human Rights and Empire, Abingdon, 2007.

Fine, Robert, Cosmopolitanism, Abingdon, 2007.

Glennon, Michael J, The New Interventionism: the search for a just international law, Foreign Affairs 78 (1999), pp. 2-7. www.guardian.co.uk/katine/2009/apr/01/malnutrition-threat-uganda

Habermas, Jürgen, Between Facts and Norms: Contributions to a Discourse Theory of Law and Democracy, Cambridge MASS., 1996.

Habermas, Jürgen, The Postnational Constellation, Cambridge MASS., 2001.

Habermas, Jürgen, Interpreting the Fall of a Monument, German Law Journal 4 (7) (2003) pp. 701-708. The essay originally appeared in the Frankfurt Allgemeine Zeitung on April 17, 2003.

Hirsch, David, Law Against Genocide: Cosmopolitan Trials, London, 2003.

Hirst, Paul, Space and Power. Politics, War and Architecture, Cambridge, 2005.

Kagan, Robert, Paradise and Power, London, 2004.

Kochi, Tarik, The Other's War, London, 2008.

Osborne, Tom, What is Neo-Enlightenment? Journal of Human Rights 2 (4) (2003), pp. 523-530.

de Sepulveda, Juan Ginés, Democrates Segundo of De las Justas Causa de la Guerra contra los Indios, Madrid, 1951.

Simma, Bruno, NATO, the UN and the Use of Force: Legal Aspects, European Journal of International Law 10 (1999), pp. 1-22.

Teitel, Ruti, "Humanity's Law": Rule of Law for the New Global Politics, Cornell International Law Journal 35 (2002) pp. 355-388.

Todorov, Tzvetan, The Conquest of America, Oklahoma, 1999.

Ullman, Berthold L, What are the Humanities? Journal of Higher Education, 17/6 (1946), pp. 301-337.

Wallerstein, Immanuel, The Insurmountable Contradictions of Liberalism, Southern Atlantic Quarterly 94 (4) (1995), pp. 1161-1178.

Post-Colonial Legality and Legitimacy: The Challenge of Indigenous Peoples

Gavin W Anderson

Introduction

The contemporary resurgence of indigenous peoples is one of the most challenging developments facing legal and political theory today. As other chapters in this collection make clear, the emergence of forms of law and politics beyond the state provokes some difficult questions for received understandings of the relation between law and power. However, the assertion of rights by the original inhabitants of modern states such as Canada and Australia to live according to the traditional norms of Aboriginal culture poses a qualitatively different challenge in a number of respects. First, an indigenous worldview operates outside some of the core assumptions of Western legal and political theory. Thus, while debates over the nature of new legal forms, such as international lex mercatoria, tend to assume the state-based paradigm of law as the antecedent from which conceptual innovations may develop,[1] indigenous notions of legality do not presuppose any original association between law and the institutions of the modern state. Second, while their roots may lie in a different cultural framework, indigenous normative systems today inhabit the same territorial space as the official legal order, and moreover are regarded by some as evidence of a continuing sovereignty which was not extinguished during the colonial period. As such, the challenges they pose do not speak solely to particular ways in which political authority can be justified, but question the very foundations of the post-colonial state itself.

The basic issue here is that 'many Aboriginal peoples do not understand their rights in terms that are amenable to the state's legal and political discourses.'[2] In other words, the language of Western legal and political thought may not be the language best suited to addressing claims of Aboriginal justice.[3] This general wariness finds a more particular expression with regard to the themes of this collection, as indigenous peoples are mindful of the general ways in which the language of legality and legitimacy was deployed in support of the colonial project. It is less than a century since the Privy Council deemed Aboriginal peoples 'so low in the scale of social organisation' that they were incapable of engaging on anything approaching equal terms with 'the institutions or legal ideas of civilized society.'[4] However, over

---

1 *Teubner*, "Global Bukowina", p. 3.
2 *Turner*, This is not a Peace Pipe, p. 4.
3 *Ivison/Patton/Saunders*, Introduction, p. 2.
4 Re Southern Rhodesia, p. 233.

the past few decades there has been a significant shift in official attitudes, and indigenous issues now regularly feature in the deliberations of public bodies such as legislatures, Royal Commissions and the superior courts. Moreover, it is through the language of legality, and specifically legal rights, that indigenous peoples are increasingly prosecuting their claims, sometimes securing headline victories,[5] and apparent gains in terms of the recognition of their cultural practices.[6]

For some, these developments provide an opportunity for advancing different conceptions of legality and legitimacy, and to rethink our understanding of the relationship between them. Working within a framework of constitutional pluralism[7] (or in some versions 'post-national constitutionalism'[8]) developed at the general level by theorists like Neil Walker, scholars such as Jim Tully[9] and Patrick Macklem[10] have proposed a thicker conception of legality which acknowledges the continued existence of indigenous legal orders. Furthermore, grounding our approach in the fact of Aboriginal difference is seen, in this account, as a necessary precursor to reorienting the exercise of power to redress past injustices suffered by indigenous peoples, thereby placing it on a more legitimate footing. For others like Dale Turner,[11] John Borrows[12] and Stewart Motha,[13] the key question is why Western discourses of legality proved an effective vehicle in legitimating the colonial project, which requires adverting to its epistemological dimension. The concern of this emerging school of critical indigenous theory is that while a reworking of legality and legitimacy may address some of the ethnocentric biases of the colonial period, it ultimately reproduces an exclusionary logic, ensuring indigenous peoples remain in a politically subordinate position. These differing outlooks present contrasting accounts of which methodological divide is most relevant to our discussion. For the first approach, the key divide is between sociological and normative accounts of legality and legitimacy, and it can be seen as an attempt to reconcile the dichotomy between them by emphasising their necessary connections. We can contrast this with a different faultline: here the crucial distinction is between those approaches which challenge, and those which assume, the epistemological foundations of the postcolonial legal and political order.

This chapter explores what is at stake between these two approaches in terms of how we think about law, power and legitimacy. While we will pursue this question primarily in the context of claims for indigenous justice – with specific reference to

---

5   See Mabo (no 2).
6   *Asch*, From Calder to Van der Peet, p. 429.
7   *Walker*, The Idea of Constitutional Pluralism, p. 317.
8   See *Chalmers*, Post-nationalism, p. 178.
9   *Tully*, Strange Multiplicity.
10 *Macklem*, Indigenous Difference.
11 *Turner*, This is not a Peace Pipe, p. 4.
12 *Borrows*, Recovering Canada.
13 See *Motha*, The Sovereign Event in a Nation's Law, p. 311.

Canada and Australia[14] – which approach we find more persuasive has broader ramifications. The first approach has been adapted to other fields where traditional notions of legality and legitimacy are under pressure,[15] and so may be potentially regarded as the elusive transferable paradigm; while the second reflects the growing importance being attached to epistemological argument as a core device of critical theory.[16] The structure is as follows: the first section places the discussion in historical and contemporary context, outlining how the exclusion of indigenous law furthered colonial strategies, and the ways in which challenges to this exclusion now feature on the public policy agenda. The second and third sections set out the background theoretical orientations of the two approaches delineated above, and focus in more detail on the differences between them, in particular whether recent official rapprochement with indigenous peoples represents a potentially decisive break with colonial notions of legality and legitimacy, or operates within a frame of continuity. The final section considers the prospects for advancing indigenous justice in light of a comparative analysis of these two approaches. This leads to the conclusion that while there has been some opening up of the discourse of legality and legitimacy to accommodate indigenous cultural difference, the limit is reached when Western legal and political discourses perceive a threat to the ultimate authority of the postcolonial state. Thus, framing the debate in terms of reworking legality and legitimacy may be counterproductive to the cause of indigenous justice.

Indigenous peoples in historical and contemporary context

The colonisation of North America and Australasia, brought into contact two very different worldviews. The colonists were, or were to become, children of the Enlightenment, and subscribed to the idea that by the deployment of reason, humanity could control its environment and achieve potentially limitless progress. They exported this model and engaged in the process of building new modern states, with attendant processes of industrialisation and urbanisation, in the lands which they settled. What the Europeans had encountered there were large numbers of diverse peoples, each with their distinctive cultures, and who followed largely agrarian and nomadic way of life – one in which nature was to be revered, not tamed – which had continued undisturbed for the preceding centuries. However, this form of existence was to come under intense pressure, and the resultant rise of the colonial state led to indigenous disempowerment and dispossession.[17]

---

14 That is not, of course, to suggest that there are not important differences between the debates in Canada and Australia, or even that that there is a homogeneity to debates within each jurisdiction. Rather, the choice here reflects the fact that it is in these jurisdictions where debate on the nature of indigenous legality is most developed.
15 See *Shaw*, Postnational Constitutionalism in the European Union.
16 See De Sousa Santos (ed), Another Knowledge is Possible.
17 See Havemann (ed) chs. 4-6.

Our interest here is the role played by ideas of legality and legitimacy in promoting the colonists' ascendancy. To be sure, force was often a potent weapon of imperialist advancement, but from the beginning, the colonial project was not simply a bare exercise of might, but sought to justify itself in the language of right. The significance of this becomes clear when we consider that Aboriginal societies were marked as much by legal, as cultural, diversity. As John Borrows recounts, at the time of first contact, indigenous societies encompassed a rich variety of legal systems 'grounded [in] complex spiritual, political and social customs.'[18] Initially, European legal norms were but one part of this fragmented picture, and we should be careful not to see the colonial state emerging from the start as a comprehensive political system, nor to regard its dominance as historically inevitable.[19] Rather, its hegemony was the result of prolonged struggle, including struggle over law; however, by the nineteenth century, this struggle had effectively been resolved, with the important consequence that notions of Aboriginal law had all but disappeared from the official narrative.

The most notorious justification of European sovereignty over colonial territories was the doctrine of terra nullius, or vacant lands, as the justification. This borrowed from John Locke's 'stages of world history' thesis in two important respects: first, that only European societies had reached the stage of development where they had gained the capacity to make laws – in contrast, Aboriginal social organisation, which was regarded as a relatively arrested condition, could not be said to live under a system of law. Second, given the European peoples' unique capacity to regulate rights in land, this provided the basis for the exercise of sovereignty over areas occupied by Aboriginals (whose consent was unnecessary as they had no legal rights to the land).[20] While on one reading, 'vacant' would seem an inaccurate description of the lands on which Aboriginal peoples hunted and gathered, for Locke they were still empty as they had not attained levels of agricultural cultivation then found in Europe. The terra nullius doctrine was the basis for the original claim to Australia in the name of the British crown,[21] while in North America, the position was for a while more ambivalent.[22] However, in terms of the justification of British sovereignty, Canada was to be treated as terra nullius, with the primitive condition of the indigenous peoples preventing them from grounding a rival claim.[23] Thus, by the time of

---

18   Borrows, Recovering Canada, p. 4.
19   See Benton, Law and Colonial Cultures, p. 9.
20   Tully notes that for Locke, in contrast with Aboriginals who were 'commonly without any fixed property on the ground,' the European settlers ('those who are counted the Civiliz'd part of Mankind') 'have multiplied positive laws to determine Property', for 'in governments the Laws regulate the right of property, and the possession of land is determined by positive constitutions': *Tully*, Strange Multiplicity, p. 72.
21   See *Reynolds*, New Frontiers: Australia, pp. 130-131.
22   Following Imperial instructions for inhabited territories, the settlers entered into negotiations 'to take possession with the Consent of the Natives: *Reynolds*, New Frontiers: Australia, p. 130.
23   *Asch*, First Nations and the Derivation of Canada's Underlying Title, p.155.

the St. Catherine's Milling case in 1888, the Judicial Committee of the Privy Council could confidently state that the Crown's underlying title to Canada had 'all along been a present proprietary estate in the land, upon which the Indian title was a mere burden.'[24]

As indicated above, in North America at least, there was some early acknowledgement that the Aboriginals enjoyed legal and political agency to enter into nation-to-nation agreements with the Europeans. For example, in the Treaty of Niagara of 1764, the British sought military and economic co-operation by providing various guarantees for their existing indigenous territory against European settlement without consent. Moreover, the process by which it was solemnified – the giving and receiving of wampum belts – and the substantive principles it embodied – including the idea that land is held in trust and should be shared – seemed to indicate recognition of the distinctive norms and practices of Aboriginal legal culture. From an Aboriginal perspective, this was, and remains, a binding agreement between equal parties.[25] However, these treaties had a dual character, and reference to Aboriginal lands as the Crown's 'dominions and territories' was regarded by the colonial administration as a means of removing Aboriginal control from their lands.[26] Thus, in the spirit of terra nullius, in construing such treaties, it was the settlers alone who understood 'the modes and forms of creating the various technical estates known [to] law.'[27] Accordingly, the treaties could be unilaterally departed from using the legal forms of the colonial state, such as when Aboriginal lands protected by the 1764 Treaty were the subject of transactions of sale to non-Aboriginals.[28]

The exclusionary logic which underpins terra nullius thinking advanced colonialism through related processes of reduction and elision which narrowed the prevailing conception of legality to the formal law of the colonial state, and collapsed questions of legality and legitimacy such that the correlation between the two became 'deeply inscribed in the dominant modern conception of law.'[29] James Tully's historical analysis of constitutional thought amplifies the significance of this reduction. Tully contrasts an older tradition of 'common constitutionalism'[30] – where recognition of different types of legality meant that legitimacy required a negotiated modus vivendi – with the rise of the 'imperial language of modern constitutionalism'[31] which sought to establish a homogeneous society with a uniform set of legal and political institutions.[32] It is at this point that legality and legitimacy become almost self-referential: establishing a single system of official law, and thereby removing

---

24 St Catherine's Milling58.
25 *Borrows*, Recovering Canada, pp. 125-6.
26 *Coates*, The "Gentle" Occupation, p.146.
27 *Asch*, First Nations, 155, quoting Jones v Meehan pp. 10-11.
28 *Borrows*, Recovering Canada, pp. 35-6.
29 *De Sousa Santos*, Towards a New Legal Common Sense, p. 19.
30 *Tully*, Strange Multiplicity, pp. 116-124.
31 *Tully*, Strange Multiplicity, p. 127.
32 See *Tully*, The Unfreedom of the Moderns, p. 209.

the 'irregularity'[33] of alternative sources of legal and political authority, was regarded as essential to realising the universal jurisdiction of the colonial state.[34] In this way, embedding the singular legality of the formal constitution at the foundation of the colonial order provided a 'licen[c]e for empire'[35] with respect to Aboriginal peoples and their lands. While acting through law was thus seen as necessary to building the modern state, it was at the same time sufficient to justify the latter's actions, including, and perhaps especially so, when engaged in the pursuit of assimilationist policies.

The idea that legality provides its own legitimacy has in recent times come under sustained critique. For many, it is not obvious that constitutional texts are self-interpreting or self-executing. As has been observed (with regard to the Canadian constitution), it is the assumption that the state enjoys inherent power which leads to the interpretation of specific constitutional provisions as granting it authority over Aboriginals, not the other way round.[36] Questioning this assumption lies at the heart of indigenous challenges: instead, it is contended not only that Aboriginal sovereignty survived the founding of the colonial state, but that it continues to this day.[37] Here, the claim that the colonial state achieved comprehensive jurisdiction as the sole repository of legality is seen less as historical fact than a normative claim, itself a legacy of eighteenth century ethnocentric approaches to public policy. This potentially leads to a direct challenge to received understandings of legitimacy: if we reject the notion that indigenous peoples and their forms of government were simply absorbed into the colonial state, the legitimacy of official laws, particularly where they seek to eradicate indigenous practices in the name of uniformity, appears far from self-evident.[38]

At the same time as these scholarly objections have been raised, there has been a change in official attitudes which might seem to move away from terra nullius type thinking. For example, the Canadian Royal Commission on Aboriginal Peoples' recommendation that Aboriginal peoples should regain 'a fair proportion' of their ancestral lands in the spirit of 'true partnership,'[39] could be regarded as a return to the nation-to-nation relations of the early treaties. Negotiations over indigenous title claims are now a regular feature of contemporary governance in Canada and Australia.[40] The 2008 apology by the Australian Prime Minister for the 'suffering and

---

33   *Tully*, Strange Multiplicity, p. 66.
34   *Tully*, Strange Multiplicity, p. 66.
35   *Tully*, Strange Multiplicity, p. 94, quoting *Jones*, License for Empire.
36   *Asch/Macklem*, Aboriginal Rights and Canadian Sovereignty, p. 510. Asch and Macklem's discussion focuses on s. 91(24) of the Constitution (formerly British North America) Act 1867, which ascribes legislative power over 'Indians and lands reserved to Indians' to the federal Canadian Parliament.
37   *Macklem*, Indigenous Difference, pp. 73-74.
38   *Macklem*, Indigenous Difference, p. 74.
39   Royal Commission on Aboriginal Peoples, p. 688.
40   See *Macklem*, Indigenous Difference, ch. 9, and *Parry/Davies/Howitt/Jarvis/Williams*, Comprehensive Native Title Negotiations.

loss' visited upon Aborigines by '[successive] laws and policies' would have been unimaginable well beyond the half point of the preceding century.[41] These changes of tone and practice at the governmental level have been accompanied by modifications in legal doctrine which might seem to reflect the idea that legitimate conduct towards Aboriginals requires taking into their account their distinctive cultural traditions. Thus, in Calder, the Supreme Court of Canada stated that the indigenous peoples were 'organized in societies and occupying the land'[42] at the time of European settlement, and on that basis, possessed pre-existing rights, to occupy their land, and use it to hunt and fish.[43] In the seminal Mabo No 2 case, the High Court of Australia held that the original presence of the Meriam people in the Murray Islands of the Torres Strait, meant they were not in fact empty lands, and so the islanders enjoyed 'native title' as a matter of common law.

These, and other, developments have led to a theoretical re-examination of the relationship between legality and legitimacy. At the heart of this rethinking are two related questions. First, if we require to rethink the relationship between legality and legitimacy in light of the evolving political climate, what theoretical tools are best suited to the task? Second, to what extent do these developments provide the opportunity for moving to a new conception of this relationship which can redress past injustices suffered by indigenous peoples. In the following two sections, I contrast two different sets of responses to these questions: the first is located within changing perceptions of the nature of sovereignty, while the second places greater emphasis on epistemological questions. Contrasting these two responses, I suggest, clarifies what are the key issues in terms of establishing the theoretical preconditions for advancing indigenous justice.

Relational sovereignty:
Towards a new understanding of legality and legitimacy?

The first response seeks to refashion the relation between legality and legitimacy through a radical rethinking of our conception of sovereignty. The principal target here is the traditional view of sovereignty as the means by which the state exercised absolute and exclusive authority over all within its territorial bounds.[44] This provided a powerful legitimating discourse for colonialism, establishing a positivist paradigm of law in which indigenous notions of legality were a conceptual non-starter.[45] Accordingly, from an indigenous rights perspective, a reworking of sovereignty appears to be an important prize in opening up established understandings of legality and legitimacy. This first response attempts such a reworking to meet two

---

41 Apology to Australia's Indigenous Peoples
42 Calder v 156 per Judson J.
43 In the instant case, though, the Court found that these rights had been extinguished.
44 See *Loughlin*, Sword and Scales, ch. 9.
45 See *Macklem*, Indigenous Difference, pp. 113-119.

broad objectives: first, to demonstrate that the state-based, positivistic, approach always rested on a misunderstanding of sovereignty, and that properly understood, the latter requires taking account of indigenous forms of legality; second, to substantiate the argument that the legitimacy of the colonial state, and in particular its policy with respect to indigenous rights, rests on its co-existence with Aboriginal sovereignty.[46] As such, this approach can be characterised as seeking to transcend existing dichotomies between sociological and normative approaches to legality and legitimacy; moreover, it suggests that we can incorporate multiple sources of law into the analysis and still provide legal discourse with normative content.

We can locate this response in recent developments in constitutional theory which outline a relational understanding of sovereignty. According to Martin Loughlin, sovereignty consists of two linked, but irreducible, facets: competence and capacity. The first – also right, or legal sovereignty – connotes the institutional framework of juridical power, the second – political or real sovereignty – the actual location of power.[47] Lawyers tend to focus on competence to the exclusion of capacity, but this is a mistake as the political conception expresses the 'basic political relationship' between rulers and ruled.[48] The two conceptions are not only strongly related, but mutually implied, and so diminution of the state's ability to implement its policies will affect the scope of its legal competence. While for Loughlin, sovereignty remains intrinsic and exclusive to the state, others have taken up his idea that 'the doctrines of legal sovereignty must march alongside political reality'[49] to argue that the capacity of non-state bodies to achieve their policy objectives, e.g. in competition with the state, means they also exercise legal authority. Such ideas of post-national constitutionalism have been developed in the context of supranational organisations: here, a pluralistic account of constitutionalism is grounded in the empirical recognition that traditional state functions, such as regulating institutions or elaborating the tenets of citizenship, are now performed by entities such as the EU or WTO.[50]

This argument that the capacity, or political sovereignty, of non-state entities translates into competence or legal sovereignty introduces a further relational dimension into the discussion, namely the relation between different sites of constitutional authority. On this account, sovereignty is not conceived of as something which can be objectively measured, but instead as a speech act which in a post-national era gives rise to a multiplicity of plausible claims to possess legal and political authority.[51] Crucially, because these claims overlap and often compete with each other, there is no ultimate sovereign, and this empirical state of affairs generates its own normative criterion. According to Neil Walker (addressing the relation between national and supranational government in Europe), this fact of constitutional plural-

---

46 *Macklem*, Indigenous Difference, p. 123.
47 *Loughlin*, Sword and Scales, pp. 145-6.
48 *Loughlin*, The Idea of Public Law, p. 85.
49 *Loughlin*, The Idea of Public Law, p. 185.
50 See *Walker*, The EU and the WTO.
51 *Walker*, Late Sovereignty in the European Union, p. 6.

ism necessarily leads to a new 'ethic of political responsibility' based on 'mutual recognition and respect' among the various sites of legal and political authority.[52] In terms of the present discussion, highlighting the necessary connection between the empirical and normative aspects of sovereignty has been a key strategy for those seeking to recover the legal and political agency of indigenous peoples. Tully, for example, has argued that in post-colonial societies the monistic view of sovereignty can now be regarded as an 'abstract forger[y],' and that the lived experience of such societies reveals a relational 'sovereignty of culturally diverse citizens.'[53] Furthermore, he sees this approach as a catalyst for opening up debate over the legitimate exercise of power: procedurally, it encourages a 'practical dialogue' in which no single contribution is privileged on account of its provenance (i.e. recognition of competence translates into the right to be heard);[54] substantively, it invites constitutional differentiation in place of uniformity, (where, obversely, we might say that the recognition of right reinforces capacity).[55]

Patrick Macklem argues that it is important to elaborate why indigenous difference is legally and politically significant to understand more precisely how a relational conception of sovereignty recasts what is to be regarded as a legitimate exercise of power. He outlines four aspects of this difference which are most relevant to the contemporary interests of indigenous peoples: the threat to their distinctive cultures, their prior occupancy of and exercise of sovereignty over the territory of the modern state, and their participation in the Treaty processes discussed above.[56] For Macklem, what unites these aspects is that they engage questions of distributive justice:[57] thus, indigenous difference is to be protected not simply because of its difference,[58] but because this promotes 'a just distribution' of power.[59] Thus, while not every aspect of indigenous difference should be upheld, it does place a high premium on claims of prior sovereignty: according to Macklem, these claims should be sustained to the extent they relieve Aboriginal peoples of the 'costs associated with reproducing their cultures in the face of alien institutional cultures.'[60] On this view, what counts as valid legal rules cannot be separated from the threshold question of whether Aboriginal people exercise 'control over their collective and individual identities.'[61] Accordingly, legitimacy can no longer be satisfied by a uniform conception of legality, but by recognising the latter's plural nature, which in practice

---

52 *Walker*, The Idea of Constitutional Pluralism, p. 337.
53 *Tully*, Strange Multiplicity, p. 183.
54 *Tully*, Strange Multiplicity, p. 183.
55 *Tully*, Strange Multiplicity, p. 172.
56 *Tully*, Strange Multiplicity, p. 167.
57 *Tully*, Strange Multiplicity, p. 71.
58 *Macklem*, Indigenous Difference, p. 42. According to Macklem, to hold otherwise, unnecessarily reduces indigenous rights to cultural rights, and lapses into an unhelpful and potentially regressive cultural relativism where difference is validated for its own sake.
59 *Macklem*, Indigenous Difference, p. 287.
60 *Macklem*, Indigenous Difference, p. 127.
61 *Macklem*, Indigenous Difference, p. 127.

entails allowing Aboriginal legal norms to prevail if that advances restorative justice. Thus, Macklem regards decisions like Sparrow,[62] where the Supreme Court of Canada accorded the Musqueam nation broader fishing entitlements than non-Aboriginals, as satisfying the test of legitimacy as it accords indigenous peoples greater autonomy in areas where their rights had been systematically denied; whereas he finds the same court's approach in Delgamuukw, where it stated that inter alia 'the development of agriculture, forestry, mining and hydro-electric power'[63] could in principle justify limiting indigenous rights, wanting as this still seeks to impose Western social and economic norms in the guise of uniformity.[64]

The idea that rethinking legality and legitimacy requires acknowledging the necessary connections between the normative and sociological dimensions of legal and political discourse has become increasingly influential, and in many ways is setting the parameters of debate. Judges now expressly characterise their task in indigenous rights cases as effecting a 'reconciliation' between the sociological fact of Aboriginal prior occupancy and the (previously) self-contained set of normative assumptions which supported assertions of colonial sovereignty.[65] The progressive critique of the emerging jurisprudence is often directed to a perceived failure to take the fact of indigenous difference sufficiently seriously, and so leaving postcolonial understandings of legitimacy inadequately transformed.[66] Perhaps the most revealing development is the extent to which the opposition to indigenous rights now seeks to maintain existing normative boundaries by arguing that claims of indigenous sovereignty are not substantiated by socio-historical analysis.[67] It might appear then, that we have a come a long way since the systematic denial of indigenous legality was at the root of the colonial constitutional order.

The epistemological dimension to legality and legitimacy: plus ça change...

We can contrast the foregoing with a second mode of thought, grounded in critical indigenous and post-colonial scholarship, which introduces an epistemological dimension into the analysis of recent changes in official and jurisprudential practice. Its theoretical orientation is directed less to overcoming the differences between normative and sociological approaches than exploring the shared assumptions which underpin debates on legality and legitimacy. This places more emphasis on a narrative of continuity than the previous approach. This continuity arises both between normative and sociological methodologies and between the legal and political practices of the colonial era and the apparent recent departures therefrom – both of

---

62 Sparrow.
63 Delgamuukw 1111.
64 *Macklem*, Indigenous Difference, ch 6.
65 *Macklem*, Indigenous Difference, p. 188, discussing La Mer CJC's judgment in Delgamuukw.
66 Havemann, A Formative Conclusion, p. 474. See also *Macklem*, Indigenous Difference.
67 *Flanagan*, First Nations? Second Thoughts, ch. 4.

which are said to contribute to maintaining key epistemological elements which played an instrumental role in the suppression of indigenous peoples. While this second response is sympathetic to the political motivations of the attempt to rework sovereignty, as we shall see, it is dubious as to whether this latter approach appreciates the full extent of the challenge posed by adverting to indigenous questions. To do so, it is suggested, we need to understand how questions of knowledge are located at 'the foundation' of the colonial order.[68]

Post-colonial studies argue that colonialism should now be seen as much as an epistemological, as an economic and political, enterprise. That is of course not to downplay the often very direct exercises of power which built the colonial state, nor to minimise the material effects of this on the existences of indigenous peoples, which were in many instances placed in jeopardy. The point rather is to underscore how the destruction of local forms of knowledge played a central role in maintaining colonial power and domination.[69] Western forms of legal and political knowledge became established as the ground-rules for social life through the discarding of alternative ways of knowing the world which were portrayed as manifestations of irrationality and so rendered effectively invisible in the epistemological 'abyss.'[70] In other words, the legitimacy of the colonial project was to be predicated not simply on establishing its pre-eminence against rival worldviews, but in eradicating the idea that there could be such alternatives. In this way, knowledge strategies contributed to hierarchical power relations in colonial society, entrenching as natural baselines for legal and political debate both capitalist forms of political economy, and the conceptualisation of social life in terms of the division between the state and civil society. Moreover, relations of power based in inequalities of knowledge can subsist long after the formal institutions of colonialism have been dismantled, leaving open the question of 'how much of the colonial past remains in the post-colonial present.'[71]

Regarding law as an artefact of the politics of knowledge deepens our understanding of how the doctrine of terra nullius operated to shore up colonial hegemony: its purpose was not simply to trump competing accounts of legality, but to reduce the range of determinants over what counts as legal or illegal to the singular law of the modern state. As with politics and economics, the aim here was to ensure that alternative conceptions were simply not recognised as conceptions of legality at all. The effect was to leave out 'a whole social territory' where the binary classifications of Western law made no sense as an organising idea, including 'the territory of the lawless, the alegal, the nonlegal, and even the legal or illegal according to nonofficially recogni[s]ed law.'[72] On this account, both empirical and normative methodologies

---

68 See *De Sousa Santos/Nunes/Meneses*, Opening up the Canon of Knowledge and Recognition of Difference, xix.
69 See *De Sousa Santos/Nunes/Meneses*, Opening up the Canon of Knowledge and Recognition of Difference, xxxiii et seq.
70 See *De Sousa Santos*, Beyond Abyssal Thinking, p. 45.
71 See *De Sousa Santos/Nunes/Meneses*, Opening up the Canon of Knowledge and Recognition of Difference, xxxv.
72 See *De Sousa Santos*, Beyond Abyssal Thinking, p. 48.

made important contributions to the artificial narrowing of legal knowledge. Legal-sociological approaches employed the scientific vocabulary of legal positivism to affirm the equation of law with the state as an incontrovertible fact.[73] In legal-philosophical terms, while colonialism could be ultimately justified as the manifestation of a collective right to development, it was made clear that the content of this legal would only draw on rational, Western, notions of what amounted to development.[74] Crucially, for some, an important element of the colonial enterprise consisted of the interplay between the two approaches, as the predominant positivist mode of legal discourse both rested on, and through its analytical method masked, the epistemicidal roots of colonialism, making it difficult to challenge this in political terms.[75] Thus, it would appear that there is nothing particularly new, nor anything necessarily progressive, about highlighting the connections between sociological and normative conceptions of law.

The argument that by reproducing modernist forms of knowledge, legal and political discourses play an important role in the subjugation of indigenous peoples is for some still highly relevant today. On this view, the increased judicial protection of indigenous rights, which for the first approach indicated some recognition, at an empirical level, of a continuing Aboriginal sovereignty, does not mark the post-colonial watershed as might first appear. Instead, indigenous scholars have highlighted how in practice this recognition conditions Aboriginal legality according to the standards of modern Western legality.[76] Thus, the landmark ruling in Mabo upholding prior native title turned on Aboriginal peoples satisfying (what were to them) alien concepts of property law, in particular that they enjoyed dominium over their traditional lands, as opposed to imperium which remained vested in the Crown. Moreover, to enjoy these (and other) rights, it has to be established to the court's satisfaction that they were an integral part of Aboriginal culture at first contact (and have not been extinguished since). The consequence is to fix the scope of Aboriginal rights to that time, so denying the possibility of any indigenous legal innovation over the past few centuries.[77] As such, the interaction between indigenous and western legal cultures is specifically excluded as a source of indigenous rights.[78] The same limitations do not apply to Western law, and so the construction of Aboriginal legality which emerges

---

73 See *De Sousa Santos/Nunes/Meneses*, Opening up the Canon of Knowledge and Recognition of Difference, xxxiii-xxxix.
74 See *Baxi*, The Future of Human Rights, pp. 30-31.
75 *De Sousa Santos*, Towards a New Legal Common Sense, p. 190. As de Sousa Santos observes, it is perhaps ironic that this strategy proved particularly successful in the very colonial and post-colonial societies where legal positivism might have appeared to be at its weakest.
76 *Borrows*, Recovering Canada, p. 66
77 Thus, as Michael Asch observes, it makes it very difficult for indigenous peoples to argue that title to land would include 'non-renewable resources' such as the discovery of oil: *Asch*, From Calder to Van der Peet, p. 426.
78 For example, in Van der Peet the Supreme Court of Canada held that selling fish was not an integral part of Sto:lo culture, and had only developed after contact.

can be depicted as partial and backward looking, premised on colonial stereotypes of the indigenous subject.[79]

Consequently, it is not surprising that most advances have tended to be where courts have upheld 'way of life' rights, based on traditional practices such as hunting and fishing.[80] For some, it is instructive to compare the recognition of these rights with that accorded to political rights. Here, there is agreement that there has been markedly little progress, with both judicial and governmental definitions of indigenous rights excluding a right to self-determination.[81] Instead, official practice often emphasises that recognising the rights of indigenous peoples should not be mistaken for acknowledging the latter's political equality. Accordingly, where land treaties have been concluded, this has in practice conceded only limited portions of ancestral homelands, but in return for the relinquishment of all future claims.[82] Also, where way of life rights are granted, it has been made clear that these are subject to unilateral extinguishment through ordinary legislation.[83] Indeed, the continued exercise by state authorities of jurisdiction to adjudicate these claims underlines that while the legitimacy of some colonial policies may now be subject to review, what remains off limits is the basic assumption of the state's inherent power.

Conclusion: Political inequality as the limit of epistemological equality

In this final section, we consider the prospects for advancing indigenous justice in light of a comparative analysis of the above two approaches to post-colonial legality and legitimacy. While they emerge from different methodological traditions, it is not uncommon to find elements of each approach within the same scholarship. Thus, the limitations of existing jurisprudence outlined by the second approach can both be acknowledged by those advancing a reworking of sovereignty, and provide the basis for further normative development of the ethic of constitutional pluralism.[84] Indeed, together they can be seen to generate complementary propositions about the theoretical conditions for indigenous justice: for the second, overcoming colonial politics of knowledge is only possible through a basic epistemological equality; while the logical conclusion of the first approach would seem to be that taking epistemological equality seriously entails political equality and the full recognition of the legitimacy of Aboriginal sovereignty.

---

79 *Borrows*, Recovering Canada, p. 60.
80 See e.g. Hamlet of Baker Lake.
81 *Asch*, From Calder to Van der Peet, p. 437.
82 See *Tully*, The Struggles of Indigenous Peoples for and of Freedom, p. 49.
83 See for instance the reference in Sparrow (p. 404) that there was from the outset never any doubt that sovereignty and legislative power [...] to [Aboriginal] lands vested in the Crown.'
84 See *Macklem*, Indigenous Difference.

For indigenous scholars, the stakes here are high. Aboriginal ways of knowing the world are not readily located on the continuum of Western legal and political thought, as Borrows's account of the indigenous notions of federalism makes clear:

Our loyalties, allegiance, and affection are related to the land. The water, wind, sun, and stars are part of this federation; the fish, birds, plants and animals share the same union.[85]

According to Turner, listening to the 'the myriad voices of Aboriginal peoples'[86] reveals that 'sovereignty lies at the very core of Aboriginal existence.'[87] For him, there is a mutually reinforcing relation between epistemological and political equality: it is precisely because a conception of sovereignty arises 'directly from the [Aboriginal] community itself,' i.e. according to the traditional tenets of knowledge such as those expressed above, that it is a 'strong' conception of sovereignty where the legitimacy of the post-colonial state remains in question, and indeed where some Aboriginals do not regard themselves as citizens of the post-colonial state.[88] Obversely, weaker conceptions of sovereignty, which assume that the post-colonial state can trump Aboriginal rights, are unable to come to terms with the epistemological factors at play here. Thus, any diminution of Aboriginal citizenship effected by colonial policies is seen as a problem within the discourse of minority rights, rather than ensuing from indigenous peoples' disenfranchisement 'from the land, water, animals and trees.'[89] Consequently, it can be redressed through more robust forms of cultural protection rather than treating indigenous peoples as 'philosophically equal participants.'

From this discussion, we might agree with Macklem that sovereignty is not a concept which debates about indigenous legality can wish away. Addressing the argument that Aboriginal peoples legitimise hierarchical power relations by engaging in such debates, he suggests such criticisms are misplaced. The object of this engagement, as he sees it, is not to mimic European-style authority structures, but instead advance debate about how indigenous peoples might exercise sovereignty '[once] viewed as sovereign within their spheres of authority.'[90] But this somewhat begs the question of whether they will come to be viewed in such a way: there is a difference between characterising sovereignty as normatively open and transforming it according to different normative visions of indigenous justice. In the concluding passages of this chapter, I argue that the development of an indigenous rights discourse, while serving as a catalyst for demands for greater political equality, should

---

85 *Borrows*, Recovering Canada, p. 138.
86 *Turner*, This is not a Peace Pipe, p. 59. In a similar vein to Borrows, Turner (166) quotes a Gitxzan view that the basis of Aboriginal law lies in the 'marriage' of the Chief and the land: 'Each Chief has an ancestor who encountered and acknowledged the life of the land. From such encounters come power. The land, the plants, the animals and the people all have spirit – they all must be shown respect.'
87 *Turner*, This is not a Peace Pipe, p. 67.
88 *Turner*, This is not a Peace Pipe, pp. 66, 68.
89 *Borrows*, Recovering Canada, p. 140.
90 See *Macklem*, Indigenous Difference, p. 112.

also be viewed as part of a containment strategy which ensures that no significant political concessions are granted which will undermine the ultimate authority of the post-colonial state.

Stewart Motha's analysis of the High Court of Australia's decision in Mabo (No. 2) locates this containment strategy in the structure of sovereignty discourse. He suggests that the decision 'both repeated and retreated from the foundation' of the legal authority of the post-colonial state.[91] On the one hand, the Court held that it was a 'fallacy' to equate the Crown's sovereignty, or absolute title, with beneficial ownership, of the Meriam peoples' lands, thus appearing to rethink the doctrine of terra nullius by recognising that Aboriginal society consisted of a 'government of laws.'[92] However, at the same time, the Court affirmed that the imperium (or radical title) of the post-colonial state still subsists, which of course was the basis of the original dispossession of Aboriginal lands and the extinguishment of their rights. For Motha, the co-presence of these two accounts of sovereignty raises the question of whether the continued reception of colonial law makes sense absent its foundational theory.[93] He argues that the Court seeks to have it both ways, rewriting colonial history in accordance 'with our present knowledge and appreciation of the facts'[94] – as a result, what was previously regarded as an exclusionary founding moment is now found always to have contained the distinction between radical and beneficial title, which enabled the Court to uphold native title in the instant case.

This potentially leads to a position of strong epistemological equality: if we are to take the Court at its word, this seems to acknowledge a ''plurality' at the original moment of the purportedly 'singular' sovereign event.'[95] But while this may seem to confirm sovereignty's 'alterability by law,'[96] for Motha, there are limits as to how far this can and will be altered, militating against its further transformation. He finds a logical impossibility at the heart of the Court's approach, namely that 'the narrative of law's foundation cannot be contained or renounced as a past abomination by a sovereign power outside the law that instituted a state, nation or society.'[97] Thus, it is no surprise that the Court is unequivocal that the question of whether colonial lands were legally acquired by the Crown is non-justiciable: in this way, the ultimate sovereignty of the post-colonial state continues to be assumed. Accordingly, upholding aboriginal land interests cannot take place outside the post-colonial law which, despite its rhetoric, the Court is unable to disavow, and so decisions such as Mabo

---

91 *Motha*, The Sovereign Event in a Nation's Law, p. 317.
92 *Motha*, The Sovereign Event in a Nation's Law, p. 322 (quoting Brennan J in Mabo No 2, p. 39).
93 *Motha*, The Sovereign Event in a Nation's Law, p. 321
94 *Motha*, The Sovereign Event in a Nation's Law, pp. 316, 322 (quoting Brennan J's judgment in Mabo No 2, 50-1, 39).
95 *Motha*, The Sovereign Event in a Nation's Law, p. 317.
96 *Motha*, The Sovereign Event in a Nation's Law, p. 311.
97 *Motha*, The Sovereign Event in a Nation's Law, p. 322.

No. 2 do not recognise a different, aboriginal, source of law,[98] but instead subordinate indigenous interests to a 'polity of proprietors.'[99] As a result, the potential for epistemological equality to be translated into political equality is 'smothered'[100] by the singular conception of sovereignty which, according to the Court, was transcended ab initio.

Michael Asch finds a similar logic in operation in the seemingly more expansive jurisprudence of the Supreme Court of Canada. He considers what is being worked out in La Mer CJC's dictum in Van der Peet that the 'special status' conferred upon indigenous peoples by the 1982 Canadian constitution provided a 'framework through which the fact that Aboriginals lived on the land in distinctive societies [...] is acknowledged and reconciled with the sovereignty of the Crown.'[101] Thus, in echoes of Mabo No 2, we are projecting a discourse of indigenous rights backwards in time both to destabilise an exclusionary narrative of sovereignty and also to save it, by underscoring its (previously misunderstood) compatibility with the 'fact' of indigenous legal traditions. Addressing what might seem the best case scenario for advocates of indigenous rights, namely extending their coverage to include political rights, he concludes that this would be unable to disturb the political inequality at the root of the post-colonial constitutional order: 'the concept of Aboriginal rights could never challenge Crown sovereignty, for, logically, a means to reconcile prior facts cannot also challenge the nature of those facts.'[102]

Thus, adverting to debates about legality and legitimacy in this context may be a double-edged sword, highlighting the centrality of epistemological equality to indigenous justice, while revealing the barriers which dominant forms of legal and political discourse pose to achieving this in practice. On the one hand, there seems some cause for optimism, as claims of indigenous rights cannot but require decision-makers to address the epistemological issues which colonialism suppressed; but the bad news is that when confronted with the full consequences of epistemological equality, the institutions of the post-colonial state retreat to the maginot line of political inequality to avoid the potentially toxic threat their own authority. In these circumstances, the most we can hope for are some modifications of the existing framework of sovereignty, rendering it more palatable to present sensibilities, but not its transformation, placing indigenous peoples on the plane of political equality. In other words, the epistemological continuity outlined above is indicative that we have reached a limit in terms of granting indigenous peoples greater political autonomy through a reworking of sovereignty.

---

98 As Motha puts it elsewhere, there is no significant change in 'which collective's law has the status of normativity': *Motha*, Reconciliation as Domination, p. 71.

99 *Motha*, The Sovereign Event in a Nation's Law, p. 337. As discussed in the preceding section, one of the ways in which this subordination is manifested in practice is by the post-colonial institutions establishing themselves as the arbiters of 'true aboriginality' which has to be satisfied before beneficial title can be conferred.

100 *Motha*, The Sovereign Event in a Nation's Law, p. 312.

101 Van der Peet, p. 303.

102 *Asch*, From Calder to Van der Peet, p. 440.

This might seem a bleak note on which to conclude, but in other ways it can be seen to herald a potential new direction for debates about legality and legitimacy, one in which the basic methodological imperative, adapting Edward Said, is to understand the 'strength of Western [political and legal] discourse[s].'[103] Bringing epistemological issues to the fore thus helps clarify some choices which are currently obscured within those discourse, and which may require giving up much that has been taken for granted. This conclusion receives some support in the recent scholarship of Jim Tully. While formerly strongly associated with the position that the first approach outlined above is a means of opening up debate not just within, but about, the constitutional rules of the post-colonial order, of late he has focused on how indigenous rights discourse operates as part of an 'informal imperialism,' ensuring that indigenous self-determination is exercised in conformity with existing power structures.[104] In contrast with his earlier work, this makes a core question for investigation whether we have to give up on the idea that effecting a reconciliation between normative and sociological approaches can open up legal and political debate. It also clarifies that an affirmative answer to this question should only be regarded as 'bleak' if the prevailing epistemological framework is the only one we can imagine. Thus, acknowledging and elaborating the limits within which current debates on legality and legitimacy take place is a potentially liberating step, freeing theoretical resources from reiterating unproductive lines of argument and diverting them to search for different forms of legal and political knowledge. For others, there may be too high a price to pay in terms of our conceptual understanding of legality if we abandon the current epistemological framework; instead, a more appropriate response would be to scale down the emancipatory claims made on its behalf.[105] But to put it this way reveals how the politics of knowledge come to the surface once the epistemological dimension is fully acknowledged – the objective of this chapter has been to show that engaging with these politics is central to the issue of indigenous justice.

Acknowledgements

I would like to thank Akbar Rasulov and Eilidh Whiteford for their helpful comments on an earlier version of this chapter.

---

103 *Said*, Orientalism, p. 25.
104 *Tully*, On Law, Democracy and Imperialism, p. 69, 90-95. See also *Tully*, The Imperialism of Modern Constitutional Democracy, p. 315.
105 See *Loughlin*, Reflections on The Idea of Public Law, pp. 47, 55-59.

Bibliography

Apology to Australia's Indigenous Peoples, House of Representatives, , Paraliament House, Canberra, 13 February 2008: http://www.pm.gov.au/media/speech/node/5952

Asch, Michael/Macklem, Patrick, Aboriginal Rights and Canadian Sovereignty: An Essay on R. v. Sparrow, Albert Law Review 29 (1991).

Asch, Michael, From Calder to Van der Peet: Aboriginal Rights and Canadian Law, 1973-96, in Havemann, Paul (ed), Indigenous Peoples' Rights in Australia, Canada and New Zealand, Auckland, 1999, pp. 428-446

Asch, Michael, First Nations and the Derivation of Canada's Underlying Title: Comparing Perspectives on Legal Ideology, in Cook, Curtis and Lindau, Juan D. (eds) Aboriginal Rights and Self-Government: The Canadian and Mexican Experience in North American Perspective, Montreal and Kingston, 2000, pp. 148-167

Baxi, Upendra, The Future of Human Rights, New Delhi, 2002.

Benton, Lauren, Law and Colonial Cultures: Legal Regimes in World History, 1400-1900, Cambridge, 2002.

Borrows, John, Recovering Canada: The Resurgence of Indigenous Law, Toronto, 2002.

Calder v British Columbia (Att-Gen) [1973] 34 DLR (3d) 145.

Chalmers, Damian, Post-nationalism and the quest for constitutional substitutes, Journal of Law and Society 27 (2002).

Coates, Ken, 'The "Gentle" Occupation: The Settlement of Canada and the Dispossession of the First Nations' in Havermann, Paul (ed), Indigenous Peoples' Rights in Australia, Canada and New Zealand, Auckland, 1999, pp. 141-161

Delgamuukw v British Columbia [1997] 3 SCR 1010.

Flanagan, Tom, First Nations? Second Thoughts, Montreal and Kingston, 2000.

Hamlet of Baker Lake v Canada (1980) 107 DLR (3d) 513.

Havemann, Paul, A Formative Conclusion, in Havemann, Paul (ed), Indigenous Peoples' Rights in Australia, Canada and New Zealand, Auckland, 1999, pp.468-475

Ivison, Duncan/Patton, Paul/Saunders Will, Introduction, in Ivison, Duncan, Patton, Paul, and Saunders, Will (eds), Political Theory and the Rights of Indigenous Peoples, Cambridge, 2000, pp. 1-21

Jones v Meehan (1899) 175 US 1

Loughlin, Martin, Sword and Scales: An Examination of the Relationship Between Law and Politics, Oxford and Portland, 2000.

Loughlin, Martin, The Idea of Public Law, Oxford, 2003.

Loughlin, Martin, Reflections on The Idea of Public Law, in Christodoulidis, Emilios/Tierney, Stephen (eds), Public Law and Politics: The Scope and Limits of Constitutionalism, Aldershot, 2008, pp. 47-65

Mabo v Queensland (no 2) (1992) 175 CLR 1

Macklem, Patrick, Indigenous Difference and the Constitution of Canada, Toronto, 2002.

Motha, Stewart, The Sovereign Event in a Nation's Law, Law and Critique 13 (2002).

Motha, Stewart, Reconciliation as Domination, in Veitch, Scott (ed), Law and the Politics of Reconciliation, Aldershot, 2007, pp. 69-91

Parry, Agius/Davies, Jocelyn/Howitt, Richard/Jarvis, Sandra/Williams, Rhian, Comprehensive Native Title Negotiations in South Australia, in Langton, Marcia, Palmer, Lisa, Tehan, Maureen, and Shain, Kathryin (eds), Honour Among Nations?: Treaties and Agreements with Indigenous People, Carlton, Vic, 2004, pp, 203-219.

R v Sparrow (1990) 70 DLR (4th) 385.
Reynolds, Henry, New Frontiers: Australia, in Havemann, Paul (ed), Indigenous Peoples' Rights in Australia, Canada and New Zealand, Auckland, 1999, pp. 129-140
Royal Commission on Aboriginal Peoples, Final Report, Ottawa, 1996, vol I.
Said, Edward, Orientalism, New York, 1978.
Shaw, Jo, Postnational Constitutionalism in the European Union, Journal of European Public Policy 6 (1999)
Santos, Boaventura de Sousa, Towards a New Legal Common Sense, London, 2002.
Santos, Boaventura de Sousa, Beyond Abyssal Thinking: From Global Lines to Ecologies of Knowledge, Review (Fernand Braudel Center) XXX (2007).
Santos, Boaventura de Sousa (ed), Another Knowledge is Possible: Beyond Northern Epistemologies, London, 2008.
Santos, Boaventura de Sousa/Nunes, João Arriscado/Meneses, Maria Paula, Opening up the Canon of Knowledge and Recognition of Difference' in Santos, Boaventura de Sousa (ed), Another Knowledge is Possible: Beyond Northern Epistemologies, London, 2008, pp.xvix-lxii
Southern Rhodesia (1919) AC (PC) 210
St Catherine's Milling and Lumber Co v. The Queen (1888) 14 App Cas 46.
Teubner, Gunther, 'Global Bukowina': Legal Pluralism in the World Society, in Teubner, Gunther (ed), Global Law Without a State, Gateshead, 1997, pp. 3-28
Tully, James, The Struggles of Indigenous Peoples for and of Freedom, in Ivison, Duncan, Patton, Paul and Sanders Will (eds), Political Theory and the Rights of Indigenous Peoples, Cambridge, 2000, pp. 36-59.
Tully, James, The Unfreedom of the Moderns in Comparison to Their Ideals of Constitutional Democracy, Modern Law Review 65 (2002).
Tully, James, The Imperialism of Modern Constitutional Democracy, in Loughlin, Martin, and Walker, Neil (eds), The Paradox of Constitutionalism: Constituent Power and Constitutional Form, Oxford, 2007, pp. 315-338.
Tully, James, On Law, Democracy and Imperialism, in Christodoulidis, Emilios/Tierney, Stephen, (eds) Public Law and Politics: The Scope and Limits of Constitutionalism, Aldershot, 2008, pp. 69-101.
Turner, Dale, This is not a Peace Pipe: Towards a Critical Indigenous Philosophy, Toronto, 2006.
Tully, James, Strange Multiplicity: Constitutionalism in an Age of Diversity, Cambridge, 1995.
Van der Peet v The Queen (1996) 137 DLR (4th) 289.
Walker, Neil, The EU and the WTO: Constitutionalism in a New Key, in de Búrca, Gráinne/Scott, Joanne (eds), The EU and the WTO: Legal and Constitutional Issues, Oxford and Portland, OR, 2001, pp. 31-57.
Walker, Neil, The Idea of Constitutional Pluralism, Modern Law Review 65 (2002), pp. 317-359.
Walker, Neil, Late Sovereignty in the European Union, in Walker, Neil (ed), Sovereignty in Transition, Oxford and Portland, OR, 2003, pp. 3-32

From legitimacy to legality: The problem of the global legal form

Kirsten Campbell

In 2004, the United Nations Secretary General's High-Level Panel on Threats, Challenges and Change released its key report on contemporary international collective security, *A More Secure World: A Shared Responsibility*.[1] The Report emphasised the importance of the international legal order in a new security paradigm of global insecurities, interdependence, and responsibilities. For the Panel, the authority of the international community derived from the agreement of its members to be bound by international legal rules rather than upon its coercive powers. Accordingly, *A More Secure World* characterised effective international governance as resting upon legal legitimacy rather than coercive force.

However, the Report also acknowledged that '[t]he effectiveness of the global collective security system, as with any other legal order, depends ultimately not only on the legality of decisions but also on the common perception of their legitimacy - their being made on solid evidentiary grounds, and for the right reasons, morally as well as legally'.[2] The Report identified the legitimacy of the international community as being most problematic where its decisions concern 'large-scale life and death impact'.[3] It contended that the 'question of legality' and the 'question of legitimacy' became particularly problematic in relation to the regulation of violence in the international system. Throughout the Report, the relationship between legality and legitimacy became a clearly paradoxical problem in relation to the international legal regulation of violence. On the one hand, the legitimacy of law founds the regulation of violence in the international system, since the agreement to be bound by an international legal order is the basis of international collective security. However, that violence also undermines legal legitimacy as a foundation of a rightful international order, as force uncouples the presumption that legality provides legitimation.

This problematic relationship between legality and legitimacy in *A More Secure World* suggests that older juridical models of legal legitimacy may no longer be useful for understanding the international legal regulation of conflict in new global orders. This paper explores how the undoing and remaking of law, sovereignty, and community in globalisation produces a form of juridical relations that is not reducible to the legitimation of rule. It argues that this legal form expresses the new *social* associations of globalisation as *legal* relations. Those legal relations reconstitute these new forms of social relations as global, and thus themselves become an integral part of the process of globalisation.

---

1 *United Nations*, A More Secure World: Our Shared Responsibility, Report of the Secretary-General's High-Level Panel on Threats, Challenges, and Change.
2 *United Nations*, A More Secure World, para. 204.
3 *United Nations*, A More Secure World, para. 205.

Reading the laws of Violence

i. The question of legitimacy

How, then, should we analyse the contemporary international legal regulation of conflict? Uwe Ewald identifies two key approaches to understanding globalisation and the international legal regulation of conflict, which he describes as 'universal protection vs. interest-related risk management'.[4] These models are perhaps better described more broadly as cosmopolitan governance, exemplified by the work of David Held, or imperial rule, most often identified with the work of Hardt and Negri (as Ewald does). Importantly, Ewald notes that 'the common point of departure for both concepts is an awareness of a new age of global risks and a different form of war which results in a new concept of security, which is, at the outset, confronted by a lack of legitimacy in the use of international and national state violence'.[5] Both these approaches claim that there is a 'legitimation crisis' concerning the international governance of coercive power. For example, Held argues that new global insecurities require new forms of legitimate international governance, while Hardt and Negri contend that the international law no longer functions as the basis of legitimate violence in the general global state of war.[6] Yet while both paradigms insist upon the absence of legal legitimacy in the new global disorder, at the same time they also insist upon the necessity of the legal legitimation of the new global order. For example, Held characterises international law as the legitimate foundation of 'cosmopolitan social democracy'.[7] In contrast, Hardt and Negri reject '*liberal cosmopolitan* arguments' and argue instead that international law serves to legitimate imperial rule. Common to both arguments is the idea that law also operates as a legitimating form of rule, which permits the exercise of power without coercive force. These models of cosmopolitan governance and imperial rule thus reiterate the same paradoxical relationship between legality and legitimacy in the international relation of violence that can be found in the Report. On the one hand, there is a crisis of legal legitimacy concerning the regulation of violence. On the other hand, the legitimacy of law is also the basis of the international regulation of violence.

Martii Koskenniemi argues that 'the structure of international legal argumentation' constantly moves between concreteness and normativity, or between apology and utopia. For Koskenniemi, this structure of argumentation entails that international law 'remains both over- and underlegitimizing: it is overlegitimizing as it can be ultimately invoked to justify any behaviour (apologism), it is underlegitimizing because it is incapable of providing any convincing argument on the legitimacy of

---

4   *Ewald*, Large-Scale Victimisation and the Jurisprudence of the ICTY, p.177.
5   *Ewald*, Large-Scale Victimisation and the Jurisprudence of the ICTY, p.177.
6   *Held/McGrew*, Globalization/Anti-Globalization, pp. 223-4; *Hardt/Negri*, Multitude, pp. 29-30.
7   *Held/McGrew*, Globalization/Anti-Globalization, pp 218-219, 224; *Hardt/Negri*, Multitude, pp. 234, 277.

any practices (utopianism)'.⁸ These models of the international regulation of armed conflict repeat this structure of international legal argumentation. In what we can call the 'apologist' account of imperial rule, international law reflects relations of force, and hence derives its efficacy from force. In the 'utopian' model of cosmopolitan governance, international law reflects ethical values, and so derives its power from morality. In both models, international law can affect social action only insofar as it functions as the legitimation of force or legitimating ideal. However, if law only has effect as legitimated force or normative legitimacy, then how do we explain the role of law in the international system? This formulation leaves unanswered the question of how international law has efficacy or effect *as law*. These arguments do not explain how law functions as a constitutive element of the global order as than as a form of the legitimation of rule.

However, the ongoing undoing and remaking of law, sovereignty, and community in the processes of globalisation suggests that it is necessary to move away from this older juridical model of legal legitimacy in order to understand the current international legal regulation of conflict. The notion of legitimacy has an intimate philological relationship to the notion of legality because its connected meanings of lawful filiation and power derive from its common etymological Latin root, *legis*. If the first sense refers to lawful belonging to family and community, the second sense refers to the lawful power of the sovereign. The concept of legitimacy uses law to bind both sovereign rule and community membership. However, the etynomologically intimate relation between the legal and the legitimate points to the emergence of this notion from the older form of rule that Foucault characterises as the 'juridical monarchy', in which the political order is founded upon the lawful exercise of sovereign rule over a community.⁹ If there has been an uncoupling of older forms of legality and legitimacy in current global insecurities and interdependences, then it is necessary to develop a model of law that does not reduce law to legitimacy. Instead, we require a new way to understand international legality that can address the specificity and efficacy of the legal in the new global world, and the constitutive power of legality in the making of this world.

ii. The problem of legality

Both cosmopolitan governance and imperial rule arguments understand humanitarian law as symptomatic of new global dis/orders, whether functioning to found global governance, or to 'neutralize and pacify conflict' in a state of global war.¹⁰ In these symptomatic readings, law reproduces broader global structures. However, these approaches fail to address law 'in its specificity as a historical practice which operates through particular forms and mechanisms which are real, effective and dif-

---

8 *Koskenniemi*, From Apology to Utopia, p. 67.
9 *Foucault*, The History of Sexuality, Volume I, p. 89.
10 *Held/McGrew*, Globalization/Anti-Globalization, p. 224; *Hardt/Negri*, Multitude, p. 276.

ferentiated, and which are related to irreducible to broader social relations'.[11] In particular, neither of these accounts explains why the regulation of international violence should necessarily take a legal form. There are clearly many forms of global ordering. However, the international community seeks to regulate armed conflict in terms of law. China Miéville describes this as the 'basic ontological question': *'why law?'*. Miéville suggests that there is 'something in the structure of the modern social relations which maintains the integrity of the peculiarly legal form of conceptualising and articulating claims'.[12] In the global context, we need to ask: why do these social relations take the form of legal relations? And what legal form do these global relations take?

iii. The laws of war

If the use of violence at the international level is legally regulated by the *jus ad bellum* (the rules governing the resort to force), and the *jus in bello* (the rules governing the conduct of conflict, or international humanitarian law ('IHL'), only certain breaches of these rules are criminalised under international law. These so-called 'core crimes' are war crimes, genocide, and crimes against humanity. With the important exception of crimes against peace, a criminal breach of the *jus ad bellum*, these crimes are violations of international humanitarian law.[13] These crimes form the subject-matter of the jurisdiction of the International Criminal Tribunal for the former Yugoslavia, the International Criminal Tribunal for Rwanda, and the International Criminal Court, the leading international criminal bodies having jurisdiction at the international level, and give rise to universal jurisdiction at the level of the state. They are typically considered to be 'the most serious crimes of concern to the international community as a whole' (Article 5, ICC Statute).

Popovski and Turner describe how 'the recourse to the use of force [the *jus ad bellum*] has an exceptional and controversial character and is the most critical domain of international relations in need of robust legality and legitimacy'.[14] The body of rules regulating the use of force, then, clearly reveals the crisis in older juridical models of legal legitimacy at the international level. However, they do not reveal the new forms of legality that are emerging in their place. By contrast, the body of rules regulating the conduct of conflict are rapidly proliferating, increasingly enforced,

---

11   *Norrie*, Law and the Beautiful Soul, p. 30.
12   *Miéville*, Between Equal Rights, p. 43.
13   While crimes against peace, or the crime of aggression, are international crimes under customary law, this crime has not been prosecuted since 1947. While its modern incarnation can be found in the ICC Statute, the Court only has jurisdiction once the crime has been defined and its scope agreed, an issue which was not formally considered until July 2009; see *Schabas*, An Introduction to the International Criminal Court, pp. 31-34. Moreover, even when the crime comes within the jurisdiction of the Court, it is likely to be severely restricted through regulation by the Security Council: *Zolo*, Who Is Afraid of Punishing Aggressors, p. 799.
14   *Popoviski/Turner*, Legality and Legitimacy in the International order, p. 2.

and increasingly significant. For these reasons, IHL is a better example of the global remaking of legality at the international level. Rather than focusing my analysis upon the laws governing the resort to force, the most 'exceptional and controversial' area of law regulating international violence, I will focus upon the least contested area, the laws governing the conduct of conflict. In particular, I will focus upon those violations of IHL that are criminalised at the international level, namely, the international criminal law ('ICL') of the core crimes of war crimes, genocide, and crimes against humanity.[15]

I use two analytic strategies to explore this international legal regulation of violence. First, I develop the 'methodology' of the pre-eminent theorist of the legal form, Pashukanis, to analyse the legal subjects and relations of ICL, and hence to describe their juridical form. My second strategy reads this early Marxist model of law together with Hardt and Negri's injunction: 'to follow in Marx's footsteps one must really walk beyond Marx and develop on the basis of his method a new theoretical apparatus adequate to our own present situation'.[16] I read Pashukanis' theory of the legal form with the accounts of contemporary forms of association offered by Latour and Hardt and Negri to describe the emergence of this new legal form of global relations. This second strategy uses the specific example of the Yugoslavian wars of the 1990s, together with the institution and jurisprudence of the International Criminal Tribunal for the former Yugoslavia ('ICTY'), to explore the emergence of this global legal form.

Strategy one: The international legal form

i. The methodology of the legal form

> Is it possible to understand law as a social relationship in the same sense in which Marx termed capital a social relationship?[17]

Pashukanis aimed to understand law as a 'historical form of regulation' that emerged from the social relations of capitalism.[18] To avoid both economist and idealist theories of law, Pashukanis' 'general theory of law' develops what I shall call the 'methodology' of the legal form, namely, a set of principles for undertaking an analysis

---

15 For clarity regarding this distinction between the core crimes and the broader body of international humanitarian rules (which include rules whose breaches are not necessarily criminalized at the international level), I will use 'IHL' to refer to the broader body of international rules regulating the conduct of conflict, and 'ICL' to refer to the narrower category of international crimes.
16 *Hardt/Negri*, Empire, p. 43.
17 *Pashukanis*, Selected Writings on Marxism and Law, p. 55.
18 *Fine*, Democracy and the Rule of Law, p. 154.

of law as specific form of social relationships.[19] In this methodology, an analysis of law should first identify 'the basic juridic abstractions' of juridical norms, subjects, and relations.[20] These legal categories are the abstract expression of the fundamental elements of the legal form. These 'basic juridic abstractions [...] which are the closest definitions of the legal form, in general reflect specific and very complex social relations'.[21] The second task of this legal theory, then, is to understand the relationship between this system of legal concepts and the concrete historical social relations from which they emerge.

Pashukanis argues that in the *legal form* of social relations, atomistic legal subjects exist in juridical relations of exchange. The legal form is a particular form of social relation, in which that relation takes the form of juridical obligations or entitlements of exchange between abstract, free, and equal subjects.[22] Pashukanis argues that under certain historical conditions, namely, capitalist relations of exchange, 'the *regulation* of social relationships assumes a *legal* character'.[23] This legal form of the social relation reaches its highest level of abstraction in the commodity exchange of developed capitalism.

ii. The legal form of international law

In his earlier extended essay on international law of 1925, Pashukanis argues that the subject of international law is the state as the bearer of sovereign authority. This abstract subject is able to enter into exchange with other states, which are understood as 'individual property owners with equal rights'. In this contractual relation, bourgeois states interact 'on the basis of equivalent exchange, i.e. on a legal basis (on the basis of the mutual recognition of subjects)'. However, like contractual relations in national legal systems, 'bourgeois international law in principle recognises that states have equal rights yet in reality they are unequal in their significance and their power'. Because of the absence of an organisational force able to coerce states to observe international legal norms, the only guarantee of these international legal relationships is 'the real balance of forces'.[24] For Pashukanis, '*modern international law is the legal form of the struggle of capitalist states among themselves for domination over the rest of the world*'.[25] In this formulation, the material conditions of the international legal form are the struggle between imperialist, capitalist states. International law, then, is the legal form of the imperialist relation between capitalist states.

---

19 See *Pashukanis*, Methods of Constructing the Concrete in the Abstract Sciences.
20 *Pashukanis*, Selected Writings on Marxism and Law, p. 43.
21 *Pashukanis*, Selected Writings on Marxism and Law, p. 43.
22 *Pashukanis*, Law and Marxism, p. 68.
23 *Pashukanis*, Selected Writings on Marxism and Law, p. 58.
24 *Pashukanis*, Selected Writings on Marxism and Law, pp. 176-179.
25 *Pashukanis*, Selected Writings on Marxism and Law, p. 169.

For Pashukanis, the laws of war exemplify the legal form at an international level, because this body of law 'assumes juridical equality and unequal violence'.[26] At first reading, this analysis of contemporary ICL seems convincing for three reasons. First, ICL does appear to assume juridical equality between sovereign states, because these norms derive from treaty or custom, that is, from the express or tacit consent of states to be bound by these rules.[27] Second, ICL also seems to reflect the principle of state sovereignty, as different rules and enforcement mechanisms apply to international or internal conflicts, and to state or non-state actors. For example, the rules governing the conduct of international conflict between states are considerably more developed and restrictive than those of internal armed conflict, which has been considered as 'an internal problem, governed by domestic law'.[28] Third, it appears that the 'unequal violence' of state interest and power shape both the norms of IHL and their enforcement. For example, the principle of proportionality (that injury to civilians must not exceed military necessity) certainly reflects the military (and political) interests of states.[29] Similarly, the international community rarely enforces these norms against its most powerful members, as exemplified by the recent antagonism of the USA towards the ICC.[30]

However, as both cosmopolitan governance and imperial rule arguments concerning new forms of legal regulation of international violence suggest, these juridical categories are also undergoing an important shift. This move is best summarised by the ICTY in the leading *Tadic* Jurisdiction Appeals Decision, which held that: '[a] State-sovereignty-oriented approach has been gradually supplanted by a human-being-oriented approach.[31] This shift can be seen in the ongoing reconstruction of the fundamental juridical categories of the legal subject and the juridical relation in contemporary ICL. These new legal concepts are not fully developed, as this shift is not yet complete.[32] Nevertheless, these changing juridical categories indicate a new global legal form, which is neither international nor national in scale.[33] To understand the emergence of this new form of juridical relations, my analysis will use the 'methodology' of the legal form. First, it will examine 'the basic juridic abstractions' of juridical norms, subjects, and relations. Second, it will analyse the rela-

---

26 *Miéville*, Between Equal Rights, pp. 136-7 and 292-293.
27 *Simma/Paulus*, The Responsibility of Individuals for Human Rights Abuses in Internal Conflicts: A Positivist View, pp. 302, 305.
28 *Rogers*, Law on the Battlefield, p. 215.
29 *Normand/Jochnick*, The Legitimation of Violence: A Critical Analysis of the Gulf War, p. 387.
30 *Krisch*, International Law in Times of Hegemony, p. 369.
31 *Tadic* Jurisdiction Appeals Decision, para. 97.
32 In this reading of the legal form, I am following Norrie (rather than Warrington's) reading of Pashukanis' general theory of law as offering the theoretical basis for the study of law in changing forms of capitalist society. See *Warrington* Pashukanis and the Commodity Form Theory, pp. 1-22, and *Norrie*, Pashukanis and the 'Commodity Form Theory: a Reply to Warrington', p. 419.
33 I would like to thank Sari Wastell for this scalar point: see her Scales of Justice.

tionship between this system of legal concepts and the concrete historical social relations from which they emerge.

iii. The legal subject and the juridical relationship

In his general theory of law, Pashukanis suggests that an analysis of the legal form should begin with the legal subject, which he describes as the 'atom' of the juridical relation.[34] Moreover, the earliest and most obvious example of the changing categories of ICL can be seen in the concept of the legal subject. From the Nuremburg Trials onwards, it is clear that international criminal liability is based upon the principle of the individual criminal responsibility of persons.[35] Pashukanis points out that modern criminal law shifts from older forms of collective guilt to current forms of individual guilt.[36] The refusal of notions of collective guilt found contemporary ICL jurisprudence and institutions, which focus upon the individual perpetrator.[37] As Pashukanis suggests in relation to national criminal law, the legal subjects of ICL are 'isolated egoistic subjects, the bearers of autonomous private interests', subject to penal punishment equivalent to his or her crime.[38] In contemporary ICL, as Pashukanis describes: 'punishment functions as a settlement of accounts [in which] the notion of responsibility is indispensable. The offender answers for his offence with his freedom, in fact with a portion of his freedom corresponding to the gravity of his action'.[39]

In terms of the forms of criminal liability in ICL, the legal subject is not the autonomous sovereign state. Instead, it is understood as the autonomous individual whose actions are abstracted from social relations and judged according to the legal norms of the 'international community'. While older models of the laws of war were based upon notions of contractual and reciprocal relationships between states, contemporary ICL is increasingly perceived as a set of universal rules applicable to all

---

34 *Pashukanis*, Law and Marxism, p. 109.
35 Nuremberg IMT, pp. 172, 221. Indeed, it remains a highly contentious issue as to whether states can be legal subjects of international criminal law, see *Crawford*, The International Law Commission's Articles on State Responsibility, pp. 242-243. This issue should be distinguished from the obligations of states to punish breaches of humanitarian law, such as those arising under the Geneva Conventions, which constitute a system of enforcement rather than a system of criminal sanctions against states.
36 *Pashukanis*, Law and Marxism, p. 167.
37 For an important discussion of the relationship between individual and collective guilt, see *Hirsh/Fine*, Individual Responsibility and Cosmopolitan Law.
38 *Pashukanis*, Law and Marxism, p. 188. See *Norrie*, Pashukanis and the 'Commodity Form Theory: a Reply to Warrington' for an important defense of Pashukanis on criminal law.
39 *Pashukanis*, Law and Marxism, p. 179. Pashukanis goes on to argue that it is because of this principle that punishment must be equivalent to guilt that the principle of *nullum crimen, nulla poena sine lege* becomes an important legal norm, for the offender 'must know in advance the conditions under which payment will be demanded of him' (p. 184). Indeed, breach of this principle is a common defense argument in cases before the ICTY.

participants in conflict.⁴⁰ This shift is most obviously seen in the norms of crimes against humanity and genocide, which all persons have an obligation to observe in all circumstances. By contrast to other areas of international law, the contemporary legal subject of ICL is not the state, but the individual. ICL transforms persons into legal subjects, by constructing them as individual actors who are subject to international criminal duties and sanctions.

What, then, is the form of the juridical relation between these subjects of ICL? Given that the subject of ICL is not the state but the individual, it is not possible to simply read the juridical relation as taking the form of a contract between equal sovereign states. Moreover, Pashukanis suggests that in the modern criminal law of the national state, the other party is neither the injured person nor the state, but rather 'the abstraction of the injured public interest' that stands in for the injured person.⁴¹ At the international level, it is also true that neither the injured person nor international community function as the legal subject. How then might we understand the 'abstraction of the injured public interest' at the international level? What is the injury? And which public suffers injury?

In normative terms, ICL no longer seeks to protect state interests as such but rather to protect humanity 'as a collective'.⁴² This can be seen in the three core international crimes, from the 'principles of humanity' that are foundational to war crimes,⁴³ to the characterisation of genocide as 'a crime against all of humankind, its harm being felt […] by all of humanity',⁴⁴ to the crime against humanity, 'a crime against the whole of mankind'.⁴⁵ In all three crimes, 'humanity' functions as the 'abstraction of the injured public interest'. Unlike international human rights law, the injury is not done to the individual person. After all, international criminal law only protects certain persons, such as prisoners of war, members of ethnic groups, or civilians, and only in particular circumstances, such as armed conflict rather than civil disturbance. It does not aim to protect all individuals at all times, and neither is it enforceable as an individual claim. Rather, the injured public interest is the *collective* community of humanity. For this reason, international criminal law prohibits this conduct as 'an attack on the legitimate interests which all states have in maintaining certain standards that are essential for the coexistence of all mankind'.⁴⁶ The abstraction of the injured public interest thus shifts from being the pro-

---

40 See *Simpson*, Law, War, and Crime, pp. 59-60 and *Meron*, The Humanization of Humanitarian Law, pp. 239, 247-8. While the distinction between the rules of international and internal conflict remains important, nevertheless the boundary between the two is increasingly blurred: *Tadic* Jurisdiction Appeals Decision, para. 97. See also *Moir*, Towards the Unification of International Humanitarian Law.
41 *Pashukanis*, Law and Marxism, p. 179.
42 *Teitel*, Humanity's Law, p. 355.
43 *International Court of Justice*, Advisory Opinion on the Legality of the Threat or Use of Nuclear Weapons, paras. 78-79.
44 *The Prosecutor v. Krstic*, para. 36.
45 *The Prosecutor v. Erdedmovic*, para. 20-21.
46 *The Prosecutor v. Tadic*, para. 40.

tection of international society (understood as the mutual interests of the society of states), to being that of the community of humanity.

These juridical relations reveal a shift from the legal form of the contract of exchange between states to the global relationship between persons. The juridical relationship between these legal subjects is no longer simply based upon the 'mutual recognition' of states as subjects, but rather upon a more complex process of constituting persons *in organised conflict* as juridical subjects. These juridical subjects exist in relations of legal equivalence because they are members of the collective community of humanity. These shifts from state to individual responsibility, from the protection of state interest to the protection of humanity as such, and from the society of states to the global society of humanity, can be described as the emergence of a new global legal form. The distinctive nature of this legal form does not lie solely in its constraint of coercive power, for it is part of the coercive relations of globalisation. Nor does it simply lie in the normative recognition of our shared humanity, for this legal form does not recognise a prior and essential 'humanity'. Rather, the distinctive nature of this juridical relation lies in its constitution of 'humanity' as such.

This global legal form is not mere a 'lifeless abstraction' that has no concrete existence.[47] Rather, the emergence of this form of legal regulation of armed conflict can be seen at both national and international levels. This point should not be misunderstood as simply claiming that there is greater enforcement of these norms, which would lead to the familiar problem of the coercive power of international law. Instead, this argument follows Pashukanis in contending that coercion is not the foundation of the legal relation, but rather that it is the ordering of social relations that guarantees the existence of the legal form.[48] While the operation of these norms at the international level at first appears to remain limited to either exceptional situations (such as the establishment of the ICTY and the ICTR), or to state agreement, (exemplified by multilateral treaties such as the ICC Statute), these developments also suggest the increasing importance of this form of legal regulation of armed violence. The establishment of the ICTY, ICTR and ICC exemplify the 'post-Cold War revival of international prosecutions', after an interregnum of some fifty years.[49] The legal mandate of the establishment of the *ad hoc* tribunals was Chapter VII of the Charter of the United Nations, namely, to maintain or restore international peace and security. The power of the Security Council to establish international criminal tribunals (and to refer cases to the ICC) is now largely beyond dispute, and was used to refer the situation in Darfur, Sudan to the ICC in 2005.[50] As John Bolton, a staunch critic of the ICC and of the Bush Administration's 'tacit support' for its Darfur investigation, acknowledged that '[i]f you allow this to happen, you legitimize the ICC'.[51] The ICC has secured significant international compliance, with

---

47 *Pashukanis*, Law and Marxism, p. 85.
48 *Pashukanis*, Law and Marxism, p. 89.
49 *Schabas*, The UN International Criminal Tribunals, p. 11.
50 *Schabas*, The UN International Criminal Tribunals, p. 53.
51 *Abramowitz/Lynch*, Darfur Killings Soften Bush's Opposition to International Court.

108 countries having ratified the Rome Statute as of January 2008. These developments suggest that this new legal form is currently emerging at the international level.

At the national level, older implementation and compliance mechanisms, which range from the instruction of armed forces in humanitarian rules to the prosecution of its violations, are increasingly well established and widely accepted.[52] There is also an ongoing increase in the exercise of universal jurisdiction, use of international criminal principles, and prosecution of crimes of war in national courts.[53] Tribunals, which utilise a mixture of international and national elements to prosecute international crimes, have also been established in response to conflicts in Sierra Leone, Timor-Leste, and Cambodia.[54] Finally, the wide ratification of the ICC Statute, and the concomitant obligation to prosecute breaches in national courts, entails that new national systems of compliance and enforcement of ICL are developing.[55] What is emerging in these developments is an orientation to the 'global agendas and systems' of this new legal form within national settings.[56]

Strategy two: Towards a social theory of the global legal form

i. From coercive power to relations of force

Pashukanis suggests that the international legal form emerges from the concrete historical social relations of imperialist capitalism. This legal form derives from 'a structured process of confrontation of international legal agents thrown up by the dynamics of capitalism'.[57] Should we understand this global legal form as the legal expression of the new global imperialism? If so, the work of Hardt and Negri would most obviously seem to offer a means to update Pashukanis' analysis. However, there are two key difficulties with such an appropriation.[58]

The first difficulty is that is Hardt and Negri persuasively argue that the processes of globalisation do not simply produce a new form of imperialism. Rather, these older imperialist forms have shifted to a new 'global order, a new logic and structure

---

52 *Fleck*, International Accountability for Violations of the Ius in Bello, p. 179. See also the International Committee of the Red Cross National Implementation Data Base, http://www.icrc.org/ihl-nat.
53 See *Human Rights Watch*, Universal Jurisdiction in Europe; *Sriram*, Globalizing Justice for Mass Atrocities; and *Ferdinandusse*, Direct Application of International Criminal Law in National Courts.
54 *Schabas*, The UN International Criminal Tribunals.
55 *Werle*, Principles of International Criminal Law, p. 89.
56 *Sassen*, Territory, Authority, Rights, p. 3.
57 *Miéville*, Between Equal Rights, p. 280.
58 Leaving aside the question of the accuracy of their descriptions of the 'juridical concept of Empire', which is raised by claims such as the ICTY does not apply either international or national law: *Hardt/Negri*, Multitude, pp. 28-29.

of rule [...] this new global form of sovereignty is what we call Empire'.[59] Given this emphasis upon a new form of rule, we cannot simply substitute their account of global exchange for Pashukanis' Leninist critique of imperialism in order to theorise ICL as the legal form of this new imperialist competition between states.[60] The second difficulty concerns Hardt and Negri's characterisation of ICL as a new mode of legal domination: 'postmodern global governance'.[61] In this account, ICL is a 'mechanism legitimating imperial authority'.[62] In many respects, this analysis rearticulates the traditional *realpolitik* analysis of ICL in terms of the contemporary global moment.[63] This older critical tradition argues that the international regulation of armed conflict legitimates the existing unequal relations of the international order by masking those inequalities through doctrines of state equality, and further makes conflict itself legitimate by giving it the mask of legality. Hence this account returns us to the earlier theoretical problems of how to understand the contemporary forms of the international legal ordering of violence.

If we return to Pashukanis' account of the international legal form, then it is possible to find a more productive appropriation of Hardt and Negri for a theory of the global legal form. Pashukanis argues that 'in critical periods, when the balance of forces has fluctuated seriously [...] the fate of the norms of the laws of war becomes extremely problematic'.[64] Pashukanis understands the notion of 'force' here in terms of the coercive power of states at the international level. However, I suggest that this claim becomes analytically very useful if it is re-read using a different paradigm of force. Foucault argues that 'war can be regarded as the point of maximum tension, or force-relations laid bare'.[65] In Foucault, the notion of 'force' refers to the 'ability to affect and be affected', so that force is always relational. Violence is a *'concomitant or consequence of force, but not a constituent element'*.[66] This approach enables us to understand the contemporary fluctuation of the 'balance of forces' not in terms of the coercive power of states, but in terms of the emergence of new relations of force in the processes of globalisation.

To paraphrase Miéville, the global legal form can be understood as a structured process of the confrontation of legal agents thrown up by the dynamics of globalising capitalism. Following Hardt and Negri, contemporary capitalism intensifies and amplifies the economic, political, and social exchanges of global exchange.[67] While the very concept of 'globalisation' is highly contentious, nevertheless it captures the multiple processes involving dynamic and differential intensifications of transplane-

---

59 *Hardt/Negri*, Empire, pp. xi-xii.
60 Hardt and Negri explicitly argue that while important, nevertheless Lenin's analysis of imperialism does not explain this new global order, *Hardt/Negri*, Empire, p. 234.
61 *Negri*, Postmodern Global Governance and the Critical Legal Project, p. 27.
62 *Hardt/Negri*, Empire, p. 38.
63 *Lippens*, Tracing the Legal Boundary between Empire and Multitude, p. 389.
64 *Pashukanis*, Selected Writings on Marxism and Law, p. 179.
65 *Foucault*, Society Must be Defended, p. 46.
66 *Deleuze*, Foucault, p. 70.
67 *Hardt/Negri*, Multitude, p. xiiii.

tary relations.[68] In this sense, 'globalisation' does not indicate the emergence of a singular 'global society', in the sense of a bounded and homogenous structure. Rather, it highlights the dynamic processes that make 'globalizing societies', in the sense of the production of diffuse and differentiated interdependencies and interconnections. This description of globalisation draws on Latour's notion of the social as 'association'.[69] It emphasises the making of the 'social', the constitution of relations, and the production of connections, and interactions. In Latour's terms, 'the social [...] is the name of a type of momentary association, which is characterised by the way it gathers together in new shapes'.[70] Framed through this understanding of the social as association, the forces of globalisation produce different forms of association, that is, new forms of relation. Globalisation is then understood as a set of processes that makes novel networks of associations, and hence constitutes new social relations. The dynamic processes of these intensified and differentiated exchanges produce new associations that are both connective and conflictual.

To understand the relation between these global associations and the global legal form, I focus upon the contemporary forms of association that sustain armed violence. If we follow Foucault in understanding violence as a consequence of force rather than its constituent element, and war as 'force-relations laid bare', then armed violence becomes the ideal field to trace the new force-relations that emerge in the processes of globalisation. My analysis of this field focuses upon conflict and connection as the two key forms of association that sustain war. Globalisation produces new shapes of interaction and new forms of networks, of which some are antagonistic, coercive, and conflictual, and others are coalitional, affiliative, and connective. I explore the operation of these conflictual and connective force-relations through the example of the Yugoslavian wars of the 1990s and their legal regulation.

Globalisation did not 'create' the Yugoslavian wars, or the legal regulation of its violences. As Sassen points out, we should not understand globalisation in terms of a single causal model since to do so wrongly uses effect to explain cause.[71] Rather, this analysis suggests that the dynamics of these forces of globalisation produced new forms of conflict and connection, which shaped the Yugoslavian conflict. Moreover, 'the Yugoslavian wars' were not a single moment of armed violence, but instead named a complex and prolonged state of conflicts and connections sustaining armed violence in the region of the former Yugoslavia. As Clausewitz reminds us, war is a fundamentally social activity, and one that requires particular forms of associations to sustain it. The processes of globalization traverse and shape these social relations of armed violence, just as they traverse and shape the formation of their international legal regulation.

---

68 *Scholte*, Globalization: A Critical Introduction.
69 *Latour*, Gabriel Tarde and the End of the Social.
70 *Latour*, Reassembling the Social, p. 65.
71 *Sassen*, Territory, Authority, Rights.

ii. The conflictual and connective associations of globalisation

The new force-relations of globalisation produce new forms of conflictual association. These conflicts are not the 'new wars' described by Kaldor and other writers, because they do not necessarily indicate new *forms* of war.[72] Rather, they represent the emergence of new antagonisms, coercions, and violence in the uneven and differential processes of globalisation. To illustrate the making of these new forms of conflictual association and their legal regulation, I focus upon two key force-relations of globalisation: the political and the economic.

A key new force-relation is the emergence of new political forms in the making of the post-Cold War world. For example, the declining legitimacy of communist rule and the impact of democratisation exposed 'the conflicting political forces in Yugoslav society' that subsequently erupted into armed violence.[73] The collapse of the Cold War system at the international level also facilitated the legal regulation of the Yugoslavian wars. United Nations consensus regarding the international prosecutions of war crimes in the Yugoslavian conflict would not have been possible without the collapse of older Cold War power blocs.[74] A second key force-relation of globalisation in the production of conflictual associations is economic. Sometimes called 'negative globalisation', the economic forces of global exchange have particular and differential impacts upon existing social and political orders.[75] For example, economic globalisation had crucial political effects in the emergence of war in the former Yugoslavia, since the declining legitimacy of the communist state was combined with a severe economic crisis due to the 'structural adjustment' programme of the International Monetary Fund.[76] Equally, economic globalisation has also shaped the model and implementation of international post-conflict justice, such as the linking international criminal trials to state reconstruction, and state reconstruction to functional free-market states.[77]

The global restructuring of older political and economic orders also produces new conflicts. These processes include the rearticulation of older territories of empire through new global relations.[78] For example, Zolo reminds us that the history of earlier Ottoman and European empires shaped the modern Yugoslavia, from the great powers carving up the collapsed Ottoman Empire to the German and Italian occupations of World War Two.[79] New global relations rearticulate these older orders, from the mobilisation of regional ethno-nationalist identity in the conflict to Western European myths of archaic 'Balkan' hatreds to justify non-intervention. However, new

---

72 *Newman*, The 'New Wars' Debate: A Historical Perspective is Needed, pp. 173, 189.
73 *Hirst*, War and Power in the 21st Century, p. 83.
74 *Cassese*, International Criminal Law, pp. 726-727.
75 *Conteh-Morgan*, Globalization, State Failure, and Collective Violence, p. 88.
76 *Woodward*, Violence-Prone Area or International Transition? Adding the Role of Outsiders in Balkan Violence.
77 *Sriram*, Liberal Peacebuilding and Transitional Justice, p. 579. This link is most evident in EU and US policies in this area in Bosnia.
78 *Ahluwalia*, Empire or Imperialism, p. 629.
79 *Zolo*, Invoking Humanity.

global orders also reshape these older patterns of association. In the Yugoslavian case, this is most evident in American and European Union intervention in the conflict.[80] This reshaping includes the remaking of existing legal orders.[81] For example, the European and American engagement with the region framed the making of 'Balkan' transitional justice, ranging from crucial American support for the establishment of the ICTY to subsequent European Union support for national war crimes prosecutions (most notably in Bosnia).

These global processes not only produce new conflicts, but also new connections. They produce different transnational networks, which move through both national and international orders. These global processes form new forms of affiliation. For example, political and military actors in the Bosnian conflict sought to produce new forms of ethnic association, which were in turn instantiated by the Dayton settlement brokered by the international community.[82] Global networks also traverse contemporary conflicts. In the case of the Yugoslavian conflict, these networks included coverage by the international media, alliances between international and national NGOs, and the international flows of fighters, arms, and funds that sustained the conflict itself.[83] The legal field of international criminal justice also emerges from these intensified global connections. In the case of the ICTY, these associations ranged from transnational political networks, such as the non-governmental organisations that campaigned for war crimes prosecutions,[84] to religious affiliations, such as the pressure from the Islamic Conference Organisation for protection of Bosnian Muslims and the subsequent significant funding for the ICTY by leading Muslim countries, such as Malaysia and Pakistan.[85] They also included communication networks, such as the importance of global information circuits such as CNN and the internet in building European and American public pressure for action.[86]

The global legal form

i. Law as association

These new forms of global association, these new conflicts and connections that emerge in the processes of globalisation, are the material conditions that produce the emergent global legal form of ICL. It is not that the case that the 'concrete totality' of globalisation produces the global legal form. Rather, it is the '"rich totality of many determinations and relations"' (pace Marx) that produces this juridical rela-

---

80 *Glenny*, The Fall of Yugoslavia.
81 *Randeria*, De-Politicization of Democracy and Judicialization of Politics, p. 38.
82 *Abazovic*, Bosnia and Herzegovina: Ten Years After Dayton, p. 195.
83 *Kaldor*, New and Old Wars.
84 *Hagan/Levi*, Crimes of War and the Force of Law, p. 1499.
85 *Glenny*, The Fall of Yugoslavia.
86 *Bass*, Stay the Hand of Vengeance.

tion.[87] ICL expresses these dynamic and differential intensifications of globalisation in legal form. ICL can thus be understood as the legal form of these emergent force-relations, in that it expresses these global relations as juridical relations.

The global legal form is a specific form of association. It works to 'associate entities *in a legal way*', that is, through particular material and symbolic legal practices that organise relations and connections.[88] It is this shaping of social relations that gives the global legal form its constitutive power. The global legal form is neither antecedent nor posterior to the globalisations of social exchange. Rather, 'the juridical moment [...] is a *constitutive part* of it'.[89] The new global legal form of ICL is a constitutive part of globalisation because it functions as a new *legal* form of association. This legal association constitutes persons as global legal subjects, who have legal relationships to other legal subjects as members of 'humanity'. ICL constitutes all persons as legal subjects, and constructs their associations in juridical terms.

This legal form constitutes these new associations as *global*. Douzinas argues that '[h]uman rights construct humans. I am human because the other recognises me as human which, in institutional terms, means as a bearer of human rights'.[90] Similarly, the legal form of ICL constructs persons as existing within global legal relations to other persons, and its object of protection as the global community of all persons, 'humanity' itself. This representation of global social relations is performative in the Austinian sense. This legal form creates the object it names, 'humanity', and its juridical field instantiates this global signifier. Following Pashukanis, this performativity is not simply in the realm of ideas or at the level of ideology. Rather, the global legal form orders existing social relations through the production of new forms of global legal association. This juridical relation constructs these emergent relations of social exchange not as particular, but as global. For this reason, the global legal form is a constituent part of the processes of globalisation.

ii. The problem of the global legal form

Hardt and Negri suggest that Pashukanis saw the possibility of 'transforming public law into an institutional system based on the common'.[91] They contend that the global common is 'the only basis upon which law can construct social relationships in line with the networks organised by the many singularities that create our new global reality'.[92] However, Hardt and Negri ignore the theoretical problem for which Stalin ostensibly 'liquidated' Pashukanis: namely, that capitalist social relations produce the legal form, and hence the revolutionary transformation of those social rela-

87 *Pashukanis*, Law and Marxism, p. 66.
88 *Latour*, Reassembling the Social, p. 239. See also *Levi/Valverde*, Studying Law by Association, pp. 805, 807.
89 *Norrie*, Pashukanis and the Commodity Form Theory, pp. 419, 423.
90 *Douzinas*, The End of Human Rights, p. 317.
91 *Hardt/Negri*, Multitude, p. 253.
92 *Hardt/Negri*, Multitude, p. 208.

tions will entail the withering away of law. Their call for new global rights as an institutional system based on the common ignores this problem of revolutionary law. Moreover, the global legal form reflects the many singularities that create our new global reality, which are both conflictual and connective. International criminal law seeks to protect 'humanity' in *war*, rather than the utopian peace of the common. For this reason, the production of 'humanity' by the global legal form should not be misunderstood as the recognition of the commonality of humans, as that which unites all person in a global community. Nor can it be understood as capturing the essence of humanity or the quality of being human. Rather, the global legal form emerges from *both* the destructive and productive associations of global social exchange.

The juridical relation of the global legal form produces 'humanity'. For this reason, it functions as a constituent element of the making of persons as members of the global community of humanity. ICL does not simply reflect an already existing humanist category of our common humanity, but rather forms a juridical relation between all persons as members of humanity. ICL therefore needs to be understood as those legal regulations without which 'global humanity' cannot be constituted. ICL constitutes 'humanity' by determining the legality of the new associations emerging from globalisation. The global legal form sustains 'global humanity', for those legal relations 'are essential for the coexistence of all mankind [...] humanity at large cannot hold together without adherence to the standards in question'.[93] The norms and practices of ICL determine the conduct that destroys or sustains the category of 'humanity' by judging the legality or illegality of certain forms of association in armed conflict. ICL protects certain categories of person, such as civilians, the wounded, and non-combatants, from armed violence. It prohibits certain aims of warfare, such as genocide. It bars certain forms of armed violence, such as those causing 'unnecessary suffering'. ICL does not prohibit war as such, but only particular objects, aims, and forms of war. These rules prohibit those forms of associations that would make the juridical category of 'global humanity' impossible. They sustain 'global humanity' by prohibiting those associations that prevent the construction of the legal relation as global, that is, the formation of 'humanity' itself.

The global legal form of ICL actively shapes the transnational extension of the social by symbolising relations between persons as *global*. Koskenniemi reminds us that '[i]nternational law may act precisely as the instrument through which particular grievances may be heard as universal ones and in this way, like myth, construct a sense of universal humanity through the act of invoking it'.[94] The global legal form acts as the instrument through which particular grievances are heard as global claims. The legal relationship that constitutes persons as legal subjects existing in juridical relationship founds this order. It constructs the possibility of global humanity, extracting persons from their particular social relations and remaking them as global legal subjects with juridical relations to humanity as such.

The problem of the global legal form is not therefore, not legitimacy, but legality. Legitimacy does not sustain the global legal form, since this legal form is a constitu-

---

93   *Tadic* Judgement in Sentencing Appeals, para. 40.
94   *Koskenniemi*, What Should International Lawyers Learn from Karl Marx?, pp. 229, 246.

tive part of the making of the global world. It is not legitimacy that constructs social associations as global, but rather the legal form that constructs the global as a juridical relation. The global legal form constitutes force relations as legal relations, humanity as a legal subject, and the associations between its members as a legal relation. For this reason, the political challenge of the global legal form is not reducible to the creation of a more legitimate order of legal rules. Rather, the challenge is to create a new concept of legality itself, a task that requires that requires the production of new legal forms that can symbolize just juridical relationships and global humanities.

Acknowledgements

I would like to thank Sam Ashenden and Chris Thornhill for their organisation of the Oñati workshop, and the workshop participants for their engaging and interesting discussions. I would also like to thank David Bausor, Beverley Brown, Kate Nash, and Sari Wastell for their very helpful comments on earlier drafts of this paper. I gratefully acknowledge the financial support of the Economic and Social Research Council for this research, a section of which was undertaken as part of the project, 'Regulating Armed Conflict: From the Laws of War to Humanitarian Laws' (RES-000-22-1650).

Bibliography

Abazovic, Dino, Bosnia and Herzegovina: Ten Years After Dayton, European Yearbook of Minority Issues 5 (2005/6), pp. 195-206.

Abramowitz, Michael/Lynch, Colum, Darfur Killings Soften Bush's Opposition to International Court, Washington Post, 12 October, 2008.

Ahluwalia, Pal, Empire or Imperialism: Implications for 'New' Politics of Resistance, Social Identities 10(5) (2004), pp. 629-645.

Bass, Gary, Stay the Hand of Vengeance, Princeton, 2000.

Cassese, Antonio, International Criminal Law, Oxford, 2003.

Crawford, James, The International Law Commission's Articles on State Responsibility, Cambridge, 2003.

Deleuze, Gilles, Foucault, Minneapolis, 1988.

Douzinas, Costas, The End of Human Rights, Oxford, 2000.

Conteh-Morgan, Earl, Globalization, State Failure, and Collective Violence, International Journal of Peace Studies 11(2) (2006), pp.87-103.

Ewald, Uwe, Large-Scale Victimisation and the Jurisprudence of the ICTY – Victimological Research Issues, in Ewald, Uwe and Turkovic, Ksenija (eds), Large-Scale Victimisation as a Potential Source of Terrorist Activities, Amsterdam, 2006.

Ferdinandusse, Ward, Direct Application of International Criminal Law in National Courts, The Hague, 2006.

Fine, Robert, Democracy and the Rule of Law: Liberal Ideals and Marxist Critiques, London, 1984.

Fleck, Dieter, International Accountability for Violations of the Ius in Bello, Journal of Conflict and Security Law 11(2) (2006).

Foucault, Michel, The History of Sexuality, Volume I, London, 1981.

Foucault, Michel, Society Must be Defended. Lectures at the College de France, 1975-1976, New York, 2003.

Glenny, Misha, The Fall of Yugoslavia: The Third Balkan War, London, 1996.

Hagan, John/Levi, Ron, Crimes of War and the Force of Law, Social Forces 83 (2005), pp. 1499-1534.

Hardt, Michael/Negri, Antonio, Empire, London and Cambridge, MA, 2000.

Hardt, Michael/Negri, Antonio, Multitude: War and Democracy in the Age of Empire, New York, 2004.

Held, David/ McGrew, Anthony, Globalization/Anti-Globalization, London, 2007.

Hirsh, David/Fine, Robert, Individual Responsibility and Cosmopolitan Law, in *Hirsh, David*, Law Against Genocide: Cosmopolitan Trials, London, 2003.

Hirst, Paul, War and Power in the 21st Century, Cambridge, 2001.

Human Rights Watch, Universal Jurisdiction in Europe: The State of the Art, 2006.

Kaldor, Mary, New and Old Wars: Organized Violence in a Global Era, Cambridge, 2001.

Koskenniemi, Martti, What Should International Lawyers Learn from Karl Marx? Leiden Journal of International Law 17 (2004), pp. 229-246.

Koskenniemi, Martti, From Apology to Utopia, Cambridge, 2005.
Krisch, Nico, International Law in Times of Hegemony: Unequal Power and the Shaping of the International Legal Order, European Journal of International Law 16(3) (2005), pp. 369-408.
Latour, Bruno, Gabriel Tarde and the End of the Social, in Joyce, Patrick (ed), The Social in Question: New Bearings in History and the Social Sciences, London, 2002.
Latour, Bruno, Reassembling the Social, Oxford, 2007.
Levi, Ron/Valverde, Mariana, Studying Law by Association, Law and Social Inquiry 33(3) (2008), pp. 805-825.
Lippens, Ron,Tracing the Legal Boundary between Empire and Multitude: Wavering with Hardt and Negri (2000-2005), Leiden Journal of International Law 18 (2005), pp. 389-402.
Meron, Theodor, The Humanization of Humanitarian Law, The American Journal of International Law 94(2) (2000), pp. 239-278.
Miéville, China, Between Equal Rights: A Marxist Theory of International Law, London, 2005.
Moir, Lindsay, Towards the Unification of International Humanitarian Law, in Burchill, Richard, Morris, Justin, and White, Nigel (eds), International Conflict and Security Law: Essays in Memory of Hilaire McCoubrey, Cambridge, 2005.
Negri, Antonio, Postmodern Global Governance and the Critical Legal Project, Law and Critique 16 (2005), pp. 27-46.
Newman, Edward, The 'New Wars' Debate: A Historical Perspective is Needed, Security Dialogue 35(2) (2004), pp. 173-189.
Normand, Roger/Jochnick, Chris, The Legitimation of Violence: A Critical Analysis of the Gulf War, Harvard International Law Journal 35(2) (1994), pp. 49-96.
Norrie, Alan, Pashukanis and the 'Commodity Form Theory': a Reply to Warrington, International Journal of the Sociology of Law 10 (1982), pp. 429-437.
Norrie, Alan, Law and the Beautiful Soul, London, 2005.
Pashukanis, Evgeny, Methods of Constructing the Concrete in the Abstract Sciences, in Law and Marxism: A General Theory, London, 1978.
Pashukanis, Evgeny, Selected Writings on Marxism and Law, London, 1980.
Popoviski, Vesselin/Turner, Nicholas, Legality and Legitimacy in the International order, Policy Brief, United Nations University, 5, 2008.
Randeria, Shalini, De-Politicization of Democracy and Judicialization of Politics, Theory, Culture & Society 24(4) (2007), pp. 38-44.
Rogers, A.P.V., Law on the Battlefield, Manchester, 2004.
Sassen, Saskia, Territory, Authority, Rights, Princeton and Oxford, 2006.
Schabas, William, An Introduction to the International Criminal Court, Cambridge, 2004.
Schabas, William, The UN International Criminal Tribunals: the former Yugoslavia, Rwanda and Sierra Leone, Cambridge, 2006.
Scholte, Jan Aart, Globalization: A Critical Introduction, London, 2005.
Simma, Bruno/Paulus, Andreas, The Responsibility of Individuals for Human Rights Abuses in Internal Conflicts: A Positivist View, The American Journal of International Law 93(2) (1999), pp. 302-316.
Simpson, Gerry, Law, War, and Crime, Cambridge, 2007.
Sriram, Chandra Lekha, Globalizing Justice for Mass Atrocities: A Revolution in Accountability, London, 2005.

Sriram, Chandra Lekha, Liberal Peacebuilding and Transitional Justice, Global Society 21(4) (2007), pp.579-591.

Teitel, Ruti. Humanity's Law: Rule of Law for the New Global Politics, Cornell International Law Journal 35 (2002), p. 355-388.

United Nations, A More Secure World: Our Shared Responsibility, Report of the Secretary-General's High-Level Panel on Threats, Challenges, and Change, 2004

Warrington, Ronald, Pashukanis and the Commodity Form Theory, International Journal of the Sociology of Law 9 (1982), pp. 1-22.

Wastell, Sari, Scales of Justice for the former Yugoslavia, Transitional Justice Research Seminar, University of Oxford, 2009.

Werle, Gerhard, Principles of International Criminal Law, The Hague, 2005.

Woodward, Susan, Violence-Prone Area or International Transition? Adding the Role of Outsiders in Balkan Violence, in Das, Veena, Kleinman, Arthur, Ramphele, Mamphela, and Reynolds, Pamela (eds), Violence and Subjectivity, Berkeley, 2000.

Zolo, Danilo, Invoking Humanity: War, Law, and Global Order, London and New York, 2002.

Zolo, Danilo, Who Is Afraid of Punishing Aggressors: On the Double-Track Approach to International Criminal Justice, Journal of International Criminal Justice 5 (2007), pp. 799-807.

Cases:

The Prosecutor v. Tadic, Case No. IT-94-1, Decision on the Defence Motion for Interlocutory Appeal on Jurisdiction, Appeals Chamber, 1995.

International Court of Justice, Advisory Opinion on the Legality of the Threat or Use of Nuclear Weapons, 8 July 1996

The Prosecutor v. Erdemovic, Case No. IT-96-22, Judgement, Appeals Chamber, 1997

The Prosecutor v. Tadic, Case No. IT-94-1-T, Judgement in Sentencing Appeals, Appeals Chamber, 2000

The Prosecutor v. Krstic, Case No: IT-98-33-A, Judgement, Appeals Chamber 2004

Nuremberg IMT, Judgment and Sentences, American Journal of International Law 41 (1947).

Section III:
Legitimacy as an institutional problem

Legality and legitimacy in the European Union

William Outhwaite

> L'Union [...] a su faire le saut technologique du pouvoir supranational, mais il n'y a toujours pas de légitimité supranationale, *Pascal Lamy* (Le Temps, 28.8.09).

A shorthand version of this paper would give the EU 10 points for legality (or maybe 9 to allow for endemic financial irregularities) but only 3 or 4 for legitimacy. Legality is the EU's essence: set up by international treaties, operating through regulations and directives, and with its own legal corpus and court as one of its most successful institutional achievements.

Legitimacy is, however, another matter. In theory, the national and the supranational should complement each other in the EU like the two sides of a Euro coin. (We could complicate the image by thinking of a polyhedron to represent multi-level governance.) In practice, I suggest, the national and the European levels are not just in tension, which is to be expected, but undermine and delegitimate one another. This has serious implications for projects, which I endorse, to encourage the development of a form of constitutional patriotism which can work for the European Union as a whole.[1]

What sort of polity is the EU becoming?[2] The shift in nomenclature, from 'Communities' to 'Union', suggests progress towards the official goal, as stated in the treaties, of 'ever closer union', and there has indeed been such progress. But ra-

---

1   As Habermas, in his reply to a recent collection of articles, believes it can. 'The establishment of a European civic identity can be understood as the continuation of a process which takes place initially within the national state. Even within these limits a well-understood constitutional patriotism has developed as a foundation of civic integration, in reaction to challenging historical experiences and along with the political-cultural incorporation of immigrant groups who remain connected with their countries of origin.' *Habermas* Reply, in Niesen and Herborth (eds), Anarchie der kommunikativen Freiheit, p. 457. One might of course question both this account of what has happened at the level of the national state and its possible transnational extension. See also *Nanz*, Europolis, esp. ch. 6. For a more optimistic neo-Milwardian view of all this, see *Menon/Weatherill*, Transnational Legitimacy in a Global World. The authors (p. 411) recognise the problems identified by Vivien Schmidt, which I discuss later. Conversely, while disagreeing with them overall, I agree that 'the starting point of any interrogation of legitimacy in (but not simply of) the EU is properly the flaws of the member states...' (p. 404).

2   For a fuller discussion of this theme, see *Outhwaite*, European Society, on which I have drawn here. I am grateful for comments when I delivered versions of this paper at Oñati and again at a conference at Sussex organised by Gerard Delanty and Paul Blokker to mark the tenth anniversary of the *European Journal of Social of Theory*; this took place just a week after the 'no' vote in the Irish referendum on the Lisbon Treaty. My thanks also to David Spence for comments on an earlier version of this chapter.

ther like the development of social democracy in the twentieth century, the positive achievements tend to go alongside a scaling-down of the ultimate goals.[3] European federalism, like socialism, now seems to many Europeans either unattainable in the form in which it was originally conceived, or anyway undesirable.

We should however go back to the beginning and ask what a European federation or confederation[4] would be, and why Europeans might have wanted it in the second half of the twentieth century.[5] The idea has of course a much longer history, but one important motivation for the project of European integration was in fact to prevent the Second World War happening again. Two thirds of a century later, this aim seems quaint, and the idea of achieving it by, as a first step, coordinating the production of coal and steel between the former axis powers and some of their victims seems a roundabout route. Yet this is what happened, and it substantially shaped later developments.

It was also of course possible to want integration for its own sake, on the basis that, as Willy Brandt once said of divided Germany, that 'what belongs together should grow together'. Europeans, on this view, have the basis for the sort of solidarity aspired to, and often achieved, by its national states, and this calls for an institutional expression of a similar kind, as in the great nineteenth century projects of German or Italian unification. Somewhere between these two poles one can locate views about the need to form larger economic units, to solve economic and other problems for which the national state was too small.

Postwar European integration began, then, with a fudge between motives of these kinds – an ambiguity which persists to the present. The original institutional model of the Coal and Steel Community has shaped the whole subsequent evolution of the Union: a 'high authority' of nine members, a council of ministers and a parliamentary assembly. Finally there was a court and an advisory committee of what we would now call stakeholders. The assembly and the court subsequently had their scope extended to the EEC and EURATOM. Half a century later, we now have a larger European Commission, a larger set of councils of ministers and the European Council of heads of state and government, a larger court and a ten times larger, directly elected parliament with substantially extended, though still very limited powers.[6]

Whatever the merits of this design, it is clearly not the most obvious for a federation or confederation, where one would expect the executive authority to be subject to parliamentary control and for legislation to be passed by the parliament. Something like this was in fact proposed in the drafting of the European constitution, and the downgrading of the Council of Ministers was probably the proposal least accept-

---

3   *Shore*, Building Europe, ch. 1.
4   As Dario Castiglione points out, the EU remains 'both open with regards to the forms of integration, and indeterminate in relation to its historical movement', *Castiglione*, Reflections on Europe's Constitutional Future, p. 393.
5   *Stråth*, A European Identity. To the Historical Limits of a Concept.
6   As Brunkhorst notes, the Parliament's formal powers are actually quite extensive. The problem is its lack of a public profile. See *Brunkhorst*, Zwischen transnationaler Klassenherrschaft und egalitärer Konstitutionalisierung, pp. 343-4.

able to many member states. In this, of course, they could justifiably claim to be following the majority views of their electorates whose main focus of attention and loyalty remains the national state.

Should we just bite the bullet and call the EU a state, perhaps with a qualifying adjective such as 'network' or 'regional'?[7]

> [T]he EU has developed a single currency, a single market, a single voice in international trade negotiation, a single anti-trust authority, common policies on environmental protection, worker safety and health, a common foreign and security policy, and even the beginnings of a common defense policy. [Thus] While the use of the term state may [...] be difficult for classically trained IR theorists, there is no other word that does justice to the growing power and developing sovereignty – however contingent – of the EU.[8]

Schmidt's preference is for the term regional state; the focus of her book is on the impact of the EU on member-state polities. Clearly one has to think of the EU polity or state as significantly constituted by its interrelations with national and subnational levels. In this sense, 'multi-level governance' is simply a fact. To invert Marx's phrase: 'Europe has changed; the point is to understand it'.

Attempts to understand the European polity are however bound up with arguments for particular institutional designs, and it may be helpful to look at three of these. One of the boldest recent contributions is the political philosopher Glyn Morgan's defence of *The Idea of a European Superstate*. Morgan deliberately takes the strongest and most provocative term in the 'Eurosceptic' vocabulary, demolishes some of the arguments for and assumptions about the desirability of a European state and then, in a startling volte-face, argues that we need it after all because only a unitary European state can provide the best available guarantee of security. Morgan admits however that 'a federalist European superstate is further from being a viable option today than at any time in Europe's postwar history'.[9]

An obvious alternative response is to abandon the already stalled integration project or to wind it back in an inter-governmentalist direction. A comparably bold proposal on these lines is offered by the historian John Gillingham.[10] Gillingham's strategy of 'hibernation' and downsizing goes so far as to propose half-seriously the sale of some of the EU's real estate in Brussels. A rather more likely scenario, which may be what Gillingham really wants, would be limits to the expansion of EU activities and a future of stagnation. Whether the EU bicycle, in Walter Hallstein's memorable image, could stand up without moving forward, is another matter.

There is however a third way, a growing body of literature which is accommodated to the EU in something like its present state. John A. Hall (2006) invokes the

---

7 *Schmidt*, Democracy in Europe, p. 10.
8 *Schmidt*, Democracy in Europe, p. 14.
9 *Morgan*, The Idea of a European Superstate.
10 *Gillingham*, Design for a New Europe.

old Gaullist slogan of 'l'Europe des patries' in his argument for a steady state.[11] For Rainer Lepsius, too, the national state remains the 'central political object of identification'; the EU lacks the 'interactive density and linguistic homogeneity' required to make it an appropriate site for working out economic and cultural conflicts. 'The integrative capacity of a society organised as a national state cannot be replaced by the new European structures'.[12]

Hall and Lepsius are historical and political sociologists but, not surprisingly, much of this literature is produced by interdisciplinary legal experts such as Joseph Weiler. Weiler, in a classic discussion of Europe's *Sonderweg* or special path, writes that 'Europe has charted its own brand of constitutional federalism. It works. Why fix it?'[13] Weiler's focus here is on constitutional law, but his view seems to be shaped by the relatively smooth operation of European legal integration as a whole.

I agree with Habermas that law and democracy have to be seen in conjunction, and it is at the democratic end of the European polity that matters become more problematic. The attention of European citizens is primarily focussed on national or regional, rather than European politics, and the transfer of power to the European level has mostly not been stressed by member state governments, except when they are seeking an excuse for unpopular policies. Where the policies are popular, national governments tend, not surprisingly, to take the credit themselves. Vivien Schmidt, in her exceptionally innovative study of the interface between European and national politics, concludes that 'while the EU has *policy without politics,* the member-states end up with *politics without policy* in EU-related areas. And this makes for major problems for national democracy.'[14]

The democratic deficit, in other words, is not only in the relatively unpolitical (though of course politically *relevant*) spheres of EU policy-making,[15] with their confusing interplay of parliamentary, executive and legislative entities, but back home in the member states themselves, and also in non-members like Norway, who participate in the European Economic Area, Schengen etc. without even a formal place in EU non-politics.[16]

> National elections tend to be focussed on substantive policy issues that increasingly can only be fully addressed at the EU level, such as immigration, food safety, environment, or economic growth, while European Parliamentary elections tend to focus

---

11 *Hall*, Plaidoyer pour l'Europe des Patries, pp. 107-124.
12 *Lepsius*, Prozesse der europäischen Identitätsstiftung, p. 5.
13 *Weiler*, Europe's *Sonderweg*.
14 *Schmidt*, Democracy in Europe, p. 33.
15 As Schmidt argues: '[N]ational partisan politics has been marginalized. Ministers speak in the Council more in the name of the national interest than for governmental majorities. Members of the EP speak more in terms of the public interest than for electoral majorities. Citizens have more influence in Brussels when lobbying as organized interests than when voting or protesting in national capitals' (*Schmidt*, Democracy in Europe, p. 2).
16 See, for example, the Norwegian Study of Power and Democracy, part of a larger series of Nordic studies: www.sv.uio.no/mutr/english/index.html

more on general polity issues that can only be resolved by nationally based actors, such as how to reform EU institutions – where, that is, they are concerned with EU issues at all ...[17]

This is not so much a 'joint decision trap' as what, borrowing from Bachrach and Baratz (1970), one might call a 'non-decision trap' – at least from the citizen's point of view.[18]

To speak of the European polity, then is to address not just the EU and the individual member states (including close associates like Norway and Switzerland) but, crucially, the interplay between them. Schmidt shows how essentially unitary states like the UK[19] and France interact differently with the EU from more decentralised ones like Germany: 'Europeanization ... has been more disruptive to simple polities with unified structures like France and Britain.'[20]

Schmidt's diagnosis may seem worrying, but her conclusion is relatively optimistic. As long as we recognise that the EU should be seen as a regional state and do not try to democratise it according to the model of national democracies, we can live with something like its present arrangements. 'Its "federal" checks and balances, its voting rules ensuring supermajorities, its elaborate interest intermediation process *with* the people, and its consensus politics go very far toward guaranteeing good governance *for* the people.'[21] All that is needed is for the member states to recognise this and adapt their political discourse and practices accordingly.

17 *Schmidt*, Democracy in Europe, p. 33
18 *Bachrach/Baratz*, Power and Poverty.
19 The UK, like Spain, has of course now substantial devolution (to Scotland and to a lesser extent to Wales), and the Blair government reversed Thatcher's abolition of metropolitan institutions in London and elsewhere. Its political style however remains essentially unitary, reinforced by a strongly majoritarian voting system in which coalitions have historically been rare. This may of course be about to change, with Brown, the British Medvedev, visibly running out of steam.
20 *Schmidt*, Democracy in Europe, pp. 54-5. The details of Schmidt's analysis of her four states do not concern us here, but her concluding recommendations give a flavour of it: 'The French need to rethink their vision of leadership in Europe [...] given that they know that France no longer leads Europe, are in crisis over national identity, and increasingly blame EU "neoliberalism" for their economic problems. The British need to develop a vision of Britain in Europe, given that the discourse of economic interest does not respond to growing concerns about sovereignty and identity, while the idea of British separateness in Europe could very well lead to the reality of British separation from Europe [...]. The Germans need to update their vision of "German-as-European" in light of the changes related to unification and fading memories of World War II, especially since they increasingly question the benefits of membership and worry about the EU's impact on the social market economy. The Italians [...] need to concern themselves not so much with their vision of Italy in Europe as with their implementation of European rules in Italy, since their pride in being European is likely to suffer as a result of the fact that the EU "rescue of the nation-state" is no longer enough to rescue the nation-state' (p. 272).
21 *Schmidt*, Democracy in Europe, pp. 22-3.

In a related approach, Jan Zielonka and others have presented a vision of the EU as a kind of empire, more specifically a neomedieval one in which political authority is divided and multiple, not clearly nested as in idealised descriptions of feudalism, but a messier picture of competing sovereignties, statuses and rights. Zielonka's book is substantially concerned with Eastern enlargement, since 'it is the European integration project that needs to be adjusted to enlargement, and not the other way around.'[22]

Claus Offe and Ulrich Preuss adopt a similar answer to 'The Problem of Legitimacy in the European Polity'. They start from a similar point to Schmidt: 'the problem is not primarily that the *EU* must become democratic; it is that *member states* must *remain* democratic'.[23] They suggest the deliberately paradoxical image of a republican empire.

The appeal of a model of this kind is of course its flexibility, which Ulrich Beck and others have linked to a cosmopolitan vision that transcends old-fashioned oppositions between inside and outside, us and them.[24] Against this happy vision, however, the negative votes on the European constitution in France and the Netherlands, two states involved from the beginning in the integration project and generally reckoned among the most favourably inclined to it, carry a powerful lesson.[25]

The problem, then, as many see it, is that it may be impossible to democratise the EU without undermining the democratic states which make it up.[26] Yet other federal polities manage this, with only occasional grumbles in Bavaria, Texas or the Valais about goings-on in the national capitals. But to speak like this, Euro-realists would say, is to fail to grasp the reality of the EU, where legitimating structures are inevitably embedded at national level and the pursuit of a stronger European identity is a dangerous diversion.[27]

The problem of the EU polity, then, is essentially that of its decoupling from society, which reproduces in spades the alienation of the national political sphere diagnosed by Marx in the nineteenth and by Régis Debray in the twentieth century.[28] Delanty and Rumford point to the similarities between European and global politics: 'In Europe, as in the world polity more generally, cultural control is exerted by those who are seen to work for the common good rather than self-interest, framing their

---

22 Zielonka, Europe as Empire. This book is also a superb guide through recent literature on the EU. See also *Verdun/Croci*, The European Union in the Wake of Eastern Enlargement.
23 *Offe/Preuss*, The Problem of Legitimacy in the European Polity.
24 *Beck/Grande*, Das kosmopolitische Europa; *Lavenex*, EU external governance in "wider Europe".
25 *Van der Pijl*, A Lockean Europe? p. 36.
26 As David Bailey points out, studies of European integration might benefit from paying more attention to critical state theory, drawn from, among other sources, Marx and Foucault, which has consistently addressed contradictions generated by forms of governance themselves and what have been called 'crises of crisis management'; *Bailey*, Governance or the crisis of governmentality?
27 *Weiler*, Europe's *Sonderweg*; *Scharpf*, Legitimationskonzepte jenseits des Nationalstaats.
28 *Debray*, Critique de la raison politique. More recently, see *Crouch*, Post-Democracy; *Ginsborg*, Democracy. Crisis and Renewal; *Wolin*, Democracy Incorporated.

calls for development, progress, standardization, and rational organization in terms of the potential benefits to everyone.'[29] The European polity thus displays in microcosm the tension between the rhetorical cosmopolitisation and democratisation of modern politics, the latter marked also by the informal style of leaders like Blair, Bush, Sarkozy and Berlusconi, and the increasing alienation of marginalized and excluded populations, which in the European context tends to be expressed at best in hostility to the European project and at worst in a generalised xenophobia.[30] The pursuit of European integration was always, in a phrase applied to fascism, an 'extremism of the centre'. In its well-meaning but arrogant elitism it has now generated an anti-European extremism which may be spreading from the extreme right to the mainstream. Something, I think, *does* have to be done.

Having outlined the issues as I see them, I shall end with a few remarks more directly on the question of legitimacy. It is not surprising that the discussion of the EU's legitimation problems has largely repeated two motifs I grew up with as a young academic in the 1970s: output legitimacy, somewhat dismissively treated in the literature of the time as conducing merely to 'mass loyalty' rather than legitimacy,[31] and procedural legitimation.[32] The early functionalist justifications of European integration were cast in terms of beneficial outcomes, and this is continued in the EUROPA site's current list of '50 ways forward. Europe's best successes'.[33] The second, procedural aspect has again, as I noted at the beginning, been central throughout to a union initiated by treaties and substantially advanced by them. Whatever we like to think of as the life-blood of the Union, its sinews are surely legal.

The domestic discussion of legitimation seems to have died out at roughly the same time, in the 1980s, as attention focused on the European 'democratic deficit'. But as David Spence notes, 'If there is a democratic deficit, there must also be a legitimacy deficit.'[34] What Europe, in the sense of what was becoming the EU, lacked was something which, following Michael Billig's brilliant discussion of banal nationalism, we might call banal nationalist legitimation. The *composition* of many of the member states may have been contested, but except in the case of Belgium (which has not (yet) broken up) and Czechoslovakia (which did), the contestation is largely peripheral, in the sense that it is only on the peripheries (Scotland, the Basque Country, etc.) that the unity of the respective states is radically questioned. On the whole, the identity of the state and hence a sort of zero degree of legitimacy has been taken for granted. In the case of the EU, however, it is not difficult to find voices calling for withdrawal, or even predictions of the dissolution of the Union. [The counterpoint to this secessionist threat is the more Europeanist or integrationist question

29 *Delanty/Rumford*, Rethinking Europe.
30 *Bale*, Cinderella and her ugly sisters: the mainstream and the extreme right in Europe's bipolarising party systems.
31 *Narr/Offe*, Wohlfahrtsstaat und Massenloyalität.
32 *Luhmann*, Legitimation durch Verfahren.
33 See: www.europa.eu/success50/index.
34 *Spence*, EU Governance and Global Governance: New Rules for EU Diplomats, p. 70.

whether the *Union* might be better off without some prospective member (e.g. Turkey) or an existing one (notably the UK, whose size makes its incorrigible obstructionism particularly irritating and dangerous).[35]

The institutional architecture of the EU is also up for grabs in a way which that of the member states is not. The states may move back and forth between PR and majority voting, between less or more centralisation, but radical alternatives such as those represented by Fischer and opposed by Blair in the 2000 discussion,[36] or between Morgan and Gilligan in the more recent past, are largely absent. The principle of majority voting, which is largely unquestioned within the member states,[37] is a permanent bone of contention at the European level. The option of withdrawal for dissatisfied minorities, which is presented as hypothetical in the domestic context and a serious possibility only for minorities of regional separatists, remains a real option at the European level, where it cannot be taken for granted that we are together for ever.

The tide is flowing fairly clearly in the direction of majority voting, but it is less clear that there is a move towards what we might call a normal democracy at the European level. Three independent but complementary options are parliamentarisation, a directly elected president and a greater use of referendums. The last two can be seen as offering a plebiscitary corrective to an inevitably complex and bureaucratic federal system,[38] where even parliamentary assemblies are at several interrelated levels. Such assemblies, along with multifarious committees, may be optimistically seen as approaching the desiderata of deliberative democracy, but they fail to offer clear-cut choices between political alternatives to a European electorate.[39]

---

35 Glyn Morgan suggests that the issue is not so much of legitimacy as of the basic justification of the European project; see *Morgan*, European Political Integration and the Need for Justification.

36 Fischer's speech is reprinted and commented in *Joerges/Mény/Weiler*, What Kind of constitution for What Kind of Polity? Responses to Joschka Fischer. Fischer envisaged a second chamber of the European Parliament made up of 'elected deputies who are also members of the national parliaments' but left open the question whether a future European government should emerge from the Council or from the Commission (with a directly elected President). No doubt his preference, like mine, would be for the latter. This classically Weberian proposal for the presidency is of course open to familiar objections, but perhaps with less reason at the European level. Italy might elect a Berlusconi, or Poland a Kaczynski, but Europe as a whole is surely less likely to. Blair's characteristically Thatcherite response was that 'The primary sources of democratic accountability in Europe are the directly elected and representative institutions of the nations of Europe, national parliaments and governments' (cited in Kohler-Koch and Rittberger (eds), Debating the Democratic Legitimacy of the European Union, p. 102).

37 An excellent edited collection by Guggenberger and Offe (eds), An den Grenzen der Mehrheitsdemokratie, does address fundamental issues, including those posed by protest movements, but makes no mention of European-level politics, even in the chapter (by Heidrun Abromeit) on federalism. More recently, see *Abromeit*, Democracy in Europe: Legitimizing Politics in a Non-State Polity.

38 Abromeit's chapter on federalism uses the term 'Ventil'.

39 *Brunkhorst*, The Legitimation Crisis of the European Union, p. 174.

Without serious progress in this direction,[40] the attention to elements and fora of deliberative democracy at the European level, like the comforting efforts of Beck and Grande,[41] in what remains an extremely important contribution the debate, to square all possible circles, risk appearing as a diversion. If there *is* a European legitimation crisis, as I believe there is, it has at least two elements - in Eurospeak we might say pillars. One is structural and institutional: it concerns the intergovernmental and technocratic foundations of the original Communities, set up without significant input from European populations who were merely expected to marvel at the cargo of benefits emerging from integration. On the whole this worked: the integration process advanced by fits and starts, and the European economy, even after the oil shock of the mid-1970s, provided a large enough cake to mitigate squabbles over relative shares.[42] But European capitalism has become more irresponsible and dangerous and a justified suspicion of European political elites increasingly also takes a dangerous populist form.[43] One Berlusconi government might be an accident; three looks like carelessness. The other element of the crisis is the weakness of European civil society and the commercial degradation of the European public sphere, just as it becomes more pan-European and global in its possible scope.[44] The two elements reinforce one another: a European civil society has nothing to get its teeth into because many of the most important issues of welfare and social policy are still a *chasse gardée* for the member states.

The question, then, is whether it is possible to have more democratic legitimacy at a European level without further weakening the democracy of the national states and, where they have them, of their regional assemblies.[45] My provisional answer is

---

40 See also the editors' introduction to Kohler-Koch and Rittberger (eds), Debating the Democratic Legitimacy of the European Union, and the volume as a whole.
41 *Beck/Grande*, Das kosmopolitische Europa,.
42 Along with economic growth, the Soviet threat provided the other crucial element determining the progress of integration.
43 We should not perhaps have been surprised at the collapse of UK and US banks in 2007-8, but to see the irresponsibility and corruption also affecting such apparently respectable institutions as German *Landesbanken* was genuinely alarming.
44 As Ulrich Haltern writes '[...] European democracy will not work – in that it will not lead to a vibrant transnational political life – unless European citizens understand, and are convinced of, the communal, collective dimension of a European political community'; *Haltern*, in Kohler-Koch and Rittberger (eds), Debating the Democratic Legitimacy of the European Union, p. 51. On the European public sphere in relation to this issue, see e.g. the report by *Sifft et al.*, Segmented Europeanization: Exploring the Legitimacy of the European Union from a Public Discourse Perspective, and the literature cited there; see also *Eder/Trenz*, Pre-Requisites of Transnational Democracy and Mechanisms of Sustaining it: The Case of the European Union in Kohler-Koch and Rittberger (eds), Debating the Democratic Legitimacy of the European Union, and Kohler-Koch's own chapter in this volume, esp. pp. 267-8.
45 Hauke Brunkhorst sounded an early warning here: 'The already well advanced state of European constitutionalisation increases the chance of a transition from a weak European public sphere to a really strong one, but also the danger of a constitutionally entrenched de-democratisation of Europe and its nations': *Brunkhorst*, Verfassung ohne Staat? p. 531. See also the view in *Nanz*, Europolis, p. 181: 'Without citizen support for democratic practices

to say that federal systems are inevitably messy, but the mess can be creative. The question can I think be turned round: the presence of a manifestly undemocratic set of structures at a European level cannot fail to undermine an already shaky identification of modern Europeans with democratic parliamentary politics. The danger is of European politics, like the fish, rotting from the head down.

and identification with political institutions, the EU risks – at best – creating an environment of post-political consumer loyalty.'

Bibliography

Abromeit, Heidrun, Mehrheitsprinzip und Föderalismus, in Guggenberger, Bernd, and Offe, Claus (eds), An den Grenzen der Mehrheitsdemokratie. Politik und Soziologie der Mehrheitsregel, Opladen, 1984.
Abromeit, Heidrun, Democracy in Europe: Legitimizing Politics in a Non-State Polity, Oxford, 1998.
Bachrach, Peter/Baratz, Morton S, Power and Poverty: Theory and Practice, Oxford, 1970.
Bailey, David, Governance or the crisis of governmentality? Applying critical state theory at the European level, *Journal of European Public Policy*, 13 (1) (2006), pp. 16-33.
Bale, Tim, Cinderella and her ugly sisters: the mainstream and the extreme right in Europe's bipolarising party systems, West European Politics, 26 (3) (2003), pp. 67-90.
Beck, Ulrich/Grande, Edgar, Das kosmopolitische Europa, Frankfurt, 2004.
Brunkhorst, Hauke, Verfassung ohne Staat? Das Schicksal der Demokratie in der europäischen Rechtsgenossenschaft, Leviathan 30 (2002), pp. 530-543.
Brunkhorst, Hauke, The Legitimation Crisis of the European Union, Constellations 13 (2006), pp. 165-80.
Brunkhorst, Hauke, Zwischen transnationaler Klassenherrschaft und egalitärer Konstitutionalisierung. Europas zweite Chance, in Niesen, Peter, and Herborth, Benjamin (eds), Anarchie der kommunikativen Freiheit. Jürgen Habermas und die Theorie der internationalen Politik, Frankfurt, 2007.
Castiglione, Dario, Reflections on Europe's Constitutional Future, Constellations 11 (3) (2004), pp. 393-411.
Crouch, Colin, Post-Democracy, Cambridge, 2004.
Debray, Régis, Critique de la raison politique, Paris, 1981.
Delanty, Gerard/Rumford Chris, Rethinking Europe: Social Theory and the Implications of Europeanization, London, 2005.
Eder, Klaus/Trenz, Hans-Jörg, Pre-Requisites of Transnational Democracy and Mechanisms of Sustaining it: The Case of the European Union In Kohler-Koch, Beate, and Rittberger, Berthold (eds) Debating the Democratic Legitimacy of the European Union, Lanham, MD, 2007, ch. 7, pp. 165-81.
www.europa.eu/success50/index.
Gillingham, John, Design for a New Europe, Cambridge, 2006.
Ginsborg, Paul, Democracy. Crisis and Renewal, London, 2008.
Guggenberger, Bernd, and Offe, Claus, (eds), An den Grenzen der Mehrheitsdemokratie. Politik und Soziologie der Mehrheitsregel, Opladen, 1984.
Habermas, Jürgen, Kommunikative Rationalität und grenzüberschreitende Politik: eine Replik, in Niesen, Peter, and Herborth, Benjamin (eds), Anarchie der kommunikativen Freiheit. Jürgen Habermas und die Theorie der internationalen Politik, Frankfurt, 2007, pp. 406-59.
Hall, John A, Plaidoyer pour l'Europe des Patries, in Rogowski, Ralf, and Turner, Charles (eds), The Shape of the New Europe, Cambridge, 2006, pp. 107-124.
Haltern, Ulrich, A Comment on Von Bogdandy by Ulrich Haltern, in Kohler-Koch, Beate, and Rittberger, Berthold (eds), Debating the Democratic Legitimacy of the European Union, Lanham, MD, 2007, ch. 2, pp. 45-54.
Joerges, Christian/Mény, Yves/Weiler, Joseph HH, What Kind of constitution for What Kind of Polity? Responses to Joschka Fischer: http://www.eui.eu/RSCAS/OnlineSymposium/Josch ka-Fischer.shtml (2000).

Kohler-Koch, Beate, and Rittberger, Berthold (eds), Debating the Democratic Legitimacy of the European Union, Lanham, MD, 2007.

Kohler-Koch, Beate, The Organization of Interests and Democracy in the European Union, in Kohler-Koch, Beate, and Rittberger, Berthold (eds), Debating the Democratic Legitimacy of the European Union, Lanham, MD, 2007, pp. 255-71.

Lavenex, Sandra, EU external governance in "wider Europe", *Journal of European Public Policy* 11 (4) (2004), pp. 680-700.

Lepsius, Mario R, Prozesse der europäischen Identitätsstiftung, Aus Politik und Zeitgeschichte 38 (2004) pp. 3-5.

Luhmann, Niklas, Legitimation durch Verfahren, Darmstadt, 1969.

Menon, Anand, and Weatherill, Stephen, Transnational Legitimacy in a Global World: How the European Union Rescues its States, West European Politics, 31 (2008), pp. 397-416.

Morgan, Glyn, The Idea of a European Superstate. Public Justification and European Integration, Princeton, 2005.

Morgan, Glyn, European Political Integration and the Need for Justification, (2007) 14 Constellations, 14 (2007), pp. 332-46.

Nanz, Patrizia, Europolis: Constitutional Patriotism Beyond the Nation State, Manchester, 2006.

Norwegian Study of Power and Democracy, available at: www.sv.uio.no/mutr/english/index.html

Offe, Claus/Preuss, Ulrich, The Problem of Legitimacy in the European Polity. Is Democratization the Answer? in Crouch, Colin, and Streeck, Wolfgang, (eds), The Diversity of Democracy. Corporatism, Social Order and Political Conflict, Cheltenham, 2006, pp. 175-204.

Narr, Wolf-Dieter/Offe, Claus, Wohlfahrtsstaat und Massenloyalität, Cologne, 1975.

Outhwaite, William, European Society, Cambridge, 2008.

Van der Pijl, Kees, A Lockean Europe?, New Left Review, 37 (2006), pp. 9-37.

Scharpf, Fritz, Legitimationskonzepte jenseits des Nationalstaats, Cologne: MPIfG Working paper 04/6, November 2004: www.mpi-fg-koeln.mpg.**de**/pu/workpap/wp04-6/wp04-6.html.

Schmidt, Vivien, Democracy in Europe. The EU and National Polities, Oxford, 2006.

Shore, Cris, Building Europe. The Cultural Politics of European Integration, London, 2000.

Sifft, Stefani/Brüggemann, Michael/Kleinen-v. Königslöw Katharina/Peters, Bernhard/Wimmel, Andreas, Segmented Europeanization: Exploring the Legitimacy of the European Union from a Public Discourse Perspective, Journal of Common Market Studies 45 (1) (2007), pp. 127-55.

Spence, David, EU Governance and Global Governance: New Rules for EU Diplomats, in Cooper, Andrew, Hocking, Brian, and Maley, William, (eds), Global Governance and Diplomacy. Worlds Apart?, Basingstoke, pp. 63-84.

Stråth, Bo, A European Identity. To the Historical Limits of a Concept, European Journal of Social Theory 5 (2002), pp. 387-401.

Verdun, Amy, and Croci, Osvaldo (eds), The European Union in the Wake of Eastern Enlargement. Institutional and policy-making challenges, Manchester, 2005.

Weiler, Joseph, Europe's *Sonderweg*, in Nicolaïdes, Kalypso, and Howse, Robert (eds), The Federal Vision: Legitimacy and Levels of Governance in the US and the EU, Oxford, 2001, pp. 54-70.

Wolin, Sheldon, Democracy Incorporated: Managed Democracy and the Specter of Inverted Totalitarianism, Princeton, 2008.

Zielonka, Jan, Europe as Empire. The Nature of the Enlarged European Union, Manchester, 2006.

From Philadelphia to Vitoria via Bonn?
Why there is no Constitutional Patriotism in the Basque Country

Andreas Hess

> Guernica must be the happiest community on earth. Its affairs are governed by a council of peasants that gathers under an oak tree and that always takes the fairest decisions. *Jean-Jacques Rousseau*

> ...after those people in Europe who have had the skill, courage, and fortune, to preserve a voice in government, Biscay, in Spain, ought by no means to be omitted [...]. It is a republic; and one of the privileges they have most insisted on, is not to have a king. *John Adams*

Introduction: The importance of a lucky start

It was Tocqueville who once remarked that American democracy had been in the happy position of having had a lucky start. The unique political and historical circumstances of the early United States allowed the Founding Fathers to design a political system from scratch and with little historical baggage. Karl Marx implicitly agreed with Tocqueville's assessment. For him, America had none of the 'old shit' that had so much plagued Europe. To be sure, America's original founding was not perfect. The American republic needed, as Barrington Moore has pointed out, a second revolution – the Civil War – to give some substance to the Founding Fathers' rhetoric of rights and only with the Civil Rights Act from 1965 did African Americans get full civil rights. What matters for the following discussion is that Americans had had a lucky start in the sense that the original founding documents, in particular the Bill of Rights, provided the rhetorical framework which later generations could later use and build upon.

If we try to compare the history of American democracy, and particularly those lucky moments of political institutional design of the United States, with the long and twisted political history and apparently eternally repetitive founding phases of European nation states, not even to mention that new hybrid framework that is now the European Union, the contrast could not be starker. In terms of nation-building and legitimacy, American constitutionalism allowed for both consensus and limited, that is functional, conflict. The secret of its success lies in two circumstances, both of them important for the political rhetoric: first, in the constant re-affirmation, the ritual of evoking again and again the values and the spirit of the founding documents; and second, in its concreteness, that is that rights can actually be claimed, not by some abstract citizen of the world but by real citizens appealing to an actually functioning political framework that guarantees its constitutional principles and is prepared to live up to them. The legitimation of American governance lies in this Renan-like daily re-affirmation or plebiscite of an actually functioning rhetorical triangle consisting of citizens, nation and rights, in which each part is connected to the other two parts. Thus, in America, constitutional patriotism became a success story long before the term 'constitutional patriotism' actually became part of political discourse in Europe. I maintain that although there are no fixed historical principles or written-in-stone guidelines for achieving constitutional patriotism – as the English historian E.P.Thompson once pointed out, there are no regular verbs in history – it is nevertheless possible to identify a few developmental patterns and achievements of 'the first new nation' experience (S. M. Lipset) that, while perhaps falling short of a fully developed comparison, can serve at least as a reference point. In his groundbreaking study *The American Constitution: A Biography* – the constitutional historian Akhil Reed Amar has stressed exactly this close nexus between nation, citizens and rights.[1] It is my contention that historical credit should be given where historical credit is due. Thus, it should be the 'First Nation' American rhetorical nexus between citizen, constitutionalism/rights and nation that provides the best historical departure point for contrasting and comparing the practice of other countries or aspiring nations, including those from Europe.

Limits to constitutional patriotism in Europe

I would like to discuss here briefly three Western and two Eastern and South Eastern European examples in an attempt to illustrate that European nation-states and Europe as a whole have not only been latecomers but also continue to have major legitimation deficits that even a new European constitution will not be able to settle, never mind be able to overcome. Pre-empting my brief discussion here for a second, I maintain that Germany and Spain are the only major countries in which constitutional patriotism has become part of the public rhetoric. As we will see, this happened for very specific reasons. The brief European sketch which follows, particularly the discussion of the Spanish-Basque case, is mainly intended to provide a counterargument to the promotion of constitutional patriotism as proposed by Jan-Werner Müller in his *Constitutional Patriotism*.[2] Again, pre-empting my conclusion here, I maintain that constitutional patriotism as coined by Jaspers, Sternberger, Ha-

---

1   *Reed Amar*, America's Constitution. I should point out here that Amar does in fact not use the term 'constitutionalism' or even 'constitutional patriotism' – but then that is hard to do when your entire book is about exactly that topic. On one occasion Amar calls the actual constitutional text "America's legal city on a hill" (XI) – no better way of expressing the American attitude towards rights and its normative-political and practical-sociological dimensions.
2   *Müller*, Constitutional Patriotism. Müller decided to downgrade the American contribution to constitutional patriotism considerably. He only devotes one and a half pages on it – and then only as a precursor to the German post-WWII use of constitutional patriotism.

bermas or, for that matter, Müller is not easily exportable, never mind universally applicable. It is, in contrast, the American tradition that looks more attractive – even if it is only for historical reference purposes.

I start with the United Kingdom since it is the UK that is generally regarded as the oldest example of successful western and European democracy. One soon finds that the emphatic rhetoric of 'the world's oldest living democracy' does not really live up to reality. Although it is true that the Westminster parliament is one of the oldest political parliaments, Britain only became a democracy after three major electoral reforms in the course of the nineteenth century.[3] Most commentators confuse parliamentary history with the history of democracy. True, modern democracy is, in essence, functioning representative democracy. But this is exactly where the UK falls short. The UK's constitutional base of government still consists of a mix of parliamentary acts and traditional customs which have, institutionally speaking, led to a strange fusion of political powers in which the judiciary is, firstly, still part of the legislative assembly (although separated by role and function, i.e. the Law Lords in the Upper House) and, secondly, still not constitutionally superior when set against the majority decisions of the Lower House of the Westminster Parliament. Furthermore, in terms of modern citizenship the UK is actually a latecomer. To be fair, in recent years the British government has at least made an effort and is now promoting active citizenship in the classroom and beyond[4]. This is mainly due to the fact that the prospect of being subjects to the Crown has become less and less attractive in modern times and has, apart from some die-hard fans of royalty, little future value. (Having said that, being 'subject to the crown' still continues to be a strong legal position.) Yet, the very definition of UK citizenship remains problematic, mainly because of the UK's colonial legacy. The UK currently knows six different definitions of citizenship, depending of the individual citizen's positioning in terms of residence, age and family relations in the now dead empire.[5]

When it comes to internal coherence, the UK faces the problem of having to deal with three and a half different nations (the half is Northern Ireland) and is doing so strictly by only one principle – contingency. This attitude of 'making-it-up-as-you-go-along' has created an unprecedented institutional mess. Scotland, Wales, England and Northern Ireland – and we might add here the Isle of Man and the Channel Islands – all have a different constitutional status with very little resemblance and coherence in terms of their political representation (with England of course having none that it could call exclusively its own). However exceptional and even weak the UK may appear when it comes to constitutional matters, like the U.S., the UK has

---

3   The best studies on the subject are still *Weir/Beetham*, Political Power and Democratic Control in Britain, and *Klug/Starmer/Weir*, The Three Pillars of Liberty: Political Rights and Freedoms in the United Kingdom. Also informative is *von Ziegesar* Wie demokratisch ist England?
4   For more details see the report of the Advisory Group on Citizenship (chaired by Bernard Crick): Education for citizenship and the teaching of democracy in schools.
5   Instructive are still *Cohen*, Frontiers of Identity: The British and the Others, and *Crick*, Essays on Citizenship.

never experienced dictatorship and foreign invasion in modern times. This certainly has created a bond between the government and the governed, to such an extent that we might say that in the UK the legitimacy between the political elite and the people has never been radically questioned and is unlikely to be questioned any time soon. I suspect that exactly because of the historical nexus that is often symbolized in the rhetorical figure of the freeborn Englishman and Englishwoman, speaking of constitutional patriotism in the UK makes little or no sense at all.

The UK and the U.S. appear almost as if they were models of political continuity when compared to France. French political history in the nineteenth and twentieth century is lumbered with radical changes despite the continued rhetoric of early revolutionary republicanism. Just to recall briefly, the French after the Revolution went through Napoleonic dictatorship, another three revolutions (1830, 1848 and 1870/71) and five republics – not to mention the Vichy regime – before settling its constitutional affairs. Once known as the most centralized republic in the western world, France has over the course of the last twenty years or so embarked on a process of reform in which the grip of Paris and the centralized tendencies of the French Revolution have become less felt in the regions and *départements*. However, the current French republic still appears to be quite reluctant to relax the rules when it comes to wishing to express a concrete identity in more than a folkloristic manner. Language, schooling and some meaningful regional representation as in the cases of Alsace, Corsica and the French part of the Basque Country are still highly sensitive issues. France also still has to fully come to terms with its colonial legacy in Algeria, particularly in relation to immigration and integration issues. Again, as in the case of the UK, *constitutional* patriotism is weak and can hardly be encountered. It is rather an abstract universal sense of equality and liberty as promoted by traditional French revolutionary republicanism that still prevails. This is despite the social realities of ethnic segmentation and niches, particularly in the *banlieus* of the big cities. Against all signs that the universalism of the republican model appears to be at odds, at least when dealing with the social realities of France, it is still taboo to question the old republican consensus.

Germany tops the list of nation-building latecomers by having experienced the full spectrum of political regimes in the course of just one hundred years.[6] Germany has done it all: from Imperial Reich to the Weimar Republic, from Weimar to the 'brown revolution' of the Third Reich, and after the defeat of National Socialism the split into the Democratic Federal Republic of West Germany and the Communist German Democratic Republic, and finally the creation of the newly united Federal Republic after the fall of the Berlin Wall. In terms of constitutional issues Germany seems now to be in a much more settled position (Europe hopes). However, there seems to be a tendency to farm out problematic issues to the EU level. Particularly when it comes to apparently rather traditional nation-state performances, such as citizenship and integration issues, a somewhat misunderstood principle of subsidiarity seems now to prompt an easy escape route to Europe. After Auschwitz everything

---

6   In terms of late nation building and political extremism Italy is actually not that far behind Germany.

that smacked of national and nationalist positions, needed to be dismissed or curtailed. In this respect Germany embarked on what might be called a 'post-national' phase. This was the historical phase in which constitutional patriotism made sense. It was understood to replace the rhetoric of 'territory', 'organization' and 'monopoly of legitimate violence' with loyalty to republican and civic principles and values emerging out of some never-ending communication pattern. However, it is not altogether clear where, politically and culturally speaking, this is all heading. Germany nowadays looks like pursuing some 'quid-pro-quo' politics in which Germany constantly seeks answers from Europe – with an export-ready, nation-free constitutional patriotism now playing a cunning but ultimately not very convincing role. After all, not every country in Europe has entered a post-national phase.

This is not the place to discuss all the different nation-building processes and constellations in Europe[7] but in order to discuss some of the problems of nation-building and the role constitutional patriotism could prospectively play in the new Europe I would briefly like to add to my three Western examples two Eastern and Southeastern examples before returning to my main topic, the Spanish and Basque case and how it figures in terms of constitutional patriotism.

The fall of the Berlin Wall and the snowball effect it created led to a major delegitimization and deconstruction process in the Soviet orbit, played out mainly in the Caucasus region and on the Western fringe of the former SU, particularly the Baltic region. A similar delegitimation and deconstruction process, only slightly delayed because of additional complicating factors, happened in the former Yugoslavia.

The revolt and newly gained independence of the Baltic republics did not come as a complete surprise. Since the Ribbentrop-Molotov pact Soviet rule had always been regarded as being problematic. The westward expansion in the context of World War II and its subsequent entrenchment during the Cold War period put the SU and those local political elites that sympathized with it in charge. Once the Soviet power grid weakened, first through Poland's *solidarnosc*, then *Perestroika* and later through the fall of the Berlin Wall, the Baltic States began to find their footing in the new Europe. Like other countries of the former Eastern Bloc, Estonia, Latvia and Lithuania became democratic nation states. However, in contrast to Hungary, Poland, Romania or Czechoslovakia the Baltic states had been fully absorbed into the SU. As such they were subject to an engineered mass migration of SU citizens to the Baltic, particularly to Estonia and Latvia (less so to Lithuania), something that neither Hungary, Poland, Romania or Czechoslovakia experienced. After the SU's disintegration, these Russian migrants had no homeland to return to, a fact that has created serious tensions in the new, now independent, Baltic states. What constitutional *patriotism* could potentially mean in such a complex social and political context with such explosive demographics remains unclear.

---

7   The best writings on the subject still remain *von Beyme*, Systemwechsel in Osteuropa; *Rokkan*, Nation und Demokratie in Europa [English version: *State Formation, Nation Building and Mass Politics in Europe*]; and *Hroch*, Das Europa der Nationen.

The break-up of the former socialist federation of Yugoslavia was an even more complicated affair. While the Russian Federation provided the fall-back position for the crumbling Soviet Union, the rump that was left once communism was gone, Serbia, never managed to play the same role for Yugoslavia. Also, in the case of Yugoslavia there was no meaningful pre-World War II context to fall back upon, as had been the case in the Baltic. In the case of Slovenia, Croatia and to a certain extent even Serbia, the forming of new nation-states during the break-up of Yugoslavia could be explained by looking at their former territorial status in the Austrian-Hungarian empire. It was much more difficult to confirm or determine the existence of former pre-war countries called Kosovo, Bosnia-Herzegovina, Macedonia or Montenegro. To complicate matters even further, the existence of the former federation of Yugoslavia and the common language[8] had made it easy for its citizens to move around and settle in any part of the federation. However, in the break-up process the right of free movement that had formerly been enjoyed by Yugoslavian citizens turned now into a real demographic mess in which historic regions and territorial claims clashed with claims of newly emerging proto-states – Bosnia and its capital Sarajevo being the prime tragic examples. Even after the war and the Dayton peace agreement, the situation in the Balkans remains volatile. While Slovenia had a lucky start, Kosovo remains some form of large left-over, which in a few years time might want to enter a new federation called Albania-Kosovo.[9] Again, the fact that these new states are now democracies and rely on lawful procedures and constitutions does not imply that they will show any enthusiasm for a *constitutional* patriotism. Rather it is patriotism or nationalism that are evoking the passions of its citizens – with very little meaningful constitutionalism. I have serious doubts whether a new European constitutional patriotism will be able to gloss over all the differences not only between different constitutional traditions amongst the original member states but also in terms of including all the newcomers in a meaningful way.[10] Seen from its fuzzy and, normatively speaking, apparently rather weak content, the prospects of a European constitutional patriotism might not even appear promising in

---

8   Slovenia, Macedonia and Kosovo were the exception.
9   At current this seems to be highly unlikely because Kosovo has been looking to West for some time while Albania has not seen any great progress neither in terms of investment, productivity and growth nor in terms of great political achievements. .
10 Actually, since the Irish said 'no' to Lisbon in a referendum in the Spring of 2008, it looked for some time as if the EU was in a delicate position to get a political framework, never mind a constitution, ratified. Ever since the defeats in Denmark, the Netherlands and France, and later Ireland, the rhetoric of a European constitutional agenda has been seriously called into question. Only a few intellectual die-hards like Derrida and Habermas attempted to save the idea of not just a treaty but an actual European Constitution for posteriority. The outcome of a second Irish referendum in autumn of 2009 was more successful. In times of economic crisis the Irish voter had obviously second thoughts. The fact that a second referendum had to be held seriously damaged the democratic legitimation process of the Lisbon Treaty. The sinister irony of Bert Brecht cannot be overlooked: the Irish voter clearly has been urged to vote until it suited the EU's Lisbon agenda.

terms of providing a solution for some unresolved business as in the case of Spanish-Basque relations.

The Basque Case in Context (I): The Nineteenth Century

Spain acknowledged the independence of the Baltic republics only reluctantly and it was not just by chance that the declaration of independence of the new states that had emerged from the former Yugoslavia had been welcomed only after serious diplomatic pressure had been applied. It should also not surprise us that up to the present day Kosovo's proclamation of independence has not been acknowledged by Spain. The reason for this late acknowledgement in the case of the new Baltic states and the non-acknowledgement in the case of Kosovo lies of course not in any disrespect of the Baltic republics, or in the love for the former Yugoslavian federation, but rather in the precedent and the signals that these cases of new nation-building set for the supposed old nation-state that is Spain.

If one looks at older historical maps of Spain it is immediately obvious that Spain has for much of its history been a relatively weak nation state.[11] A closer look at Spain's history reveals long-lasting and, on occasion, unsettled conflicts – Catalonia, the Basque Country and, to a lesser extent, Galicia being the prime examples. In the Middle Ages we encounter a number of competing kingdoms, the prime players being Navarre, Aragón and Castile. Out of the power struggle, which lasted for three centuries, Castile finally emerged as the strongest player with the *Reyes Católicos* laying the groundwork for what would eventually become the *sea-borne* Spanish Empire. The Spanish empire became a major international force and its influence was to last for almost a further three centuries before it was eventually defeated, overtaken and partly replaced by the British Empire. However, the external, international power and influence of the Kingdom of Castile appeared not to be reflected in internal strength. Castile's political hegemony continued to be based on consensual agreements between powerful economic regions and cities – such as Catalonia and Barcelona and Bizkaia and Bilbao – that also managed to preserve distinctive cultural and administrative features. The same could be said about Navarre that, although shrinking in size, still continued to exert a formidable and influential force. Both the Basque provinces and Navarre continued to enjoy special rights (*fueros*) which allowed for economic independent decision-making (until 1841 customs were still located along the northern stretch of the river Ebro, rather than along the French-Spanish border). Independently from each other, Henry Kamen and John H. Elliott have stressed in their books on the rise and fall of the Spanish Empire how extraordinary weak Castile appeared internally for much of her reign and even at the height of its power,[12] Castile never really managed to translate the international influence and wealth into creating a powerful state and a national Spanish economy

---

11 See, for example, *de Cortázar*, Atlas de Historia de España.
12 See *Kamen*, Spain's Road to Empire; *Elliott*, Empires of the Atlantic World.

which was likely to have a future or that at least could lay the groundwork for things to come. The Spanish Empire and Castile almost seem to have been arrested in a time warp. In contrast, Bilbao and its environs had, trade-wise in terms of the development of international links, benefited considerably from the Empire. At the beginning of the nineteenth century, Castile was lagging so far behind that even the repeated attempts of the liberals to steer the ship through what was then the early phase of the industrial revolution, remained problematic.

To be sure, in the regions not everything was ready for industrial take-off and political change either. Especially in the Basque Country the nineteenth century was marked by a long-lasting conflict that found its violent expression in two wars. The two Carlist Wars (1833-40 and 1872-76) are notoriously hard to comprehend, even for historians.[13] This is the case mainly because there were so many layers to the conflict. On one side we encounter the more liberal, enlightened, secular, anti-royal and urban influences that were particularly strong in Bilbao, demanding not only economic and social modernization but also political reform. These forces wanted to get rid of the old rights and customs as enshrined in the *fueros*. On the other side we have the rural areas of the Basque provinces and Navarre, the so-called *Carlistas*, defending religion and the old autonomy based on old rights, privileges and economic arrangements with the Crown of Castile. The *Carlistas* defended a rural world that functioned relatively well, at least when compared to some of the other regions of Spain. True, the *Carlistas* were certainly not radical modernizers; however, it would be wrong to describe them as being simply backward or reactionary. They had a point in holding on to and defending their way of life, which seemed to have worked for that rural world that made up a big part of the Basque Country and Navarre, in particular those parts that had not been subject to the industrial revolution.

Officially, the conflict ended with the victory of the modernizers and the abolition of the *fueros*. However, it is not really possible to identify with certainty the winners and losers in this conflict, particularly not since it is hard to determine which one is the Spanish side and which one is the Basque side. In the Carlist conflict we find Spanish and Basque liberals fighting together against Spanish, Navarrese and Basque *Carlistas*.[14] The underlying cultural conflict was also to continue and would re-emerge in the twentieth century, particularly with Franco's coup d'état in 1936. The Carlist Wars never fully settled the latent and lingering conflict between the traditional rural and small-town world and the expanding urban environment, mainly of Bilbao. While the liberals gained access to power and, consecutively, introduced economic and legal reforms, this remained a Pyrrhic victory.

In the last two decades of the nineteenth century the political, social and economic conditions began to change dramatically, particularly in the urban zone around

---

13 A good account is *Orruño Legarda*, Crisis del Antiguo Régimen y Revolución Liberal (1793-1878).
14 For an impressive (visual) interpretation of the conflict see also Medem's celebrated film *Vacas*.

Bilbao.[15] Within twenty years Bilbao became transformed and was turned into a giant industrial magnet. To maintain its productivity and labor force it needed massive immigration. Tens of thousands of immigrants followed the call and migrated from the poorer areas of Spain and also from the rural areas of the Basque Country to Bilbao. A true demographic revolution was the result. The liberal modernizers had won – but only to encounter a demographically explosive and politically volatile constellation. This is where our story of Basque and Spanish patriotism and related political diverging projects (including competing constitutional visions) really begins to take off.

The Basque Case in Context (II): The Twentieth Century and beyond

At the beginning of the twentieth century there was no real or meaningful nexus between nation, rights and citizens in the region we call the Basque Country. We are dealing, first of all, with a highly fragmented territory, divided up between the Basque provinces of Bizkaia, Gipuzkoa and Alava plus Navarre, and the three provinces in France, Lower Navarre, Zuberoa and Lapurdi. Speaking in terms of citizenship, we are talking about an equally complex and complicated picture in which we have two types of national citizenship (Spain and France). On the French side the three traditional Basque provinces are not represented politically as such but form part of the much larger *département* of the Basses Pyrénées (now Pyrénées Atlantiques); on the Spanish side we have the Basque provinces of Bizkaia, Gipuzkoa and Alava with Navarre being a separate political entity. On the French side two processes rendered the traditional Basque territories powerless in terms of common political representation: a mass exodus from the countryside, mainly to America, and the change of the Basque seaside towns into holiday resorts with massive immigration from other parts of France led to a situation in which Basques were no longer in a position to claim significant political representation and rights. On the Spanish side events were much more dramatic. The dictatorship of Primo de Rivera (1923-1930) changed very little but the Second Republic made a huge difference. The major problem, however, was that the changes came too late, namely at a time when the republic itself was torn apart by what seemed then like irreconcilable and irreparable conflicts, which eventually helped to trigger Franco's military coup. It was only late in 1936 that in order to find regional allies, the Cortes and the Spanish government decided to grant the three Basque provinces of Bizkaia, Gipuzkoa and Alava more than the statute granted in 1931 – namely an improved autonomy status that fell just short of

---

15 Bilbao had become a city of wealth mainly through early trade, commerce and banking. The newly discovered mineral wealth towards the west of the city helped to kick-start the industrial revolution and led eventually to steel production and shipbuilding on a grand scale, which in turn changed and transformed the city and its environs. See also *Luengo Teixidor*, El Primer tercio del siglo XX.

sovereignty[16]. Navarre was not part of this new political framework. A government was formed consisting of a coalition of Basque nationalist, republican, socialist and communist parties under the *Lehendakari* José Antonio Aguirre. Finding itself under enormous military pressure by the insurgents, Aguirre's administration spent most of its time organizing the defense of the Basque provinces. It is at this point that the unresolved tensions with the *Carlistas* came again to the forefront. The *Carlistas* were particularly strong in the northern part of Navarre and in Alava. What had brought them to join the insurgents was the promise of a continuation of their traditional that is, mostly rural and small-town way of life, defending their special rights and remaining fervent Catholic believers. Having much local knowledge and knowing the terrain in which they were fighting the insurgents and their Carlist allies soon closed the ring around Bilbao. After the bombardment and fall of Gernika and Durango and the threat of a similar fate for Bilbao, the Basque soldiers, the *Gudariak*, still continued to fight heroically against the much better equipped insurgents but soon gave up once it became clear that General Mola would make good his threats and destroy Bilbao, putting eventually the lives of thousands of civilians at risk. After the fall of Bilbao for a short period a few Basque troops escaped and continued with their resistance further west in the Cantabrian mountains, while the Aguirre government took refuge first in Santander and then Barcelona before it was finally forced to leave Spain after the fall of Catalonia and Valencia. In exile, first in Belgium, then in Paris and London, and finally in New York, Aguirre continued to be in charge of the Basque government in exile (interrupted only by a short period when he went underground in Berlin for a few months). Later on Aguirre would also join the Spanish exile government and exercise a considerable influence in its ranks.[17]

In New York the Basque government in exile survived until the end of the Second World War. It contributed to the Allied war effort through various means: Basque soldiers continued to fight with the French *résistance*, and Aguirre himself did not cease to tour the Americas to promote the Allies' case, with at least some success in Latin America. Meanwhile, thousands of Basque refugees survived in France, Belgium, England and the Americas[18]. In the Basque Country itself a great number of Basque citizens, independent of political affiliation, minus of course Carlists and Spanish nationalists, were sentenced to either death or to enforced labor and prison. Everybody in the Basque homeland and in exile hoped that the war effort of the Allies would eventually result in the removal of the Franco dictatorship. As it turned out, the Cold War changed things considerably, against the expectations of many

---

16   To mention just three examples, the Basque government had its own army, collected taxes and issued passports.
17   Both *Aguirre*'s 1944 book Escape via Berlin and his diary, posthumously published as Diario de Aguirre, are very moving accounts about his narrow escape from Nazi-occupied Europe. *Mees*'s biographical study El profeta pragmático is so far the best historical account of Aguirre's life and times.
18   None of these exiles ever received compensation from the Spanish government. It goes almost without saying that those who were sentenced to work in Spanish labour and concentration camps or those relatives whose members had been shot or disappeared never qualified for compensation either.

(including Aguirre) who had believed strongly and for a very long time that the US was fighting for the democratic cause. To their disappointment the US soon concluded that Franco Spain was a welcome ally in the Cold War. The New York-based Aguirre government, which had been sponsored by the US throughout all those years, soon fell out of favor and was finally dropped by the American administration. Aguirre moved back to Paris to be closer to the Basque region. However, this relocation proved to be fruitless. By the late 1950s many Basque refugees had returned. Also, a new generation of political activists had emerged who saw the Aguirre government as consisting of mere rhetoricians who would not get their hands dirty. It was no coincidence that the first long official communiqué that ETA ever published was a critical obituary for Aguirre as he was laid to rest in Saint Jean de Luz in 1960. With him, the first democratically elected *lehendakari*, the hope for a continuation of the lawful and legitimate Basque government – in short Basque constitutional patriotism – had too been buried. What remained was the continuous conflict over the legitimate use of violence both by violent Basque insurgents and the Spanish security apparatus.

The next phase of legitimate Basque governance would only arise with the death of Franco in 1975 and the beginning of what in Spain and in the Basque Country is known as *la transición*. Two consultation exercises were of particular importance, that of the new Spanish constitution in 1978 and that of the modified Basque autonomy status in 1979.[19] In both cases no clear majority emerged for either project. In the first case of the new Spanish constitution this was mainly due to the call for abstention by the grand old party, the PNV, the same party which Aguirre had steered through some rough times earlier, and a clear 'no' vote by the left wing Basque nationalist parties; the "Spanish" left wing and conservative parties urged their voters to vote "yes". In the end, abstention and the 'no'-vote together ranged from 44.72% in Navarre to almost 70% in the case of Gipuzkoa. In the second case the abstention rate ranged from 40.27% in Gipuzkoa and 42.51% in Bizkaia to 36.72% in Alava. Navarre was not part of this referendum – a major concern to those voters who abstained in the Basque Country.

In 2004, a coalition led by the PNV and the *lehendakari* Ibarretxe, supported by two smaller left-leaning parties (Eusko Alkartasuna and Ezker Batua), passed Basque legislation in an attempt to overcome the political impasse caused by ETA violence and Spanish constitutional, political and cultural power play. The coalition wishes to put a referendum to the Basque people in which the voters will be asked whether they favor the right of the Basque Country to become independent and for the Basque Autonomous Community to become freely associated with Spain.[20] There is a Navarre clause in this plan but it was carefully designed not to offend the Navarrese by stating that it is only out of their free will, determined and confirmed either by election or through a referendum, that Navarre can associate itself with the

---

19 The first Gernika statute had been the result of the new Spanish constitution of December 1978.
20 The English translation of the text is available online at: http://www.estatutodeeuskadi.net/docs/dictamencomision20122004_eng.pdf.

Autonomous Basque Community. The so-called Ibarretxe plan passed the first hurdle in the Basque Parliament but was soon afterwards rejected by the Spanish Senate. In the meantime the Spanish government let nothing untried to prevent the consultation from developing beyond the planning stages.[21] While the Zapatero government indicated that more rights devolved from Madrid could be an option for the Basque Country, all modifications and reforms would have to remain strictly within the boundaries proscribed by the Spanish Constitution, which, as we know, had and continues to have major legitimation problems in the Basque Country. Both sides currently propagate mutually exclusive patriotic constitutionalisms.[22] Both projects are to some extent impositions, particularly when seen in the light of shifting demographic and identity patterns over the last few decades.[23] The Spanish and newly elected Basque governments' case will find support amongst Spanish migrants but also amongst those who identify themselves as either clearly of Spanish origin or as having both a *Spanish* and Basque identity. On the other side, the former Basque government's initiative had been welcomed by those who identify themselves mainly as Basques or those who have a *Basque* Spanish identity. To ask in this context and in the current climate for constitutional patriotism on either side is a highly explosive issue.

Some final reflections

Asked on my take on the current situation, I will probably surprise the reader by arguing for a serious case of restorative justice. I would argue that something like the now defunct Ibarretxe plan with some important modifications such as a complete halt to ETA's violent campaigns but also including the end of what can be called "lawful harassment" by Spanish legal institutions could have potential (such a proposal will also have to sail under a different name in order not to be identified too closely with one person or one particular government proposal only). Any future plan in this direction should also take into account the changed demographic situation and the complex identity patterns that one can currently encounter in the Basque lands. This implies getting rid of all-too-narrow visions of what it means to be a

---

21 The consultation has finally been prohibited by the Spanish government and its courts. The then outgoing Basque government tried to get a European Court ruling on the matter. What fate awaits this move after the last Basque elections in May 2009, which for the first time resulted in a non-nationalist Basque government, is not that complicated to predict. As promised, the new government of Patxi Lopez will try to stop and get rid of everything that even reminds Basque citizens of the Ibarretxe plan.
22 After the election of Patxi Lopez to *Lehendakari* the conflict appears now to become even more accentuated since two competing and mutually exclusive Basque visions of what patriotism could mean in this part of the world are now on firm collision course.
23 A very good account of the territorial dimensions of the Basque Country can be found in *Mansvelt Beck*, Territory and Terror. However, while the study is excellent as long as it deals with human and political geography it is highly problematic in terms of its political conclusions.

Basque patriot and support more inclusive, that means first and foremost universally applicable practices, models and visions of what it means to be a true *abertzale*.[24] Additionally, this future plan should include some independent international guidance and supervision. Such an amended new plan and particularly the political process that accompanies it could help to create a situation in which the very concepts of legitimation and legitimacy might eventually come to signify and mean something again. Whether this suffices and whether this could really make a difference in terms of an alternative to a prolonged conflict and the day-to-day cynicism that one can observe in the Basque Country remains to be seen. It is worth a try though, especially as the alternatives have not worked.[25] It is too early to say and I don't want to engage here in political prophecy but I have serious doubts whether the new first non-nationalist Basque government under Patxi Lopex will be able to deliver on any of those accounts – au contraire.

In this article I have been very critical of the unreflective, bland, often imposing and a-historical use of the term constitutional patriotism. I have argued, maybe more in an implicit way, for a serious reality check of some of the rhetoric that is currently been employed in legal, social and political thought. By referring to some European examples I have argued that it is not Germany (actually former West Germany) that we have to refer to if we are interested in comparisons, models, examples or comparative references, but that – if we decide to use the term at all – it is rather the United States that we have to acknowledge as having been the true pioneer in terms of coinage, effort and historical achievement. Of course one can argue about some of the aspects of America's legal practices such as its harsh law enforcement policies or its aberrations and peculiarities such as the death penalty (all of which have also been used in constitutionalist rhetoric). However, such arguments would miss the point of the widespread, patriotic acceptance – "legitimation" or "legitimacy" would be other fitting words – of the U.S.'s constitutionalism.

---

24 Thought-provoking attempts can be found in *Etxeberria Mauleon* et al., Derecho de autodeterminación y realidad vasca.

25 To make this work, Basque unity and political compromise or even agreement on some fundamental issues are crucial. The current political system that divides the spectrum up in 2x2 fields of political gravity makes it hard for both residents and outside observers to understand what people in the Basque Country really want. The so-called "Spanish" parties on the left and the right, the PSE and the PP respectively, and the so-called "Basque" parties from conservative Christian-democratic nationalist (PNV) and a small social democratic nationalist party (EA) on one side and the more radical left-wing *abertzale* movement in its deeply fragmented form (Batasuna, ANV, PCTV, Aralar) on the other side, not to mention a different party spectrum with important modifications in Navarre constitute a true political labyrinth. In terms of explaining how a peace deal may be achieved I recommend Ulrich *Schneckener's*, Auswege aus dem Bürgerkrieg, particularly the last chapter, pp. 474-509. It deals with conflict and with the advantages and disadvantages of collective forms of learning. Also, Paddy Woodworth, one of the best-informed observers of the Basque conflict, has made some very concrete suggestions of how to enter a constructive dialogue. I refer here particularly to two longer articles: *Woodworth*, The Spanish-Basque Peace Process, and *Woodworth*, Euskal Hiria (La Ciudad Vasca).

America has had the benefits of a lucky start; yet, as Locke famously pointed out, in the beginning all the world was America. Is it too far fetched or have we simply become too entrapped in the language of the European political elites to apply such an original and democratic position to the Basque Country, too?

Bibliography

Advisory Group on Citizenship (chaired by Bernard Crick): Education for citizenship and the teaching of democracy in schools, Qualifications and Curriculum Authority, 22 September 1998.
Aguirre, José Antonio de, Escape via Berlin, Reno, [1944] 1991.
Aguirre, José Antonio de, Diario de Aguirre, Tafalla, 1998.
v. Beyme, Klaus, Systemwechsel in Osteuropa, Frankfurt, 1994.
Cohen, Robin, Frontiers of Identity: The British and the Others, London, 1994.
de Cortázar, Fernando Garcia, Atlas de Historia de España, Barcelona, 2005.
Crick, Bernard, Essays on Citizenship, London, 2000.
Elliott, John H, Empires of the Atlantic World, New Haven, 2007.
Etxeberria Mauleon, Xabier, et al., Derecho de autodeterminación y realidad vasca, Vitoria-Gasteiz, 2002.
Hroch, Miroslaw, Das Europa der Nationen, Göttingen, 2005.
Kamen, Henry, Spain's Road to Empire, London, 2002.
Klug, Francesca/Starmer, Keir/Weir, Stuart, The Three Pillars of Liberty: Political Rights and Freedoms in the United Kingdom, London, 1996.
Luengo Teixidor, Félix, El Primer tercio del siglo XX, in Angel Leuna Pueyo, Jose, Barruso Barés, Pedro, and Alday Ruiz, Alfonso (eds), Historia del País Vasco, San Sebastián, 2005, pp. 177-235.
Mansvelt Beck, Jan, Territory and Terror: Conflicting Nationalisms in the Basque Country, London, 2005.
Medem, Julio, Vacas, Spain, 1991.
Mees, Ludger, El profeta pragmático, Irun, 2006. The English translation of the text is available online at: http://www.estatutodeeuskadi.net/docs/dictamencomision20122004_eng.pdf.
Müller, Jan-Werner, Constitutional Patriotism, Princeton, 2007.
Orruño, Legarda/José María Ortíz, Crisis del Antiguo Régimen y Revolución Liberal (1793-1878), in: Angel Leuna Pueyo, Jose, Barruso Barés, Pedro, and Alday Ruiz, Alfonso (eds), Historia del País Vasco, San Sebastián, 2005, pp. 17-77.
Reed Amar, Akhil, America's Constitution, New York, 2005.
Rokkan, Stein, Nation und Demokratie in Europa, Frankfurt, 2005. English version: State Formation, Nation Building and Mass Politics in Europe, Oxford, 1999.
Schneckener, Ulrich, Auswege aus dem Bürgerkrieg, Frankfurt, 2002.
Weir, Stuart/Beetham, David, Political Power and Democratic Control in Britain, London, 1999.
Woodworth, Paddy, The Spanish-Basque Peace Process: How to Get Things Wrong, World Policy Journal 24(1) 2007, pp. 65-73.
Woodworth, Paddy, Euskal Hiria (La Ciudad Vasca): una visión desde lejos, Hermes (2007), pp. 50-56.
v. Ziegesar, Detlef, Wie demokratisch ist England? Die Wahrheit uber einen Mythos, Köln, 1991.

The necessary secularism of legitimate authority

David Saunders

A post-secular setting and a 'believing citizen'?

In the final week of January 2008, something happened in the sky. On a Heathrow-bound Air Canada flight, the co-pilot was in communication ... not with ground control, but with God. As a result, he had to be wrested from the flight-deck, taken to the Economy section and sedated. The problem lay not with his relation to the deity but with his potentially dangerous loss of sense of office. His role was not to bring the divine command to humanity or to fly the passengers to heaven; it was to land the passengers in earthly London by maintaining the aircraft's safety and their security. The flight-deck, we might say, should properly remain a secularised setting. This in-flight incident will serve as emblem for my argument.

Air travel security aside, in more philosophical circles voices are heard calling on us to refer ourselves to something beyond the accountably secular. The secular liberal state, they claim, now confronts its crisis of legitimacy. It is as if history has reached a point where we re-orient our thinking – and our selves – to a radical possibility: that the historical political-legal order has been superseded. The concept of becoming 'post-secular' is now in play, as if this were a royal road to re-grounding political-legal order in a legitimating norm.

On 19 January 2004, in Munich, the Catholic Academy of Bavaria arranged a 'dialogue' between the then Cardinal Joseph Ratzinger and Jürgen Habermas. In presenting their exchange – published in English as The Dialectics of Secularisation – I return later to the Cardinal's contribution.[1] Habermas's discourse on 'Pre-political foundations of the democratic constitutional state?' – delivered in the persona of 'the Philosopher' – offers us a point of entry into a would-be post-secular performance.

The philosopher addresses a central question: whether it is 'possible in any way to provide a secular justification of political rule, that is, a justification that is non-religious or postmetaphysical'.[2] Initially, the answer is affirmative: in liberal constitutional states systems of law can be 'legitimated in a self-referential manner, that is, on the basis of legal procedures born of democratic procedures'.[3] This positive assessment rests, though, on tilting the balance away from law's historical forms – these remain complicit with capitalist inequalities – and towards the emancipatory potential that European legal systems have conserved, whether through their deli-

---

1 *Habermas/Ratzinger*, The Dialectics of Secularisation.
2 *Habermas/Ratzinger*, The Dialectics of Secularisation. p. 22.
3 *Habermas/Ratzinger*, The Dialectics of Secularisation, pp. 27-8.

307

berative discursive procedures or their stewardship of individual or communal rights. But the Philosopher is one whose normative gaze can now see beyond the limits of proceduralism in the historically secular juridical order. What does he see there? Looking through a 'post-secularist' ouverture to religion and religious values, he sees a set of higher-order norms on which to found a more complete 'justification'.

Conversely, the Philosopher identifies as normatively inadequate a merely law-abiding modus vivendi:

> [I]t remains doubtful, when we consider the element of human motivation, whether a society with a plurality of worldviews can achieve a normative stabilisation – that is, something that goes beyond a mere modus vivendi – through the assumption of a background understanding that will at best remain on the formal level, limited to questions of procedures and principles.[4]

This dismissive view of a 'mere modus vivendi' is reiterated, in line with the allegation that – unlike the philosopher himself – other of today's citizens lack the 'motivations' required for there to be solidarity and social stability.[5] By way of remedy for this moral shortcoming, he proposes that the time is now ready for taking the opening towards those cultural resources preserved like precious oil embedded deep in the religious tradition. By muting the 'secular forces of a communicative reason', the Philosopher can preserve himself from the old error of treating 'the continued existence of religion in a largely secularised environment simply as a societal fact'. Rather, 'philosophy must take this phenomenon seriously from within, so to speak, as a cognitive challenge'.[6] This serves as prelude to opening the normative door and entering the ecclesial domain.

The message is one of guarded respect for this erstwhile religious challenger to the secular order, a challenger itself now transformed into an ally by the philosopher's emancipating post-secular vision. He thus grants religious norms 'the respect due to persons and ways of life that obviously derive their integrity and authenticity from religious convictions'.[7] But this is by no means all: 'more is involved here than respect'; as if in deep normative deficit, the secularist habit of mind now 'has good reason to be willing to learn from religious traditions'.[8] A normative treasure lies in religion, hidden to eyes that cannot see it but fortunately preserved – as if by a prov-

---

4 *Habermas/Ratzinger*, The Dialectics of Secularisation, pp. 22.
5 See *Habermas/Ratzinger*, The Dialectics of Secularisation, pp. 48-9. Habermas's 'mere *modus vivendi*' echoes John Rawls's treatment of *modus vivendi* as failure to constitute 'stability for the right reasons'. See *Rawls*, Political Liberalism, pp. 124-44. By contrast, John Gray presents a positive account of *modus vivendi* as political compromise enabling a measure of peaceful co-existence despite incompatible world-views. See *Gray*, Two Faces of Liberalism, pp. 105-9.
6 *Habermas/Ratzinger*, The Dialectics of Secularisation, p. 38.
7 *Habermas/Ratzinger*, The Dialectics of Secularisation, p. 40.
8 *Habermas/Ratzinger*, The Dialectics of Secularisation, p. 42.

idential history – as the 'something intact in the communal life of the religious fellowships ... something that has been lost elsewhere and that cannot be restored by the professional knowledge of experts alone'.⁹

Hence today's imperative: the shift to 'secularisation as a twofold and complementary learning process'.¹⁰ This shift marks the threshold of entry to a 'post-secular society':

> The expression 'post-secular' does more than give public recognition to religious fellowships in view of the functional contribution they make to the reproduction of motivations and attitudes that are societally desirable. The public awareness of a post-secular society also reflects a normative insight that has consequences for the political dealings of unbelieving citizens with believing citizens. In the post-secular society, there is an increasing consensus that certain phases of the 'modernisation of the public consciousness' involve the assimilation and the reflexive transformation of both religious and secular mentalities.¹¹

Given this mutually transformative exchange between the secular state and 'religious fellowships', the political and legal doctrine that the former has endorsed will now have to 'modernise', reconfigured in terms of a resilient religious normative reality that it has mistakenly excluded. It is interesting to observe, though, as Anton Schütz has noted, that the voices calling on us to embrace the 'post-secular' come from the secularist side of the contemporary secularist-religionist exchange.¹²

The prospect of completing ourselves through this opening to an enriching but long hidden religious reality has an evident allure. Yet with the very concept of a 'believing citizen' – a post-secular citizen-believer – questions arise. How does such a figure operate in the historical context of a religiously neutralised political-legal order that has sought to decouple the standard of citizenship from the diversity of confessional identities? Is the moral anthropology underpinning Habermas's new model creature – the 'believing citizen' – itself new? Is the polemical function of this 'believing citizen' – as a post-secular figuration of humanity's moral completion in history – to reverse a historical separating of 'man' and 'citizen' as theorised by early modern political thinkers, including Thomas Hobbes? Then, in circumstances of religious civil conflict, drawing a distinction between the political-legal citizen and the Christian conscience served the cause of civil peace between warring confessional communities: 'The Law is the publique Conscience ... private Consciences

---

9   *Habermas/Ratzinger*, The Dialectics of Secularisation, p. 43. Elsewhere, Habermas repeats this de-repressive line, depicting 'secular citizens' as recognising in 'the normative truth content of a religious utterance hidden intuitions of their own'. See *Habermas*, Religion in the Public Sphere, p. 10.
10 *Habermas/Ratzinger*, The Dialectics of Secularisation, p. 43.
11 *Habermas/Ratzinger*, The Dialectics of Secularisation, p. 46-7.
12 *Schutz*, "Legal Critique": Elements for a Genealogy, p. 87.

... are but private opinions'. Where private conscience reigns, no man will 'obey the Sovereign Power, further than it shall seem good in his own eyes'.[13]

Religious challenges to secular legitimacy

Religiously motivated challenges to the legitimacy of the secular political-legal order have not waited for an ecclesial starting signal from the Catholic Academy of Bavaria or resolution of a historical dialectic of fact and norm from another philosophical milieu. Rather than conceptual invisibles operating 'at depth', such challenges are now surface events for all to see. Before considering Cardinal Ratzinger's response to the Philosopher's post-secular opening to a 'reflexive transformation of both religious and secular mentalities', I therefore chronicle four recent instances – two English, one French, one Australian – of strikes against the secular city. These include what would be termed a 'faith-based' policy initiative, but are not limited to that category of action.

The English political-legal scene is characterised not by a crystal-clear constitutional separation of state from church but by an established national church whose particular law is enforceable – in the last instance – by the state. If England has a longstanding state religion and national church, the current scene appears nonetheless susceptible to instability and boundary conflict between the domain of faith and the secular political-legal order.

The first English instance concerns charitable provision of welfare services, as debated in the House of Lords on 24 January 2008. In this legislative setting, one church and one church only enjoys establishment status, no fewer than twenty-six high officers of that church – the archbishops and certain bishops – having ex officio constitutional standing in the legislature as the Lords Spiritual.

In debate, the Anglican Lord Bishop of Carlisle, Graham Dow, indicates that the Government and the Anglican Church have been engaged 'in conversation' on the possibility of his church providing more 'extensive welfare services'.[14] As supporting backdrop to his speech, the Bishop identifies two major socio-political trends: first, that 'the new direction of the state, it seems, is to be a commissioning state, rather than one that has extensive institutions providing welfare'; second, that 'the nation is changing from a welfare state to a welfare society'. The 'commissioning state', he asserts, now gives way to a 'welfare society'.[15] To confirm for his church an organic closeness to 'society' that the secular state cannot match, the Bishop claims that it has 'very strong roots in local communities, making it well placed in many contexts to deliver quality services in a way that truly understands the local

---

13 *Hobbes*, Leviathan, p. 223.
14 *Dow*, Non-governmental organisations, Column 402.
15 *Dow*, Non-governmental organisations, Column 402.

situation, which government departments may not'.[16] Such Christian populism is unsurprising.

But there are surprises in store as the Bishop expands on the fact that 'We want to engage with the state in extending our considerable involvement in social care and community health provision'. There follows an ambit claim to receive long-term guaranteed public funding:

> The church is signing 25-year contracts for the new academies. Christian groups bidding to deliver dentistry are getting 20-year contracts. In all that, we are glad, but the picture is very mixed. Good social care needs long-term commitment, which we cannot emphasise too strongly.[17]

You really have to read this twice: the Anglican church will 'deliver dentistry' is what it says ... and discussions with government have been in progress for two years! Guaranteed provision of public funding, though, is not the sole or, perhaps, the primary condition. Of crucial importance for the Bishop is a further condition: such faith-based delivery is 'not controlled':

> If the church is to be a partner, it must be trusted by government and not controlled. As I perceive it, recent governments have found that very difficult. Church projects of course would be audited, but not controlled. My opinion is that, recently, we have been building a society that is very low on trust and very high on inspection and control – I see that, for example, in farming – which is very bad news for a healthy society.[18]

Predictably, the Bishop favours a mandatory 'church tax' for the United Kingdom, as exists in Germany and the Scandinavian countries.

What is the extent of this 'not controlled'? Would church welfare services be a potential instrument of religious discrimination between citizens? The issue is addressed. The Bishop's 'post-secular' line is somewhat chilling. Noting 'the possibility of a clash of views in the spheres of justice and ethical values, and the implications that this would have if the church was the recipient of large sums of taxpayers' money for the provision of welfare', he warns that 'the church sees part of its role as challenging existing assumptions and values':

> In spite of huge areas of agreement on the welfare of citizens, it is increasingly possible that differences could lead us into significant difficulty over [...] policies which challenge the Christian understanding of marriage. If the church chose to challenge certain policies and the values undergirding them, it could have government funding denied. Then it could be trapped in the unenviable position of making

---

16 *Dow*, Non-governmental organisations, Column 402.
17 *Dow*, Non-governmental organisations, Column 403.
18 *Dow*, Non-governmental organisations, Column 403.

its staff insecure or having to go along with a policy which compromised the position required by its faith.[19]

Here we must raise some practical questions of our own. Will a true believer-public welfare deliverer never compromise 'the position required by [their] faith' as a matter of private conscience or church teaching? If this new version of the 'welfare society' is to work, must the secular state trust the church to deliver services without discriminating in the process?

But there is an even sharper question: is the state's coercive power now liable to become available for a religious end? As a precautionary note, a certain warning should be sounded. Discussing 'The Catholic Church and its will to control civil society', Dominique Colas does just this: 'Still, is there not cause to believe that the only reason the Church does not impose its choices, particularly in the matter of moral custom, on all persons, Catholic or not, living in the same political community is that it may not have the political means to do so?'[20]

A qualification is nonetheless appropriate. No necessary contradiction arises if a secular state endorses and supports church activities in the domain of civil society, for instance in relation to welfare and educational provision. This is the case in modern Germany. The key condition is that the secular state exercise strict neutrality towards the multiple faiths of its constituent communities, churches being treated as tolerated social associations. In this way, even-handed state funding of all churches demonstrates the secular state's indifference towards the churches' own exclusive sense of themselves as the unique stairway to salvation.

The second English instance concerns the controversy that followed the Archbishop of Canterbury's 7 February 2008 address on 'Civil Laws and Religious Law in England: a Religious Perspective'. Delivered as a foundation lecture at London's Royal Courts of Justice, the address enjoyed a wider dissemination with the Anglican Primate's subsequent BBC radio interview. In the course of his address, Archbishop Williams explores the possibility that recognition of elements of Sharia law might become 'unavoidable' in the common law of England.[21] His concern is that 'groups of serious and profound conviction are not systematically faced with the stark alternatives of cultural loyalty or state loyalty'.[22] 'Cultural' goes proxy for 'confessional', the normative argument being that secular law should better incorporate communities' religious sensibilities. This is a call to redraw the line between the temporal order and the spiritual in a direction that favours religionists, such that a religious tribunal would acquire certain civil powers. Indeed, elsewhere the Archbi-

---

19 *Dow*, Non-governmental organisations, Column 404.
20 *Colas*, Civil Society and Fanaticism: Conjoined Histories, p. 87.
21 The UK Arbitration Act allows for recognition of agreements signed under a foreign law between adults who have consented to subject their dispute to binding arbitration by a third party. Such an agreement is enforceable in England, provided it does not breach English law.
22 *Williams*, Civil and Religious Law in England: a Religious Perspective, not paginated.

shop observes – in Anglican understatement – that the idea of 'one and only one law for everybody' was 'a bit of a danger'.[23]

Does such an address signal commitment to a socio-political project to change the present boundaries of the civil laws? If so, it will be a project that seeks precisely that same normative 'solidarity' and social cohesion to which Habermas's post-secular aspiration is directed. At the Royal Courts of Justice, the Archbishop invited his listeners to introduce themselves to one another, not the usual body gesture in juridical settings. And judging by his concluding words – quietly threatening, again in an Anglican way – the project will indeed be theologically grounded:

> It is always easy to take refuge in some form of positivism; and what I have called legal universalism, when divorced from a serious theoretical (and, I would argue, religious) underpinning, can turn into a positivism as sterile as any other variety. If the paradoxical idea which I have sketched is true – that universal law and universal right are a way of recognising what is least fathomable and controllable in the human subject – theology still waits for us around the corner of these debates, however hard our culture may try to keep it out.[24]

Here, we can observe a return to a classic Christian natural law relegation of positive law. Even as he proposes a certain legal pluralism, the Archbishop holds the positive law to a universal theological 'underpinning'. Can his proposition and his disposition be reconciled? The answer – if not for the Archbishop then most definitely for an early modern political jurist such as Pufendorf – must be no. When an early modern natural jurist such as Samuel Pufendorf rejected religious and moral-theological natural law as the ground for the positive laws, it was because he recognised, as did Hobbes – both living in the shadow of religious wars – that the secular state had to maintain peaceful coexistence between confessional communities committed each to its own particular universal theology. Historically speaking, the secularised 'positivism' of religiously neutralised legal systems was never an 'easy refuge'. To the contrary, it was an urgent and secular response to the failures of Christian universalism and religious natural law.

Absent this historical perspective, the Archbishop's discourse might soon pass unnoticed as a typical Anglican gesture towards those of other denominations and confessions. Yet, in a different context, where the separation of state from church has been constitutionally confirmed for a century, the same discourse would have registered as starkly heterodox. Nevertheless, in France – where the Law of 1905 on the Separation of Churches and the State finds formal constitutional expression in the principle of laïcité – President Nicolas Sarkozy appears intent on officiating as a voice of religion in politics, although it remains to be seen whether his words will prove anodyne or consequential.

---

23 See Williams, BBC Interview – Radio 4 World at One, not paginated.
24 *Williams*, Civil and Religious Law in England, not paginated.

Historically, and with disastrously violent consequences, early modern European states did pursue confessionalising programs. The modern French term, intégrisme, well captures the nature of these programs, each aimed at incorporating whole populations within one of the exclusive Christian truths. With this mission came a dynamism of faith but also a deadly rivalry of faiths. Where once there'd been the unity of the Respublica christiana there now was inter-confessional religious war. Once there was war, who could doubt that the precondition for survival of the state was reunification of religion, enforced as common cause by prince and bishop where political and ecclesial power were closely linked?

Was President Sarkozy at all mindful of this European history when, in his 20 December 2007 presidential address at the Vatican on the occasion of his being made Honorary Canon of Saint John Lateran, the 'mother church' of Catholics, he welcomed 'the advent of a positive laïcité'?[25] This novel conception he defined as a political disposition that 'considers religions not as a danger but rather a key advantage [atout]'. Was Sarkozy doing simple courtesy to his host, Benedict XVI, in following the latter's 30 November 2007 encyclical, Spe salvi (Saved by hope) by proclaiming 'the interest of the [French] Republic is that there be many men and women who hope'?[26] Such hope, he continued, would be 'enriched by moral reflexion inspired by religious convictions [having] links with transcendence'. A merely secular regime fails, the President argued, to be 'associated with an aspiration that satisfies the aspiration for the infinite'.

Political enthusiasm for a discourse of 'aspiration to the infinite' would seem to open space for restoring the idea that a sovereign state, to be legitimate should not be morally neutral. More specifically, coming from the Head of State, Sarkozy's Roman discourse undermines the current religious settlement in France. He does acknowledge today's 'regime of laïcité' is a constitutional freedom and 'a condition of civil peace'.[27] Yet he then adds: 'But, that being the case, laïcité could never be a negation of the past. It does not have the power to cut France off from her Christian roots'. Not to recognise these religious roots, he continues, is to 'weaken the cement of national identity'. In a country with a significant and potentially restive non-Christian minority, identifying 'Christian roots' for the state was not the most prudent way to administer governance of multi-confessionality.

Less than a month after his Vatican speech, the French President returned to the religious register. His 14 January 2008 presidential address to the Saudi Consultative Council in Riyad gives God no less than thirteen good citations in the manner of 'Transcendent God who is in the thought and heart of every man. God who does not oppress man but liberates him'.[28] Sarkozy refutes a suggestion that violence was down to religion: only the 'utilisation of religion for political ends' caused harm. If

25 *Sarkozy*, Allocution du Latran, p. 4.
26 *Sarkozy*, Allocution du Latran, p. 4..
27 *Sarkozy*, Allocution du Latran, p. 3..
28 *Sarkozy*, Presidential Address to the Saudi Consultative Council.

he recognises the necessary neutrality of the presidential office given separation of state and church, it is only to continue:

> Yet, I also have the duty of preserving the heritage of a long history, of a culture, and, I dare use the word, of a civilisation. And I know no country whose heritage, culture and civilisation do not have religious roots. I know no culture, no civilisation where morality, even if it incorporates other philosophical influences, does not have a religious origin, no matter how little. At the base of every civilisation there is something religious, something that comes from religion.[29]

Such a discourse reinserts religion into politics. Astonishing from the highest political authority of a secular state constitutionally bound to complete neutrality in matters of religion, this is an exemplary religious challenge to the secular political-legal order. Article 5 of the 1957 French Constitution requires the President to 'ensure respect of the Constitution'.

A final and somewhat less Eurocentric instance concerns the Australian Archbishop who, in 2007, came close to being charged with contempt of parliament. Like France, Australia has no established church, the Australian Constitution separating state from church.[30] In early June 2007, the Catholic Archbishop of Sydney, Cardinal George Pell, challenged members of the New South Wales Lower House regarding the prospective passage of a bill to end a ban on therapeutic cloning with stem cells obtained from embryos. In their press release of 4 June, Catholic Bishops issued a public warning: 'No Catholic politician – indeed no Christian or person with respect for human life – who has properly informed his conscience about the facts and ethics in this area should vote in favour of this immoral legislation'.

Responding to press questioning, Archbishop Pell indicated that Catholic members of parliament voting to support the bill 'must realise that their voting has consequences for their place in the life of the Church'. Following passage of the bill (by 62 to 25 votes), he wrote in a 10 June newspaper column that 'every Catholic politician who voted for this bill should think twice and examine his or her conscience before next receiving communion'. Pell thus threatened to impose a spiritual sanction – refusal of Holy Communion and excommunication – on Catholic legislators who voted in a manner contrary to teachings of their Church. This clerical directive to elected legislators occasioned referral to the Privileges Committee of the New South Wales Upper House to investigate whether a contempt of Parliament had occurred. In the event, no contempt was found to have been committed.

Behind Cardinal Pell's words stood the Catholic Magisterium and a natural law that transcended politics. His reference to the person 'who has properly informed his

---

29 *Sarkozy*, Presidential Address to the Saudi Consultative Council.
30 See Australian Constitution, section 116: 'The Commonwealth shall not make any law for establishing any religion, or for imposing any religious observance, or for prohibiting the free exercise of any religion, and no religious test shall be required as a qualification for any office or public trust under the Commonwealth'.

conscience' is a doctrinal reminder: only conformity with the conclusive teachings of the Church allows an individual conscience to transcend subjective preference and know the universal truth of an immutable divine order. A divine natural law provides the normative ground that legitimates the secular state's positive legislation.

Re-asserting a pastoral-spiritual authority, the Archbishop required the law of the secular state to be religious. At the same time, he claimed the secular right of an Australian citizen freely to express his personal views. In his office of Cardinal, Pell deployed the ecclesial power of excluding individuals – as citizens elected to political office – from their entitlement to participate – as Catholic Christians – in church observances. This is a departure from the separation of citizenship from salvation theorised by early modern secularisers such as Hobbes and Pufendorf to de-couple the political-legal domain of the civil state from the sphere of religious natural law and the powers of the church. It is a concrete illustration of the ambivalence from which the post-secular figure of the 'believing citizen' is not easily extricated.

Ratzinger's reason

With this sketch of four recent religious challenges to secular authority – challenges conducted under the respective standards of 'the position required by faith', 'theology waiting for us around the corner', 'aspiration for the infinite' and the 'properly informed conscience' – we are in a position to return to Cardinal Ratzinger's discourse in Munich in early 2004.

The Cardinal's exposition on 'That which holds the world together: the pre-political moral foundations of a free state' leads Anton Schutz (2005: 87) to characterise the 2004 exchange as between a Habermas 'lately converted to the politico-pastoral merits of "religion"', and then still a Cardinal Joseph Ratzinger answering this newly acquired post-secular open-mindedness with utter indifference'.[31] Indeed, there's no denying Ratzinger's calm deployment of a 'trumping' technique. After seeming to agree – for instance, 'with Jürgen Habermas' remarks about a willingness to learn from each other, and about self-limitation on both sides'[32] – the Cardinal will advance a qualification and get the final word.

At least three themes emerge from Ratzinger's discourse: the recognition of other cultures; the nature and sources of law; and the relations of faith and reason.

If the fact of other cultures – Chinese, Indian, Islamic – is now recognised in Western thinking, Ratzinger deploys this recognition for his particular purpose: to relativise Western certitudes. These include certitudes of religion but more so of morality and scientific reason. Set in 'global' perspective, 'ethical certainties that had hitherto provided solid foundations have largely disintegrated'.[33] Scientific know-

---

31 *Schutz*, "Legal Critique", p. 87.
32 *Habermas/Ratzinger*, The Dialectics of Secularisation, p. 77.
33 *Habermas/Ratzinger*, The Dialectics of Secularisation, p. 56.

ledge is relativised. The Cardinal's opening statement ends with an imperative: 'philosophy must sift the non-scientific element out of the scientific results with which it is often entangled, thus keeping open our awareness of the totality and of the broader dimensions of the reality of human existence'.[34]

In the name of 'our awareness of the totality', we are invited to participate in a moment of transcendental presence. Our participation, though, remains conditional on following a 'philosophy' that detaches itself from a science – positivistic and empirical – that has excluded the 'broader dimensions of the reality of human existence'. On the one hand, the Cardinal opens a door to transcendental presence in the guise of a 'philosophy' of human reason unshackled from 'science'. On the other hand, he is effectively acknowledging that natural science is indeed secular, thus something other than a transcendental reason. Yet, if natural science has required a radical separation of positive knowledge and faith, does the same apply to secular politics and law?

The Cardinal's discussion of the sources of law concerns precisely the relations of positive and natural law. Having appeared to follow Habermas's granting legitimacy to 'legal procedures born of democratic procedures',[35] Ratzinger sounds a Madisonian warning against the potential tyranny of democratic majorities, since 'the majority principle always leaves open the question of the ethical foundations of the law'. A crucial observation follows: 'Whether there is something that is of its very nature inalienably law, something that is antecedent to every majority decision and must be respected by all such decisions.'[36] No answer is offered, only an assertion that past and present candidates for this high function – human rights are cited – must now be relativised, not universalised.

As to natural law, Ratzinger returns to ancient Greece and 'the idea that in the face of a positive law that can in reality be injustice, there must be a law that derives from the nature, from the very being of man himself'.[37] He then passes to the impact of Europeans' discovery of the Americas, when encounter with non-Christian peoples raised the question of whether there is 'a law that transcends all legal systems, a law that is binding on men qua men in their mutual relationships and that tells them what to do'.[38] The reference is to Vitoria and the lex gentium, but also to early modern natural law – Grotius and Pufendorf are named – that responded to post-Reformation Christian disunion, a natural law 'which transcends the confessional borders of faith by establishing reason as the instrument whereby law can be posited in common'.[39] Citing an evolution-based disenchantment that has rendered nature anything but rational, the Cardinal sets this early modern natural law aside.

---

34 *Habermas/Ratzinger*, The Dialectics of Secularisation, p. 57.
35 *Habermas/Ratzinger*, The Dialectics of Secularisation, p. 27.
36 *Habermas/Ratzinger*, The Dialectics of Secularisation, p. 60.
37 *Habermas/Ratzinger*, The Dialectics of Secularisation, p. 67.
38 *Habermas/Ratzinger*, The Dialectics of Secularisation, p. 68.
39 *Habermas/Ratzinger*, The Dialectics of Secularisation, p. 69.

A third Ratzinger theme concerns faith and reason. Again, the approach appears even-handed, almost agnostic. Recognising religious fanaticism as a source of Islamic 'terrorism', he asks: 'Is then religion a healing and saving force? Or is it not rather an archaic and dangerous force that builds up false universalisms, thereby leading to intolerance and acts of terrorism?'.[40] If the latter, 'Ought we to consider the gradual abolishment of religion, the overcoming of religion, to be necessary progress on the part of mankind, so that it may find the path to freedom and to universal tolerance?'.[41] Before we think this a serious question, the alternative follows instantly: 'Or is this view mistaken?'. This serves as preamble to questioning 'the reliability of reason', 'reason' here identified with nuclear weapons and 'breeding and selection of human beings'.[42] Rapprochement with Habermas still seems close: 'Or should perhaps religion and reason restrict each other and remind each other where their limits are, thereby encouraging a positive path?'.[43] Indeed, no more than the rational, the 'religious formula that would embrace the whole world and unite all persons does not exist'. But then, as always, a qualifying word immediately follows: 'or, at least, it is unattainable at the present moment'.[44]

The Cardinal's finale on 'the essential complementarity of faith and reason' is visionary: 'Ultimately, the essential values and norms that are in some way known or sensed by all men will take on a new brightness in such a process, so that that which holds the world together can once again become an effective force in mankind'.[45] What does this 'once again' actually refer to? The answer has already been suggested: it refers to restoration of a transcendent theo-rational principle whereby politics and law re-join a religious faith that will have co-opted and re-purified human 'reason'. A broken circle will be re-closed. No matter how diplomatic, Ratzinger asserts the ultimate dependence of positive knowledges – including secular politics and law if these are to be legitimate – on a religious norm.

On secularisations

To this point, I have inserted a number of historical reflections into the discussion so as to build a contrastive perspective on some current post-secular enthusiasms. These reflections bring into the picture a significant strand of early modern thought on 'secularisation' – that is, on the relations of religion, politics and law – associated with Hobbes and Pufendorf, his German disciple.[46] This thought can now be complemented with recognition of an essential historical fact concerning 'secularisa-

---

40 *Habermas/Ratzinger*, The Dialectics of Secularisation, p. 64.
41 *Habermas/Ratzinger*, The Dialectics of Secularisation, p. 64-5.
42 *Habermas/Ratzinger*, The Dialectics of Secularisation, p. 65-6.
43 *Habermas/Ratzinger*, The Dialectics of Secularisation, p. 66.
44 *Habermas/Ratzinger*, The Dialectics of Secularisation, p. 76.
45 *Habermas/Ratzinger*, The Dialectics of Secularisation, pp. 79-80.
46 See especially *Palladini*, Samuel Pufendorf Discepolo di Hobbes.

tions': European religious settlements display no singular or necessary form. This proposition is crucial. Upon it rests a concluding proposition: 'secularisation' is best approached as a post-facto summation of historically varied arrangements in different territorial states, rather than an ideological doctrine. It is, of course, secularisation as an ideological doctrine that Cardinal Ratzinger's ecclesial absolutism, like Jürgen Habermas's socio-discursive dialectic of fact and norm, seeks to displace.

The French path led via an imposed Catholic conformity and the expulsion or forced conversion of Huguenot dissidents. The sixteenth-century Huguenot challenge to Catholic order under the last Valois had entailed thirty years of intercommunal conflict, eight civil wars of religion and – despite remarkable peacemaking efforts of Chancellor Michel de l'Hospital in the mid-1560s, – the St Bartholomew's Day Massacre of 1572. Acceding to the throne in 1589, a 'de-hereticised' Henri IV installed a measure of religious peace under the 1598 Edict of Nantes in what remained a religiously plural but divided society. By 1628-9, with the fall of Huguenot La Rochelle and the death of the Duc de Rohan, Catholic dominance saw Catholic conformity imposed in France. Cuius regio eius religio characterised the centralising absolutist rule of Louis XIII and Louis XIV, leading in 1685 to revocation of Huguenot religious and political entitlements. A century later, Revolutionary Jacobins reduced clergy to one among other civil statuses, only for Napoleon to institute the 1801 Concordat with Rome. Only with the Third Republic's 1901 Law on Associations and 1905 Law on the Separation of Churches and the State did something like the current constitutional settlement emerge.[47]

Unlike France since 1905, England with its privileged state church remains a confessional state in 2010. After the seventeenth-century religious civil wars, the English settlement was founded on a hegemonic Anglican Church. Non-conformists whose active faith kept them outside the settlement envelope were generally left free to worship in their chosen way, provided this was private and peaceful. Catholic recusants and more extreme Protestant non-conformists were seen as threatening the civil order and debarred – in principle if not always in practice – from public office. The Anglican 'broad-brush' settlement was thus a compromise, made possible by comparatively tolerant dispositions – the term of art is 'latitudinarian' – towards non-Anglicans. This has been termed a 'de-sacralisation' of politics: 'If religion is no more than opinion, the magistrate could afford to tolerate it'. In this sense too, 'the liberation of religion entailed a [political] minimisation of religion'.[48] English liberal constitutionalism remains anchored in this concrete modus vivendi.

Nor did all Protestant territories follow a uniform development. Between England and the emblematic German state of Brandenburg, the differences are no more stark than between Brandenburg and its German neighbour, Lutheran Saxony. From the 1650s into the early eighteenth century, a political-legal framework emerged in Brandenburg allowing peaceful coexistence among Calvinists (who included the rul-

---

47 On these two great laws of the Third Republic, see *Saunders, Anticommunautarisme* and the Government of Religion in France, p. 151.
48 *Pocock*, Religious Freedom and the Desacralisation of Politics, pp. 66, 67.

ing Hohenzollerns), Lutherans and Catholics in circumstances where no one of these confessions had managed to achieve political dominance. Although like France absolutist in its political rule, the post-Westphalian Brandenburg state was not monoconfessional; it was a religiously neutral regime designed to govern a plurality of legally recognised confessions. Individual conscience and peaceful communal worship were thereby freed from governmental intervention. This 'emancipation' had a significant corollary: church authorities were excluded from a coercive role in civil government. The historical picture is of different forms of church-state settlement, and different secularisations of politics and law. The fact of diversity does not preclude the transmission or importation of a given form of religious settlement from one territory to another, as when Kemalist Turkey imported a juridical model of church-state separation based on the 1905 French Law. A liberal state – be it France, the United Kingdom, Australia or the Federal Republic of Germany (Brandenburg's heir in its state-regulated protection of religious pluralism) – is considered secular even though religious bodies fulfil delegated roles in key areas of governmental provision: welfare, education and healthcare are familiar examples.

Liberal secularisation has not meant extirpation of religion in favour of an atheistic doctrine enforced by the state. Rather than a conceptual paradox, this is historical evidence of political-legal accommodations between states and churches, settlements pursued in the face of bitter religious conflicts, with various forms of modus vivendi achieved in the name of civil peace. These secularisations were not the irresistible product of an emergent secular philosophy of enlightenment. Nor were they the inevitable epochal product of 'modernisation'. As in the cases of early modern France and Saxony, a state could both 'modernise' its government, law, administration and economy and remain theocratic.

The German historian of law, Martin Heckel, understands secularisation in this restrictive way. His focus is on the early modern German imperial lawyers who – in the face of religious wars that had run beyond theological settlement – sought to provide legal means of ending confessional conflict. These included institution-building, such as the bi-confessional Imperial Chamber Court (the Reichskammergericht) where an attempt was made to grant parity of legal representation to Catholic and Lutheran religionists. A crucial cultural shift saw a 'translation' of political rule from the religious to the legal – a juridification of religion – embodied in the peace treaties of Augsburg (1555) and Westphalia (1648). Through complex trading and slow compromise, the jurists built a 'non-confessional or supra-confessional order of coexistence between the two great confessional blocs'.[49] A de-theologised framework enhanced chances of settlement by suspending engagement with claims to know religious truth. The domain of state and public law was made secular, but other spheres of life continued on as theologised spaces in civil society. This is secula-

---

49 *Heckel*, Das Säkularisierungsproblem in der Entwicklung des deutschen Staatskirchenrechts, p. 50.

risation in Heckel's limited sense: the construction of a political-legal framework grounded in public law, not in churches.

The point has been to recontextualise the question of their legitimacy within liberal states' historical conditions of existence. Central to these conditions was – and is – the necessity of a modus vivendi between rival communities of faith or ideology. This necessity could not be met if a state enforced on all its citizens a comprehensive normative rationale, be this religious, moral or ideological. Whatever the enthusiasms for a future 'post-secular' order of being, it is historically ignorant to conceive the legitimacy of secular political-legal orders in terms of rationales that liberal states' historical conditions of existence preclude them from enforcing.

Bibliography

Australian Constitution: http://www.aph.gov.au/SEnate/general/constitution/index.htm
Colas, Dominique, Civil Society and Fanaticism: Conjoined Histories, Stanford, 1997.
Dow, Graham, Non-governmental organisations, Hansard, 24 January 2008. Available at: http://www.publications.parliament.uk/pa/ld200708/ldhansrd/text/80124-0011.htm#08012455000390
Gray, John, Two Faces of Liberalism, Cambridge, 2000.
Habermas, JürgenRatzinger, Joseph, The Dialectics of Secularisation. On Reason and Religion, San Francisco, 2006.
Habermas, Jürgen, Religion in the Public Sphere, European Journal of Philosophy, 14, 1 (2006), pp. 1-25.
Heckel, Martin, Das Säkularisierungsproblem in der Entwicklung des deutschen Staatskirchenrechts, in Dilcher, Gerhard and Staff, Ilse (eds), Christentum und modernes Recht. Beiträge zum Problem der Säkularisation, Frankfurt am Main, 1984, pp. 35-95.
Hobbes, Thomas, Leviathan, Cambridge, 1991.
Le Monde, L'appel du Latran, editorial report, 22 December 2007:
  http://www.lemonde.fr/cgibin/ACHATS/acheter.cgi?offre=ARCHIVES&type_item=ART_ARCH_30J&objet_id=1017751
Palladini, Fiammetta, Samuel Pufendorf Discepolo di Hobbes: Per una Reinterpretazione del Giusnaturalismo Moderno, Bologna, 1990.
Pocock, John Greville Agard, Religious Freedom and the Desacralisation of Politics: from the English Civil Wars to the Virginia Statute, in Peterson, Merrill D and Vaughan, Robert C (eds), The Virginia Statute for Religious Freedom: Its Evolution and Consequences in American History, Cambridge, 1988.
Rawls, John, Political Liberalism, New York, 1993.
Sarkozy, Nicolas, Presidential Address at the Vatican, 20 December 2007:
  www.elysee.fr/download/?mode=press&filename=Allocution_Latran_20122007.pdf.
Sarkozy, Nicolas, Presidential Address to the Saudi Consultative Council, 14 January 2008:
  www.elysee.fr/document/index.php?mode=view&lang=fr&cat_id=7&press=id=880 not paginated.
Saunders, David, Anticommunautarisme and the Government of Religion in France, Economy and Society, 37, 2 (2008), pp. 151-171.
Schutz, Anton, "Legal Critique": Elements for a Genealogy, Law and Critique 16 (2005), pp. 71-93.
Williams, Rowan, Civil and Religious Law in England: a Religious Perspective, http://www.archbishopofcanterbury.org/1575 (2008) not paginated.
Williams, Rowan, BBC Interview – Radio 4 World at One:
  http://www.archbishopofcanterbury.org/1573 (2008) not paginated.

Legitimation in terms of questioning: Integrating political rhetoric and the sociology of law

Nick Turnbull

Contemporary social changes have rendered political legitimacy more problematic. The weakening of national boundaries from above and calls for more democracy from below have brought into question the mechanisms by which states establish legitimate power. This problematisation has taken the form of depoliticisation for some citizens, greater political participation by others in new social movements, and the imposition of major constraints upon the state's capacity for coordinated action.[1] In their different ways, each of these has brought political legitimacy into question. In general, the modern state is designed to enhance power but also tame coercive power,[2] with Mann noting that the power of states to dominate civil society 'despotically' is weak in modern capitalist states, in which elites are forced to negotiate with civil society groups.[3] Instead, there has been a long-term growth in the 'infrastructural' power of states, that is, 'the capacity of the state to actually penetrate civil society, and to implement logistically political decisions throughout the realm.[4] I would add that accompanying this shift, the state has become increasingly rhetorical, for with its weakening despotic power comes the necessity to argue. The problematisation of state power thus brings an increased role for rhetoric.

I claim that we should attempt to develop a rhetorical element to theories of political legitimacy. Positive and negative rhetoric is all-pervasive in contemporary politics, most prominently in expensive election campaigns and in the media where competing actors engage in a daily round of argumentation, but also in the legislature and between the many actors engaged in policy processes. Political parties have increasingly used rhetorical strategies in remaking their image to position themselves favourably in the minds of the voters, particularly in contesting what has become a 'permanent campaign' for political office.[5] The rhetorical activities of the state have been both necessitated and supported by its territorial centralization,[6] which has given it the capacity to coordinate messages through the institutionalisation of communications across a large and complex organisation. States rhetorically

---

1   *Offe*, Modernity and the State.
2   *Poggi*, The State, p 73.
3   *Mann*, States, War and Capitalism, p. 7.
4   *Mann*, States, War and Capitalism, p. 5.
5   *Blumenthal*, The Permanent Campaign. On political language, legitimation and the media in the UK, see especially *Hindmoor*, New Labour at the Centre; and Kuhn, Media management.
6   *Mann*, States, War and Capitalism.

construct the appearance of consistency and rationality to secure legitimacy with the public audience.[7]

Rhetoric is important because it is especially suited to periods of social change: in times of doubt and uncertainty, rhetoric comes to the fore.[8] It is a vehicle for change in that it is used to express what is problematic and to search for new solutions to public problems, and also a force for stability in reaffirming traditional values in new circumstances. However, rhetoric has at the very least been inadequately theorised in political studies; often regarded as trivial or purely cosmetic, and at worst entirely ignored. Even though rhetoric is accepted as necessary by political actors and routinely used to justify political power, theories of legitimacy hardly take account of its existence. Many theorists attempt to rule out rhetoric on normative grounds as manipulative discourse, but this does not alter the empirical reality of its importance: as Michel Meyer comments, 'to condemn language for being manipulative is to condemn language for being.'[9]

This chapter proposes a way by which to integrate rhetoric with law in a theory of legitimacy. Why attempt to integrate the two? One could study rhetoric on its own, as is often the case for specialist rhetoricians. However, to examine rhetoric in isolation would be only a partial view, and one which would implicitly accept the historical denigration of rhetoric as style without substance.[10] Furthermore, political argumentation does not exist outside the legal and institutional framework which supports it. From the inverse perspective, the case for linking the two is that even when political decisions are grounded in constitutional power, it is usually deemed necessary to argue this, to claim the value of such provisions and the legitimacy of resorting to them. Both rhetoric and law are political practices oriented towards dealing with public problems and legitimating the state's authority. Therefore an integrated view is essential.[11]

Integrating rhetoric and law as answers to a problematic

With regard to the question of authority, many theorists define the power of the state as its ultimate, sole right to use force within a given territory.[12] However, Poggi points out that contemporary Western states make little direct reference to their underlying recourse to force, and that everyday political experience has become highly

---

7   See *Poggi*, The State (p. 74) on rational justification by state agents.
8   *Brooke-Rose*, in *Meyer*, Rhetoric, Language and Reason, p. 35.
9   *Meyer*, Rhetoric and the Theory of Argument.
10 See generally *Richards*, The Philosophy of Rhetoric; *Vickers*, In Defence of Rhetoric.
11 I draw from Michel Meyer's philosophy of questioning, which is useful for two main reasons: 1) in departing from the problematisation of legitimacy we can theorise legitimacy itself in terms of problems, that is, as questioning; and 2) Meyer incorporates rhetoric as a central element in his philosophy, so we can theorise law as one form of answering legitimation questions and rhetoric as another, while situating both within a coherent philosophical framework which relates the two; *Meyer*, Of Problematology.
12 *Weber*, From Max Weber: Essays in Sociology, p 78.

'civilianised.'[13] The legal system provides a solid normative foundation to the legitimacy of the state. Even if we accept this view, however, law is far from guaranteeing legitimacy. Because authority in democracies is conditional,[14]—that is, in question—the political process involves extensive argumentation over public problems, which are usually formulated by organised interests as in support of, or as a challenge to, the legitimacy of the government. Social and political systems express a degree of contingency which cannot be ignored,[15] and as the discourse of contingency par excellence, rhetoric occupies an essential place in contemporary political life.

Considering rhetoric and law from a sociological perspective draws our attention to them as practices of the state. Governments respond to public problems by making law (or policymaking, more generally) and by putting forward arguments.[16] Both are practical means by which they acknowledge and attempt to deal with public problems, or by which they respond to their own internal motivations and interests.[17] At the same time as they deal with practical problems, both law and rhetoric are used to make a case for the legitimacy of a government's actions and of state authority in general. An integrated view of rhetoric and law requires an integrated view of rhetoric and reason. We can find such a view in the philosophy of Michel Meyer—problematology, or the 'philosophy of questioning.'[18] Meyer works from the idea that reason is grounded in questioning and therefore fundamentally problematic, so that any answer has two qualities; 1) that which responds to the problematic by expressing it as a question, constituting a partial or weak (problematological) answer, and 2) that which dissolves the problematic, constituting a strong (apocritical) answer. He labels this dual quality the problematological difference. A problematological answer performs a partial resolution of an otherwise indeterminate worry or concern by formulating a question,[19] whereas an apocritical answer dissolves the original question and becomes autonomous from it.[20] Applying this distinction to the

---

13 *Poggi*, The State, p 73.
14 *Tilly*, Contention and Democracy in Europe; Barker, Political Legitimacy and the State, p 162.
15 See generally, *Luhmann*, Social Systems; *Poggi*, The State; *Tilly*, Contention and Democracy.
16 On politics as problem-oriented, see especially *Dewey*, The Public and Its Problems.
17 States are independent actors in their own right; Evans, Rueschemeyer and Skocpol (eds), Bringing the State Back In. Here, we should be careful to distinguish arguing and legislating, as the former does not necessarily lead to the latter. Not all political questions are dealt with by the government making new laws, and even then, new laws can themselves throw up complications which require further deliberation.
18 Problematology is a new metaphysics, radically different from traditional philosophy. Meyer argues that questioning is the foundational principle of reason, and that the principles of thought deduced from this principle should be expressed in terms of questioning and answering; *Meyer*, Problematology.
19 Dewey also expresses the sense in which forming a question already moves us halfway towards the answer; *Dewey*, Logic, p 107.
20 The problematological difference is foundational and reflected secondarily within explicit discourse, such that every answer contains both qualities, although they can be expressed in different ways. Answering is necessary but no particular answer is necessary, in the tradition-

state's responses to questions, we can define law as a strong answer and rhetoric as a weak one.

The logic of legitimacy rests upon the key political differentiation between the governors and governed.[21] If we conceive of this state/society difference in terms of questioning, the state is that which responds to public problems, and is thus an answerer.[22] We can find a similar view in Dewey, for whom the philosophical and political orientation towards public problems produced a dual concern expressed in terms of questioning: i) what are the best solutions to public problems? and ii) how is the public to ensure its will achieves sufficient weight in decision making so that rulers do not advance their interests at the expense of the ruled?[23] The problem orientation of the state is linked to the question of its legitimacy, with both structured in particular by the interpretation and will formation processes of civil society, and the degree to which civil society actors are able to organise and mobilise in favour of state action,[24] along with the ability of the state to coercively or rhetorically influence them.

Using the conception of questioning outlined above, we can expand upon the idea of legitimation as questioning to consider two dimensions of the state as answerer. The state is apocritical in that it is an answer, but it is also problematological in that the state itself is not the solution to public problems, but rather a partial solution, the mechanism by which answers are sought. Because it is an answer it is autonomous, its apocritical aspect separating it from civil society and giving it the general authority to deal with problems, for which the state must seek a new answer each time. In the problematological conception, the state has authority as answerer but is also simultaneously in question. Hence we can distinguish between aspects of the state's authority which resist questioning and those aspects which are vulnerable to it. As answerer, the state frames problems and searches for solutions, sometimes enshrining these solutions in law, at other times allocating funding and other resources via the executive and bureaucracy, and in other cases answering by rejecting the problem as a matter for the state. The question of legitimacy is explicitly structured through various legal and institutional mechanisms, the most important of which is the popular plebiscite, in which the legitimacy of the state is most explicitly in ques-

---

al sense by which we think of necessity, for example in cause and effect logic. One cannot help but answer, but any answer must refer to an initial question in order to make sense so that, at any time, we can 'problematise' an answer and affirm the fundamentality of questioning. Meyer opposes the foundation of questioning to 'propositional' reason which presupposes a necessary link between question and answer such that real knowledge only resides in the elimination of the problematic. Problematology is thus an alternative conception of rationality which establishes the necessity of questioning while also affirming the inevitable contingency it generates; *Meyer*, Problematology.

21   *Coicaud*, Legitimacy and Politics, p. 26.
22   Many theorists have written of legitimacy as a 'question' or 'problem'. See for example *Coicaud*, Legitimacy and Politics; *Connolly*, Politics and Ambiguity, p. 74; *Habermas*, Legitimation Crisis; and *Lipset*, Political Man, p. 80. However, none have theorised legitimacy in terms of the logic of question and answer.
23   *Dewey*, Public and Its Problems. On the logic of questioning, see especially *Dewey*, Logic.
24   See especially *Offe*, Modernity and the State, pp. 112-113.

tion. However, in democracies, we might say that legitimacy is always implicitly in question and repeatedly resolved through each new resolution of a public problem since the action (or non-action) of the state implies an answer to the related question of the legitimacy of its authority. This logic of implication is rhetorical, confirming the legitimacy of state power in its practical exercise, which also figuratively symbolises its authority. Returning again to the difference between state and society, this difference can be expressed in problematological terms as a dialectic of question and answer, in which the identity of each and the distance between them is continually negotiated on a practical basis through the treatment of public problems. The negotiation of this distance is rhetorical, and therefore expressed in terms of logic, emotions, and identity.[25]

Situating both rhetoric and law within the theory of questioning, we can articulate the difference between the two in terms of how they respond to—answer—public problems. Law is a strong solution which seeks to dissolve the problematic in new enforceable answers, while rhetoric is a weak, partial solution which answers a question but also maintains it for further deliberation: rhetoric and law are complementary.[26] Law is a strong way of providing solutions to problems, fixing reference points about all kinds of social action along with reflexive determinations which define the extent of state powers. Law secures rights, protecting citizens from arbitrary treatment by providing consistent, generalised answers to problematic situations and making it easier to decide what is in question and what is not in public affairs. But social complexity means that law cannot account for every situation (indeed, in many cases good laws are not overly prescriptive since these stifle their ability to adapt to new contexts). New problems for which we have no ready-made solutions need to be expressed and answers sought through more contingent means—this is the domain of rhetoric. Problems are rhetorically debated in the public sphere, including through the media and in the legislature. Whereas law limits and rationalises the passions, rhetorical discourse admits them because it concerns values and the differences between us, who is deserving of praise and who of blame. Multiple solutions are not ruled out but developed and deliberated upon. Even in cases for which existing law applies, we sometimes require rhetoric to deliberate upon which interpretation and application of that law is to decide the question. And when the law fails to cope with a situation, we use rhetoric to argue for changes to the law to reflect new circumstances, new opinions, or new claims to recognition. The constitution sets limits on the state but rhetoric is the necessary discourse of variability which the law cannot entirely eliminate.

The legitimacy of the state is put in question and it can respond through the dual

---

25 Tilly notes that political identities have been important in the historical development of democracies insofar as people hold ties to governments in either a hostile or favourable way. These run along a continuum from 'embedded' to 'detached' identities; *Tilly*, Contention and Democracy, pp. 59-65.

26 In Meyer's terms, an answer is a 'repression' of the problematic. Strong repressions are apocritical, and weaker ones are problematological.

mechanisms of answering. Rhetoric and law correspond to two forms of answering stemming from the bifurcation made possible by the problematological difference. Both forms of answering, taken as a whole, generate legitimacy. Law provides stable, autonomous reference points which guide social action and reduce problematicity. That is, law generates legitimacy because it deproblematises. The strong solution of law establishes legitimacy so well that, in general, legality itself becomes an argument for the legitimate exercise of authority. In contrast, rhetoric responds to problematicity by expressing it; rhetoric generates legitimacy because it problematises, the indeterminacy of rhetoric functioning as a legitimating device insofar as it expresses what is problematic, making room for public sentiment in maintaining the openness of a question, which is also a necessary step in enabling the public to deliberate upon its problems. The people's will is formed in the public sphere in all its complexity and passions, where the participants are given recognition through their position in regard to problems. This brings the audience into deliberative practice and is more substantial than a residual conception of due process.[27] Aristotle noted well that rhetoric is most likely to persuade an audience when it involves them in the argument than when it is presented as a fait accompli.[28] Argumentation in the public sphere which involves a wide variety of participants is thus persuasive for the question of legitimacy. Rhetoricity does not establish legitimacy in the same way as legality; simply reciting an argument is insufficient to reach a solution because rhetoric is by nature a weak answer. However, it does generate legitimacy insofar as it is inclusive and persuasive to the audience. Here, rhetoric can certainly be manipulative or 'black', pretending to leave questions open for the public when in fact they have been resolved behind closed doors by an elite. This possibility results from the state holding authority, and while that authority can be questioned, to do so requires extensive political mobilisation. Even if questions are not widely debated, the solutions can still be considered legitimate as long as there is no effective opposition, since established authority wins the argument by default. Here we find the importance of a strong political culture and public sphere which effectively questions state decisions and brings to bear sufficient pressure on its legitimacy so as to persuade it to act in accordance with the public will.[29] Having established the state as a rhetorical actor, we can use rhetorical concepts to define its characteristics.

---

27 The idea that public sphere debate contributes to legitimacy is developed in the literature on deliberative democracy which emerged to examine the quality of political discourse and propose alternative, more democratic deliberative forms. See, for example, *Bohman*, The Coming of Age of Deliberative Democracy; *Bohman/Rehg*, Deliberative Democracy; *Dryzek*, Deliberative Democracy and Beyond; Elster (ed), Deliberative Democracy. Some deliberative democracy scholars have begun to acknowledge the importance of rhetoric—for example, Dryzek—however, for many in this field, especially those following Habermas, rhetoric is dangerous because of its potential for manipulation and populism which contradict the ideal of rational persuasion.
28 *Aristotle*, On Rhetoric. Hence, rhetoric uses the enthymeme rather than the syllogism.
29 *Habermas*, Between Facts and Norms, p. 304.

The rhetorical modern state

The modern state is often thought of as non-rhetorical and instead highly rationalised, characterised by the legal/rational basis of its authority[30] and its use of scientific techniques of governance. However, the sociological literature on states gives many pointers towards a more rhetorical aspect to modern governance. The rationalising character of the modern state is emphasised by Poggi, who defines the institutionalisation of political power as consisting of three aspects: depersonalisation, formalisation, and integration.[31] However, despite significant depersonalisation and formalisation in the modern state, human societies require other rhetorical characteristics to achieve integration and for the first two elements to be accepted as legitimate. Indeed, Strayer notes that, historically, personal loyalty to the ruler and the state (and later still, to the nation) was a key factor in legitimating the modern state as the dominant form of governance.[32] Whatever depersonalisation has taken place in the twentieth century, personal identification with rulers and nations has far from been abolished. Weber's discussion of charismatic authority situates the role of leadership in democracies. Charisma was important for Weber as a source of freedom and creativity, particularly when it left an impact on institutional structure.[33] Weber's schema is limited in many respects, for example in not clearly differentiating between the charisma of responsible democratic leaders and dictators, nor between charismatic leadership and charismatic domination.[34] I argue that the subtleties of political charisma can be successfully expressed using a rhetorical perspective which allocates an equal place to ethos.

In stressing the autonomy of states, Skocpol notes that states are independent actors which 'influence the meanings and methods of politics for all groups and classes in society.'[35] State actions are thus rhetorical in the sense of constructing interpretative frames for citizens and external audiences. Given that rhetoric is a key practice of the state, evident not only in written and spoken discourse but also in political decisions and policy mechanisms, we can bring rhetorical concepts to bear upon it. The problematological view presents the state as a questioner/answerer in relation to civil society and to other states. This can be combined with the Aristotelian triptych of ethos, pathos and logos to articulate the rhetorical relationships between the state and other actors, providing a complete account of the modes of persuasion which importantly includes the dimensions of character and the passions alongside logical argumentation. Using these rhetorical concepts, it is possible to develop a perspective upon the modern state which articulates elements other than rationalisation in its development and extends the view of state and society as rhetorically related.

30 *Weber*, From Max Weber.
31 *Poggi*, The State, p. 18, drawing on Popitz.
32 *Strayer*, On the Medieval Origins of the Modern State, p. 107.
33 *Weber*, On Charisma and Institution Building.
34 *Mommsen*, The Age of Bureaucracy, pp. 91-93.
35 *Skocpol*, Bringing the State Back In, p. 28.

The modern state is characterised by increasing differentiation in dealing with more complex social problems and in expanding its own power and legitimacy. There is a division of powers within the state, and a division of rhetorical characteristics which accompanies this institutional differentiation: ethos belongs to the executive[36] and the legislature, while logos belongs to the bureaucracy and the courts. In the polity more broadly, we find a further differentiation in which pathos belongs to civil society. While legal-rational authority is central to the modern polity, the other elements are also present in different ways. Taken together, the three form a rhetorical whole, each separate from but also complementing the others in an ideally integrated form.[37]

In the ideal of rational planning, government is administered by a depersonalised bureaucracy which acts according to general rules which guarantee universality and logical consistency, guarding against bias and corruption in favour of particular interests.[38] Hence ethos and pathos are absent: the administration of the state is characterised by logos. The demand for legal/rational legitimacy limits and structures what is to be allowed in argumentation. Administration does involve argumentation, however this must be persuasive on rational grounds, avoid contradiction, and involve claims based in law, established procedures, and scientific assessments. The bureaucracy is concerned with statistical monitoring and quantitative performance targets (logos) rather than discourse on values (pathos). In modern states, the procedural link between rhetoric and law is typically 'rationalised,' such that arguments—or at least their outcomes—are presented as following a linear order of question and answer commencing in the public sphere, through deliberation in the legislature and executive decision, and then to implementation and monitoring by the bureaucracy, which maintains highly rationalised operations. The state converts the public will into rational, non-rhetorical executive decisions and law. However, in practice this linear path is itself a rhetorical construction—policymaking is a much more disorganised, reflexive, and political process than the rational model supposes. Nonetheless, the legitimacy of the modern state rests greatly upon its 'rationality,' so constructing this rhetorical rationality remains an important task for governments even in the face of confusion, incompetence, and mistakes. Similarly, the courts are impersonal, operating on rational grounds according to logical rules of evidence and procedure.

However, people do not accept an entirely impersonal and rationalistic state, so there must be some compensatory personalisation in order to secure the people's acceptance of state rule. So, ethos belongs to the executive and the legislature, and in particular to the leaders of government and opposition. The legislature is populated by the citizens and its procedures legitimate the resulting, rational law. Whereas the ethos of the bureaucrat is suppressed in favour of logos, ethos is allowed and necessary for the politician, who must be one of, and stand for (metonymy), the people.[39]

---

36 The head of state is an important symbolic figure, however only the character of the elected leader is problematised in elections.
37 Within each location the practice of argumentation involves all three elements.
38 *Weber*, From Max Weber.
39 Rhetoric involves both the figurative and argumentative dimensions; *Meyer*, Meaning and

This promotes the legitimacy of the state in that a person, rather than a functionary, directs the administrative apparatus. It presents a vision of the state as controlled by the people, a rhetorical representation of a state which grounds legitimate rule in the people. So, even though the executive and the legislature produce formal laws and decisions, they are distinguished from the bureaucracy by a form of identity as well as in terms of their formal powers to act.

People interpret the world more easily through narratives and characters than legal-rational discourse, so they follow political action and debate the legitimacy of the government through the ethos of the players. This is why political commentators attribute 'character' to a government and seek an identity in it which matches popular perceptions of national culture and the spirit of the times. The character of the government in turn legitimises certain aspects of the culture—it matters that leaders can be of working class background, that Barack Obama has been elected President of the United States, and that the professional middle classes dominate public office. Arguments against government policy by its opponents link policy arguments to the ethos of the leaders of the government. For example, failing to stop a run on the Northern Rock bank in 2007 became an argument against the personal competence of the Prime Minister of the United Kingdom. Much political debate loses its focus on the efficacy of policy alternatives to become an endeavour of hyperbolic characterisation, with leaders cast as strong/weak, democratic/authoritarian, experienced/inexperienced, too old/too young, and so forth. The division between government and opposition is a choice between individual leaders as much as between ideologies, a choice which has become even more important with the waning of sharp political cleavages. Policy argumentation must contribute to the construction of political narratives, which occupy the parties along with policy development. Framing the question of the legitimacy of the government through the ethos is more meaningful for the public because it is a question of identity, about which we can feel passionate and take sides, giving the impression that the government is not a monolithic power but requires our active support for its legitimacy.[40]

This personalisation applies to all the ministers of the executive. The minister is responsible for all matters within her portfolio, for the actions of her department, and personally responsible for its success and failure. Hence ministers in charge of key portfolios become public personalities. The leader of the government is allowed and expected to show the strongest personality, so as to be distinguished from other members of the executive over whom he exercises effective and symbolic authority. Mechanisms of appointment are different for the executive than for the bureaucracy, being made with regard to personal character and public perceptions of it as much as for policy outcomes, so that ministerial 'performance' takes on a more rhetorical meaning. The leader judges her performance and rewards or demotes the minister accordingly. It is important that the minister is personally responsible, such that

---

Reading.
40 Weber took for granted the emotional appeal of the charismatic; *Eisenstadt*, Introduction: Charisma and Institution Building, p. xxii. Differentiating such appeals by types of ethos and pathos provides an opportunity for research to articulate their form and strength.

when there is a breach of procedure or a failure to deal with a problem the minister is blamed, by the opposition in parliament, by the media, and by the public. If this rhetorical pressure is strong enough the leader might replace her to save the legitimacy of the whole. The appointment of ministers to certain departments is also interpreted according to the ethos. For example, a leader might appoint a hard character, known for cutting expenses, to a department seen to be profligate. When the government wishes to appear softer or firmer in particular policy areas, it changes the minister or spokesperson on the issue, often through gendered appointments.

Pathos is the remaining element of the rhetorical triptych. The administration of the state is characterised by logos, but it accepts that the passions have a place so it leaves them to civil society where pathos forms the logic of identity and difference between people. The modern state is faced with the problems of integrating a large territory of diverse peoples and all their structural divisions, such as gender, race and class. These divisions are marked by the passions, in that we feel compassionate or impassionate, resentful or solidaristic, hostile or welcoming towards others. When it comes to particular problems, the public pathos towards others is directed through the state itself, for example negatively in anger at the state for not acting in response to the fear of outsiders generated by immigration, or positively in the spirit of seeking reconciliation with native peoples. Modern states also seek legitimacy by promoting a passionate nationalism which acts to integrate an otherwise divided people through a common identity. In liberal capitalist democracies, the dominant pathos is the desire for economic advancement, with its accompanying pleasures of consumption. The performance of governments is monitored regularly through statistical measures of economic growth (logos) and business and consumer confidence (pathos). Reflecting the importance of the economy, the leaders of the government must project the ethos of the competent manager, so they adopt business dress.[41] At the same time, economic ideologies rule out alternative visions of the good life as illegitimate. And even if we would no longer consider culture in structural terms, we can say that consumer culture generates hegemonic legitimacy through a rhetorical effect of seduction.[42] But within this passion for growth is also the question of the distribution of wealth, around which continue to lie many of the most passionate social divisions and which structure the dimensions of the legitimation question for the state, since inequalities generate differences expressed emotively as aspiration, resentment, or envy. In general, pathos concerns our relationship with the other, what brings us together or separates us.[43] If we accept that pathos cannot be eliminated in an entirely rational political discourse, we admit the passions but we are also made aware of their dangers. The modern state cannot rule out pathos, but instead denies it power and legitimacy by relegating it to one sphere, which in turn creates the impression of public irrationality among the officials of the state—who also reject politicians' appeals to the passions as populism—and inversely giving the impression to

---

41 *Poggi*, The State, p. 74. In authoritarian states, the legitimacy of the ruler is at the discretion of the military, so he dresses in uniform.
42 The Frankfurt School approach to culture is still important in this respect.
43 *Meyer*, Rhetoric and the Theory of Argument.

the public of an impersonal and inhuman bureaucracy. Legal-rational values threaten the lifeworld when they encroach on its territory,[44] and when they fail to recognise the legitimacy of public questioning articulated through the passions. However, bureaucracies must operate on rational principles, because they become dangerous not when pathos is eliminated, but when pathos merges with logos and becomes a passion for rules which turns against humanism.

In the public sphere, the three rhetorical institutions meet and the difference between state and society is continuously questioned and answered. Here, the passions of the people are expressed in debates about the best policy solutions, the competence of the government and the character of the leaders, all driven by what it means for the legitimacy of the state, which exercises a dominant power over the whole through its institutional authority to answer. Law forms the backdrop to these debates, and putting the law into question requires considerable political will. While the state concedes the necessity to include the public and to persuade it rather than coerce it, the practice of argumentation is often top-down, informed by the differential access to expertise held by state officials. Values are questioned and affirmed in public debate, values which are themselves expressions of pathos as much as they are logical principles governing action. The state must respond to the passions of the population, and its legitimacy depends in part on how well it articulates but also controls them, suppressing some sentiments while promoting others. When the state fails to deal with the political claims of newly identified social groups, they mobilise through emotional responses to form social movements.[45] The media is the primary vehicle through which public debate is channelled and questions of legitimacy are formed, so its ownership, structure and tone are all-important in rhetorical debate. This rhetoric is not only deliberative. It also includes epideictic rhetoric which is used to denigrate or praise particular social groups (for example, welfare recipients and immigrants, sporting heroes or soldiers), and at key moments is used to define the nation and reaffirm or redirect its values.

Legitimation problems in the modern state

The emphasis on legal-rational authority in the modern state can be understood fully not as the rejection of emotions and character but as rhetorically and institutionally distinct from them. The separation of these aspects contributes to the authority of the modern state and how it pursues its task of legitimation. In practice, of course, the picture is more complicated. While supposing a rhetorical whole, this separation produces its own legitimation problems, for example with the impersonality of the state alienating the public, and the dangers of governments seeking office through the personality of the leader detached from concerns for effective policy. In practice, the public do not accept total state control (even though the centralization and con-

---

44 *Habermas*, Theory of Communicative Action.
45 Goodwin, Jasper and Polletta (eds), Passionate Politics.

centration of power supports it) and seek influence over policymaking in between elections. The distance between state and society is continuously negotiated with regard to particular policy problems and the broader question of legitimacy through which people express their expectations of the state. This is further complicated by the state's entanglement with international organisations and relationships with other states.

From the 1970s, some commentators argued that the capitalist welfare states experienced a severe legitimation deficit, as 'overloaded government,' from the right, or as legitimation crisis, from the left.[46] Held argues convincingly against the notion of crisis, pointing out that despite challenges to the state, political distrust and the resulting conflicts were often diffuse and fragmented, so that states could maintain their authority as long as some conflict could be displaced and they could secure the acquiescence of key organised interests.[47] So, instead of a crisis we can redefine the recent period in terms of questioning, as the state experiencing legitimation 'problems.'[48] The legitimation problems of the 1970s found public expectations of the welfare state in conflict with other demands for retrenchment and economic liberalisation.[49] Neoliberal institutional reform acted to limit the responsibilities of the state for solving problems, some of which were shifted back to civil society, and to the economy in particular. State actions to restrict fiscal latitude and limit its debt were accompanied by an ideological repositioning in favour of market mechanisms and withdrawal of the state, seen for example in rhetorical criticisms of the 'nanny state' and the policy discourse of individual responsibility. Although neoliberalism's strongest proponents were less successful than they hoped[50] – and indeed states continue on the path of fiscal expansion and coordination, against arguments to the contrary[51] – the ideology of this state-society reconfiguration remains a powerful rhetoric, even in countries where reform has been far more moderate. Lately, 'globalisation' has been used as an argument for necessitating similar policy reform, as much as it is a description of empirical economic and social change. In the most neoliberal welfare states, policy instruments effect an identity politics which sustains majority support, for example in 'workfare' schemes which entrench the social distance between deserving and undeserving classes of welfare recipients. In the liberal, residual welfare states, an epideictic discourse of character denigration of welfare recipients is enacted through policy mechanisms and policy discourse, appealing to the downward envy of the workers and at the same time affirming the latter's good cha-

---

46 For a summary, see *Held*, Models of Democracy, pp. 184-216.
47 *Held*, Models of Democracy, p. 199.
48 Here, it is worthwhile noting that the German title of Habermas's *Legitimation Crisis* was *Legitimationsprobleme im Spätkapitalismus,* and throughout emphasises problems rather than crisis. This work is replete with discussion of problems, questions, and alternatives. Habermas did not argue an entirely determinist position that capitalism would necessarily produce its own crisis as a consequence of its internal logic. Rather, he emphasised problems of legitimation which required strategies of resolution; Habermas, *Legitimation Crisis*.
49 *Offe*, Contradictions of the Welfare State.
50 *Pierson*, Dismantling the Welfare State?; *Poggi*, The State, p. 126.
51 *Offe*, Modernity and the State.

racter. A cross-party, neoliberal consensus is thus established by politically marginalising the losers from such reforms.[52] The tabloid media sustains these characterisations so that the possibilities for policy change become rhetorically limited by them. New policy measures therefore enshrine the different identities not so much by reducing income transfers (which is politically difficult) as through control mechanisms, whereby the poor are penalised by being subject to interventionist state controls in contrast to other, more autonomous citizens. When a reconfiguration of the redistributive system is off the table because of the need to limit state financial liabilities, its legitimacy is affirmed through symbolic rhetoric and complementary mechanisms of differentiation in formal policy mechanisms. In all this we see the intersection of the politics of identity (ethos), envy and resentment (pathos), policy and political strategy (logos). When the various parties offer similar policies, the rhetorical logic of identity and difference becomes all the more important in sustaining some form of choice for the public.

So, liberal democracies are not in crisis but their legitimacy has been 'problematised'. In light of these legitimation problems, and restricted state resources, previous answers to legitimation challenges which involved extending citizens' rights were rejected by many states. The resolutary effect of strong legal responses which established citizens' rights weakened, with rhetorical answers to legitimation questions becoming increasingly important in justifying government actions. With the increasing significance of rhetorical legitimation, the state is concerned not only with the technical and/or judicial correctness of policy and law,[53] but also with the appearance of decisions and their reception by the audience (the media, experts, interest groups, and voters). States take a greater interest in public opinion measurement and media management. The advent of mass media technologies has brought the rhetoric of images to the forefront of politics, so that today media strategy—and especially television—is as important as concrete policymaking. Rhetorical functions have been institutionalised in the bureaucracy, which has seen a growth in the number of media positions and in their ranking to the point of taking seniority over and above many civil servants directly involved in policy development. Media officers are now often involved in designing policy itself. Political parties make strenuous efforts to manage the appearance of the leader and the government in general, mounting a daily rhetorical programme of interpretation for the purpose of legitimation. As the opportunities for reform are more circumscribed, the contest for legitimacy becomes a media narrative dominated by the character of the leaders. In these circumstances, political argumentation can become dangerously ad hominem, for example, in the United States, where significant public resources were deployed by public prosecutor Ken Starr in attacking President Clinton's character. When the focus on ethos is too great it can weaken the ability of the public sphere to support informed debate and judgement upon social problems.

The new-found rhetorical sophistication of the state challenges the media's claim to be the arbiters of public opinion, to which the media has responded by declaring

---

52 *Taylor-Gooby*, Welfare Reform in the UK: The Construction of a Liberal Consensus.
53 *Poggi*, The State, p. 32.

governments to be obsessed with 'spin.' The danger here is that the message of the government is lost as all its communications are regarded as pejoratively rhetorical, prompting some members of the public to switch off and become depoliticised, which itself raises the danger of an alternative political figure mobilising a counter-politicising, populist rhetoric. When the effect of rhetorical discourse becomes weak, legitimation can become excessively problematised, and a stronger resolution may be necessary. Such a shift might take form in the entry of new parties or new institutional mechanisms which extend public participation in decision making.

Conclusion

In considering legitimacy in terms of questioning, we do not require a foundational proposition which declares what legitimacy, unproblematically, is, but instead an understanding of how states respond to the task of legitimation questions in more or less contingent circumstances. Legality provides a strong basis to the legitimacy of the state, however it is not the same thing as legitimacy, which is more in question today. States undertake many actions in response to the problematisation of their legitimacy, including many types of rhetorical practices related to, or independently of, policy action. Therefore we can say that states are founded on both the 'rule of men' and the 'rule of law,' without opposing the two.[54] Indeed, they are complementary. Certainly, political systems reflect upon their own operations and articulate norms which underpin law. However, these are themselves answers which can be questioned through the contingent mechanisms of political deliberation. Developing an integrated theory of rhetoric and law supports the consideration of day-to-day politics alongside legal principles. Rhetoric is thoroughly political since it deals with the contingency which characterises political relations between people by reflecting and maintaining questions so we might deliberate upon them. Law is stronger, encapsulating our rights with regard to each other, rights which must remain out of the question to protect individuals and provide structure to public life. By considering rhetoric and law in terms of questioning we can locate them within a singular epistemological framework which accounts for their role in the legitimation of states. And, in doing so, we need not construct them as dependent on some foundational metaphysical proposition or norm, but rather understand how such norms arise as the result of political answering, contingent phenomena which take on the appearance of necessity via their autonomisation from the historical questions to which they initially responded. The rule of law achieves a kind of necessity through its autonomy as a strong answer to political questions, and thus attains a normative power of its own, even if it cannot be metaphysically secured beyond all possible doubt. In contrast, rhetoric is always temporally contained. Its virtue is that it responds to the context, renewing values each time by constructing relevant narratives to interpret events and include the public in political deliberation. Even though it seems to be

---

54   See generally, *Bobbio*, The Future of Democracy.

insubstantial insofar as it requires constant renewal, its legitimating power is considerable precisely for this characteristic.

Problematology supports an integrated view of rhetoric, institutions, and law through the concept of questioning. In problematology, the foundational place of the problematic secures a systematic view, even as it establishes a place for the contingency expressed in rhetoric. By situating the rhetorical within a foundational philosophy, we understand the human as the problematic itself, for we are always in question, and thus we have a guiding principle for the operation of democracy in dealing with our shared contingency. But this does not deny the necessity to produce answers in order to guarantee the rights of each in relation to the other nor the necessity to answer in order to repress unregulated questioning which would lead to social disorder. To restate the point above, were we to consider the answer to the question of legitimacy as only that which abolishes the problematic, the authority of the state would be reduced to the 'authoritarian' by default. By reconceptualising answering in the dual sense described here, as problematising and deproblematising, we broaden our understanding of democratic legitimation.[55]

This is only a sketch of such a view of the state. The balance between rhetoric and law, and their various forms, expresses wide variability. Beyond further theoretical elaboration, an empirical task is to uncover the relationship between legal-institutional forms and rhetorical practices.

---

55 Even in authoritarian regimes there is a legitimation question to answer, except that the public is not allowed to question the authority of state decisions, so legitimacy is diverted almost entirely through the ethos of the leader to whom public praise is demanded in the form of large and frequent epideictic displays.

Bibliography

Aristotle, On Rhetoric: A Theory of Civic Discourse, translated by GA Kennedy, New York, 1991
Barker, Rodney, Political Legitimacy and the State, Oxford, 1990.
Blumenthal, Sidney, The Permanent Campaign: Inside the World of Elite Political Operatives, Boston, 1980.
Bobbio, Norberto, The Future of Democracy: A Defence of the Rules of the Game, translated by R Griffin and edited by R Bellamy, Cambridge, 1987.
Bohman, James, The Coming of Age of Deliberative Democracy, Journal of Political Philosophy 6(4) (1998), pp. 400-425
Bohman, James/Rehg, William, Deliberative Democracy: Essays on Reason and Politics, Cambridge, Mass, 1997.
Brooke-Rose, Christine, A Rhetoric of the Unreal: Studies in Narrative and Structure, Especially of the Fantastic, Cambridge, 1981.
Coicaud, Jean-Marc, Legitimacy and Politics: A Contribution to the Study of Political Right and Political Responsibility, Cambridge, 2002.
Connolly, William E, Politics and Ambiguity, Madison, 1987.
Dewey, John, The Public and Its Problems, Denver, 1927.
Dryzek, John S., Deliberative Democracy and Beyond, Oxford, 2002.
Eisenstadt, S.N., Introduction: Charisma and Institution Building, in Weber, Max, On Charisma and Institution Building: Selected Papers, edited by SN Eisenstadt, Chicago and London, 1968.
Elster, Jon (ed), Deliberative Democracy, Cambridge, 1998.
Evans, Peter B., Rueschemeyer, Dietrich, and Skocpol, Theda (eds), Bringing the State Back In, Cambridge, 1985.
Goodwin, Jeff, Jasper, James M, and Polletta, Francesca (eds), Passionate Politics: Emotions and Social Movements, Chicago, 2001.
Habermas, Jürgen, Legitimation Crisis, translated by T McCarthy, London, 1976.
Habermas, Jürgen, Theory of Communicative Action, translated by T McCarthy, Boston, 1984-1987.
Habermas, Jürgen, Between Facts and Norms, translated by W Rehg, Cambridge, 1996.
Held, David, Models of Democracy, 3rd edition, Cambridge, 2008.
Hindmoor, Andrew, New Labour at the Centre, Oxford, 2004.
Kuhn, Raymond, Media Management, in Seldon, Anthony (ed), Blair's Britain: 1997-2007, Cambridge, 2007, pp 123-142.
Lipset, Seymour Martin, Political Man: The Social Bases of Politics, Garden City, 1960.
Luhmann, Niklas, Social Systems, translated by J Bednarz, Jr with Dirk Baecker, Stanford, 1995.
Mann, Michael, States, War and Capitalism: Studies in Political Sociology, Oxford, 1988.
Meyer, Michel, Meaning and Reading: A Philosophical Essay on Language and Literature, Amsterdam, 1983.
Meyer, Michel, Rhetoric, Language, and Reason, University Park, 1994.
Meyer, Michel, Of Problematology: Philosophy, Science and Language, translated by D Jamison with A Hart, Chicago, 1995.
Meyer, Michel, Rhetoric and the Theory of Argument, Revue Internationale de Philosophie 196 (1996), pp 325-357.
Mommsen, Wolfgang J., The Age of Bureaucracy: Perspectives on the Political Sociology of Max Weber, Oxford, 1974.

Offe, Claus, Contradictions of the Welfare State, edited by J Keane, London, 1984.
Offe, Claus, Modernity and the State: East, West, Oxford, 1996.
Pierson, Paul, Dismantling the Welfare State? Reagan, Thatcher, and the Politics of Retrenchment, Cambridge, 1994.
Poggi, Gianfranco, The State: Its Nature, Development and Prospects, Cambridge, 1990.
Richards, I.A., The Philosophy of Rhetoric, New York, 1965.
Skocpol, Theda, Bringing the State Back In: Strategies of Analysis in Current Research, in Evans, Peter B., Rueschemeyer, Dietrich, and Skocpol, Theda (eds), Bringing the State Back In, Cambridge, 1985, pp. 3-37.
Strayer, James R., On the Medieval Origins of the Modern State, Princeton, 1970.
Taylor-Gooby, Peter, Welfare Reform in the UK: the Construction of a Liberal Consensus, in Taylor-Gooby, Peter (ed), Welfare States Under Pressure, London, 2001, pp 146-70.
Tilly, Charles, Contention and Democracy in Europe, 1650-2000, Cambridge, 2004.
Vickers, Brian, In Defence of Rhetoric, Oxford, 1988.
Weber, Max, On Charisma and Institution Building: Selected Papers, edited by S.N. Eisenstadt, Chicago and London, 1968.
Weber, Max, From Max Weber: Essays in Sociology, translated and edited by H.H. Gerth and C.W. Mills, London, 1970.

Notes on contributors

Gavin W. Anderson is Senior Lecturer in Law at the University of Glasgow

Samantha Ashenden is Senior Lecturer in Sociology at Birkbeck College, University of London

Hauke Brunkhorst is Professor of Sociology and Head of the Institute of Sociology at the University of Flensburg

Kirsten Campbell is Senior Lecturer in Sociology at Goldsmith's College, University of London

Costas Douzinas is Professor of Law, and Director of the Birkbeck Insitute for the Humanities, Birkbeck College, University of London

Robert Fine is Professor of Sociology at the University of Warwick and co-convenor of the European Sociological Association Network on Racism and Antisemitism

Pierre Guibentif is Professor of Sociology at ISCTE (Instituto Superior de Ciências do Trabalho e da Empresa) and at the Universidade Nova, Lisbon

Andreas Hess is Senior Lecturer in Sociology at University College Dublin

Blandine Kriegel is Professor of Moral and Political Philosophy at the University of Paris X – Nanterre, and President of the Haut Conseil à l'Intégration in France

William Outhwaite is Professor of Sociology at Newcastle University

Inger-Johanne Sand is Professor of Public Law at the University of Oslo

David Saunders is Professor Emeritus in the Sociolegal Research Centre at Griffith University

Darrow Schecter is Reader in Intellectual History at the University of Sussex

David Sciulli is Professor of Sociology at Texas A&M University

Chris Thornhill is Professor of European Political Thought at the University of Glasgow

Nicholas Turnbull is Lecturer in Politics at the University of Manchester.